Self-Portrait of Percy Grainger

Self-Portrait of
Percy Grainger

Edited by

Malcolm Gillies, David Pear,
and Mark Carroll

OXFORD
UNIVERSITY PRESS
2006

OXFORD

UNIVERSITY PRESS

Oxford University Press, Inc., publishes works that further
Oxford University's objective of excellence
in research, scholarship, and education.

Oxford   New York
Auckland   Cape Town   Dar es Salaam   Hong Kong   Karachi
Kuala Lumpur   Madrid   Melbourne   Mexico City   Nairobi
New Delhi   Shanghai   Taipei   Toronto

With offices in
Argentina   Austria   Brazil   Chile   Czech Republic   France   Greece
Guatemala   Hungary   Italy   Japan   Poland   Portugal   Singapore
South Korea   Switzerland   Thailand   Turkey   Ukraine   Vietnam

Published by Oxford University Press, Inc.
198 Madison Avenue, New York, New York 10016

www.oup.com

Oxford is a registered trademark of Oxford University Press

Library of Congress Cataloging-in-Publication Data
Grainger, Percy, 1882–1961.
Self-portrait of Percy Grainger / edited by Malcolm Gillies, David Pear, and Mark Carroll.
p.   cm.
Includes bibliographical references (p.   ) and index.
ISBN-13 978-0-19-530537-1
ISBN 0-19-530537-X
1. Grainger, Percy, 1882–1961. 2. Composers—Biography.
I. Gillies, Malcolm. II. Pear, David. III. Carroll, Mark, 1955–
IV. Title.
ML410.G75A3 2006
786.2'092—dc22   2005019957

1 3 5 7 9 8 6 4

Printed in the United States of America
on acid-free paper

To Kay Dreyfus

Acknowledgments

For permission to include the essays and extracts of Grainger's writings found in this volume, we acknowledge the kind agency of the Estate of Percy Grainger, and especially Stewart Manville (White Plains, NY).

The texts of materials found in this volume are drawn from unpublished manuscripts or typescripts found in the Grainger Museum at The University of Melbourne, Australia. We are grateful to the Baillieu Librarian and successive curators at the Grainger Museum, and especially Brian Allison, for granting access to the Museum's collections, both textual and photographic, for the purpose of preparing this volume. We have also appreciated the support and advice of successive staff of the Grainger Museum, including Kay Dreyfus, the late Rosemary Florrimell, Alessandro Servadei, Rowena Pearce, and Amelia Peachment.

For translations of materials in Danish and some in German, and general advice on matters of translation, we are indebted to Hans Kuhn (Canberra). For initial work on reading and summarizing Grainger's autobiographical writings, we acknowledge the pioneering work of Simon Perry (Brisbane). For work on the Grainger Studies project, which has enriched the annotational perspective of this volume, we are grateful to Bronwen Arthur (Brisbane), Anne-Marie Forbes (Hobart), Jennifer Hill (Melbourne), Paul Kildea (London), Sandra McColl (Melbourne), and Kathleen E. Nelson (Sydney). We also recognize the bibliographic assistance to this volume of Gordon Abbott (Adelaide) and the work carried out by Bruce Clunies Ross (Copenhagen) under the joint Australian–Danish Grainger Essays project.

We have received generous advice and support for the work of this volume from the Australian Music Centre (Sydney); the British Library (London); the Danish Music Information Centre (Copenhagen); the Library of Congress (Washington); the National Library of Australia (Canberra); the Library of the Australian National University (Canberra); and the libraries of the universities of Adelaide, Queensland (Brisbane), and Sydney.

We acknowledge the considerable assistance to the annotations of this volume gained from the specialist literature about other Frankfurt Group composers written by Stephen Banfield (on English song); Valerie Langfield (on Roger Quilter); Stephen Lloyd (on Balfour Gardiner); Ian Parrott (on Cyril Scott); and from the specialist Grainger publications of Teresa Balough, John Bird, Phil Clifford, the late Eileen Dorum, Kay Dreyfus, David Josephson, and Jane O'Brien. Of profound assistance to this volume has been Kay Dreyfus's two-volume catalogue of Grainger's music and her edition, *The Farthest North of Humanness: Letters of Percy Grainger, 1901–14*, which, two decades on, remains the *tour de force* of Grainger scholarship.

M. G.
D. P.
M. C.

Contents

⇝ Part I. THE MAN

Part II. THE MUSICIAN

Early. You Must Wait Till You're Dead' (1941); **97** Facts about Percy Grainger's Year in Europe (1923); **98** ['The King Is Dead, Long Live the King': World, Racial and Tone-Art Loyalties] (1933); **99** [Parry's 'Judith'] (1935); **100** [The Gifted and Half-Gifted] (1935); **101** Balfour Gardiner's Judgement on Vaughan Williams [Holst and Bax] (1949/52); **102** Grieg on His Romanticism, My Scientificness, re Folksong (1952); **103** Mother Liked Sibelius. P. G.'s Estimate of Him & Other Nordic Music (1953); **104** The Cheek of Band-Bosses ((Conductors)) (1945); **105** Rudolf Ganz Praised Reger & Mahler to Busoni (1953); **106** Busoni & P. G. (1953); **107** My First Hearing of Fritz Kreisler, with Mrs Lowrey (1945); **108** Melbourne Miss Rowe and Ernő Rappé's Stolen Music (1953); **109** Balfour Gardiner: 'Obscure Successes' (1953); **110** Tonery (Japanese Singer, Javanese Tone-Tool, Pablo Casals) (1945); **111** Intelligence versus Education (1943)

Photo Gallery appears after page 162

List of Illustrations

Illustrations appear after page 162

Chronology

Malcolm Gillies and David Pear

1882	Born George Percy Grainger in Brighton (near Melbourne), Victoria, 8 July.
ca.1886	Starts formal education at home.
ca.1888	Commences piano lessons with his mother.
1890	His parents separate.
ca.1891	Starts to study acting, painting, and drawing.
ca.1892	Commences piano study with Louis Pabst in Melbourne (to 1894); first reads Icelandic sagas.
1894	First appears in public as a pianist. His parents seek support for him to study abroad.
1895	Commences studies at the Hoch Conservatory in Frankfurt-am-Main with James Kwast (piano) and Iwan Knorr (composition, theory); studies composition informally with Karl Klimsch; develops over following years deep friendships with British students Henry Balfour Gardiner, Roger Quilter, and Cyril Scott, and the Dane, Herman Sandby.
1897	First reads works by Kipling.
1898	Begins his Kipling settings (on which he continued to work until 1958).
1899	First reads Whitman's poems; starts to teach piano. His mother's health declines.
1900	Visits France, Britain, and Holland with his parents; presents first public solo recital in Frankfurt.
1901	Moves with his mother to London, where he appears in many 'society' concerts as accompanist or assistant artist; commences his *Marching Song of Democracy*, inspired by Whitman.
1902	Gains his first concerto appearances, in Bath; undertakes first regional tours in Britain; makes initial arrangement of *Irish Tune from County Derry*; completes first setting of *Hill-Song* No. 1.
1903	Studies with Busoni in Berlin; undertakes extended concert tour of Australasia and South Africa with the contralto Ada Crossley (to May 1904).

1904	Tours Denmark with Sandby; meets Karen Holten (later Kellermann), who soon becomes his girlfriend (to 1913).
1905	Starts serious collection and arrangement of English folk music; gains more concerto engagements, but most concert appearances are still as associate artist.
1906	Forges friendship with Grieg; first uses the phonograph to record folksongs; composes *Brigg Fair* setting.
1907	First meets Delius; visits the Griegs in Norway; presents memorial performances of Grieg's piano concerto in Britain and Denmark; first sets *Molly on the Shore*.
1908	Publishes major article about the use of the phonograph in folk-music collection; makes first gramophone records; departs on second Australasian tour with Crossley (to May 1909).
1909	Is greatly influenced by Polynesian and Maori culture while in New Zealand; begins to present his compositions in public; completes *Father and Daughter* setting of Faeroe Islanders' music.
1910	Establishes himself as a solo recitalist and orchestral soloist, averaging about one hundred concerts per year to 1914, the majority in continental Europe. *Mock Morris* and *Molly on the Shore* are premièred in Copenhagen.
1911	Changes his professional name to Percy Aldridge Grainger. Schott (London) starts to publish his compositions.
1912	Hears several of his works performed at the first Balfour Gardiner concert series in London; holds first public concert solely of his own works; starts regularly to write articles for publication; suffers minor nervous breakdown during German concert tour; completes *Handel in the Strand*.
1913	Participates in second Gardiner series; is briefly engaged to his piano student Margot Harrison; starts to compose his 'imaginary ballet' music, *The Warriors*.
1914	Postpones or cancels concert engagements when war is declared, August; soon sails to the United States, ostensibly out of regard for his mother's health; contracts with New York music publisher G. Schirmer; first appears in New York, playing the piano part in *Shepherd's Hey*.
1915	Scores a stunning success with his début recital and concerto performance in New York; contracts with Duo-Art Company to make piano rolls (to 1933); undertakes first American tour.
1916	Collaborates with Melba in recitals in support of the Allied war effort; completes *The Warriors*, dedicated to Delius. Première of *In a Nutshell* suite.
1917	Enlists in a U.S. Army band playing oboe and soprano saxophone; makes first gramophone recordings with Columbia (to 1931); starts relationship with Mrs. Lotta (Lotte) Mills Hough (to 1922). *The Warriors* and *Marching Song of Democracy* are premièred. Grainger's father dies in Melbourne.
1918	Expects to be sent with the band to France and makes many recordings of unfinished works; is instead appointed an Army band music instructor and remains in America; assumes U.S. citizenship; completes his most famous piece, *Country Gardens*.

1919   Is discharged from the U.S. Army; first teaches at the Chicago Musical College (intermittently, in summers, to 1931); completes *Children's March*, for band.

1920   Undertakes long concert tours of the American Far West and Cuba; makes first attempts at 'elastic scoring' with an arrangement of his *Irish Tune*; increasing interest in questions of racial identity.

1921   Moves with his mother to their final home, 7 Cromwell Place, White Plains, NY; rescores a number of his early works.

1922   His mother's mental state deteriorates, and she commits suicide in April; he cancels most performing engagements and sails for Europe, where he collects folk music with Evald Tang Kristensen in Jutland and visits old friends; starts to pen recollections of his and his mother's life together (to 1956).

1923   Lives for six months in Frankfurt, where he assists Delius; arranges production of a memorial volume of photographs and writings of his mother; collects folk music again in Jutland. Publication of his *Guide to Virtuosity*.

1924   Arranges concerts in Carnegie Hall, New York, in memory of his mother and in honour of Delius; sails via Polynesia to Australia, where he visits relatives and presents recitals; adopts vegetarianism.

1925   Arranges New York concerts devoted to his own and other recent chamber music; undertakes another expedition to collect folk music in Jutland.

1926   Travels to Australia for a concert tour; in Hobart, meets the linguist Robert Atkinson, who revitalizes his interest in 'Nordic' (or 'Blue-eyed') English; comes to know the Swede Ella Ström, his future wife, while returning to America.

1927   Undertakes final folk-music expedition in Jutland; proposes to Ella Ström; begins the autobiographical narrative, 'The Love-Life of Helen and Paris', his first major essay in 'Nordic' English (to 1928).

1928   Marries Ella Ström in the Hollywood Bowl, Los Angeles. *To a Nordic Princess* is premièred at his wedding.

1929   Visits Europe with his wife; organizes performances of 'Frankfurt Group' compositions at a festival in Harrogate; first formally outlines his views on 'elastic scoring'.

1930   First association with the National Music Camp, Interlochen, MI. Orchestral première of *Spoon River*.

1931   Attends Haslemere Festival in Surrey, organized by Arnold Dolmetsch, rekindling his interest in early music; starts to adopt a more promotional approach (such as reduction in his performing fee) to encourage performances of his own compositions. Première of *Tribute to Foster*.

1932   Takes first steps toward building a museum at The University of Melbourne; accepts a year-long appointment as associate professor and music departmental head at New York University, where he delivers a series of twenty-nine lectures entitled, 'A General Study of the Manifold Nature of Music'.

1933   Travels from Copenhagen to Australia with his wife aboard the sailing ship *L'Avenir*; writes his longest autobiographical essay, 'The Aldridge-Grainger-Ström Saga', while on board.

1934   Undertakes his most comprehensive tour of Australia and New Zealand (to late 1935), presenting many concerts and broadcasts; writes a long article in memory of Delius; presents twelve lectures (to February 1935) entitled, 'Music: A Commonsense View of All Types', for the Australian Broadcasting Commission, including the première (by string quartet) of his first 'Free Music' work (later rescored for theremins).

1935   Supervises building of the first stage of Grainger Museum in Melbourne; concert and lecture engagements in Australia and New Zealand.

1936   Returns to the United States; travels to Britain, where he attends Haslemere Festival and undertakes first BBC broadcast, conducting his own works.

1937   Writes most famous band work, *Lincolnshire Posy*, for immediate premièring in Milwaukee; begins annual teaching at Interlochen summer camp (to 1944).

1938   Revisits Australia to supervise building (with Gardiner's financial assistance) of Museum's second stage and to arrange its exhibits; clarifies his ideas about 'Free Music'.

1939   Visits Europe, returning just before outbreak of war; completes *The Immovable Do* and arrangement of '*The Duke of Marlborough' Fanfare*; begins glossary of his 'Nordic' English.

1940   Employs Henry Cowell as his 'musical secretary' for one year; copies and disperses his correspondence and important musical items, fearing invasion of America; moves to Springfield, MO (to 1945); writes his 'Deemths' [Opinions] essays (to 1944).

1941   Travels widely, giving many concerts for the Red Cross and troops (to 1945).

1942   Attends a Grainger festival in Madison, WI. Première of *Kipling 'Jungle Book' Cycle*.

1943   Completes *The Power of Rome and the Christian Heart*; underwrites costs of production of *False Foundations of British History* by James Mackinnon Fowler; writes seminal essay, 'The Specialist and the All-Round Man'.

1944   Commences a series of recordings with Decca; starts the slow reduction in his concert commitments (to 1960); starts to write his recollections, 'Ere-I-Forget' (to 1947). His favourite aunt, Clara Aldridge, dies in Adelaide.

1945   Comes to know the scientist Burnett Cross, with whom he soon starts to work on his 'Free Music' ideas; collaborates with Stokowski in Hollywood Bowl concerts.

1946   Undertakes first post-war visit to Scandinavia. Première of *Youthful Suite*.

1947   Hears brilliant performance of his *Hill-Song* No. 1 from West Point Band; writes his 'Bird's-eye View of the Together-life of Rose Grainger and Percy Grainger'; presents his first piano recitals in Britain since 1914.

1948   Embarks on his last formal concert tour in America, although continues to perform frequently for many years, mainly for educational institutions; writes his 'Notes on Whip-Lust'.

1949   Commences his collection of 'Anecdotes' (to 1954); starts to make new arrangements of several of his popular pieces for a Stokowski recording.

1950   Starts to experience problems with his hearing. Henry Balfour Gardiner dies.

1951   Constructs the 'Estey-reed Tone-tool', with Burnett Cross, for playing 'Free Music'; writes the introduction to his projected autobiographical volume, 'My Wretched Tone-Life'.

1952   Invents, with Cross, the 'Kangaroo-pouch' machine.

1953   Undergoes operation for prostate cancer in Århus, Denmark, recovering only slowly. Roger Quilter and Karen Kellermann die.

1954   Undergoes further operations for cancer; is awarded St. Olav medal for services to Norwegian music; writes the essay, 'Tone-Cribs'.

1955   Travels to Australia, for the last time, to work on exhibits at his museum in Melbourne.

1956   Returns midyear from Australia to New York.

1957   Presents one of his last major performances in Århus; gives only television appearance with the BBC in London; starts to suffer from occasional mental disorders affecting speech and coordination; undergoes a further cancer operation.

1958   Visits Britain, where he meets many folk-music acquaintances and Benjamin Britten.

1959   Travels to Britain for the last time; considers adding another storey to his Melbourne museum; draws up his final will, leaving the bulk of his artistic legacy to his museum.

1960   Undertakes final work on 'Free Music' machines; gives last concert in Hanover, NH; further deteriorates mentally and physically; writes his last essay on *Hill-Song* No. 2.

1961   Dies of cancer in White Plains Hospital, 20 February.

Note: Grainger's compositions are difficult to date concisely, as they were often conceived over many years and then repeatedly revised and rearranged for a variety of performing resources. Dates provided mainly refer to the initial, substantially complete form of a work. For a more detailed listing of Grainger's compositions, see, for instance: Malcolm Gillies and David Pear, 'Grainger, Percy', in *The New Grove Dictionary of Music and Musicians*, 2nd ed. (London: Macmillan, 2001), vol. 10, pp. 269–73; David Josephson, 'Grainger, Percy', in *The New Grove Dictionary of American Music* (London: Macmillan, 1986), vol. 2, pp. 272–74; and Kay Dreyfus, *Music by Percy Grainger*, 2 vols. (Melbourne: University of Melbourne, 1978, 1995).

Introduction

Malcolm Gillies

Few musicians have lived their lives with as intriguing a symmetry as Percy Grainger. Born in 1882 in Victoria, Australia, he died seventy-eight years later, in 1961, in John F. Kennedy's America.[1] In precise midlife, aged thirty-nine, Grainger suffered his greatest shock: the dramatic suicide of his mother on 30 April 1922, when she leapt from a New York skyscraper. Their relationship had been so close, their thoughts and passions so shared, that Grainger's life could not go on as before. Over those first thirty-nine years, he had rarely been apart from his mother for more than a few weeks. His immediate response was to neglect his concert career and to make repeated visits to Europe and Australia in an attempt to recapture their shared intimacies through visiting friends, sights, and sounds of old. For nearly five years—until December 1926, when Grainger met his wife-to-be—he wandered the world in mourning. Even thereafter, despite a generally happy marriage, he never found the 'soul-mate' to rival his mother. His life's second half did not manage to maintain the confidence and optimism of its first half.

The events of 1922 brought to the surface a retrospective mind-set that had been lurking in Grainger since his decision to join the U.S. Army in 1917. Concerned that he might be killed in the war, he had ordered his musical and written manuscripts and recorded some of his intentions for musical works conceived but not yet fully born. From these later war years also emerge the first coherent ideas of founding his own museum. Rose Grainger's death catapulted Grainger beyond practical archival thoughts into a strongly retrospective mood, which only intensified over the remaining four decades of his life. It led to the construction of his own Grainger Museum at The University of Melbourne in the 1930s. It led to lesser, and more

---

1. See the chronology at the beginning of this volume for a year-by-year overview of Grainger's life.

tentative, production of new compositions (although there are still some gems, such as *Lincolnshire Posy*, from the 1930s, and the 'Free Music' experiments of his final years) and a growing concern to tidy up and (re)present the works and musical ideas of his earlier years. In fact, Grainger had, in many ways, laid down the blueprint for his compositional life by his early twenties,[2] and he stuck to it with surprising exactitude over the following six decades.

From 1922, Grainger began to pen his reminiscences. These many recollections were intended as raw materials for finished biographies, but somehow Grainger could never bring himself to write up those definitive stories. Between 1922 and the late 1930s, he laid down over one hundred 'sketches' for the intended half-autobiography, 'The Life of My Mother & Her Son',[3] but that book never emerged, although he would return constantly to write and rewrite aspects of their life together until well into his seventies. His massive 'The Aldridge-Grainger-Ström Saga', written in 1933–34 while aboard a sailing boat between Europe and Australia, was intended as a gathering of recollections 'before beginning the real end-some [final] form of the book telling the life-story of his mother, himself, his friends, his art, his business-paths',[4] but that 'end-some form' eluded him. When compiling his 'Bird's-Eye View of the Together-Life of Rose Grainger and Percy Grainger' in 1947, he expressed the fear that he might die before the definitive saga of their lives was written and offered this sketch as 'a rough chart of her life's voyage, a rough summing-up of what she was & what sways she exerted upon me and my art-life'.[5] Similarly, in 1951, he drafted an introduction to an autobiography, 'My Wretched Tone-Life',[6] and in 1953, a longer explanatory essay, 'Why "My Wretched Tone-Life"?',[7] but he never went on to write the 'Wretched Tone-Life' itself.

2. As articulated, e.g., in his collected writings from 1901 to 1904, 'Methods of Teaching and Other Things' (Grainger Museum, Melbourne). See sections from that collection in essays 46, 47, 93, and 94 of this volume and in Malcolm Gillies and Bruce Clunies Ross, eds., *Grainger on Music* (Oxford: Oxford University Press, 1999), essays 2 and 3.

3. See the List of Sources for identification of the fifteen sections from these 'Sketches' included in this volume.

4. Introductory paragraph, W37-1, dated 28 September 1933. See the List of Sources for the eleven sections of this 'Saga' included in this volume. (The first number in Grainger's own source identifications refers to his own numbering of essays, or essay collections. The second number generally refers to subsections, not pages.)

5. 'The Purpose of This Brief Sketch', 399-1, dated 5 January 1947. 'Bird's-Eye View' is reproduced, in its entirety, as essay 20.

6. Reproduced in Malcolm Gillies and David Pear, *Portrait of Percy Grainger* (Rochester, NY: Rochester University Press, 2002), 206–8.

7. See essay 63 in this volume.

Owing to Grainger's increasing retrospectivity of mind, he left to posterity more than half a million words of autobiographical reminiscences, nearly all of them dating from the second half of his life, but the considerable majority of them recalling events from the first half of his life: his childhood in Australia (1882–95), his music college years in Germany (1895–1901), his early professional years in Britain (1901–14), along with less comprehensive attention to his earliest years in America (1914–18). Because of the tragic circumstance of his mother's death, and Percy Grainger's complicated private life in the preceding few years, he was most coy about the years of 1918–22. When he did mention those years in his writings,[8] he sometimes resorted to pseudonyms to disguise the identities of those personally involved with him, nearly all of whom he banished from his life following his mother's death. As Grainger moved through the 1920s to the 1950s, the tone of his autobiographical writings changes from nostalgic to wistful to bitter. That progression is reflected in the titles and stated purposes of the various essays, ranging from his saccharine 'The Love-Life of Helen and Paris' (1927–28)[9] and more objectively titled 'The Aldridge-Grainger-Ström Saga' (1933–34), through his 'The Thots I Think as I Grow Old' (1937),[10] 'Growing Nasty-Spoken as I Near My Sixties' (1940),[11] and 'Ere-I-Forget' collection (1944–47),[12] and on to his lengthy 'The Things I Dislike' of 1954[13] (from 'Grainger's Anecdotes'[14]) and the preparatory writings in the early 1950s for 'My Wretched Tone-Life'. Over these decades, many changes in Grainger's self-perception are apparent, as he sees himself sliding off the pedestal of world fame—at least as a pianist and composer[15]—then heading toward the abyss of 'has been' mediocrity, and finally lashing out at the growing restrictions brought on by illness and old age. His voluminous autobiographical legacy is remarkable in the way in which it so precisely and comprehensively captures this slow change in self-perception over nearly four decades. There is also an element of prospective vanity in Grainger's punctilious and self-conscious documentation. In 1917, he first suggested that 'My music expresses only certain sides, in any event, and I almost think that my emotional life and the life

8. See essays 20 and 82, in particular.
9. Essays 38 to 42.
10. Essay 54.
11. Essay 56.
12. See the List of Sources for the thirteen sections from 'Ere-I-Forget' included in this volume.
13. Essay 58.
14. See the List of Sources for the thirty-nine sections from 'Grainger's Anecdotes' (1949–54) included in this volume.
15. Grainger's best-known composition, *Country Gardens*, dates from 1918–19; the years 1914–22 were also, if measured by real income or critical reception, the zenith of his performing career.

of my thoughts have more to say than my artistic life, and will, in the future, be regarded as being of the same, or even greater, significance.'[16]

This volume, then, joins existing volumes of letters and essays[17] in documenting that world of Grainger's emotional life and his 'thoughts'. These autobiographical tracts are Grainger's most intimate writings, most of them penned—unlike his letters or published essays—with no thought of immediate consumption or exposure. They are candid sketches, some little more than rough notes, for those eventual 'finished' biographies. They provide the most compelling counterpart to the image of the fresh, vibrant Grainger that emerges from the contemporary record of the first half of his life and that has inevitably gained the lion's share of attention in existing biographies.[18] The private nature of this medium of sketch and memory-aid allowed him the freedom to probe the topics that interested—and sometimes obsessed—him, in particular the sharper edges of his sexual, racial, and nationalistic beliefs that he dared not share beyond the closest circle of his friends. The informal style of these writings also offered up valuable unpremeditated snapshots of his thinking, whether caught between stations on a train trip, scribbled down during spare minutes in hotels while on tour, or elaborated while in hospital for an operation (as were many of his 'Anecdotes').

The evolution from such sketches, as left by Grainger in his museum, to the annotated selection found in this volume was a much greater challenge than that presented by his letters or published essays. These autobiographical texts are mainly written by hand and are in highly varied states of preservation (hence, occasional references to illegibility). They present the widest range of connection and also disconnection. Just as with Grainger's 'round letters', many of his more sustained reminiscences are intellectual rambles of epic proportion, none more so than his seamless 'Aldridge-Grainger-Ström Saga', written when Grainger had the unusual luxury of large amounts of free time.[19] Many of the later writings from the 1940s and 1950s, however, make no pretence at continuity. They lurch around, as with his 'Ere-I-Forget'[20] and

---

16. Letter, Grainger to Karen Kellermann (née Holten), 16 June 1917 (Grainger Museum, Melbourne).
17. See Select Grainger Bibliography.
18. The biographies of John Bird (*Percy Grainger*, 3rd ed., Oxford: Oxford University Press, 1999) and Eileen Dorum (*Percy Grainger: The Man Behind the Music*, Melbourne: IC & EE Dorum, 1986) both devote nearly two-thirds of their text to the first half of Grainger's life. The film *Passion* (1999) only portrays Grainger's London years, 1901–14.
19. See Ella Grainger's account of their time aboard the windjammer *L'Avenir* during 1933 in Gillies and Pear, *Portrait of Percy Grainger*, 140–44.
20. Noted by Grainger on its title page as 'jottings-down (for use in 'Aldridge-Grainger-Brandelius saga') of close-ups ((details)) that otherwise might go un-writ-hoarded ((unrecorded))'. For Grainger's use of double parentheses, see later in this introduction.

also his 'Anecdotes', the latter which he introduced as 'things I heard people say, thoughts I myself have had, gossip about people, things I have read, epigrams, aphorisms—in short, all sorts of aids-to-memory.'[21] Despite this seemingly random approach, Grainger, ever the archivist, made sure that its sections were titled, numbered, and provided with data of date and place.

This volume has fashioned Grainger's diverse raw materials into something of the shape that he himself suggested in the opening of 'The Aldridge-Grainger-Ström Saga', namely, 'the life-story of his mother, himself, his friends, his art, his business-paths'.[22] To tell that life-story by reproducing all of his autobiographical writings would have been neither commercially feasible, given their extent, nor practically useful, given their frequent repetition, disconnection of materials, and even illegibility. We, therefore, began with the most intimately autobiographical aspects of Grainger's plan—'himself' and 'his art'—and then looked at the other themes—'his mother', 'his friends', 'his business-paths'—considering how comprehensively they accounted for the themes emerging, in total, from his autobiographical writings. Hence, the final shape of the volume, with two parts: 'The Man' and 'The Musician'. Within each part, we then sought the most convenient chapter divisions, first of his broader personal relations—Forebears, Father, Mother, Friends, Wife, Self—and second of his approach in his art—Composer, Performer, Commentator, with this last category encompassing a wide range of musical and broader artistic interests. These nine chapters are, however, only rough corrallings of Grainger's often rogue materials. As a musician, and with friends who were almost all musically aware if not professional musicians themselves, he did not hesitate in flicking between personal and professional concerns, even within a single sentence. Likewise, in looking at compositional questions, he would frequently slew into inspirational issues of poetry, visual art, race, sex, or personalities. Within the chapters, the ordering of materials is neither systematically chronological nor thematic, although we did attempt both. Rather, each chapter is a collection of materials with a stronger or weaker focus on the chapter's title and arranged in such a way as to pursue evolving subthemes of person, place, artistic output, or time. Although we have tried to provide a coverage of issues that is roughly representative of Grainger's own coverage, we have consciously over- and underrepresented certain materials. If raw wordage were the measure, then the chapter on 'Mother'—already the largest in the volume—should probably be several times longer, so perenni-

21. 'Grainger's Anecdotes', p. 1, dated 7 September 1952.
22. Introductory paragraph, W37-1, dated 28 September 1933.

ally dominating was this theme in the aging Grainger's mind.[23] So, too, issues of race and sex would have needed to be somewhat more emphasized.[24] Conversely, we have sought to draw out the diversity of Grainger's opinions of his friends and the broader musical output of others and so have, to some degree, overly devoted space to these issues in comparison with their representation in the totality of his autobiographical writings. On a couple of occasions, a letter is included where it occurs within an autobiographical context.[25] So, too, two of the autobiographical passages included came into life as briefings for the press.[26]

Ultimately, in crafting the balance of this 'self-portrait'—*our* portrait using *Grainger's* materials—we have been guided by the belief that, despite Grainger's espousal of 'all-roundedness' and his self-appointed role as Antipodean 'over-soul' (genius), athletic exhibitionist, amateur sexologist, linguistic pioneer, or racial seer, the world, now as then, remains most interested in him as a musician. This 'self-portrait', then, has sought to effect a compromise between what Grainger was most interested in writing about and what the world now recognizes as most distinctive about him. It also tries to balance what Grainger wanted future readers to know about him with what they themselves might (or might not) wish to know. Do we need to know such details of his sex life, as found in chapter 5,[27] or of his interests in flagellation and sadomasochism, as found in chapters 5 and 6?[28] Grainger's answer is unequivocally 'yes', through his desire that such documentations help future ages to understand 'the nature & habits of creative Australians'.[29] But he goes further in his more intimate writings to explain just how these racial and sexual 'stirs' informed his musical composition,[30] as well as his broader approach to

23. This volume has not, e.g., included Grainger's lengthy 'Rough Sketch of My Mother's Nature' of 1954 (from 'Grainger's Anecdotes', 423-86) because of its repetition of much included in 'Bird's-Eye View' (essay 20). Nor has it included her Museum Legend of 1956 that parallels the Legend provided for Grainger's father (essay 5). We do, however, include the only passage of this volume published during Grainger's lifetime, namely, the 'Dates of Important Events and Movements in the Life of Rose Grainger' of 1923 (essay 11).

24. An early plan for this volume attempted to draw these diverse autobiographical materials under the five headings suggested by Grainger's letter of 7 October 1911 to his mother (Kay Dreyfus, ed., *The Farthest North of Humanness*, Melbourne: Macmillan, 1985, p. 428)—'I hardly ever think of ought else but sex, race, athletics, speech & art'—but foundered on Grainger's cross-linking of these five characteristics of his 'all-roundedness', as well as the difficulty of successfully placing his mother.

25. See essays 77 and 79.

26. See essays 85 and 97.

27. See essays 40 to 42.

28. See, e.g., essays 44 and 59.

29. Essay 59.

30. See, e.g., essay 61.

art and to life.[31] In fact, he saw it as his *duty* to reveal these intimate details for the benefit of all:

> It seems to me my duty to place before the public, as far as I can, the intimacies (the stories, the facts, the photos, the letters, etc.) that have created love in my case & no doubt will create love in the hearts of others as well. Everything withheld makes for lovelessness, in my opinion. Everything included (however trifling it may seem at first glance) makes for greater love, greater peace, greater harmony in the world—in my opinion.[32]

Despite the curiosity, titillation, even horror that parts of *Self-Portrait of Percy Grainger* will give to some readers, we have sought neither to censor nor to sensationalize Grainger's conscientious open-mindedness.

A challenge to any reader of Grainger's autobiographical writings is his use of language, for his recollections are written as much to house Grainger's linguistic experiments and ploys as to record facts and ideas. He started to learn Danish from his student-friend in Frankfurt, Herman Sandby, and continued to refine his knowledge of the language during his London years through that friendship and also through his seven-year-long relationship with his Danish girlfriend, Karen Holten. Quite frequently in these autobiographical writings, Grainger darts between English and Danish. He explained in 1947, in the opening of 'Bird's-Eye View of the Together-Life of Rose Grainger and Percy Grainger', that he placed less problematic facts and opinions in English, but resorted to Danish where the materials demanded a more mature response: 'The Scandinavian reader is not frightened to face unusual, unexpected & up-setting data; therefore, the more tragic & puzzling details of my mother's and my together-life are addressed to him, while those details presenting no problems to a timid & evasive mentality are recorded for English-speaking readers.'[33] He also tends to record in German statements originally made to him in German—for instance, during his Frankfurt years[34]—or concerning his relations with Ferruccio Busoni.[35] Occasional words or phrases in Swedish (the first language of his wife) or in Maori (which he preferred for describing more intimate parts of the human anatomy)[36]

---

31. See, e.g., essays 50 to 53.
32. Letter, Grainger to Roger Quilter, 21 September 1941 (Grainger Museum, Melbourne).
33. In 'The Languages in which This Sketch Is Written', 399-2, dated 5 January 1947 (in essay 20). For further discussion of Grainger's use of Danish, see the 'Editor's Note' and 'Translator's Note' in Dreyfus, ed., *The Farthest North of Humanness*, xviii–xxiii.
34. See, e.g., essay 20.
35. See, e.g., essay 106.
36. Grainger claimed to have first become interested in Maori while a boy in Melbourne through the influence of the artist and linguist A. E. Aldis, then a lodger with the Graingers. See use of Maori (or pseudo-Maori) words in essays 41 and 42.

enliven some other essays. At other times, Grainger uses nonsense words, or perhaps a code we have not yet been able to crack,[37] or just leaves a blank space where he cannot remember a word or name or does not want to be specific. In this volume, while generally presenting individual foreign-language words in the text, with translations in the notes, we have presented passages of greater foreign-language continuity in English translation only, lest the reader or the meaning become lost in the interplay between two, or three, languages. In every case, however, the original language is clearly indicated.

The most persistent linguistic challenge, however, lies not with foreign languages, but with Grainger's idiosyncratic use of Nordic, or 'Blue-eyed', English. This language, largely of Grainger's own devising, had been evolving in his mind since his childhood. Although it can appear simply as a long-winded and tedious game, Nordic English was completely consistent with Grainger's broader Nordic obsession. He desired to turn English, and the English people, back to more northerly, Scandinavian, and Anglo-Saxon ('blue-eyed') roots and away from the more southerly, Graeco-Roman ('dark-eyed') roots that Grainger saw as having infected the country, its culture, and language, at least since 1066.[38] After meeting the linguist Robert Atkinson in Tasmania in 1926, Grainger was spurred to renew and consolidate his experiments with Nordic English. Indeed, for many years, he subsidized Atkinson in his authoring of a never-completed book, *Our Mothertongue*.[39] Grainger's first full-length essay written in Nordic English was 'The Love-Life of Helen and Paris' (1927–28).[40] Thereafter, until the end of his life, Grainger wrote frequently in his made-up language—sometimes entire tracts, at other times merely passages or key phrases, depending on the topic or intended audience. As he once observed: 'one cannot write freely when one is trying to create & reform a language at the same time'.[41] The best tutorial in Grainger's Nordic linguistic purposes is undoubtedly given in the foreword, 'On Blue-eyed English',[42] to his 'Love-Life' essay, part of which is reproduced in the following excerpt. (Grainger's double parentheses show the 'dark-eyed' synonyms he himself provided. Unfortunately, his knowledge of Latin, Greek, and French was less strong than of German and Danish, hence occasional slips in etymology.)

37. E.g., essay 31, where Grainger uses the term 'tmpe tljf', probably meaning 'break wind'.
38. In 1943, Grainger even underwrote the costs of production of *False Foundations of British History* by James Mackinnon Fowler.
39. See letter, Grainger to Atkinson, 16 April 1931, in Gillies and Pear, eds., *The All-Round Man: Selected Letters of Percy Grainger, 1914–1961* (Oxford: Clarendon Press, 1994), 103–8.
40. See essays 38 to 42. 'Helen' referred to Grainger's wife-to-be Ella Ström, and 'Paris' to Grainger himself.
41. From 'The Languages in which This Sketch Is Written', in essay 20.
42. Dated 8 November 1927, on board the S.S. *Republic* in the Atlantic Ocean.

The English stretches of this story are written (as well as I can) in 'Nordic English'. I have always believed in the wish-for-ableness ((desirability)) of building up a mainly Anglo-Saxon-Scandinavian kind of English in which all but the most un-do-withoutable ((indispensable)) of the French-begotten, Latin-begotten & Greek-begotten words should be side-stepped ((avoided)) & in which the bulk of the put-together ((compound)) words should be wilfully & owned-up-to-ly ((admittedly)) hot-house-grown out of Nordic word-seeds.

My nature-urge ((instinct)) tells me that speech (like tone-art ((music)) & all other arts) ought to be over-weighingly ((preponderantly)) a forth-showing ((manifestation)) of race, place & type, & that nothing is gained (at least from an artist's mind-slant ((attitude))) by making speech a gathered-together-ness ((conglomeration)) of worn-out Europe-wide word-chains ((sentences)) such as 'in commemoration of this illustrious anniversary', 'this involved situation demanded a readjustment of the entire machinery of representation', & the like. I have little quarrel with those shorter & simpler French-begotten words that have wormed their way so deeply into English as to have taken on a more or less English-like sound-type—words such as train, pride, single, simple, urge, type, place, power, bottle, pure, clear, common, person, manner, second, paper, price, and so on. In many cases such words have so utterly ousted their older Anglosaxon or Scandinavian forerunners ((predecessors)) that we can find nothing Nordic to put in their stead.

But I have every quarrel with those longer, stuck-up, would-be-learned put-together ((compound)) words (such as 'incompatibility', 'corrosive', 'contemptible') that are as un-English in their put-to-use-ness ((application)) as in their whence-come-ness ((origin)) & which (on top of being sickeningly ugly & typeless) seem to me to stand like a fence between the plain man & his road to wider Knowledge. For I believe that such sham-English words as 'transparent', 'insurmountably', & 'indispensability' are not as clear to the plain man as 'durchsichtig', 'unüberwindlich' & 'unentbehrlichkeit' are in German, as 'gennemsigtig', 'uoverkommeligt' & 'uundværlighed' are in Danish,[43] and that the fondness of English-speaking mind-tilth-swayers ((influencers of education)) for these dead 'pundit-words' (made up of roots that are not alive in English in their single, simple forms) plays its evil part in keeping the bulk of English-speaking folk needlessly backward in mind-tilth ((education)) & soul-tilth ((spiritual culture))—as set alongside Scandinavians, for instance.

Therefore I welcome the plan-born ((systematic)) begetting ((creation)) of such new, unnaturally put-together same-place-takers ((substitutes)) as 'see-thru-able' ((transparent)), 'unclimb-over-ably' ((insurmount-

43. That is, the equivalent in German and Danish, respectively, of the three given English words.

ably)) & 'undo-without-able-ness' ((indispensability)), as well as the natural growth of such popular forms as 'stick-to-it-ive-ness', 'get-at-able-ness', 'never-give-up-ness'—however clumsy they may seem to some ears and eyes.

Out-of-the-way ((especially)) sickly seem to me those cases where a wholly un-English shift of rhythm takes place in some of the sundry forms of a given French root (such as 'reveal' & 'revelation', 'invent' & 'inventivity')—due no doubt to the un-Nordic stresslessness of French. It is mind-balming ((consoling)) to note that such stress-crippling of Nordic-begotten words never (to my knowledge) happens; showing that many of the foreign-root words were, after all, handled as things aloof by English tongues. In all such cases it would seem to me well (even where French roots are kept) to cure these hunch-back words by treating them along the lines of true English speech-wont ((linguistic habits))—turning 'revelation' into 'revealment', 'inventivity' into 'inventiveness', and so on. Where good type-true ((characteristic)) Nordic forms (such as 'play-wright', 'wheel-wright') already thrive in a certain line of thot [thought] I would rede ((advise)) their example being followed by others of kindred type (such as 'tone-wright' ((musical composer)), 'book-wright' ((literary author))).

Although Grainger frequently provided these 'dark-eyed' synonyms to his Nordic English words, in his most private writings, he sometimes did not. Hence, our occasional editorial clarifications in square brackets where the meaning of a word cannot easily be guessed or the accumulation of 'blue-eyed' words is likely to lead to verbal indigestion for all but the most dedicated of readers.

This volume has been heavily annotated because of the obscurity of so much that Grainger writes about to a twenty-first-century audience. Annotations are also needed in the frequent instances where Grainger's memory is faulty, his quotations are inaccurate, or he simply leaves blanks intended for later filling. Although we have attempted to present whole sections of text (without excisions)—and under the titles given by Grainger or their abbreviation—this has sometimes not been the case where passages have been illegible (particularly at the tops or bottoms of handwritten pages); where his section divisions are a poor guide to the real division between materials; or where, as in 'The Aldridge-Grainger-Ström Saga', Grainger has given neither titles nor clear section divisions. Although we have attempted to reproduce the many linguistic and spelling idiosyncrasies of Grainger, we have, with the benefit now of a large database of his writings, silently corrected obvious slips of the pen, erratic hyphenation of Nordic English words, and occasional phonetic spellings. So, too, we have standardized his emphatic use of capitals (often in typing) and underlinings (in handwriting) as italics, as also his use of all forms of brackets and parentheses, reserving the use of square brackets for our own editorial interpolations, double parentheses solely for his 'dark-eyed' synonyms, and single parentheses for most other usages. Grainger's endearing train sketches—meaning that he was writing the passage while on a train—have been represented verbally by '[on train]'. His occasional musical examples have been represented in transcription, unless otherwise indicated.

Finally, I record my appreciation of the close collaboration with David Pear and Mark Carroll in preparing this *Self-Portrait* and, variously, the four Grainger volumes that have preceded it. Their folk-lore-some ((historical)), writ-grooming ((editing)), and tone-art-fact-search-y ((musicological)) skills have been invaluable in producing this volume.

Self-Portrait of Percy Grainger

PART I

The Man

1

FOREBEARS

≈1   [The Aldridge Saga Begins] (1933)

My mother always told me that her mother and father[1] came from Kent (England), but they were both born in London (England), her kin tell me. Likely they were born in London of Kentish forebears. All the Aldridges have a fairness of hair, a blueness of eye that hints a countryside background—none have the darker strain one looks for in Cockneys. It is harder to guess from what class in England the Aldridges came: in the breed-group ((family)) there is a story that my mother's father was a leech [doctor], with leech fathers behind him; Uncle Charlie (mother's next youngest brother)[2] saw a grave, or graves, of one or more 'Dr Aldridges' in a London churchyard. The thing needs looking into. My own guess would be that the Aldridges are true-to-type yeomen; for most of us with Aldridge blood have a love of beasts ((animals)), a yearning for country life, a sturdiness, a tholesomeness ((patience)), a quiet glowing self-belief and self-enoughness ((individualism)), a hatred of tally-lore ((arithmetic)), or other clerkish skills, a blend of slowness of wit with speed of body—all these type-signs ((characteristics)) being, as I see it, fruits of the yeoman tree, & quite othersome from the shallow-rooted, flighty, untholesome ((impatient)), smart-witted shiftiness of town-rat—such as my father, for sample ((for instance)).

Around 1908–9 Uncle Charlie told my mother that their birth-givers ((parents)) were not wed when Uncle George (my mother's eldest, & best-beloved, brother)[3] was born in England, a tale that delighted my law-unworshipping

---

1. Sarah Jane Brown (1821–1895) and George Aldridge (1817–1879).
2. Charles Edwin Aldridge (1858–1932).
3. George Sydney Aldridge (1847–1911).

mother, for she told me it tickled her that just Uncle George—the most proud, lofty-minded, study-fond & high-class of all her brothers—should have been born out of wed-lock. (Uncle Charlie, on the other hand, likely viewed it as a rue-worthy ((regrettable)) bit of breed-group past-lore ((family history)) & I can mind-hear [recall] him telling it to my mother somewhat under his breath.) Uncle Charlie told the old story: that my grandfather was not happy with his wedded wife, and so on. Doubtless the upshot of this law-unbehallowed love-life drove my grand-birthgivers ((grandparents)) to Australia, with my grandmother's mother[4] as fellow-farer. They came on a sailing ship, 10 months from England to Australia. Mother said that my grandmother loved the sea in all its moods & had herself lashed to a mast so that she might witness storms on deck. (Yet it is as hard for me to mind-fancy ((imagine)) the sweet, over-quiet, selfward-inturned old woman I knew in early boyhood, joyfully weathering a sea-storm on deck as it is for me to think of her swept outside the law-wonts ((legal conventions)) on a sex-stream. That is maybe our harshest unfairness to the old: we cannot, for the life of us, see them seething in the youth-heats.)

When the 3 of them landed (at Port Adelaide?)[5] there were still plenty of Blacks about & my mother's grandmother always said that all the years she was in Australia she never could get the smell of the Blacks out of her nostrils. She could not bring herself to like the new land & always belittled Australia—longing for England. But my mother told me that grandmother stood out against all belittlement of Australia, saying that it was laugh-at-able ((absurd)) to make-believe that life was better in the old country: 'we have all sorts of advantages here we never had at home.'

My grandfather tried his hand at all sorts of trades—was a baker on the goldfields, had a shop in Adelaide & later on he acted as an 'agent' for 'concert-artists', & other 'entertainers'. But mainly, it seems to me, he was a hotel-keeper, & from the way he well-did at the job & from the way no less than 4 of his sons took to hotel-keeping as ducks take to water, my thots lean towards the likelihood that he came out of a hotelkeeping background (rather than out of a leech background, as my (in class matters) upward-yearning Uncle Charlie might better-deem to think).

By the time my mother was born her father had a hotel in the ring-core ((center)) of Adelaide. He was a headstrong, wilful, noisy man, fond of doing things in a grand way & very public-spirited. He did 'catering' along big lines & the morning after some big 'banquet' the poor might be seen standing in line to get masses of free food. He would not thole ((endure)) a Jew or a

---

4. Sarah Brown (née Butler), married to Timothy Brown in Westminster, 1820.
5. In August or September 1847.

bookmaker in his hotel; if such a one got in, unbeknown to him, he would (on learning the awful truth) storm up to the poor man's door, shouting: 'I'll have no Jews (or bookmakers) in my hotel. Out you go!', throwing the man's luggage down the stairs. (Bark 'L'Avenir', nearing Skagen, Sept. 28, 1933)

On Sundays he loved to pile his whole breed-group ((family)) into a joy-wagon of some kind, himself driving some half-wild horse or horses—the more kicking, rearing, jibbing & thrashing the better. My grandmother hated these heroic outings, but never crossed her husband's will in this or any other matter. She and her brood hung on for dear life, shamming to like it. If anyone murmured their fears they were told, 'there is nothing to be frightened of'. My grandfather thrashed his sons as he thrashed the horses, laying scornfully into them with a horsewhip in a hair-raising way, my mother said—most so Uncle Jim,[6] whom with his deep love of frith-life ((nature-life)), I can easily fancy playing truant from school, or otherwise order-flouting along sweet boyish lines. Uncle Charlie got merciless lambasteings at his father's hands. But mother said that her father never struck Uncle George, who, with his quiet, study-full ways & heed-full, worth-weighsome gaze, brought calm & order into any group he neared. She said that if folk were noisy or wrangling (be it her father, her brothers or outsiders) it was enough for Uncle George to enter the room to set up calm at once. Mother felt Uncle George to be the good angel of the breed-group & always longed for his at-ness ((presence)) when things got stormy. Mother worshipped Uncle George's calm, manly ways, slow melody-full voice and youthful body, for he was handsome like a young knight. Like most Englishmen who early settled Australia, my grandfather was too fond of the bottle & towards evening would grow quarrelsome, or at least loudspoken, with his wife, but he would pipe down when Uncle George showed up. Once, when grandfather was talking more or less roughly to grandmother, my mother, then in her early teens, stepped up to him in that uprisesome ((rebellious)) up-flaring so inborn in her, saying, 'How dare you speak to our mother like that?' Grandfather checked himself & left the room. As soon as he was gone grandmother boxed my mother's ears, saying 'Don't you *dare* speak like that to your father!' Grandmother utterly and unuplettingly served her husband and his will in all things, not as a willless slave, but as a self-chosen willfulfiller to him. This is the reward a man often has of reaching out for love beyond wedlock—a rightful woman deeming herself sex-scorned by a man who waits for the law.

Grandmother worked hard in the hotel kitchen all day & got bad swollen veins in her legs from standing so long. When her day's work was done she liked to shut herself up in her room, with her feet raised up, away from the life

6. James Henry Aldridge (1849–1925).

of the house. Maybe she was always a bit of a hermit, or maybe her hard-working days tired her out so that she needed some lonely hours in which to gather herself together. And maybe this too; that those who have stepped outside life-wonts ((conventions)) of the man-herd—however little—learn of the cruelness & scaith-will ((mischievousness)) of the man-herd & feel safer & happier withdrawn from it. For whatever reason, grandmother sought no friends in Adelaide, enoughed ((content)) with her own brood-group ((family)) & the tasks it brought. This linked up with the snobbishness of my grandfather, who thot no other hotel-keeper's brood-group good enough for his brood-group to mix with. Such better-class brood-groups as he would have thot good enough he most likely was not in touch with, or by such, again, he & his were not thot good enough.

The upshot of all this was that the upgrowing Aldridge children had next to no friends in their own class, with the outcome that the boys, when sex-ready, had to flirt & mate with bar-maids & servants—no bad sex-field to pluck one's sex-flowers in, may be. Jim, Fred,[7] Ted[8] & Charlie all wedded bar-maids & servants.

Source: Untitled section, in 'The Aldridge-Grainger-Ström Saga', W37-3 to 37-5, dated 28–29 September 1933 (Grainger Museum, Melbourne).

➤ 2   [Aldridge Family Strengths] (1933)

There seems to have been a great deal of reading aloud in the Aldridge life—a lovely home-wont; one that one would guess true mind-tilth [education] & soul-tilth [spiritual culture] to be firmly rooted in. (Sure enough, it is the un-slakeable book-hunger of the Norwegians that makes them the out-of-the-ordinarily gifted folk they are at book-art ((literature)). Little Norwegian boys, of the most manly types, will un-hide ((reveal)) to one the books they have read in the way Anglosaxon boys will talk of football, cricket or baseball, or the way German boys, before the war, would boast of the German navy. In spite of this long been-thru-someness ((experience)) of Norwegian bookfainth ((fondness for books)) both Ella[9] & I were wonder-struck ((amazed)) when Herman Wildenvej[10] stayed with us in White Plains, to note how boundlessly

---

7. Frederick Clement Aldridge (1853–1926).
8. Edward (Ted) William Aldridge (1851–1909).
9. Ella Ström (1889–1979), Grainger's Swedish-born wife from 1928. See chapter 5, 'Wife'.
10. (1886–1959), Norwegian poet and husband of Ella Ström's friend, Gisken Wildenvej (Wildenvey).

fond a man could be of reading.) Uncle Ted (or was it Fred?) seems to have been a great reader & very fond of the play-house ((theatre)). He be-married the brood-group with his wit, with his great store of jokes from Mark Twain, Dickens & other joke-artists ((humorists)), & with all sorts of catch-saws culled from the play-house, such as 'T. E. tea, Jane Mould', and the like. I seem to remember my mother word-painting ((describing)) her father's speech as rife with jolly saws and quote-ments ((quotations)). Mother seems to have rated Uncle Ted as the most art-gifted of her brothers. He had an ease for drawing & painting & one of the delights of my childhood was a card he painted with a view of a richly red Stuart Pea[11] & Broken Hill Mines linked-together ((combined)). He gathered together a far-famed gatherment of ore-stuffs & mining-wares—things bewitching in their cold sparkle, their shimmering, many-coloredness, their weird shapes. Mother always thot he showed true art-sense in this gatherment of his & she rued that it was spread to the 4 winds on his death[12] with true-to-type Anglosaxon worth-wastefulness. Uncle Ted's reading & play-house going, such as it was, does not seem to have in any way lifted him out of the round of mean-some ((normal)) Anglosaxon thot, while the home-reading does seem to have turned both Auntie Clara's[13] and mother's minds out of the wonted English or Australian ruts. I would word-paint the English-speaking thot-rut as follows: a belief in luck, good or bad, rather than a belief in work; a blind belief in the rightness of the law, even when it goes against one's inner feeling; a liking for carriage-folk (nowadays motor-folk) and other well-to-do rascals.[14] Auntie Clara has never seemed to care whether a sex-pair were hallowed with wedlock or not, & during & after the war[15] she seems to have had no turning against such Germans or German-Australians as she knew, nor has she ever showed any signs of disliking or liking folk because they had or lacked money, made or lost it. Such very un-Anglosaxon behaveness needs some cause-showing & I would lean towards the view that Auntie Clara's mind to some length was un-English, & tuned to all-mankind-some stirs by much early reading of pity-fraught 19th-hundred-year-groupsome [19th-century] book-writers. Or was it the quietly self-enough soul of my grandmother—so beyond all winning & losing, so willingly fair & good in her judgements—that entered into both Auntie Clara & my mother? In that case, should my grandmother's world-deaf-hearing ((world-ignoring)) mood be laid to Dickens & other fondness-mongering

---

11. *Swainsona formosa*, better known as Sturt's desert pea.
12. In 1909.
13. Clara Jane Aldridge (1856–1944), elder sister of Grainger's mother.
14. Grainger here later inserted a largely illegible sentence, beginning, 'It lies almost within the realm of the unprobable . . . '.
15. First World War.

writers, that she read? Whatever its roots, this unworldly view of the world went further in mother's case than in her mother's or her sister's. What in their case added up to a rather nice evenweight between worldliness & unworldliness, between out-winth ((success)) & out-loss ((failure)) swung over, in my mother's case, to a marked taking of sides with the fallen angel, the hunted hero, the bewitching sinner. It was as if the uprisesome ((rebellious)) spirit of Heine & Byron (two poets she early-worshipped) entered into her blood & led her to turn her back forever on smug English-speaking get-on-someness. The blind worship of beauty & genius within her raised her hand forever against that middle-class 'you-butter-my-bread-&-I'll-butter-yours' plan of life that holds the reins in the British Empire & U.S. now-time-life & which brings to naught all the strivings of seers & geniuses to usher in a more frith-true [true to nature], wholesome, joy-lit, beauty-worshipping wont of life.

(L'Avenir, tacking in Skagerrak, off Norway, Sept. 30, 1933)

Source: Untitled section, in 'The Aldridge-Grainger-Ström Saga', W37-9 (Grainger Museum, Melbourne).

➤ 3   [Aldridge Family Weaknesses] (1933)

One cannot help being hopethwarted ((disappointed)) in such as the Aldridges when one finds that they are *never* tired of clinging to outworn stirs such as snobbishness, horseracing, money-fainth ((fondness for money)) (tho I freely own up that they are less steeped in such poisons than most Anglosaxons), never tired of choosing life jobs hanging (as do hotel-keeping, money-securing in mining, motor-car selling & handling, stud-farming) on the askment 'How can I *waste* my time & my money?' instead of hanging on the askment 'How can I *use* my time & my money?' Australia is a land of the glory-full sunrise for mankind's finer, fuller fate. Should not Australians (speak-likementishly speaking ((figuratively speaking))) rise early to joy-use their wondrous dawn? But no, they sleep late (speak-likementishly speaking) in the old English way after a razzle-dazzle English night-before. It stands to reason in a poor-sun-lighted, foggy, hunger-stricken land like England that men should lie late a bed & strive to sidestep the poorness & wretchedness of their landfolkish ((national)) life in a drunken forgetfulness of life-facts. But can sun-blessed, easy-living Australians never creep out of the old snakeskin of their forefathers' old-world sottishness, luckworship, prudery, listlessness?

When I think of these things & real-see the short tether of the yeomanlike Aldridge mantype ((nature))—how it swirls round in a ring, like a dog biting its own tail—I can understand that my mother yearned away to a bright-witted man like my father, who—even if he was afraid of horses—could use his mind, could pin his thots to beauty & forget money & who could, when he was sober, mindbirth a bridge that was worth looking at & could make buildings sit firm in soggy ground, in short, a man abreast of his times, for whom the Greeks, the geniuses, had not lived in vain.[16] The Aldridge love of Dickens or Mark Twain was, if I guess aright, still rooted in mankindliness ((humanitarianism)), still rooted in something brimful of meansome ((normal)) beast-like ((animal)) cravings & fulfillments. Such braininess as my father had his share of was, it must be owned-up-to, a leap off the earth's flatness into some realm of thot-withdrawness ((abstraction)) & lifespurningness; the heraldment, maybe, of mankind's coming powers. I can quite see how my mother must have felt herself tempted to take the leap off the yeoman Aldridge furrow into the airier, less earthbound Grainger brain-life. And I say this who am incurably Aldridge-fain & gainst-Graingerish. I never really felt at home or at one with my father—his looks, his wonts, his moods, his views, his aims, his letters, his worthprizements ((admirations)). On the other hand, the Aldridges (when I am with them) wrap me round with bliss, with heavenly balm. Their looks, their speech, their ways thrill me to the core. I feel no gainst-stir ((reaction)) in their at-ness ((presence)). The Aldridges seem to me so proper, so wholesome, so evenweighted ((balanced)), so loving, so mild, so stalwart, so yielding, so kindly. I wish I could mix my spunk with theirs, that I could help onward-breed their type. So much do I feel all this that I cannot help gainst-stirring ((reacting)) towards those that the Aldridges wed. I feel that no not-Aldridge brood is good enough, clean enough for them to breed with. I long for Aldridges to breed only with Aldridges & to the very core of me I scorn all merely half-Aldridge offspring (the outcome of an Aldridge breeding with a not-Aldridge) as bastards. The wives and husbands that have mated with Aldridges I gainst-feel as tween-lopers ((interlopers)).[17]

Source: Untitled section, in 'The Aldridge-Grainger-Ström Saga', W37-29, dated 13 October 1933 (Grainger Museum, Melbourne).

16. See chapter 2, 'Father'.
17. During his visit to Australia of 1934–35, Grainger completed a series of interviews about family history with his aunt, Clara Aldridge. He had started these interviews during his 1926 Australian visit. The resultant 'Aunty Clara's Aldridge History' was finalized in 1941 (Grainger Museum, Melbourne). It contains 142 entries, including family trees, document copies, and Grainger's transcripts of Clara Aldridge's reminiscences.

➤ 4   [Frank and Clara Aldridge] (1933)

Now Uncle Frank[18] was like the Tsar-son of mankind, cured of the ills of townskillsomeness [civilization] by the tween-comst,[19] not of the gifted ones with their mankindly redes [advice], but of his sculldwarfment & the freedom from mean-some life that it brot with it. No brutal herd of schoolboys turned his work-willingness into gainst-matchment-madness ((the madness of competition)), his breedgroupsome [family] pride into snobbery, his liking for women into sex-slavery, his love of reading & writing into wontsome book-art-craft. So Uncle Frank the feebleminded, & myself the overminded, met & found each other like ourselves—liker than were to us any of those poor other meansome ones that struggled in pain & darkness & heatkeenth outside the pale of our mild feebleminded, our mild overmindedness. (When I met him again in 1924 & 1926 I real-knew ((realized)), stronger than ever before, how like he & I were; so much liker than I felt myself to be to any of my other uncles or cousins—above all, how like his call-to-mindment was to mine, how like his diary[20] to this book I am now writing.)

Aunty Clara is tall & somewhat gaunt, with the utter Aldridge fairness of skin, hair & eyes; a long straight nose; body, longish-built thru out, but with longer length of leg; hands, big-boned and wellworked-looking. At rest her eyes look somewhat staring, not at the spoken-to but into space; when her gaze is turned on the spoken-to it is apt to be sparkling & a bit saucy. Like most Aldridges, Aunty Clara is fidgety & sudden in her movements, staying long in a dreamy restful holdment & then unlookedforly flinging her head aside, or her shoulder up, with a jerk of unequalled suddenness. She is also apt to take unreasonably forceful flicks at specks or other offending scraps on plates or elsewhere; likewise, she dashes out of a room when one would never guess she would. There is no doubt that there is a lot of the startled doe, the hiding hare, in us Aldridges: grandmother of shutting herself up in her room, Aunty Clara flinging & flicking & darting out of reach, Uncle Jim stopping bolting horses & saying nought, my mother hiding under the bed when my father as wooer came to call on her, Uncle Frank running into the bathroom & sweet-sulking there, myself running up to the

---

18. (1867–1931), Rose Grainger's youngest brother, looked after throughout his life by Clara Aldridge.
19. Probably meaning, 'by his handicap'.
20. Uncle Frank's diary, held in the Grainger Museum, Melbourne, mainly records the weather and key family events. Nothing could be less like Grainger's extended saga than its laconic utterances.

highest gallery of the hall in Liverpool & hiding there when 'Irish Tune from County Derry' for blent-choir [mixed chorus] gave me my first great fight-winth [success] as a tone-birther & the listen-host ((audience)) was hand-clapping for me to show up.[21]

Source: Untitled section, in 'The Aldridge-Grainger-Ström Saga', W37-77, dated 30 October 1933 (Grainger Museum, Melbourne).

---

21. 25 September 1909, when *Irish Tune* and *Brigg Fair* were performed by the Liverpool Welsh Choral Union, conducted by Harry Evans.

2

FATHER

            John H. Grainger (1956)

Born Nov. 30, 1855.[1] Died April 13, 1917.
Husband of *Rose Grainger*. Father of *Percy Grainger*.

My father was born in London (England) November 30, 1855.[2] But he came from a Northumbrian family of builders, architects & engineers & he grew up in Durham (England). I have always been told that 'Grainger Street' in Newcastle-on-Tyne was so called because an uncle, or other relative of my father, had built most of the houses in the street.[3]

My father got most of his education at a monastery school at Evetot, France,[4] & at Westminster School, London.[5] His early experiences in France seem to have kindled in him a lifelong devotion to French Gothic architecture. Indeed, he was on fire for beauty everywhere & all his life he collected photos of lovely buildings, pictures, statues, bridges & pasted them into albums, himself adding information about the origin & history of the works of art depicted. This was known as 'Graingerising'. (Many of these 'Graingerised' albums are in this museum.)[6]

---

1. An unused, probably earlier, version of this Legend to a 1956 Grainger Museum display gives his father's year of birth, erroneously, as 1854.
2. In the unused version, Grainger stated that his father was born on a train crossing Blackfriars Bridge, London.
3. Newcastle's Grainger Street was named after the architect Richard Grainger (1797–1861), who fundamentally redesigned the city.
4. Yvetot, 40 kilometres east of Le Havre.
5. Westminster School records make no mention of a John Grainger at this time.
6. Grainger Museum, Melbourne.

My father was apprenticed to a civil engineer & was soon put to work on the construction of King's Cross Railway Station, London.

At the age of 22 (1877) he came to Australia & became Assistant Architect & Engineer to the South Australian Government. The offices where he worked, in Adelaide, were next door to the 'Prince Alfred' Hotel kept by my mother's father (George Aldridge) & my father got to know the Aldridges (my mother's family). Of that period there are gifts of books from my father, showing his fondness for poetry & other artistic subjects. He seems to have thrown himself wholeheartedly into the musical life of Adelaide, having heard much music in London before leaving England. He organised the first string quartet in Adelaide & when he & my mother, newly wed, lived at 'The Stowe Manse'[7] I believe the string quartet (which consisted of Herman Schrader, J. Hall, Jules Meilhan & Frank Winterbottom[8]) rehearsed in their rooms.

While in Adelaide my father won first prize in the competition for Princes Bridge, Melbourne.[9] Out of 21 competitions to which he entered designs at about that time (the last seventies & early eighties) he won 19 first & second prizes.

The construction of Princes Bridge brought my parents to Melbourne, where I was born in 1882. All seemed promising for the Grainger family. Yet only a few years later my father had lost his health & his prosperity.

When I was about seven years old my father became seriously ill & took a sea trip to England for his health. Our dear friend Dr R. Hamilton Russell[10] (who, like ourselves, lived in Glenferrie at that time) said to my mother: 'Jack will not live to see Colombo'. But my father was always fond of the sea & by the time he reached Colombo he was taking part in all the shipboard games. On his return to Australia he settled in Adelaide (living for a year or so with my Uncle George & Aunty May—Mr & Mrs George Sydney Aldridge) & from then on he never lived again with my mother & me, although we always wrote to each other & sometimes met. Most of his water-colour paintings (of which there are 10 in this museum) date from this second Adelaide period.[11]

My father was Chief Architect to the Western Australian Government from 1897 to about 1905, when he retired from that post owing to ill health. Later he returned to Melbourne, where he died in 1917.

---

7. Stowe Manse Chambers, on Flinders Street, where John Grainger lived in 1879 and established his architectural office.

8. Respectively, viola, violin, piano [sic], and cello.

9. Across the Yarra River.

10. (1860–1933), an English medical specialist, academic, and amateur pianist, who befriended the Graingers in 1890 shortly after arriving in Melbourne. See essays 22 and 23.

11. I.e., early to mid-1890s.

My father was always drawn to artistic personalities, such as Jules Meil-han, the French composer, in Adelaide (Meilhan's *Missa Solemnis* is in this museum[12]), and in Melbourne, Dr Henry O'Hara,[13] Dr R. Hamilton Russell, A. E. Aldis the English painter (6 of whose paintings hang in this museum),[14] & Thomas A. Sisley, the English author, painter & elocution teacher (one of his paintings & much of his writings are in this museum).[15]

My father had a decisive effect upon my compositional life. On December 22, 1897 (by which time my mother & I had been two-and-a-half years in Frankfurt, Germany) he wrote to Miss Amy Black (later Mrs A. E. Chalk[16]) as follows: 'I am sending you a copy of Percy's last letter to me, which I am sure you will enjoy. Rose says he gets more Germanised every day, so I shall have to touch him up a bit with Rule Britannia & Hearts of Oak, etc.'

My father sent me a patriotic book 'Deeds that won the Empire' & several Kipling books. The latter captivated me immediately & I soon started writing choral settings of Kipling's poems, especially those in the *Jungle Books*. In these (above all, in 'The Beaches of Lukannon',[17] composed in 1898) I developed my mature harmonic style, that is to say *harmony in unresolved discords*. To the best of my knowledge such a procedure was unknown at that time & must be considered an Australian contribution to musical progress. So through the books my father sent me in 1897 I became what I have remained ever since: a composer whose whole musical output is based on patriotism & racial consciousness.

In matters musical my father was always judging between the quick & the dead. He would say: 'the E flat isn't a patch on the Jupiter'.[18] This put me in the enviable position, even as a young child, of feeling that there was nothing—not even the greatest 'classics'—that I might not sharply criticise.

My father was quick-tempered. If he wanted my mother to play him a certain bit of Beethoven & she said that she would have to look at it first, he would storm out of the room & we would not see him for two or three days. On the other hand, he was never harsh. Once when we were living in Glen-ferrie (where there had been several burglaries & where we had seen a man leap over our fence on coming home one evening) & my father was just fin-

---

12. *Messe solennelle*, for four voices and orchestra, published in Paris in the early 1880s (MG J1/MEI-1).

13. (1853–1921), neighbour of the Graingers in Brighton and their family doctor. He delivered Percy in 1882. See essay 21.

14. (1870–1921), botanical and landscape painter, who boarded with the Graingers in the early 1890s. The Grainger Museum holds, in total, nine works of Aldis.

15. (d. 1925), the Museum holds his *Albert Park Lagoon*.

16. (b. 1868/9), near neighbour of the Graingers in Brighton. For her recollection of the Graingers during the 1880s and 1890s, see Gillies and Pear, *Portrait of Percy Grainger*, 13–15.

17. With text from 'The White Seal' in *The Jungle Book*.

18. Mozart's K.543 and K.551 Symphonies.

ishing an important design, I went to the back part of our house, which was in darkness. Overcome by a sudden panic—born out of fear of the dark, no doubt—I rushed to the lighted, forward, part of the house, screaming 'Thief, thief'. This caused my father to overturn his India ink bottle over his design. Yet all he said to me was: 'You *are* a silly chump'.

He never expressed any pleasure at my playing or compositions. About a somewhat Brahms-like piece I wrote when I was about 15 he said to his friend Mr Schrader, years later: 'If the boy had only stuck to this kind of thing', showing that he was disappointed in my mature style. After taking a cure for his arthritis in Harrogate (England) he happened to be passing through London & heard—unknown to my mother or me—the Balfour Gardiner[19] concert of May 1st, 1912, at which I conducted my English Dance for orchestra[20]—after all, one of my 3 or 4 best works. He rang me up the next morning & said to me: 'it is amusing to hear you young chaps trying your hand'.

At about this time he was very scornful of my earning capacity. He wanted money in order to settle in British Columbia, Canada. He must have been about 58 at the time. 'But you don't know anybody there, do you, father?' I remonstrated. 'That's why I want to go there,' he retorted.

He was also scornful when I arrived in Fremantle in 1908[21] with a black eye—the result of playing cricket on board the boat too late into the twilight the night before. 'I never thought that a son of mine would stop a cricket ball with his eye', was his remark.

In his last years, when crippled with arthritis, my father still had enough enthusiasm for music to spend the evening hours playing his pianola, after his day's work was done.

The following list of the bridges & buildings designed by my father is far from complete:

Princes Bridge, Melbourne
Swing Bridge, Sale, Gippsland
Masonic Hall, Melbourne
Reconstruction of Collins House, Melbourne
Grand Stand of the Ellerslie Race Course, New Zealand[22]
George & Georges, Melbourne
Administrative Block of Town Hall, Melbourne

19. Henry Balfour Gardiner (1877–1950), Grainger's fellow student in Frankfurt and lifelong friend, who organized a series of eight concerts of mainly contemporary English music in 1912–13.
20. (1899–1902, rev. 1906–9).
21. On Grainger's second Australasian tour in the party of the Australian contralto, Ada Crossley.
22. Auckland.

The Law Courts, Perth
Parliament House, Perth
Town Hall, Kalgoorlie
Town Hall, Boulder, W.A.
Federal Coffee Palace (later Hotel), Melbourne
Albert Street Bridge, Adelaide[23]
Public Library, Auckland, New Zealand
Reconstructions of Cliveden Mansions, Melbourne
Town Hall, Hobart
Maryborough Town Hall, Queensland
State Savings Bank, Elizabeth Street, Melbourne
Government House Ballroom, Perth
Town Hall & Port Office, Perth
Post Office, Kalgoorlie
Post Office, Boulder, W.A.

This museum houses two very sympathetic, revealing & informative accounts of my father's personality & artistic enthusiasms, both accounts in manuscript: *Memories of John H. Grainger*,[24] by Mrs Amy E. Chalk (Miss Amy Black); *The Life and Works of John H. Grainger*, by Miss Winifred Falconer.[25] My own memories & anecdotes of my father will be found in this museum in my manuscripts *The Aldridge-Grainger-Ström Saga* and *Ere-I-Forget*.

Percy Aldridge Grainger
March 15, 1956

Source: 'John H. Grainger', Museum Legend (with two variants) (Grainger Museum, Melbourne).

➤ 6   [John H. Grainger in Adelaide] (ca. 1933)

She [Mrs Fred H. Tothill][26] first saw my mother in the theatre (Hindley Street, Adelaide), when my mother was about 8 or 9 (Jessie Renner was herself about 15 at the time[27]). Dick Knucky (see Aunty Clara's 'Aldridge His-

---

23. Now The Albert Bridge, Adelaide.
24. Written in June–July 1934.
25. Unpublished manuscript 134–1 (Grainger Museum). Falconer was companion ('niece') to Grainger's father in his later years.
26. Née Jessie Renner.
27. I.e., about 1869–70.

tory', p. 20[28]) was J. R.'s adopted brother. My mother (when first seen by J. R.)
was with Jim Aldridge (P. G.'s Uncle Jim). 'Jim & George never went anywhere without yr mother in those days. They adored her. She wore her hair
loose—standing out.' At her first ball (Freemasons' Ball) she still had kept her
hair just as fair. Her dress was a silvery grey. Dick Knucky was much older.
When her father (Dr Frederick Renner) was in town (Adelaide), he went to
'The Southern Cross' & Rose (my mother) would come in. Dr Renner was
the doctor of the expedition Telegraph Construction Party, started at Port Au-
gusta, & went right up to Port Darwin. They were away nearly 2 years. The
Renners lived at Kapunda.[29] My father arrived about 1877. The 3 (Jessie Ren-
ner, Fred Tothill[30] & J. H. Grainger) were a lot together until J. Renner's mar-
riage in 1880. Fred Tothill & J. H. Grainger batched together the year before.
About Easter of 1880 J.H.G. brought the musicians together for the 4-tet.
Meilhan (dark, short, French in figure, but with a look about him that was
not French quite) (Alsatian, maybe—Mühl-Hans?) came out from Europe &
J. H. Grainger interested the people of Adelaide—sent out invitations for
Meilhan's recital, & it was only a few weeks later that the string 4-tet concerts
commenced. Frank Winterbottom was such a splendid cellist, [John] Hall
was the chief violinist—a beautiful violinist (chief violinist at the theatre).
Breitenstein the pianist often played with them. It may have been with Breitenstein my mother studied. Heuzenroeder may have been the piano teacher at
whom Rosa[31] threw the music. What helped music even more than the string
quartet were the Sunday mornings at my father's (J.H.G.) rooms—at his office, Flinders Street, next to the old church near the post office (The Manse?).
All the musical spirits seemed to be there on Sunday mornings. My father interested Sir Thomas Elder in music at that time.[32] My father went in for
everything—if he bought Eno's fruit salad[33] he'd buy a whole case of it. 'He
was so young, so youth[ful], too—only 22 when I first knew him. He quickly
got command of things—he was very generous. He came out with letters to
the engineer-in-chief & got a position right away. You could imagine yr father

28. That section (T-181, section 20) is entitled 'Dick Knucky & his wife (Eva Hawke)'. Knuck[e]y
    had worked with Grainger's Uncle George on the telegraph line in the Northern Territory in the
    early 1870s.
29. 80 kilometres northeast of Adelaide.
30. At this time, a bank clerk; he shared lodgings with John H. Grainger in 1879.
31. I.e., Grainger's mother.
32. In 1883, the pastoralist and philanthropist Thomas Elder (1817–97) would endow the first Aus-
    tralian chair in music at the University of Adelaide, and in 1897, his further bequest led to the
    founding of the Elder Conservatorium.
33. A digestive powder.

would not stay long in the office. He soon got on his feet. A contractor called Davies got interested in him & yr father designed the Albert Street bridge—they carried it out together. Then the firm Grainger, Naish & Worsley was formed & it was [in] their room at The Manse. Naish was a grand little man. Then yr father drew the designs for Princes Bridge. The firm didn't last very long, but Naish stayed with yr father, while Worsley went up to N.S.W. It was there (office at The Manse?) yr father designed the beautiful house for the Barr Smiths & Sir Thomas Elder.[34] A house he was always very proud of was "Werocata", built for young Bowman, near Port Wakefield.' Mr & Mrs Tothill went up near Crystal Brook, S.A.,[35] to open up the country. 'That seemed really far North then. J.H.G. was groomsman at my wedding.' J.H.G. built some buildings on the Terrace.

Reyher was the name of an old musician. 'I feel quite sure that the Conservatorium came into Elder's mind in yr father's rooms. It was no small thing in those days to have got the men together & kept them up to it. You couldn't buy Beethoven's sonatas when I was a girl of 16. Music was so difficult to get. There were only 8 mails a year from home [Britain]. Ketten[36] came about 1880. I was so disappointed not to be able to hear him. Father (Dr Renner) had a song he was very fond of: "The lark now rises from her watery nest". All the cities were just in the making. J. H. Grainger won designs in many places: something in Sydney, a bridge in Brisbane, and so on.'

Source: 'Mrs Fred H. Tothill's (born Jessie M. Renner) Information about Rosa Aldridge (Mrs J.H.G.) & John H. Grainger (P.G.'s Parents)',[37] in 'Sketches for My Book "The Life of My Mother & Her Son"', W35-77, undated (about 1933; Grainger Museum, Melbourne).

7 My Father's Comment on Cyril Scott's Magnificat (1953)

When my father came to Paris to build the West-Australian Court of the 1900 Paris Exhibition (as West-Australian Government Architect)[38] he came to Frankfurt for a few days (probably in 1899) to see mother & me. (We had

---

34. Joanna Lang Elder, sister of Thomas Elder, married Robert Barr Smith (1824–1915) in 1856. John Grainger designed 'Auchendarroch', their summer retreat at Mt. Barker, in 1880.
35. 210 kilometres north of Adelaide.
36. Henry Ketten (1848–83), pianist.
37. Grainger added 'written out by P. G. in first person'.
38. For further comment on John Grainger's role in this exhibition, see essay 79.

not met since 1895.)[39] Father went with us to the Klimsches[40] for an evening. It seems that he talked all the time about himself & said next to nothing about mother & me. Dear old Karl Klimsch was awfully against father. 'You should never go back to that man,' Klimsch said to mother. It must have been at the West End Pension that father met Cyril Scott[41] & heard Cyril play thru his Magnificat,[42] which was just finished, or half-finished, at that time. 'Very reverent', was father's comment on the work. This amused Cyril extremely, for the last thing he had in mind, in writing the Magnificat, was reverence. That is the difference between conventional Englishmen like my father & German-trained Britishers like Cyril & me. Any interest in religion on our parts was totally excluded. (But some years later, after being long enough in England to be re-Anglicised, Cyril could be religious—in the Yogi way.)[43]

Århus Kommunehospital,[44] Aug. 10, 1953.

Source: 'My Father's Comment on Cyril Scott's Magnificat: "Very Reverent". Klimsch's Estimate of Father', in 'Grainger's Anecdotes', 423-36 (Grainger Museum, Melbourne).

➤ 8   Mother's Experience with Scotch & Irish (1953)

Some time before father left us (when I was 7?) he had delirium tremens very badly. Mother had to take him by train from that country place where the cockies[45] descended on the fruit trees in thousands (leaving me with Mrs McGee[46] there—the place where Mrs McGee smacked Faerie [in Danish] on the bum[47]) [in English] down to Melbourne. Mother was alone with father in a railway compartment & he was very violent & mother said she was frightened. Mother got father into a hospital or somewhere, but had no money to

---

39. When Rose and Percy Grainger had left Melbourne for Frankfurt.
40. The family of Karl Klimsch (1841–1926), a printer who acted as Percy Grainger's male mentor during his years in Frankfurt.
41. (1879–1970), English composer, fellow student of Grainger's in Frankfurt, and lifelong friend.
42. (1899), for chorus, orchestra, soloists, and organ. Grainger transcribed it for solo piano in 1899.
43. Grainger refers to Scott's interest in mysticism and the paranormal. In later life, he wrote books about occultism and medicine 'rational and irrational'.
44. In Denmark, where Grainger was to undergo surgery for prostate cancer on 20 August.
45. Cockatoos.
46. Mrs. John McGee, at whose home in North Brighton Percy Grainger frequently played. Her daughter, Faerie (Mary) McGee, was one of his most frequent playmates.
47. See, further, essay 59.

pay for things. So she went to a Scotchman she knew father was working for, preventing this Scotchman's factory, built too near the Yarra, from sinking. 'Foundations' were one of father's specialities, & mother knew that the Scotchman—who had previously tried other architects to stop his factory from sinking in the soft ground near the river—was delighted with father's non-sinking treatments. But when she asked this Scotchman for some money to pay for father's illness he said, 'But how do I know you *are* Mrs Grainger?' On the stairway an Irishman, whom mother knew only slightly, saw mother with tears in her eyes, & asked her what was the matter. On hearing how matters stood the Irishman took a hundred pounds (or some ample sum) from his pocket & handed it to mother. That incident typified for mother the difference between the Irish & the Scotch. I think the doctor said that father was suffering more from nicotine poisoning than from his drinking. Mother used to make cigarettes for father (roll them) by the hundreds—cheaper that way.

Århus Kommunehospital, Aug. 19, 1953.

Source: 'Mother's Experience with Scotch & Irish', in 'Grainger's Anecdotes', 423–83 (Grainger Museum, Melbourne).

9   How Would We Ordinary Men Get On If the Clever Ones Did Not Destroy Themselves? (1953)

I suppose it was about the time of my father's delirium tremens & nicotine poisoning that mother overheard 2 men talking about my father in a train (she could not see them, but heard them over the ½-wall separating the compartments). They were talking about his illness & one of them remarked how strange it was that so many exceptionally clever men did things that destroyed their health & spoilt their careers. The other answered: 'How would we ordinary men get on at all if the clever ones didn't destroy themselves?' I seem to remember that there was some story about me talking to a whole compartment of train-travellers between Brighton [48] & Melbourne—showing my un-shy-ness & trust in people. I would like to know when I developed my shyness & diffidence.

Aug. 19, '53, Århus Kommunehospital

48. Where the Graingers lived until 1885.

Source: 'How Would We Ordinary Men Get On If the Clever Ones Did Not Destroy Themselves?' in 'Grainger's Anecdotes', 423–84 (Grainger Museum, Melbourne).

➤ 10   My Father in My Childhood (1954)

My father was never cruel or bad-tempered with either mother or me—only quick-tempered. If he got into an argument (as to the height of the Cologne Cathedral as compared with the length of the cable-laying steamer 'The Great Eastern',[49] for instance) & was proved wrong he would slam the door, storm out of the house & not turn up for 2 or 3 days—his clothes filthy from having lain drunk in a gutter, or the like. Mother said he was always very nice with his workingmen. One evening (in Glenferrie) he asked mother to read a movement of a Beethoven sonata, but mother said she could not read it without trying it thru first. Father got angry, snatched the music away & stormed out of the house, saying he knew someone who would read it for him. (That was a barmaid at a hotel in Glenferrie.) On this occasion he stayed away a few days & came back in a bad state. Then he would swear off the drink for a while & then a more pleasant, lively & happy man couldn't be found, mother said—nor a more contrite. (His letters to his father were full of what a wonderful wife he had, & how wonderfully she was bringing up her little boy.) Sometimes mother would feel that he shouldn't be left to himself & would then go with father to his office every day. He would then be so energetic, clearminded, happy & sensible that mother said she couldn't possibly believe he could ever be weak again & drink. So she would let him go alone to town, & in a few days he would be back where he had been—drinking, wretched, quick-tempered. He would take me for a walk & tell me not to bend my knees like a working man. He would come back to mother & say, 'I can't do a thing with the boy'. Mother wondered whether he lied, or just forgot facts. He would say, 'My dear old dad is dead', showing a great deal of feeling. A few months later he would say, 'I've just written a letter to my dear old dad'. Mother would say, 'I thought you said he had died'. 'Nothing of the sort.' He did his designing in a middle room at 'Kilalla' (Glenferrie)[50] & wonderfully neat it all was. I suppose he was designing for competitions. (About the first time he came to Melbourne (from Adelaide—about 1881 or 1882) he entered 21 or 22 competitions & won 18 or 19 first & second prizes.) One evening at Kilalla I had been in the unlighted back part of the house & rushed back in a

49. When launched in 1858, the largest ship in the world; from 1865 until 1872, used to lay cables.
50. 36 Oxley Road, Hawthorn, where the Graingers lived from 1888 to 1892.

fright (I was always afraid of the dark) shouting 'thief'. My father sprang up in a great hurry & overturned the India ink over his design. Father said 'What a stoopid chump you are', but didn't get angry, altho he had to draw his design all over again.[51]

Once my dog would go with father to the station, tho I tried to induce the dog to stay with me. I was so peeved, I threw a chair at a chest of drawers. (I think that was the last time I gave way to anger in my life.) We had a nice bull terrier & father's delight seemed to be for us to go walking with the dog, & for the dog to kill as many cats as possible. (We gave away this dog to a butcher. It was hard to get the dog to stick to his new home, but he did, after a time. Later the railway ran over one of his legs & he came back to Kilalla, hiding under the house, & died there.)

In those days (when I was 6 or 7) there was a lot of tennis, & I picked up the balls. Father liked tennis, cricket, long walks & most games. On Sundays we went mushroom-gathering, generally with some supposed-to-be danger-ous bull somewhere. I think it was on Saturdays we took the steamer to Por-tarlington[52] (gathered periwinkles at our destination?). Young volunteer sol-diers would be on board, lifting up each other's feet & smacking each other's behinds, drawing from my father the word 'louts'. I think I have written else-where of mother & me going with father to the cricket matches between Eng-lish & Australian teams. When the Australians came onto the field father said indignantly, 'Look at the louts. No gloves.' And when the Australian team won there was nothing but bad temper, of course.

Mother sometimes said to father: 'I don't think I'm the right kind of wife for you. I'm too easy-going. If you lived with someone stricter, who got angry when you drank, you might give it up.' Perhaps this idea worked upon him & played its part in making him stay in South Australia after his trip to England, when I was 8. I think he took the trip for his health. This was after the delir-ium tremens & nicotine poisoning. Dr Russell took him to the boat ('Oruba') & came back & said to mother, 'Jack won't live to reach Colombo'. But father had always been fond of the sea, & by the time he reached Colombo was tak-ing part in all the games. His father would not see him when he got to En-gland (had heard of his drinking, or his love affair with Mrs Smayle[53] maybe; or maybe was still horror-struck at father having left the girl in England who had a child by him before father came out to Adelaide), so father came back to

---

51. Cf. recollection of this story in essay 5.
52. 40 kilometres southwest of Melbourne, across Port Phillip.
53. This affair, with a local widow in Brighton, took place in 1882, before Percy Grainger was born. He always believed that his father had contracted syphilis from Mrs. Smayle and thereby in-fected his mother.

Australia by the same boat he had gone to England. This is borne out by 2 entries in Uncle Frank's Diary:

> Sept. 10, 1890: Jack started out to England, in the steamship Oruba.
> Dec. 18, 1890: Jack arrived today, with steamship, Oruba.

Why father didn't come back to Melbourne, but stayed in Adelaide with Uncle George & Aunty May, I don't know, unless it was mother's idea (stated above) that he might give up drinking if he lived with someone he stood more in awe of. Around 1924 or 1925 Aunty May told me that Uncle George never talked to father of father's drinking & always had the whisky decanter within sight, so that father should feel he was trusted in Uncle George's home. And the story is that father never drank after that trip to England—a story mother never quite believed. Father got on well with the Aldridges & got out of them benefits that might otherwise have gone to my mother—I don't think. If mother had ever let her mother & other members of the Aldridge family know that father had given mother Spanish Sickness[54] they mightn't have been so keen on father—Uncle George, Uncle Charlie, and so on. But mother was glad that her family liked father & didn't want to do or say anything that might make him less liked by them. If Aunty Clara had known the real reason why mother sometimes dashed over to Adelaide with me—her horror of giving birth to a child blind or mad or otherwise tainted by Spanish Sickness—she would not have spoken of these trips as she did: 'When your mother had one of her flying fits'. Father got a job with the Anguses—to build houses for workmen or station hands near Clare, S.A. Mother & I went to visit him there, & I remember father pointing out the height of the ceiling in the room we were to have: 'They don't build that way nowadays'. There was something wrong in mother's eyes about the arrangements for her & me, there near Clare. The room, or the beds, were not prepared, or something. So we dashed off to a hotel in Clare (English-speaking huffiness). With the trip to Clare is linked up a long drive in an old stage coach & the smell of hot leather being scraped off the leather brake by the iron wheel. Linked up with Clare is also the sweet sound of my mother playing the slow movement of Beethoven's E minor-E major Piano Sonata.[55]

[on train], N. York–Chic., May 12, 1954

Source: 'My Father in My Childhood', in 'Grainger's Anecdotes', 423–85 (Grainger Museum, Melbourne).

54. Syphilis.
55. Op. 90. Grainger here, somewhat inaccurately, quoted the opening notes of the slow movement.

≈ 3 ≈

MOTHER

≫ 11   Dates of Important Events and Movements
in the Life of Rose Grainger (1923)

Maiden Name: Rose Annie Aldridge
Married Name: Mrs. John H. Grainger

July 3, 1861 Born at Adelaide, South Australia; daughter of George Aldridge and Sarah Jane Aldridge (maiden name: Grant).[1] Both parents came from Kent, England.

1861–1880 (up to 19 years of age) In Adelaide; happy devoted family life with her parents and grandmother, with her sisters Clara and Emma,[2] with her brothers George, Jim, Ted, Fred, Charlie and Frank; fond of animals, a fearless rider and driver; known as a 'tom-boy'; studying the piano of her own accord (first from a school chum) and from childhood on devouring masses of literature (specially fond of Hans Christian Andersen's and other fairy tales, Greek Mythology, *The Arabian Nights*, and poetry).

October 1, 1880 (aged 19) Married John Harry Grainger (aged 25; born in London, England, of a Durham family), architect and civil engineer, designer of: Princes Bridge and Masonic Building, Melbourne (Australia); Swing Bridge, Sale, Gippsland; Law Courts, Perth (Western Australia); Town Hall, Coolgardie; and other public buildings in Australia and New Zealand. He organized the first string quartet in Adelaide (about 1880?), painted and sang, but played no musical instrument.

---

1. Elsewhere, in essay 1, Grainger gives this maiden name as Brown.
2. Emma Elizabeth Aldridge (1855–81).

About 1881–middle of 1895 (aged 20–33) Life mainly in Melbourne (Victoria, Australia); tho with rare trips to Sydney, N.S.W., and frequent trips to see her relatives in Adelaide.

July 8, 1882 (aged 21) Birth of her son (only child) George Percy Grainger (pen-name as composer: Percy Aldridge Grainger; 'Aldridge' adopted because he thought, or hoped, that his music reflected some of the beloved qualities of his mother's family) at Brighton, suburb of Melbourne. Henceforward, for the rest of her life, was never separated from her son for more than a week or so at a time (longest separations; about 6 weeks in 1904, and the last 8½ weeks of her life).[3] All subsequent events and movements on this list are to be understood as having been experienced by Rose Grainger and her son together, unless otherwise stated.

About 1887–about 1892 Sat beside her son (aged 5–10) for 2 or more hours daily while he practised the piano.

About 1891 or 1892[4] Her husband went to England for his health. After this they never lived together again, tho they very occasionally met, throughout the years, and corresponded, off and on, up to his death in 1917. (In May, 1912, she, her husband and her son, together, heartily enjoyed Harry Lauder[5] in a London music-hall.)

About 1891–middle of 1895 (aged about 26–33) Despite delicate health and torments of neuralgia earned the livelihood for herself and her son as piano teacher in Melbourne. During this period she appeared in public at least once as pianist.

1892 or 1893 First public appearance of her son (aged 10) as pianist, in Melbourne.[6]

About 1894 Received from her son, as 'birthday-gift' for her birthday, July 3, several of his compositions (the first, or one of the first, of his musical manuscripts) presented in an elaborately decorated cover or bag sewn by him and consisting of cardboard, lace, scrapwork, kitchen curtains, part of a stocking, small stars of silver paper, etc.

Middle of 1895 (aged 33) Departure for Germany, after her son having appeared several times in concerts in Melbourne and once in Adelaide.

---

3. Rose Grainger did not accompany her son on his six-week tour of South Africa in February–March 1904, nor did she accompany him on his tour of Canada and central-western United States that started with a concert in Winnipeg on 7 March 1922.
4. Correctly, 1890.
5. (1870–1950), Scottish baritone and composer.
6. Grainger's first public appearance as a pianist appears to have been on 9 July 1894 in Melbourne's Masonic Hall.

Vivid Esthetic Impressions of the Australian Years (1861–1895)[7]

Literature (somewhat in the order probably read): H. C. Andersen's *Household Stories* (Fairy Tales), *Arabian Nights*, Homer, Greek Mythology, Byron (especially *Lara, The Bride of Abydos, Manfred, Don Juan*), Goethe (*Hermann and Dorothea*, etc.), Heine (*Poems, Notes of Travel*), Shakespeare, Tennyson (particularly *The Idylls of the King*), Dickens, Thackeray (especially *Vanity Fair*), Bulwer Lytton, Ouida,[8] *Little Lord Fauntleroy, Jackanapes*,[9] Adelaide Anne Procter's poetry, Zola's *Nana*, Balzac's *Droll Stories*, George Moore's *A Mummer's Wife*, Hardy's *Tess*, Kipling's *The Light that Failed*, R. L. Stevenson's *Treasure Island*. Music (somewhat in the order probably experienced): Old English songs, Stephen Foster's songs, Beethoven sonatas, selections from Verdi and Gounod, Mozart operas (piano scores), Heller's *Restless Nights*, Grieg's and Schumann's piano compositions, Schubert's, Schumann's and many other songs.

Italian opera troupes in Adelaide (about 1877?). Ketten's piano recitals in Adelaide (about 1879?). First hearing of Wagner, Gounod's *Funeral March of a Marionette* and other orchestral music, conducted by Frederic Cowen,[10] at Melbourne exhibition of about 1890.[11] Charles Hallé's[12] piano recitals in Melbourne, between 1890–1892.

Natural beauties of the Blue Mountains, N.S.W. (about 1881).

Natural beauties of Heidelberg, Narbethong, Wood End, Fern Tree Gully, etc., all in Victoria (between 1883–1892).

'Mushrooming' excursions in rural country around Melbourne (about 1890).

Taking part in Shakespearean performances in Melbourne (between 1889–1895).

(European) Summer 1895–Xmas 1900 (aged 33–38) Life in Frankfurt-am-Main, Germany, earning the livelihood for herself and her son by giving

---

7. Detailed annotations are not provided for these extensive listings of 'esthetic impressions'; rather, annotations are provided when independent mention is made of persons or works in this or other essays.
8. Louise De La Ramée (1839–1908), English novelist.
9. (1883), by Juliana Horatia Ewing (1841–85).
10. (1852–1935), English conductor, pianist, and composer.
11. Correctly, 1888, at the Centennial Exhibition.
12. (1819–95), German-born English pianist and conductor.

English lessons—greatly overtaxing her frail health. Her son studying music at Dr. Hoch's Conservatorium, drawing and painting landscapes, old buildings, ruins, etc., in and round Frankfurt, on the Rhine, etc. Rose Grainger greatly beloved and kindly treated by her pupils; her artistic and spiritual self nurtured and satisfied by the rich world of culture suddenly opened up to her; a sense of great liberation.

About 1898 Her son (aged about 16) matures his compositional style and his consistent activities as a musical composer begin (tho holding his compositions back from public performance until about 1911—with 2 or 3 exceptions). From now on he prepared and dedicated to her compositions (as 'birthday-gifts' and 'yule-gifts') for wellnigh every remaining birthday and yuletide of her life.

1898 or 1899 First acquaintance with Walt Whitman's *Leaves of Grass*[13]—destined to become a leading spiritual and artistic influence in her and her son's life.

Xmas 1899–Autumn 1900 (aged 38–39) Serious breakdown of health. Short stays in San Remo, Nice, Paris, London, Glasgow.

Autumn 1900–Summer 1901 Life in Frankfurt resumed. Second serious breakdown of health (lying for months on iced pipes, chiefly nursed by her son). Her son begins earning the livelihood for her and himself as pianist, piano teacher and accompanist.

Vivid Esthetic Impressions of the Frankfurt Years (1895–1901)

Wagner's music dramas, music of Brahms, Tchaikovsky, etc., *Nora* and other plays of Ibsen, Hauptmann's *Die versunkene Glocke*, Sudermann's *Katzensteg*, Ludwig Fulda's poem *Immer sind wir so allein*, death-bed story by Schnitzler, Burns's poems, Kipling's prose and poetry, Walt Whitman's *Leaves of Grass*. Ludwig Wüllner's[14] singing and platform personality. Trips along the Rhine and to Heidelberg; bicycling around Frankfurt and in the Taunus; holiday at Brückenau (Oberfranken).

Summer 1901–Summer 1914 (aged 39–53) Life mainly in London (England), her son chiefly active as concert pianist.

---

13. The various editions of *Leaves of Grass* by the American poet Walt Whitman (1819–92) date from the 1850s to the 1890s.
14. (1858–1938), German actor and baritone.

About July 1903–about April, 1904 First Australian concert tour. On the sea-voyage to Australia started to learn Danish. Returning to England by way of South Africa, greatly impressed by the first sight of Table Mountain, Cape Town.

Summer 1907 First trip to Scandinavia (several weeks at Svinkløv, Jylland, Denmark).

Summer of 1908 (?)[15] Keenly enjoyed a few days' folksong-collecting in North-East Lincolnshire (England) with her son and friends; vividly impressed and touched with the vital and affectionate personalities and pregnant art of several of the old rural songsters.

June 1908–(European) spring 1909 Second Australasian concert tour. In Christchurch (New Zealand) museum instantly impressed with African and South Sea Island beadwork, an enthusiasm in which her son soon joined her. During this tour he made as a gift to her a beadwork neck and breast ornament in South African style that took 60 hours of work. She and her son thrilled with Maori dancing, singing and reciting at Rotorua, New Zealand. Soon after this they started learning the Maori language.

1910–1914 (aged 49–52) Often accompanying her son on his concert tours in Norway, Denmark, Holland, Germany, Russia, Finland.

Outstanding Esthetic Impressions of Trips on European Continent (1910–1914)

Happy collecting old Scandinavian embroideries, 'aaklaer', wood carvings and other relics. Relishing, in Kristiania,[16] theatre performances of Lengyel's *Taifun*, Oscar Wilde's *Lady Windermere's Fan*, Björnson's *Sigurd Slembe*, Tolstoy's *Anna Karenina*, Ibsen plays, etc., also *slåtter*[17]-playing by peasant fiddlers at Kristiania *Bondeungdomslaget*. In Berlin (about 1912) impressed with stage performance of Strindberg's *Totentanz*. In Norway (1912 or 1913) translated into English, with her son, the Faerösk text of his composition *The Merry Wedding* (*Brúnsveins Visa*). Greatly benefitted by the climate of Slemdal (outside Kristiania); never so well as there. Much relished hearing Sibelius conduct his orchestral compositions, Herman Bang read from his novels and stories, both in Kristiania. Greatly tickled with humorous film in Copenhagen. While on a visit to Frankfurt (1912 or 1913) read Huxley and

15. Late May 1908.
16. Oslo.
17. Norwegian folk dances.

Lubbock with delight. Greatly struck with the almost oriental lavishness of the Hermitage Palace, Petrograd[18] (1913). Impressed with the breaking up of the ice at the junction of the rivers, seen from Bellevue Hotel, Dordrecht, Holland (1912?).[19]

About 1911 Urged her son (then about 29) to publish and publicly perform his musical compositions; to which, after much consideration, he agreed.

1911–1914 Enjoyed hearing orchestral, choral and chamber performances of compositions by her son and by his fellow-composers Cyril Scott, Balfour Gardiner, Roger Quilter, Frederick Delius, Frederick Austin and others, at concerts in London, Bournemouth, Torquay, etc. Herself played elaborate guitar part in her son's *Scotch Strathspey and Reel* at his chamber concert of his own compositions, May 21, 1912, at Aeolian Hall, London. She also played the resonophone (bass glockenspiel) in orchestral performances of her son's compositions in London and Bournemouth in 1914.

Other Chief Esthetic Impressions and Interests of the London Years
(1901–1914)

Sir Walter Scott's *Minstrelsy of the Scottish Border* and other Scotch Border Ballads, Björnson's *Paa Guds Veie*, Kipling's books as they appeared, Darwin, Herbert Spencer, Weininger's *Geschlecht und Charakter*, Meredith's *Diana of the Crossways, The Egoist*, etc., Swinburne's *Before Dawn, Atalanta in Calydon*, etc., Dowson's poems, Bernard Shaw's *Candida*, Lafcadio Hearn, Maeterlinck's 'Life of the Bee', Jekyll's *Jamaican Folk Tales*, Hjalmar Thuren's collection of Faerösk folksongs, Danish texts of Evald Tang Kristensen's *Jydske Folkeviser* (some of which she learned by heart), Tolstoy's *Anna Karenina*, J. P. Jacobsen's novels (especially *Mogens* and *Fru Föns*), Selma Lagerlöf's *Tössen fra Stormyrshuset*, etc., Herman Bang's *En glad Dag* and *Ved Vejen*, Cranmer-Byng's *A Lute of Jade*, Herbert A. Giles' *Chinese Poetry in English Verse*, Gustav Wied's *Dansemus*, etc., Strindberg's *Paaske*, Stanley Houghton's play *Hindle Wakes*, Max Beerbohm's *A Christmas Garland*, George Moore's *Hail and Farewell*, Pierre Loti's novelettes, Björnson's *Over Evne*.

Especially remembered performances were: Lecture by Shaw on *The Middle Class*, ushered in by grand Bach Prelude and Fugue on the organ; Ed-

18. St. Petersburg, where Grainger played the Grieg Concerto under Siloti's direction on 8 November 1913 (Western dating).
19. Perhaps at the time of Grainger's concert in Dordrecht on 10 January 1912.

vard Grieg's London concerts of his own compositions, himself conducting and playing (1906); Cecil J. Sharp's *Morris Dance* performances; several hearings of Harry Lauder (1909–1914).

Enjoyed collecting old English furniture, Russian and Tartar woodcarvings, embroideries and fabrics, etc. Translated (with friends) part of Herman Bang's *Oscar Heinrich* from Danish into English (between 1911–1914).

After return from second Australasian tour she and her son made several copies of South African and South Sea Island beadwork (1909–1914).

September 1914 (aged 53) Arrival in Boston, Mass., U.S.A.

About October 1914–June 1921 (aged 53–59) Life mainly in New York City, U.S.A.

November–December 1916 First Far-Western trip (California, Colorado, etc.). Snowed up in train for 2 or 3 days, at Medicine Bow, Wyoming, at yuletide.

July 12, 1917–January 6, 1919 Her son soldier in U.S.A. Army. With him at Fort Hamilton, South Brooklyn (Long Island, U.S.A.), summer of 1917, and at Bay Ridge, South Brooklyn, early 1918. Early in 1918 she played resonophone with his band (15th Band, Coast Artillery Corps, U.S.A.) in performances of his compositions.

February 1918 (aged 57) Record made by the Duo-Art reproducing piano of her and her son's playing, on two pianos, of his settings of *Hermundi illi* (Faerösk folksong) and *As Sally sat aweeping* (English folksong from Dorsetshire).[20]

June–August 1919 First summer in Chicago.

March–May 1920 Second Far-Western trip (Oregon, California, New Mexico), with several heavenly days alone with her son at Barstow, in the Californian desert (herself learning Spanish, her son working at his compositions and trying to draw the magic beauties of the desert hills); also seeing much, and collecting some, fine Indian work at Albuquerque, N.M.

June–August 1920 Second summer in Chicago.

December 1920 Short trip to Havana, Cuba.[21]

June 1920 (aged 58) Became U.S. citizen; her husband having died in 1917; her son having become U.S. citizen, June 3, 1918.

June 5, 1921–April 30, 1922 Life mainly at her and her son's home at White Plains N.Y.[22]

---

20. These two works were published as *Two Musical Relics of My Mother* by Schirmer (New York) in 1924.
21. Grainger gave three solo recitals in Havana during 16–21 December 1920.
22. 7 Cromwell Place, where Grainger continued to live until his death in 1961.

Summer 1921 (aged 59–60) Musically very active; playing ukulele in her son's guitar and ukulele rehearsals and playing at 2 pianos with her son and others—thus fulfilling her wish, expressed long years before, that she would play duets with her son when she was 60 years old.

January 1922 Serious breakdown of health.

April 30, 1922 (aged 60) Tragic death in New York City (her son absent in California).

Strongest Esthetic Impressions of the American Years (1914–1922)

New York Clef Club (Negro chorus and orchestra) in Will Marion Cook's *Rain Song* and *Evocation,* Hampton (Negro) vocal quartet, Natalie Curtis Burlin's rendering of Indian folksongs and Indian-Spanish music, George Moore's *The Brook Kerith* and *Evelyn Innes*, performances of Herman Sandby's compositions, 'Emily Sparks', 'William Jones' and 'Lucinda Matlock' in Edgar Lee Masters's *Spoon River Anthology*, 'General William Booth enters Heaven', 'The Congo' and 'The Santa Fé Trail' by Vachel Lindsay, Henry T. Finck's *Primitive and Romantic Love* and *Gardening with Brains*, Swedish film of Selma Lagerlöf's *The Girl from the Marsh-Croft*. Enjoyed hearing performances of her son's compositions in New York City, Chicago, San Francisco, Worcester, Mass., Norfolk, Conn., Evanston, Ill., Bridgeport, Conn., etc.

Thrilled by the Columbia River, Ore., and other natural beauties of New Mexico, Arizona, California, Oregon, Wyoming, Utah, etc.—mainly seen from train windows and often at dawn or early morning.

Source: 'Dates of Important Events and Movements in the Life of Rose Grainger Compiled by Her Adoring Son, Percy Grainger', dated 30 April 1923, in *Photos of Rose Grainger and of 3 Short Accounts of Her Life by Herself, in Her Own Hand-Writing, reproduced for her kin and friends by her adoring son, Percy Grainger* (private publication, 1923), 3–5.

➤ 12 [How I Have Loved Her, How I Love Her Now] (1922)

How poignantly I remember now that night in the Taunus, about 1898, when boarding at Guern's house in Kronberg[23] with mother—the night following the evening when I first kissed Mimi,[24] the night I tossed wakeful & crying;

23. About fifteen kilometres northwest of Frankfurt.
24. Mimi Kwast (1879–1926) was Grainger's first girlfriend. Her father, James Kwast (1852–1927), taught Grainger the piano at the Hoch Conservatory. She later married the German composer Hans Pfitzner.

crying that my boyhood had passed & that with the coming of sexual love the door was being shut upon my Australian childhood & its central resolve—the resolve of never marrying, but of living always with my darling mother, shielding & supporting her, trying to make good to her, thru my love & ministry of love, the tragedies of her marriage & disease. 'Faithless to my boyhood & its resolves' was the thought uppermost in my mind, that night at Kronberg as I lay & wept—& how vividly the spears of the garden fences & my old preoccupations with armour came to my mind.

Because I admitted to her, during the last months of her life, that I had, in the past in Europe, longed deeply for marriage, did she think my love for her, my life with her, partly a sham? And did she therefore get ill as she did, lose hold on life & hope & music as she did? If only she could know the truth: *How I have loved her, how I love her now.*[25]

Kristiania,[26] early Sept, 1922.

Source: Untitled section, in 'Sketches for My Book "The Life of My Mother & Her Son"', W35-4 (Grainger Museum, Melbourne).

➤ 13   Thought Mother Was 'God'. Something of This Still Remains (1923)

As a child (at the first 'Kilalla' in Melbourne[27]) the thought often came to me that mother was really God. She was the only creature I had seen who seemed as if she had created everything, was responsible for everything. So I suspected she really was God & that she had the Bibles written & the Church services going just to fool me. Something of this innate conception of her supremeness has stayed with me always & I notice it, now that she is gone, in a funny way about buying clothes. I so seldom bought anything for myself, except army boots & an occasional bright blue tie, in her time. She would have shirts, socks, collars, pyjamas, etc., ready for me at home, me only having to try them on. And how lazy I was in doing that tiny end of the task, how often I'd keep her waiting for days before carrying out her wish to have me try on this or that! How seldom I voiced a hearty thankfulness for all she took off my shoulders! How natural it seemed that they should be waiting there for me at

---

25. Grainger's mother had committed suicide in April 1922.
26. Oslo, where Grainger began a Scandinavian concert tour on 8 September.
27. Grainger lived in two houses named 'Kilalla' during his Melbourne childhood, the first in Hawthorn (Glenferrie) during 1888–92, the second in South Yarra during 1894–95.

home, but what a tiresome branch of life, anyway! But now that they are part of my own task of life, now that the right choice of clothes, & a proper fore-sightedness & order with regard to them, is part of the success or failure of my career, I feel a keen resentment that mere I can find such nice things in almost every city. These things seemed part of *her* magic, part of *her* powers as my providence, & it is bitter to me that I can find & pick out things as good as those she chose so lovingly for me, or nearly so. It seems a desecration & I find myself realizing that, in some subconscious way, I thought of the good things in men's clothing stores as things that she alone had the 'open sesame' to. I prize all those events & people that tend to make me think of her as God, or godlike, & resent everything that puts her on a level with myself or other people & makes her able to be replaced in any way.

Janesville, Wis. Station.[28] Nov. 16, 1923.

Source: 'Thought Mother Was "God". Something of This Still Remains', in 'Sketches for My Book "The Life of My Mother & Her Son"', W35-62 (Grainger Museum, Melbourne).

14   Arguments with Beloved Mother (1926)

Too often I would argue with her about small things like these: she was not good at knowing who could see thru a window into a lighted room from a certain angle, or at knowing when something was in her light or not. She would want to pull a blind down because she thought folk could see in. I too often would argue in a stuck-up way about it, saying: 'If you knew anything of perspective you'd know that was utterly impossible'. Or she would say: 'You're in my light, dear', when I could see by my moving shadow that I was still several inches off being in her light. I would try too much to prove myself right to her: 'Look, mumsie, there is my shadow. You follow it, as I move, & you will see I *can't* possibly be in yr light. How is it possible that one cannot know such a simple fact of nature! etc.' I generally calm & stuck-up; mother often nerve-racked & irritable.

I do not mean that our life, in these ways, was full of vulgar bickering. But it is just in such little things that the younger, healthier party can show his devotion, love & understanding, & that is just what I fear I too often failed to do. I did not go so far as to show bad or rough manners (I am *naturally* po-lite). Trust me to stay on the safe side of the fence, coward that I am. But I

---

28. Grainger was traveling from a concert in Rockford, IL, to one in La Crosse, WI.

failed to show sweetness, that hour-by-hourly tender care and thoughtfulness that balms a loving suffering being & makes her sure of one's devotion.

Feb. 9, 1926

Source: 'Arguments with Beloved Mother', manuscript appended to 'Sketches for My Book "The Life of My Mother & Her Son" ', W35 (Grainger Museum, Melbourne).

➤ 15   Mother's Neuralgia in Australia (1926)

I have [never] seen my darling mother's face show bodily suffering so much as at the time of her neuralgia in Australia, which began about 2 or 1½ years before we left for Germany.[29] No doubt it was all part of the deeper illness & worsened by her overwork of that time—giving too many lessons & having to walk from one pupil to another (for she gave almost all lessons at the homes of the pupils) far beyond her strength. She would come home looking with her poor face so drawn with torment & with that peculiar look around the eyes that goes along with nervous pains. The sight of that pain entered into my boyhood & helped, maybe, to make my nature what it became. One result of the neuralgia was that mother could not bear rasping noises, or to see folk cut their nails, pick at things & the like. She told me that when she saw folk do such things in railway trains she had to ask them to stop, telling them how it was with her & such things. At that time she often felt she could bear it all no longer & told me the thought of killing herself came to her often. One day, in special agony, she felt driven to try the power of prayer & prayed God to lead her to relief. She had just come out of the Railway station (we were living at Rathmines Rd) & went into a chemist's shop just opposite the station (on the [ ] side of the tracks, on the side of [ ][30] Road) & asked him if he could 'recommend anything for neuralgia'. He answered that he had something particularly effecatious [efficacious]. Mother took the bottle home, took a dose, & had no more neuralgia (that I remember/can mind) from then on.

Feb. 10, 1926

29. I.e., 1893–94, while living in 'Solfiero' on Rathmines Road, Hawthorn.
30. Left blank by Grainger. He probably meant at Auburn Station, north of the tracks on the side of Victoria Road.

Source: 'Mother's Neuralgia in Australia', manuscript appended to 'Sketches for My Book "The Life of My Mother & Her Son"', W35 (Grainger Museum, Melbourne).

16   Mother on My Love of Being Pitied (1926)

Mother thought the wish to be pitied an overmastering passion with me. She would say: 'I am afraid you tell your sweethearts a lot of silly things in order to make them pity you and that spoils everything & gives them a wrong idea of me & you, & takes all the fun out of everything. You are awfully fond of being pitied, you know. It's too bad; for you're really quite a happy little man.' Mother undoubtedly thought me happier than I thought myself. It was part of her brave, sunny nature to see me happier than I was. It was one of the steady griefs of my life that my darling mother did not see me in my full piteousness.

For there is nothing my soul craves so much as to have my true wretchedness known to those I love best. True, the full state of my misery was reached only with & after her death. But the germ was always there, or rather a curious lack of being able to enjoy things, life, folk. A dull, sulky, low-hearted state has always been natural to me, relieved only by quick bursts of excitement (not happiness) over my own art, other men's art, sex & sport. I have never deserved to be happy, for my feeling-life is rooted in cruelty, pride, selfishness.

Findlay, Ohio, Feb. 11, 1926

Source: 'Mother on My Love of Being Pitied', manuscript appended to 'Sketches for My Book "The Life of My Mother & Her Son"', W35 (Grainger Museum, Melbourne).

17   Beloved Mother's Swear-Words (1926)

'Damn devil take' was, I think mother's chief swear. It seemed as if she was loth [*sic*] actually to say, 'Devil take *you*'. She made awful grimaces when she swore, twisting the ends of her mouth up & open, & she hardly ever swore out of irritation, but with real fury. If furious she would often say: 'God will punish you for yr cruelty to me'—tho I never took her as meaning that very seriously, & do not now, tho someone *has* punished me for my cruelty, or, rather, my lack of tenderness & vision. We should not resent that those we love deeply play upon us as on an instrument, revealing to us many sides of life & their nature.

March 16, 1926

Source: 'Beloved Mother's Swear-Words', manuscript appended to 'Sketches for My Book "The Life of My Mother & Her Son"', W35 (Grainger Museum, Melbourne).

18   Mother a Nietzschean? (1926)

So often mother would say: 'Why must the superior always be sacrificed for the inferior?' For instance, in railway trains & other public places, so shockingly overheated & airless as they mostly are—why must the wishes of those with healthy tastes, who love fresh air, always be set aside for the so-thought comfort of those that care less for their health & give no thought to fresh air? Why should those who are too selfish [or] sensitive to be able to stand the noise of music practise be considered before some hard-working musician who is trying to improve himself & his art? (Why did John Barrymore,[31] because he was a nervous weakling thru drink or other unwisdom have to have *all* the consideration at 'The Southern',[32] and I none? I was even willing to meet him the whole way, why not he willing to meet me part way, or half way? No the weakling under our civilisation gets the *whole* consideration. There is a thin thread of connection between the Barrymore incident and much that led up to the mood that caused mother's death, by the way. Without Barrymore, no White Plains.[33] Without Wh. Pl., perhaps, no Isabel-Else-Hyde[34] episode, who knows? Not but that *the whole guilt* is not mine, in any case.) Why, in music, is the opinion of the inferior musician (critics, ordinary performers, teachers, etc.—those who have not proved that they have special gifts) almost unfailingly taken before that of the geniuses & proven talents (composers, creative types)? Mother's whole life was one great fondness for *the*

31. (1882–1942), Shakespearean actor and early film star.
32. Hotel at 680 Madison Avenue, New York, where the Graingers stayed variously from 1915 to 1918.
33. I.e., a move out of central New York, as the Graingers did in 1921.
34. The complex of relationships that developed in 1921–22 involving Grainger (and his mother) along with Isabel Du Cane, Else Permin, and Miss Hyde, and also Lotta Hough. See essay 20, following.

superior, happiness in finding it, eagerness in helping it. In her behaviour to me, in her training of me, she was glorious towards my superior sides, almost merciless towards my inferior sides. One of the deep griefs of my army time for her was to find how contented I was in a humdrum, useless life, how contented I was with mediocre, 3rd-rate companions. Her fondness for men, her often ill-at-easeness when *too long* together with women (for one could not say that she *disliked* women, at all) was not, I feel sure, the usual sexual drawnness of women towards men as much as her better-liking of man's superiority to woman's inferiority.

Was not mother's death, if definitely planned as I think it was, a proof of her utter fealty towards this urge of favoring the superior? She saw (I think likely) me as the younger, superior, healthier, more gifted one, saw herself as the older, weaker, inferior one, thinking her mind was going. And she hated to think of the one she saw as the inferior one becoming a burden to the superior one, a handicap to his very superiority. And she did not flinch to die for her opinion. The Anglosaxon interpretation of democracy as an unfailing love for mediocreness (third-rateness), an untiring interest in newspapers & other shallow & unimportant things made it impossible for her to be ever really thoroly happy in Australia, England or America. For undoubtedly mother was a Nietzschean,[35] a worshipper of better-things-to-come (Übermensch), & undoubtedly the deep-rooted Nietzscheanism (whether beknown or unbeknown) of Germany & Scandinavia made her happier there—more at rest. She could be happy wherever genius was worshipped—any genius, all genius. L—[36] once said to me: 'You & yr mother are the greatest intellectual snobs I have ever heard of'—meaning that we liked the company of genius, liked to talk of genius & quote their opinions & were not able to like or enjoy folk for ordinary every-day qualities. True. And a more beautiful setting forth of mother's genius-worship could hardly be found than mother's letter to L— of March 1918, at the time of my army measles.[37]

What, at bottom, is the difference between this Nietzscheanism of mother's, this love of hers for superiority & the American 'uplift', the English love of 'character' (quote English 'character' joke),[38] the Christian sense of 'spirituality'. Their idea of what is good, desirable & superior is always according to a *Code*, a moral system, the opinion & judgement of the many, or of authority. Mother's feeling for superiority was only an instinct, a thing of

---

35. Follower of the German philosopher Friedrich Nietzsche (1844–1900).
36. Grainger is referring to Lotta Mills Hough (Mrs. Williston Hough), with whom he maintained a relationship between 1917 and 1922.
37. This letter appears not to be extant.
38. Presumably, when Grainger wrote the envisaged final *Life* volume.

nature, not of civilisation; a thing of intuition, not of obedience; the difference between the primeval[39] & the orthodox.

Source: 'Mother a Nietzschean?', manuscript appended to 'Sketches for My Book "The Life of My Mother & Her Son"', W35, dated 17 February 1926 (Grainger Museum, Melbourne).

19 Thots of Mother while Scoring
To a Nordic Princess (1928)

As I lay resting a moment (between scoring the end of *To a Nordic Princess*[40]—I scored most of the day yesterday till 1 at night & was up soon after 6 this morn & have worked all day, no food but oranges & grapefruit for 26 hours) the sensation suddenly came to me of the hot dry smell in Frankfurt in the summertime, & I thot of such days spent together in happiness by my beloved darling mother & me—painting, or biking, or reading aloud, & her merry laugh, & myself serious as always at some work. And I realized that this is what is meant by 'auld lang syne'—the things that are so far back in time that they are strange as well as homish, the things that could never be brought back. It would be no use going back to Frankfurt to recapture the hot dry summer smell—that smell comes to life only with my mother beside me, or along of thots of her. It is in 'auld lang syne' that we who are dead find our full despotic kingdom at last—that oneness of sway that even the truest, sweetest love can never assure us of while living.

My little mother—who in Frankfurt was so gay & reckless, so careless of the morrow, so natural in having sweethearts & so innocent & happy with them—my little mother, who in her older age was to become so harassed, so fear-ridden, so never quitting her work. I can see her in White Plains, the last year of her life, writing, writing always, & calling out to me in earnest, warning, or energizing tones[41]—reminding me of something to be done, urging me to this or that—with but little of her gaiety left & none of her recklessness. Is that merely old age & sickness? More likely the signs of a broken heart—she no longer felt sure of my *whole-hearted* love for her, & she had no other loves, now, to fill the gap, as at Frankfurt. Also it is the strain of living beside genius—the nearness to never-up-letting *problems*. Also it was the war. But

---

39. Grainger originally wrote 'primitive'.
40. This 'Bridal Song' was Grainger's wedding gift to his wife. It was first performed on 9 August 1928 at their wedding in the Hollywood Bowl. Grainger's programme note proclaimed the work as 'honor-tokened in pride of race and personal love'.
41. Text unclear, perhaps 'energy tones'.

mostly, no doubt, it was old age & sickness & my un-enoughness ((insufficiency)), my failing her in my *soul*.

Source: 'Thots of Mother while Scoring *To a Nordic Princess*', in 'Sketches for My Book "The Life of My Mother & Her Son" ', W35-88, dated 3 March 1928 (Grainger Museum, Melbourne).

➤ 20   Bird's-Eye View of the Together-Life of Rose Grainger and Percy Grainger (1947)

The Purpose of This Brief Sketch

When my Aldridge-Grainger-Brandelius-Saga[42] is written I hope the reader will have a clear view of my mother's personality & of the life she & I had together; & even from the various sketches for the above-mentioned A-G-B-Saga (Ere-I-Forget,[43] Sketches for the Life of my Mother & Her Son,[44] etc.) I hope this clear view will transpire. But it might be that I will die before the saga is finished & before I have compiled enough sketches for the saga to furnish not only a full account of her personality but also of the mainstream of her aims, longings, accomplishments that colored our together-life—also of the changes of mood & outlook happening during her life. This sketch aims at being a rough chart of her life's voyage, a rough summing-up of what she was & what sways she exerted upon me & my art-life.

The Languages in Which This Sketch Is Written

There is no attempt to write this sketch in my 'Blue-eyed English' (Nordic English),[45] because I want this bird's-eye-view to be written as freely & naturally as possible—& one cannot write freely when one is trying to create & reform a language at the same time. The parts written in English give an account of those events & points of view that are not likely to give any trouble to the somewhat childish & undeveloped (irresponsible) mentality of English-speaking readers. Passages written in Danish require the more grown-

---

42. Grainger clearly looked on his 'Aldridge-Grainger-Ström Saga' (1933–34) as only a sketch for this never-written definitive saga. Ström was the name of his wife's foster parents, while Brandelius was the name of her genetic father.
43. (1944–47).
44. (1922–38).
45. For an explanation of Grainger's use of Nordic English and Danish, see this volume's Introduction.

up, responsible attitude of Scandinavian readers. There is probably no part of the world where the reading public is so aware of the part played by literature & history in fitting mankind to develop a sense of our duties toward the future of mankind. In particular, a knowledge of the workings of artistic minds & a truthful & comprehensive record of artistic lives seems to the Scandinavian a means of reaching a more delicate insight into the workings of nature in man & of laying the foundations of a more kindly, understanding, tolerant & scientific pattern of life to come. The Scandinavian reader is not frightened to face unusual, unexpected & up-setting data; therefore, the more tragic & puzzling details of my mother's & my together-life are addressed to him, while those details presenting no problems to a timid & evasive mentality are recorded for English-speaking readers. The names of some persons have been changed.

Some of My Mother's Qualities

I suppose my mother's most outstanding qualities were wilfulness, recklessness, fearlessness, gaiety, fair judgement, drasticness, helpfulness, lightning changes of mood & policy, outspokenness, forgivingness, exaggerated devotion to the arts, a Dickens-typed championship of the under-dog, complete cosmopolitanism interrupted by flashes of British patriotism, utter classlessness, genuine dislike of the bible = inability to join any religious group, free outlook on sex-behaviour combined with a general 'wholesomeness' (instinctive lack of interest in abnormal or 'perverse' tendencies in erotic affairs), protective attitude towards persons of genius (equally whether myself, or others), worship of physical beauty, carelessness about money with occasional panics about same, quite equal fondness for men & women, need for having some friends round her (sometimes to her undoing), self-formed judgements in the arts, [in Danish] admiration of erotic qualities both in men and in women, [in English] bossiness, violentness if opposed, some possible vein of hypochondria (yet combined with a hatred of illness), irrepressible leaning towards warm expressiveness & affectionateness in the arts (Dickens, H.C. Andersen, Walt Whitman, Tennyson, Byron, Heine, Ernest Dowson,[46] Herman Bang,[47] Strindberg, Beethoven, Brahms, Gabriel Fauré, Grieg, [ ][48]), theatrical leanings (presentation of events in lurid colors, subject to a sudden shift to humor & debunked laughter), possible vein of jealousy (never can make up

---

46. (1867–1900), English poet.
47. (1857–1912), Danish novelist.
48. Grainger left additional space here, clearly intending to add further names.

my mind as to this), extreme self-restraint & self-effacingness when for business purposes (for instance, complete lack of any wish to be invited to the parties or homes of those 'society' people in London from whom I earned my living), completely impartial judgement of my artistic efforts & on my behaviour in life, preference for goodness over cleverness or giftedness, dislike of 'chaffing,' dislike of joculence [*sic*] about mating & flirting & love-making, lack of prudery (as compared with her mother, for instance) & extreme decency-cult, fury when told about errors in playing music or speaking languages, wish to provide me with sweethearts (followed at any moment by the wish to get rid of same sweethearts), standing with her son 'against the world' (on his side against conventions, etc.), happiness in trains & in railway stations & in public places generally, tendency to burn food in cooking (turn toffee into enamel), strong rather than neat sewing, apt to wound even her best friends by ruthless outspokenness, constant willingness to admit the worst (a possible explanation of her suicide), keenness on business (overworking herself as a consequence), determination not to see me money-minded, easily upset by too much prosperity round her, love of riding & driving when young, possible severity with her piano pupils & with me, fondness for 'Lord Fauntleroying' me (dressing me up),[49] [in Danish] lashing activity in her family and with her, which possibly led to lashing sensuality in me, [in English] championing of her less worthy friends, ability to carry out drastic resolutions in diet & other fields (suicide ability?), unwillingness to develop herself artistically, propensity for scaring & testing me, disposition for disloyalty, fondness for the manly in me despite her wish for me to be an art-man, nonfussiness about money, lack of jealousy toward my father, criticalness toward her kin & Australia, recognition of English as trouble-makers, ability to get on with servants, unfailing sense of the practical (businesslike, monetary) as a background to the ideal & the emotional (in art, love, etc.), stick-to-itiveness [persistence] in spite of impatience, horror of policemen & officials.[50]

Mother's Wilfulness, Recklessness, Fearlessness, Bossiness, Violence if Opposed, Tendency to Burn Food When Cooking, Vehemence

Mother had a Hitlerian streak—she was sure of what was right, felt sure of those she approved of & therefore had no halfheartedness in espousing the cause of those people & things she liked. Self-restraint didn't enter into it. She

49. *Little Lord Fauntleroy* (1886) was a novel by Frances Hodgson Burnett. In it, a young American boy is made an earl; he is dressed up, accordingly, in lace and velvet suits, and he sports long, curly hair. .

50. Grainger left further space here, in which to add in additional qualities of his mother.

was always planning helpful things for those she approved of (getting them jobs, for instance). So if anyone opposed her in the things she had set her heart on—the things she deeply felt to be good—she was violent, bossy, ruthless in putting her will thru. By the same token, if she was cooking food, her instinct was to cook it good—cook it a lot. In the early days in Frankfurt (in her early thirties) she got keen on making toffee; & she cooked it so well it stuck to the plate like enamel. The plate would break before the toffee would. And how heartily she would laugh at all such—half gay, half annoyed.

In her late teens her recklessness was shown in driving to the hunt, following the hound on the roads, going round corners on 2 wheels (think of the accident in Melbourne that led to the first Mrs O'Shannessy's death);[51] & in her attitude in marrying my father. 'Do you think you will be happy with Jack?' asked her mother. Mother answered, 'If I'm happy with him for a fortnight, that's enough'. She married on a Friday, on the 13th of the month.[52] (Mother was one of those that didn't have to have everything so good, so propitious, all the time.) Her fearlessness with horses is elsewhere described. If she thought people (like Miss Hyllested[53] in London) were trying to get the better of me, or cash in on my polite or mild ways, she could talk straight to them all right.

If mother's will was opposed, I have never known anyone to successfully oppose her. I never could. And the thought that she killed herself because she felt herself growing weak & saw that as a result she might have to surrender her will makes me glad that she killed herself—if that's what she did. I would have hated to see her *defeated*. I would have hated others (including myself) to triumph over her. People are wrong who think that children suffer from having tyrannical parents. They suffer from having willy-nilly parents. A proper child gloats in the tyranny, bossiness (even cruelty) of a wilful mother. See mother-&-child couples in the train. As long as the mother acts mild, the child is unconvinced & bored. As soon as the mother lifts the child up & bumps the base of his spine down good & hard upon the seat the child looks satisfied. 'What a wonderful mother I have', his eyes say. If any hyenas round my mother, at the end of her life, were starting to lick their chops, thinking 'our time is coming', I am glad that her suicide put a spoke in all such wheels. (And I am thankful that any plans, conscious or subconscious, that I may have had for setting up my will against hers were hamstrung by her death. I am glad I never saw her

51. Grainger may be using a false name here, intending to refer to the first wife of Dr. Henry O'Hara. In October 1883, Rose Grainger had been driving the O'Haras' carriage, with pregnant Mrs. O'Hara as a passenger. For some reason, Mrs. O'Hara fell from the carriage, suffered a miscarriage, and died a few days later.
52. John and Rose Grainger had married in Adelaide on Friday, 1 October 1880.
53. Gutrum Hyllested, one of Grainger's Scandinavian piano students.

will blunted.) Mind you, all I am saying about a mother's wilfulness & tyranny hinges on whether or not the mother feels herself charged with good & right-ness, as mine did. Bossiness, without this certainty of being inspired by right-ness on a mother's part, I am not talking about.

Mother was full of resources. She would smack my face, which I found very annoying, the more so as I neared 40. If I then held her wrists, to prevent her doing so, she could say, 'Someday you'll kill me, exciting me so'; or she would say, 'I can see how much you hate me, when you look at me like that!' To which I would say, 'Do you expect me to look pleased, when you smack my face?' When I praise my mother's wilfulness (& say I am glad I never saw it broken down by old age or weakness), I am merely admiring it as an attrib-ute of hers, as part of her. I never liked being domineered by her. And I never like any form of love, or anything else, that leads one person to seek sway over another. (That's why I say I hate love; that love is the cruellest thing in human affairs.) I like only those things in life that leave men & women perfectly free. The only kind of love I like is platonic love. But there was heaps of that be-tween mother & me. (The reason why I say I worship lust, but hate love, is because lust, like platonic love, leaves people absolutely free.) The thing I adored about my mother was not anything she did to me or for me (not the way she helped me with my career; or anything she did to 'improve my char-acter'—I am not aware of such influences). I adored her for herself—for her beauty, her high-mindedness, her grasp of art, her fair-mindedness, her courage—and her wilfulness (in itself, not directed towards me).

Was My Mother Jealous about Me?

That is a question I can never satisfactorily answer. I have no doubt that Ingerid Traegaard[54] would answer that it was my mother's jealousy that pre-vented my marrying Ingerid. But mother often urged me to marry Ingerid, or asked me if I didn't want to. What could I say, but that I didn't feel soulfully at-tached to Ingerid—[in Danish] however much joy I reaped from her, however grateful I was to her, generous lover that she was. [In English] Class outlooks sundered us—she had that middle-class feeling that things should go well with her; I had the low-class, or art-man's, outlook, that tragic things should happen to me. Other sweethearts, such as Janet Johansen[55] & Bertha Knowles,[56] might

54. Probably Karen Holten (1879–1953), Grainger's Danish girlfriend between 1905 and 1912.
55. Perhaps Else Permin, a Danish piano student of Grainger's, who lived with the Graingers in Lon-don and stayed with them at White Plains in 1921–22.
56. Probably Lotta Mills Hough.

say the same as Ingerid. Yet I am not convinced. Mother had thrown me into the arms of both of them (is that jealousy?). There were times when she turned her wilfulness into the service of getting me married to them. Of course, there were also *good other reasons* (than jealousy) that made mother less keen on such sweethearts than she otherwise would have been. Mother was a realist: she had steered me from a musically talented boy into being a full-fledged well-earning professional world-pianist. When women like Janet & Bertha talked about life, or about my affairs, to mother, it was obvious that they talked like groom-gardener-amateurs—like people who do not understand art & life, *& don't have it in them ever to master it.* Everything is class & nationality. Australians, when they go abroad, have to face the world without support (remember G. B. Shaw on Ireland, the perambulator & the Pickford van![57]). All that gives one a different class slant.

In a sense, mother may have been said to be jealous about me in branches of life far removed from marriage or sweethearts. At the very beginning of my concert engagements in England (1902?) mother was very annoyed when I came back from Bath (played there under Heymann's conducting) & said what a very happy time I'd had there with the Heymanns—not so much with Mrs Heymann (Edith Meadows from Frankfurt) as with him (a German Saxon) whom I'd never met before. Mother felt it was a disloyalty on my part to be *so very happy* the very first time I'd escaped from her apron strings.[58] Just as she was much more riled at my still greater happiness on tour with Herman Sandby[59] & Alfhild De Luce[60] on the 1904 Danish concert tour. And so she was to find how happy I was in the army (1917). On the other hand, she was never jealous of my happiness with such composer friends as Balfour Gar-

---

57. Perhaps a reference to Shaw's *Fanny's First Play* (1911).
58. Grainger had twice performed Tchaikovsky's First Piano Concerto under Max Heymann in Bath on 6 February 1902. Grainger knew Heymann's wife, Edith Meadows, from Frankfurt, where she had studied under Clara Schumann. In 'A Rough Sketch of My Mother's Nature' ('Grainger's Anecdotes', 423-86, dated 12 and 19 May 1954), he elaborated:

> 'I think the first engagement I got in England (1902?) was to play the Tchaikovsky Concerto with Max Heymann & his orchestra at Bath. He was married to Edith Heymann (whom we knew at Frankfurt) & no doubt it was thru her I got the engagement. Heymann upbraided me for playing wrong notes in the arpeggios near the beginning. But he & I were blissfully happy in a boat on the river there. Mrs H. was furious, because neither her husband nor I could manage a boat properly. She was not used to being in a boat with men who couldn't handle it properly, she said. When I got home & told mother what awful fun I'd had with Heymann on the river, mother was much riled. She didn't like me to enjoy vulgar pleasures with vulgar men & women'.

See, further, essay 84.
59. (1881–1965), Danish composer and cellist, fellow student of Grainger's in Frankfurt.
60. (1876–1961), Norwegian-born musician and writer; from 1909, Herman Sandby's wife.

diner, Roger Quilter,[61] Cyril Scott. What mother felt was disgust at my disloyalty, not merely my joy in being with other people than herself, but my joy in common place things & people. She had brought me up to enjoy superior things & people, & here was I hilariously happy in getting close to common things & people. Hatred for disloyalty is not the same thing as jealousy. Alfhild has written that Herman was hurt in his soul, when he came to London, to find that I 'had no manly freedom'. What does a composer want with manly freedom? A composer needs *protection*, so that he can forget outside things & concentrate on the much nicer things he has in his own mind.

My Mother Was Certainly Not Jealous of My Father

Mother never spoke bitterly about father's love affair with Mrs Thynne,[62] at Brighton, when I was an infant. And around 1909, when she thought he had found someone who was devoted to him[63] & ideal for him, she said to father, 'If you have found someone you like & would like to marry, I will never stand in your way. You can have a divorce any time you like. You can get it for desertion & I will never contest it.' But, of course, at that time father was not mother's success, or her provider. I had become those things to her.

Mother never felt jealous toward Emma Green's[64] pure-hearted childish devotion to my father. And she always felt grateful to those, like Aunty May, Aunty Jack[65] & Uncle George, with whom father found happiness & support—even tho the result was that the Aldridge support flowed my father's way instead of us-ward.

Mother's Matchless Devotion to the Arts

I don't suppose I've ever met anyone who was so steadily & exclusively devoted to the arts as mother was. Not that she didn't have lots of other interests; but they always sank into insignificance beside her devotion to the arts. In her teens, as she writes in one of those letters reproduced in the *Pictures of Rose Grainger Book* (1923),[66] she always had some sweetheart or other—

61. (1877–1953), English composer and pianist, fellow student of Grainger's in Frankfurt.
62. Mrs. Smayle. See essay 10.
63. Referring to Winifred Falconer, who would join John Grainger on his last visit to Britain in 1912. See essay 5.
64. Mrs. Amy Chalk (née Black). See essay 5.
65. Annie Maria Quesnel (née MacFie), sister of Grainger's Aunty May. She was a talented pianist and singer.
66. Grainger refers to a letter of 5 May 1918, produced within *Photos of Rose Grainger*.

'nothing serious,' as she added. But it was my father she married—not one of the most marriageable of young men, for it was already said that he drank, & he was not manly like her brothers ('wouldn't pick up a child & carry it around' like they would, in their strength)—but he *did* read poetry by the hour to the Aldridge girls, he *did* organise the first string quartet in Adelaide, he *did* strew books around, he *did* have collections of reproductions of the world's pictures & of Greek statues. In spite of coming from a family that enjoyed 'Donna è mobile'[67] & the 'bright' things of music, mother's taste turned irresistibly to the slow movements of Beethoven sonatas & other deeply expressive music. In Melbourne she felt deep sympathy for the forlorn (later fan-painter) Conder[68] & poor little Aldis. It was not just that she liked artists & the arts, but that the arts carried to her a continual message of sorrow, compassion & liberation. Thru Heine, Byron, H. C. Andersen, Dickens & other humanists her heart was weaned away from the temptations & satisfactions of prosperity until she found herself, in her mind's eye, on the side of prostitutes, sinners, unfortunates & Byron's luckless heroes. This is what devotion to art means: that art has replaced Christianity as a method of softening the human heart & directing man's thoughts to justice. Tho mother liked people of refinement & often prominent people, yet I can *never* remember her voicing an opinion that could be described as 'conservative'—an opinion typical of the 'having' classes.

She was always on the side of the lawless. And always on the side of the emotional in art—never captivated by brilliance. She was always happy with composers—whether they were close friends like Cyril or Roger, or a just-met one like Josef Holbrooke.[69] Mother was always interested in *the art itself*, & not in what it led to. Her conversation with Mrs Teague (Australian) in Chelsea, around 1905, was typical. Mrs T. had read in a paper that Arthur Balfour[70] had had a luncheon for me (as a matter of fact that I should meet a great mathematician,[71] to talk about a machine to record folksongs scientifically—by the number of vibrations) & she said to mother: 'That Arthur Balfour has given a luncheon for Percy means more than all Percy's concerts; it means that he has really arrived.' Mother said: 'But the luncheon is only the

67. 'La donne è mobile', from Act III of Verdi's opera, *Rigoletto* (1851).
68. Charles Conder (1868–1909), English-born artist, with whom the Graingers were acquainted during both Conder's Melbourne residence (1888–90) and his final years in London.
69. Joseph Holbrooke (1878–1958), English composer, pianist, and conductor.
70. (1848–1930), British prime minister (1902–5) and, at this time, leader of the Conservative opposition.
71. Lord Rayleigh, John William Strutt (1842–1919); from 1908, Chancellor of Cambridge University. He had published a theory of sound in 1877. This luncheon took place on 10 April 1908.

result of the concerts. If the concerts stopped, there would soon be no more luncheons at Arthur Balfour's.' Mother sometimes said to me: 'If you should die, I would try not to be too desperate. I should devote myself to the career of some other great composer, such as Cyril'. The case of mother wanting me to read aloud the newly-found Irish author Stephens,[72] in the bathroom at 31A King's Road, Chelsea,[73] when I had just told her I had broken my betrothal with Doris Morrison,[74] was typical.

I think this preoccupation with art (to the extent of ignoring 'life' for its sake) may have stemmed from her mother & grandmother. The grandmother (described in one of mother's letters in the *Rose Grainger Book*[75]) had been a school teacher. And mother's mother often said how eagerly they awaited the appearance of the weekly chapter of a new novel by Dickens, in their London paper. The fact that grandmother (mother's mother) never went to any of her children's homes, when they got married, but just welcomed the new families at *her* home (Claremont, 37 East Parade, North Kensington, Adelaide) seems to hint that she didn't have much of that appetite for 'real life', called inquisitiveness. Such a life-pale philosopher, eager to read the new Dickens chapter, but uneager to see her sons' homes (for however good a reason), might easily bear a daughter keener on art than life. Not that mother was *aware* of any coolness towards life, on her part. Some of father's friends have liked to portray him as the warm-hearted, affection-craving husband wedded to the cool, detached wife—seeking therein, maybe, an explanation of his drinking [in Danish] his frequent visits to 'loose women', [in English] his love affair with Mrs Thynne. I can only say that I found him, throughout life, the cool (skill-loving) one, & my mother the warm, outspoken, unreserved, unrestrained one.

Mother's Unwillingness to Develop Herself in the Arts (Her Dislike of Being Corrected in Music or Languages)

But for all her devotion to the arts & her interest in learning new languages (part of her very genuine cosmopolitanism), her stubbornness & self-sufficiency made her always a bad pupil. There is Aunty Clara's story of mother throwing the music-book across the room when her German music teacher in Adelaide criticized something in her playing—'I'm doing all right,

---

72. James Stephens (1882–1950), Irish poet and novelist. His first novels were *The Charwoman's Daughter* (1911) and *The Crock of Gold* (1912).
73. The Graingers' home, excepting a couple of short breaks, between 1907 and 1914.
74. Margot Harrison, to whom Grainger was briefly engaged in 1913.
75. Letter of 5 May 1918.

aren't I?' In the last few months of her life, when she was practising to play a part in the piano 3-some version of my *English Dance* together with Louise Knowles[76] & me (there is a photo of mother & me at the piano with the English Dance music[77]), mother was furious when I said that some things in the rhythm (irregular barrings) were not quite right. I think she said something about 'it's all part of your wish to put me in the wrong in everything & Louise in the right'. When we played cards together, around 1895 or 1896, mother always said I looked so triumphant if she made a mistake, or lost. The fact was I looked upon her as a kind of god, & was, maybe, relieved when she made human mistakes.

But there is no doubt that mother had that typically womanly (self-effacing) instinct *not* to shine herself in the arts she worshipped. A thousand times I told her that her memories (of her family, of early Adelaide days, of the gulf she had leapt in moving from a hotel-keeper, horse-loving life into a world-wide, art-following life) told in her own direct English (a thousand times more vital than any pundit speech I, in my 'educated above my intelligence' condition, could cough up) could be a golden leaf of literature. But she hardly heeded me (except for those letters in the *Rose Grainger Book*). And it was clear that she never seriously tried to become a professional pianist, altho she was quite conscientious, as a teacher, with her piano pupils.

The only time I remember her playing in public was shortly before we left Australia for Germany, around or before 1895, when she took part in a 'breaking up' concert at a school at which she taught the piano. She played that polka-like show piece by Popoff (or some such name) which was her great display piece.[78] (The piece is in that album Aunty Jack gave me.) I can see her in my mind's eyes, sitting up so straight & looking so girlish, with her arms flailing from middle to sides. She was very keen on playing Beethoven's violin & piano sonatas with Mr [ ][79] at the first 'Kilalla' (particularly the E flat[80]). But best of all I remember her playing expressively the lovely slow movement of Beet[hoven]'s E min. Piano Sonata[81] (at Clare, S.A., when I was about 7 or 8) & Grieg's early Lyric Pieces (Volksweise in E min. & F sharp min., Walzer

76. Lotta Hough. Grainger appears to be confusing his Knowles pseudonyms.
77. Picture 46, dated 17 July 1921, in *Photos of Rose Grainger*.
78. Probably 'Töplitz' by Julius Schulhoff (1825–98). In an annotation to the album given by 'Aunty Jack' (Grainger Museum, MG Q1/SCHUL-1), Grainger wrote that he was 'almost sure' this was the work played at the Melbourne school concert and stated that it was Rose Grainger's 'Country Gardens'.
79. Left blank by Grainger. Probably the violinist Caulfield Barton (b. 1852/3). See his recollection of their duos together at this time in Gillies and Pear, *Portrait of Percy Grainger*, 9–10.
80. Op. 12, No. 3.
81. Op. 90.

Op. 12, Waechterlied[82]) & Humoreske, Op. 6, No. 3. She played Heller's *Restless Nights*[83] a lot, too. Later in life, in London, she enjoyed playing Debussy's *En Bateau* in duet form[84] & we had great fun playing together my special 2-piano setting (written for her and me) of *Mock Morris*.[85] Perhaps the things I enjoyed best was her playing the (bar 40) chords (very robustly) of Spoon River,[86] while I played the tune on my sopr. sax (West 93 Street, after or during the first German War[87]). And I liked playing piano duet arr. of 'Charfreitagszauber'[88] with her (late London & USA). Best in her playing I enjoyed its robustness—grip (like the strong Aldridge hand). Least I liked was a kind of spasmodic expressiveness—gushes of louderness & softness that seemed to have little bearing on the course of the musical phrases. Maybe it was a widespread habit of that generation, for such a musical man as old Klimsch (Karl K.) used a somewhat similar upsetting, meaningless expressiveness. She had great pleasure in translating into English that Danish story of Herman Bang's, in which fun-task Isabel Du Cane[89] joined.

Mother's and My Piano Playing Compared by Mischke, to My Disadvantage

In spite of the fact that I was from the first such an earnest & highbrow musician, & had enjoyed such stunningly good training from mother & Louis Pabst[90] before we reached Germany in 1895, it was possible for mother's lover (or lover-like friend) Dr Hermann Mischke to insist that her playing was far more pleasing & touching than mine—a statement that filled me with surprise; for I thought my playing much smoother than mother's, & smoothness is the first thing in art that charms me (first prelude, 2nd book of [Bach's] Wohltemperiertes). [In German] 'Percy will never reach your soft, expressive touch.' [In English] In his own (musically untrained) way he perhaps felt what I, too, have always sensed: that mother was fundamentally more artistically gifted than I—more humanly rich & deep, &, therefore, with more

---

82. 'Waegtersang' (Watchman's Song), from Grieg's Lyric Pieces, Op. 12.
83. By Stephen Heller (1813–88), Hungarian-born French composer of piano character pieces.
84. From Debussy's *Petite suite* (1886–89).
85. (1910).
86. Grainger's only 'American Folk-Music Setting', started in March 1919.
87. The Graingers rented 309 West 92nd Street, New York, during 1918–21.
88. The Good Friday music from Wagner's *Parsifal*, Act 3. Grainger's library contains this music in a four-hand transcription by Humperdinck (MG C1/Wagn-4-2).
89. Friend of the Graingers in London during 1908–14 and occasional musical copyist. She stayed with them in White Plains in 1921–22.
90. (1846–1903), German pianist, resident in Melbourne in 1887–94. He taught Grainger piano and harmony during 1892–94.

to express, even if she couldn't so well express it. But it is no wonder that mother liked Germany (1895–1902 [*sic*]), where men like Mischke (such a pure, sweet, gloriously handsome giant, too) & old Klimsch revered her soul so devotedly, where a passionate Jew like Ederheimer kindled her womanliness so feverishly (she said she had never seen a man burn so brightly with sexual fire as he) & where her genius as a *mother* was so universally understood & sympathised with. In Norway, too, it could be said that she was truly appreciated (wooed by Sigurd ****,[91] liked by all kinds of young girls, dramatised by old buffers like Brandius[92] in Lillesand); whereas in Australia, England, Denmark, America *never*. (Where I was happy, mother was less liked. Where she was idolised, I was vaguely dissatisfied. Are human beings always competitors, however much they love each other? It burns me 'deep in the soul, & black' that, deep down, I was always such a selfish & disloyal son—& that mother was clever enough to sense it, in spite of all my devoted-seeming ways.)

Mother's Dislike of Humor, Smartness, Chaffing in Art & Life

I remember one evening at the von Glehn's[93] in London (about 1911?) when the von G's, Roger (Quilter) & I were all crazy with delight at Max Beerbohm's *A Xmas Garland*,[94] which must just have appeared. On the other hand, we were all (except mother) *against* something of Strindberg's (*Death Dance*? *The Father*?[95] More likely *Påske*,[96] to the purity & inspiredness of which mother was especially devoted) that had just appeared on the London skyline. Mother (for once—it wasn't her habit to talk controversially to groups) was very outspoken in her condemnation of the 'conventionality' of our standpoint. 'How can you prefer something that is merely smart & a rehash of other men's ideas to something which is really original & inspired?' On such occasions mother despaired of me. I can hardly ever remember her enthusing about funniness, wit, or humor in art. I am sure that she (with her so deeply up-buildsome & positive nature) resented humor as exerting a

91. Sigurd Fornander (1865–1945), a Swedish masseur; the Graingers and Fornander stayed at the same pension in Frankfurt during 1899.
92. Norwegian bookshop owner and concert organizer, of whom Rose Grainger was fond.
93. Wilfred von Glehn (1870–1951), English impressionist painter, and Jane von Glehn (1873–1961), American-born painter, introduced to Grainger by John Singer Sargent.
94. *The Christmas Garland* by Max Beerbohm (1872–1956) was published in 1912. Its stories parodied contemporary writers' stylistic faults.
95. *The Dance of Death* (1901), *The Father* (1887).
96. *Easter* (1901).

check (a cooling-off influence) to inspiration, impulsiveness, feeling. She liked it in Germany (1895, etc.) that no one had any humor—in spite of the fact that the German comic papers had the best humor in the world. For she had always hated all the chaffing that went on in Australia. In particular she loathed all fun at the expense of love, mating, sweethearting, etc.—'I can see you're a great hand with the ladies' & the like. She classes such tactics with baldness & other showings of worn-out manhood & 'old-fogey-ism'. On the other hand, mother had a brisk vein of impishness & mischievousness in her. But it was always apt to be directed against the pompous, the ensconced, the fatuous—never against the loving, the crazy, the half-witted, the naughty, the rebellious, the pure, the unconventional, the urge-impelled.

Mother's Non-Moral Assurance Stemmed from Basic Wholesomeness

When I felt hamstrung in my erotic life & blamed it on conventions & laws mother would say 'I don't know why you feel like that. The laws have never stood in the way of anything I wanted to do'. (And yet she had a great horror of policemen—especially in Germany. She had never been dragooned before, & there was always that tendency in the German police that could easily develop into Gestapo. But if she saw a policeman, anywhere, she would be apt to say: 'I hope he isn't coming for me'.) Mother was a good example of the point Otto Weininger[97] made in his 'Geschlecht und Charakter'[98] (which both mother & I read in the early London days; mother with 'restraint in its manifestation', I with unbalanced abandonment to its pessimism), about mother-types & prostitute-types: the mother-type is rootedly brave & confident, because she feels at one with the stirs of the universe & senses the support of humanity behind her; the prostitute-type is fundamentally cowardly, suspicious & un-confident, because she instinctively feels her life & aims are at variance with nature & life & that human society will always be 'down' on her.

Mother could preach 'free love' (to Mrs Lane in Adelaide, 1903 or 04;[99] to Bertha Knowles in 1916 or 17), voice interest & at-oneness with prostitutes (as young woman in Adelaide), rant against baby-worship & the cult of the family, espouse the cause of the sweetheart-seeking woman as against the brood-hen & the 'clinging vine' (The Doll's House[100]), approve of Becky

97. (1880–1903), Austrian philosopher.
98. (1903), in English as *Sex and Character* (1906).
99. Probably Mrs. Zebina Lane, wife of an Australian parliamentarian.
100. Henrik Ibsen's *A Doll's House* (1879).

Sharp,[101] Nana,[102] Hedda Gabler,[103] because, at bottom, she was so *wholely mother* & so utterly devoid not only of any perversity, but even of any understanding of what perversity was. Mother simply *could not* listen to anyone talking about 'perverse' habits, cults, personalities—a far-away, bored look came into her face; not that she was 'down' on the poor Oscar Wildes & Herman Bangs[104]—she always talked compassionately & tolerantly of their troubles. But she had no *interest* in perversity; it held no *charm* for her. [In Danish] Therefore, it was an incredible injustice that some of those three women (either Miss Hyde, or Miss Permin or Miss Du Cane—for my part, I am inclined to think it was mainly Hyde, for one day, in 'The Southern', she talked in a strangely hysterical-perverse manner about her relationship to her female students) could get the idea, or tolerate the idea, that I and my mother lived in an incestuous relationship. [In English] I think life lost all hope & flavor for mother, from the moment that utterly un-us-like thought was forced (thru Miss Permin's Xmas-1921 letter, & what it led to[105]) across the threshold of her mind.[106]

101. Chief character in Thackeray's *Vanity Fair* (1847).
102. (1880), by Émile Zola.
103. (1890), by Henrick Ibsen.
104. Because of their homosexuality.
105. I.e., Rose Grainger's suicide.
106. In 'A Rough Sketch of My Mother's Nature' ('Grainger's Anecdotes', 423-86, dated 12 and 19 May 1954), Grainger elaborated on the complex issues leading up to the death of his mother:

> 'With my American sweetheart mother was always friendly. Mother asked me to see Mrs— [Lotta Hough] home one evening & Mrs— said, 'I quite agree with every word yr mother said about free love. I think it is the only sensible thing.' Later on (a few years later) mother said, 'Do you think — is cruel?' Of course mother did not like to see me so infatuated as I became in my American sweetheart—[in Danish] for my mother must have guessed that I lied about train arrival times (on my concert trips) to be together with my American sweetheart—[in English] if one can call someone a sweetheart who for about 4 years felt little but resentment & hostility at some stupidity I committed in Buffalo. [In Danish] When mother's European friends Du Cane and Permin talked about incest between mother and me, my mother was as good as annihilated, but all the same she said: [in English] 'When you are away I feel happier when they are around me.' It could easily be mother's forgiving nature just wiped out what they said. Or did she secretly & self-unawaredly sympathise with Permin, Du Cane, Mrs Simonds & Mrs Weichmann in their jealousy of my American sweetheart? I have no clue at all to any of these things, except I know that those friends were mad with jealousy. The thought that continually tormented mother was, 'Who could have started the [in Danish] incest [in English] rumor?' So when my American sweetheart visited mother on the Thursday before mother's suicide [25 Apr. 1922], mother asked her if she had started the rumor. This naturally angered my American sweetheart, & it was walking out of the front door that old Mrs Miner met her, as described a few pages back [in this 'Rough Sketch']. My American sweetheart wired me to San Francisco, 'The unmentionable has been laid at my door'. My mother wired me to San Francisco

My Own Cowardice May Be Rooted in My Comparatively
Unwholesome, Twisted Nature

They say that the bully is always a coward; & of me that seems to be true. I kicked a cat round a room when I was 6 or 7 (at Mrs Bruce's, Adelaide). I early gave proof of my brutal & nasty nature. To have power has no point for me unless I can use it brutally, cruelly & unjustly. I admit that such a nature as mine is low & nasty. But I will not easily admit that it is perverse or unnatural. It seems to be natural in most boys to be cruel & nasty. And I have simply remained like a boy, instead of growing up to be that tiresome thing 'a proper man'. What use is it that woman is yielding, soft & smooth-fleshed if man cannot be domineering, harsh & wicked with her? Is it not to waste & spurn the lovely traits she offers to be chivalrous & gentle with her? Brave & proper men may be nicer & worthier than I; but I will not easily admit that they are more natural. In me, by me, the sex drama is worshipped & honored. [In Danish] That I am lash-crazy (that I am given to lash cruelty, which in the following I will call 'birch worship') is not so surprising—I was much lashed as a young (and as an older) boy; and I am of a grateful nature. I adore what I have experienced—is that so reprehensible? And lashing activity is in my memory linked to nakedness (my own and Dixie O'Donovan's)—and nakedness is a very important matter. (I am convinced that all wars would stop if nudism became generally accepted.) [In English] I grew up seeing reproductions of Greek statues & body-showing paintings (such as Rubens & Titian) in our home,[107] & I spent a large part of each day doing drawings of such pic-

---

'If— wires you you must reply truthfully that you do not understand, that all will be explained on your return' (or some such words). I wired to mother that nothing mattered but her health, 'longing to hold you in my arms'. It may be that those last words of mine seemed to be dangerous in view of the [in Danish] incest [in English] rumor. Or it may be that sleeplessness, & the fear of going out of her mind & being a burden to me, drove her to suicide. She often spoke in a way to support such an explanation. But I believe explicitly that it was the sweetheart business (spread over many years & a few different personalities) that made her desperate. She felt that my happiness no longer veered around her, but that my longing for pleasure was aimed outside my life with mother, & was thwarted by her. This was largely true. Yet it is also true that I loved none of my sweethearts as I did my mother & I never aimed seriously (if at all) at marriage while mother was alive. None of my sweethearts, none of my friends, had such a fearless, lordly, generous, gifted nature as my mother, or were so devoted to beauty & art as she was. None were so free of 'biological' nonsense as she or so free of cowardly nonsense about religion, superstition, righteousness'.

107. In the collection of Grainger's father.

tures & statues or in drawing faces, hands, etc., from life. So the body, the naked body as well as the clothed, became for me a vehicle of expression (a tally of life, a symbol of nature's will)—just as music, poetry & prose did. In art I saw the pure, the unspoilt, the natural, the unblemished exalted & deified. And in the talk of my parents & of art-loving friends I heard the artificial & the pretentious (such as artificial flowers, modern clothes, the use of scent, powder & rouge) derided & criticised. So as I grew up to be 14, or 16, or 20 years old, I looked upon grown women with horror (as being dirty with beauty-grease, foul in their powder & rouge, disgusting in their indolent grossness, repellent in their lovelessness & worldliness), mid-teen-age girls as half-spoiled goods, but girls of 13, 12 & down to 6 or 5 as being the only representatives of womankind that answered the requirements of an art-wonted mind & eye. I was not anti-woman; I was only anti-filth, anti-decay. I was not pro-infantile; I was merely pro-pure, pro-clean, pro-fit, pro-natural, pro-sweet, pro-nice. I was not so lacking in manly feeling (the love of the nasty for the nice) as to tolerate seeing females looking & behaving as revoltingly as men! I was a trained artist, which is the same as saying that 'I was one of those fitted to exert good taste in all matters, including sex'.

But the combined results of these various epicurean tastes, when I described them to mother (as I was growing up & as long as she lived & we talked together), were often alarming & distressing to her—largely because I presented them to her in exaggerated or uncompromising forms, which I felt I had to do, for good reasons. I had sworn to myself to make good to my mother those things my father had disappointed her in: money, security, manliness, loyalty, forseeingness, companionship. I saw I had to build up in her the health my father had broken down ([in Danish] when he infected her with the 'Spanish disease'). [In English] I knew her longing to see me really great (not merely successful) in art. I realised that her whole human happiness hinged on an unbroken together-life with me. So I knew that marriage was not for me—not for a long time, at any rate. Yet by 16 or 17 I was already sex-crazy [in Danish] (although not engaging in sexual acts—on the contrary. On the other hand, I burned my flesh against hot stove tiles; I stuck needles through my penis; in my imagination I exercised far-fetched cruelties on the female body.) [In English] A bad situation, one might say? Not at all! An artist grows keen & vocal by postponement, ecstatic & life-worshipful thru agony. I was all right—willing to live a large part of my life in the 'temptations of Saint Anthony'.[108] But I had to use drastic means when mother came to me asking: Didn't I want to marry? [In Danish] 'Yes, I would dearly love to own a wife

108. The early ascetic, St. Antony of Egypt (ca. AD 251–356).

whom I could lash [in English] to my heart's content.' Wouldn't you like to have children? [In Danish] 'Yes, I would highly value having intercourse with my own daughters. I would be ecstatic to lash my children until they bled,' etc. [In English] That staved mother off—at times, I think, making her happy (in the thought that marriage was not a duty she would have to immediately face); at other times making her deeply distressed, so that she would sometimes say, fiercely, 'Don't be surprised if I come in with a knife, some night, & cut off that part of you that makes you have such wicked thoughts'. (Menlo P[ark], Jan. 7).

As for my cowardice, it is obvious enough. I love to go walking in the desert, but my pleasure in so-doing is marred by my fear of dogs. I could improve all sorts of situations in my life if I only had the manhood to 'speak up'. My career as a concert artist has been spoiled by platform-timidity. If I'd not been so afraid of my mother's willfulness & anger I could have explained all sorts of things better to her & saved her a lot of wretchedness.

During the only school-going I had in my life (South Yarra, around 1894–95) I ran home madly as soon as school was out, to avoid fights with other boys. Yet as a younger boy (first Kilalla) I had fights with boys in the street & didn't seem to mind much. When I was about ten, in the 1st Kilalla, we had some nice flowers growing near the garden gate. The boys used to slip in & steal them. I warned them I'd fight them if they did. A boy (bigger than I) did & I went out & fought him, between our house & the Allsops'. We both got knocked about. The other boy pulled a piece of loose hanging skin off his knuckle, handed it to me, saying, 'You can use that as sticking plaster for your (face, hand, nose? Something he'd damaged)'. By this time he'd veered off. I suppose we'd both had enough. I remember dashing into the music room (where mother was giving a piano lesson to one of the Husband girls—I think Molly[109]), bloody, & shouting out: 'I've done it'. So I must have dreaded fighting, even then.

Does My Ris-Dyrkeri[110] Merely Stem from the Horsey Aldridge Background?

In a life such as my grandfather (mother's father), uncles, & my mother lived, the carriage whip & the riding whip were part of everyday life—were always at hand. My grandfather was always horse-whipping his sons. And every Sunday he took his horse-fearing wife & some of his children out driving, to

109. The Husband family was friendly with the Graingers during their Hawthorn years. Molly and at least one of the other daughters (Kitty, Jenny) studied the piano with Rose Grainger.
110. Birch-worship (in Danish).

show off before them his mastery over a mettlesome horse. It was a common sight at the first Kilalla (before father went away—when I was 7) to see my mother driving father out of the room with a riding whip. [In Danish] I think it has to be explained this way. Because of the 'Spanish disease' my father had acquired and infected my mother with, my mother did not want to have further children with him—she did not wish to give birth to blind or mentally deficient children, she told me. When he was sober he understood that and respected it. But when he was drunk, maybe he did not obey in this respect, and then my mother had to have recourse to the horse-whip. Her horse-whip was always in the hall, [in English] in one of those drain pipes father had painted with Chinese dragons. And the 'feather duster' (which word was synonymous with 'cane-ing' and used with much mischievous fun by her—the word, I mean) was always close to hand. I came out of a whole chain of whip-deeds-men who horse-whipped each other, men who enslaved horses & dogs with the whip, parents who brought up their children with the whip. So for me—an artist (one who used the things of life decoratively and playfully)—the whip (which had been a serious tool in the hands of my more serious elder kinsmen) became merely a source of fun, delight, enticement; a desirable horror, a bewitching fear.

Mother Tended to Be Theatrical & Drastic in Her Tests of Me

Mother was always wanting to find out if I really loved her very much or not. So she would 'sham dead'—lie quite still & corpse-like, while I would get distraught & beg her to speak to me. As soon as she was convinced that I was not at all indifferent she would say 'I see you do care for me, all right' & go about her affairs as if nothing had happened. 'I just wanted to find out what your real feelings for me were'. This test she did as late as 1919 or 1920, when we were in West 93rd [sic] Street. And threats to kill herself, or to get ill and die (if she were very displeased with something, or thought herself un-loved) were always on the cards. Why not? Why not use the material at one's disposal? Yet she would not guess what I meant when I made a protest in my own milder way. When I set Swinburne's 'The Bride's Tragedy'[111] to music I felt it was (in a way) describing my own case—the young man who loses his sweetheart because his mother delays him. I even dedicated the work to mother, as if to say 'This is partly your work'. But she sensed it so little, took it so lightly, that she was always confusing the 2 titles 'The Bride's Tragedy'

---

111. As a ballad for chorus and band (1908–14).

(which symbolised the British tragicness mother had colored my love-life with) & 'The Merry Wedding'[112] (dedicated to Ingerid Traegaard[113] in thankfulness for the Danish happiness she had injected into my life), saying 'They seem almost the same thing, don't they?' I would say 'To me [they] seem just the very opposite'. You cannot down innocence. Mother was as innocent (& as wilful, sometimes as destructive) as a child. Yet if mother's behavior gave me 'The Bride's Tragedy' & Ingerid's gave me 'The Merry Wedding', mother's was a richer gift.

Mother's Worship of Bodily Beauty

For some months before I was born mother had a picture of the Apollo Belvedere (or some similar famed-for-beauty Greek statue) facing her as she lay down on her bed or sofa for her afternoon nap, or before sleep at night— I forget which. She hoped that her thoughts, resting on Greek beauty, would invest the unborn child with the same. [In Danish] In our last days, when I was running around naked in our bedrooms in White Plains, she often said to me: [in English] 'It's such a joy to me to have such a Greek-looking son', or 'It's such a blessing to me to have such a handsome son', or the like. Her delight in the beauty of 'Little May' (who used to help serve at our tea parties[114]) & her comparison of L. M. with Miss Fleetstream[115] (to the former's advantage) is mentioned elsewhere.[116] (I must say, Little May was fair as an angel, with those small daisy-like well-chiselled English features, light English frame, blue eyes & shining gold hair that justified the phrase 'Angels, not Angles'.)[117] I think mother got on with Janet Johansen[118] as well as she did, because she enjoyed her beauty. I can never remember mother showing the least jealousy, or dislike, or criticism to anyone really beautiful—such as Mrs Edmond Wodehouse,[119] for instance. And the things mother was apt to quote from poetry such as Byron's or Tennyson's ('I brushed & combed his comely head, he

---

112. A bridal dance for solo voices, chorus, piano, and strings (1912–15).
113. Karen Holten.
114. During the Graingers' time in Chelsea.
115. Probably Grainger's pseudonym for Miss Elena Rathbone (1878–1964). See, further, essay 37.
116. 'Grainger's Anecdotes', 423-2.
117. Grainger refers to the statement of Pope Gregory I (AD 540–604) reported by Bede: 'Non Angli, sed Angeli'.
118. Perhaps Else Permin.
119. Adela H. Wodehouse (d. 1921), who had helped Grainger with learning Icelandic in his early London years.

looked so grand when he was dead'[120]) bore witness to her unfailing worship of bodily beauty.

Mother's Cosmopolitanism, Shot Thru with Streaks of British Patriotism

Ederheimer, her pupil,[121] was short, I think, & not good-looking. But his Jewish unattractiveness did not hinder her from being repeatedly touched by his genuine passionateness, woman-fondness. Mother responded to whatever genuine quality any person had to offer, without her being shooed off by their lack of other qualities. Dr Hermann Mischke she considered the most lover-like man & most attractive man she had ever met—his manliness, kindliness, unselfishness. Yet she could not marry him, when he asked her to, because she couldn't see me brought up a German. She told me that going out riding at Woodend[122] (in her twenties) with the son of Mr Coope (the inn-keeper) or some other workman-class man, convinced her that it would be as easy for her to be interested in a working man as in a gentleman—something in the shape of his legs, or the way he sat [on] his horse. But her Britishness (if challenged) would rear its head too. On the steamer 'Gera', going from Melbourne to Genoa, in 1895, somebody must have asked why the New Zealand town Wellington was called thus. 'After the Duke of Wellington, who won the Battle of Waterloo.' Said the (German) 3rd mate, 'But it wasn't Wellington who won the Battle of Waterloo. It was Bluecher'[123] (of whom mother hadn't even heard, I suppose). So the set-to began, then & there. And when (1898?) Helene Klimsch,[124] mother & I were summering together in lovely Brueckenau (Oberfranken, Bavaria) and sat talking one evening in the back garden, mother & Helene got onto the rights & wrongs of the English-German question—I, of course, like the little colorless eunuch that I always am, siding first with one, then with the other & giving satisfaction to neither. The summer guests said the next morning, 'Whatever was going on last night? We heard the two ladies' voices, talking vehemently, with the words England, Deutschland distinguishable in almost every sentence; and then Master Percy's voice, sounding more conciliatory'. Yet in spite of mother's easily arousable British

120. 'I curl'd and comb'd his comely head, / He looked so grand when he was dead' (Tennyson's 'The Sisters' Shame').
121. In Frankfurt.
122. 75 kilometres northwest of Melbourne.
123. Gebhard Leberecht von Blücher, who led the Prussian forces, fighting with Wellington, in the Battle.
124. A daughter of Karl Klimsch.

patriotism, she could be awfully down on English or Australian people. She was quite happy at the Pension Schoen[125] (1899? 1898?) until some English woman turned up there. Then we left. 'The English are always trouble-makers', mother said. And mother was always emphatic in saying that she had had little but cruel treatment in Australia (up to 1895). And America left nothing but bitter impressions. When we first settled in England (1902) she said: 'I shall never feel at home here. All is sham'.

Mother No Bohemian (The Practical to Serve the Ideal)

Mother was a puritan (according to B. Shaw's definition) rather than a bohemian—but she was neither. But it was *natural* in her (not 'moral') to aim at the high, & she had a highly practical sense of the need for money & other worldly supports to stand behind the ideal. That is why she urged me (in my 20s) to concentrate on the piano, so that I could earn good money [while] young, in order to use it on composition in later life. (But I couldn't. I had to mix my ideal & my practical as I went along. I couldn't 'forget about sex & lead a healthy vigorous life'. I couldn't forget about composition in order to specialise on the piano.) One idea—entirely her own—she was very insistent on: 'As you are experimenting with new ideas in music, you yourself must prove to the world that they are practical. If you don't prove it yourself, no-body else will. Beethoven & Wagner are about the most famous of composers, & they both financed concerts of their own music, & showed the world how their music should be conducted,' etc. Nevertheless, it was I (when I was 16 or 17), not mother, who first hatched the thought that we must save money. I will never forget how surprised my mother looked when I pronounced the word 'save'. I don't suppose she'd ever heard it mentioned before—in her family, or by father.

Mother's Idea That Genius Flourished on Immunity, Not Experience

She was always full of the thought that a genius should be protected from the harsh or depressing things of this world (amongst which sorrow[126] is not to be counted), should, in other words, enjoy *immunity* from all sorts of ordinary influences & experiences, rather than have a wide experience. This theory she carried out, in my life, with amazing thoroness. She never wavered

125. Pension Schön, Oberlindau, Frankfurt, where they lived during 1898–99.
126. Grainger first wrote 'misery'.

from her determination to screen me from the common, the ordinary, the normal. Under this comes her hardfought battle to keep me away from children's illnesses. That was one of the reasons I wasn't sent to school, except for 3 months. She was frantic when I caught measles in the army (1917 or 18). She had no tolerance at all for the toughening theory—that men are the better for roughing it. That is why she was so unhappy that I thrived so well in the army—it was a disloyalty on my part towards her immunity effort. She hated to see me love the low & the commonplace so easily. Maybe it reminded her of something in my father she didn't like—she always said he got on so well with his workingmen, was needlessly chummy with them. There was nothing 'democratic' about mother—in spite of her classlessness. That is why I call her a kind of puritan, because she was so keen on the highest, in any class or situation.

Mother's Efforts to Prevent My Becoming Money-Minded

One of the reasons she didn't bother about my learning arithmetic properly was that she almost prized my inability to add, to count money. When I was under 10 I came home from having met some Jewish children, one of whom asked me what my shoes cost. Mother was horrified: 'I'll never let you see those children again'. Shortly after we arrived in Frankfurt (I about 13) mother got the notion that I was getting too grown-up, that my face was losing its angel-look & getting too hard-looking or practical-looking. So she brought for me a child's game called 'The Farm' (with pigs, horses, animals, barns) which we played together, & for which I showed too exaggerated a liking. So she took it away from me. 'I can see you're quite childish enough. That's all I wanted to know.' There was no basking in comfort with mother; no being allowed to really *enjoy* a propensity. One was right out in the middle of things happening all the time; if one wasn't doing some wonder-feat of self-betterment, every moment, the thing one liked (was enjoying) would be whisked away from one.

Mother's Lightning Changes of Mood, of Attitude

It was the same with sweethearts. 'Don't you ever want to have a nice sweet-heart? Wouldn't you like to take Mimi's arm as you walk home from the Forsthaus[127] tonight?' And so on. But the moment one responded really well

127. Forester's house (in German).

to such a suggestion the opposite counsel was turned on. 'You can't think of nothing but sweethearting. You mustn't be so self-indulgent in everything you do.' Or, 'You have a drunkard's nature like your father—always overdoing everything'. The end with Mrs Lowrey[128] was typical. Mother wrote me in a letter, 'Perhaps this *very great* friendship with Mrs L. should come to an end'. Never extreme in her suggestions, always tolerant, yet critical. It was the same with composing & practising. If I practised hard for a few days & shunned composing she would say: 'I wonder whether I shall ever hear you compose again'. If (heeding this) I turned round & concentrated on composing for 2 or 3 days (& one can't do much in composition with less!) she would say, 'What is to become of us if you do nothing but compose & neglect your practising?' She would not only change quickly from pro-sweethearting to anti-sweethearted, but equally quickly back again. One moment she would say, 'I don't know what to think about Louise.[129] Sometimes I think she's cruel.' The next day, 'I'm going to try & think nothing but nice thoughts about Louise'. When my mind & attitude, in obedience, veered around, for or against whatever she had been saying, she would say, 'You mustn't take everything I say too literally. When I talk with you it's just like talking to myself. I say whatever comes into my head. I don't expect you to act upon it' (which I was much too inclined to do—sometimes, not always, alas!).

At Bottom, Mother Was Never Strict about Money

She would try to think strictly about money, but couldn't, most of the time. The money from the Dutch tour was a typical case. I'd had a tour in Holland, perhaps 20 or 30 concerts (1911–1914)[130] & maybe I had sent home some of the money I had earnt. But towards the end of the tour the payment for a whole lot of concerts—paper money—I had just thrown in the bottom of my suit case, under some brown paper, & packed on top of it. When I came home mother (& Mrs Kelford, or whoever was helping or charring for her then) unpacked the bag, down to the brown paper, but didn't look below. Months later, when I [was] off for another tour & mother & her aid(s) were packing up for me, the money was found. But the point was that neither mother nor I missed the rather large sum I had earned on the Dutch tour. Mother trained me to *think about the ability to earn*, but not always about the money itself. And so I, too, have always been. Actual *sums* mean little to me.

128. Lilith Lowrey (d. 1911), Grainger's first 'love-serve-job' in London, ca. 1902–4. See essay 32.
129. Lotta [Hough].
130. Grainger gave twenty concerts in The Netherlands between 12 January and 8 February 1914.

[In Danish] Mother's Pronouncement on My Birch Worship. [In English] ('Kindest Man I have Known')

[In Danish] Her dismay concerning my birch worship was possibly more based on anxiety on *my* behalf (fear of what could occur to me in the way of unpleasantness or bad luck if my birch-worshipping inclinations became known) than in moral revulsion *per se*. For at times she said to me: [in English] 'Mind you; if I were a young girl & were in love with you, I wouldn't be afraid of any of your queer tastes. For I have always found you the kindest man I have known in my life.'

Mother for Me, Against the World (& Its Conventions)

I suppose the thing that meant the most to me—the thing that made me the happiest—in my together-life with mother, was my knowledge that she would always stand *with me* against the world & its conventions, however much she might *advise me* not to do this or that unconventionality (unless I was very stuck on it). When we first settled in London & were living in Kensington (1902 or 03) father's Scotch friend Mr Aytoun[131] was spending the late afternoon with us. I had to go out somewhere (as always, *merely* for business, never for liking) & it was a question whether I should put on evening dress or not. Mother advised me to, & I heard old Aytoun old-fogeying along with mother on these lines: 'Yes, let the boy put on evening dress. It's good discipline for a young man', which immediately brought down on him mother's 'I don't agree about that at all. I think evening dress is perfect nonsense, & I wouldn't like to see Percy fond of dressing up or otherwise being a namby-pamby. I only advised him to put it on tonight because I think it might be better for his career to do so.' That was typical.

Mother's Outspokenness to Her Friends

I daresay mother was outspoken all her life. But living with me must have tended to make her more so, because I never resent anything said. But others always did; Roger (Quilter), for instance. While his father[132] was still alive

---

131. George Aytoun, of Perth, Western Australia.
132. Sir Cuthbert Quilter (1841–1911), baronet, parliamentarian, and businessman.

Roger was always talking to mother (he came & saw us, or her, every Thursday, for years, I think) about what he'd do about publishing my music when his father died & he came into his money. But when his father did die, Roger made [a] lot of excuses, why he couldn't afford to do what he'd talked about (publish my music) for a while. Mother told me she said to him, 'All right! But don't make such a song about it. You've talked so much about what you'd do when you got your money, & if you can't do what you said, that's all right. Percy's got enough money to publish his things when he wants to, I suppose. I always thought it so lovely of you to want to help him publish his things. But it doesn't matter if you can't just yet. But don't make such a song about it!' I don't think Roger ever forgave that, or got over it. I don't think things were the same between Roger & mother after that. And it may be that outspoken things mother may have said to Miss Permin or Miss Du Cane, in mother's last year, led to despair or distrust on their part.

Mother at [Peter Jones, Chelsea][133] ('Perhaps You Want Your Lunch?')[134]

As a rule her outspokenness (of which, as such, she was never aware) was reserved for me & her friends. But she could sometimes speak out to strangers in a way that flabbergasted them—a result she never intended; for mother was wholly free from stratagem, plan, intention. She (& Else Permin, I think) were shopping at [Peter Jones] (that big store, at Sloane Square, Chelsea, just opposite our 31A King's Road) around midday. The man serving mother seemed rather listless. Suddenly mother got an idea. 'Perhaps this is your lunch-time—perhaps you are wanting your lunch?! Why don't you go & get it, & I'll come back when you've had it as I live just across the street?' 'Oh no, madam. I can assure you I am in no hurry at all to have my lunch', & he quite livened up, Miss Permin said. Mother said such a thing out of the goodness of her heart—plus the wish to get things done. But never with any calculation, or any awareness (at the time) that she was acting even impulsively.

Miss Permin's First Day at 31A King's Road

The day she arrived[135] (to board with us at 31A, & to take lessons from me) was a hectic one. I was to play somewhere that night (at Mrs Charles Hunter's?[136]) & had had a mass of pupils all day. The moment the last pupil

133. Left blank by Grainger.
134. A variant of this story is found in 'Grainger's Anecdotes', 423–64 (16 August 1953).
135. Probably in July 1909.
136. Mary Hunter (1857–1933), arts patron and violinist, sister of the composer Ethel Smyth.

left some half-friend (was it Baron de Meyer?[137]) arrived & had a long conversation with me in my music-room, early in the evening. Mother was on pins & needles, wanting him to go, but he being a type of man mother didn't like to drive away. On top of this, Miss Permin, tired from her sea trip, wanted to go to bed early & didn't like to do so without saying 'goodnight' to mother. So she knocked at mother's door. 'Who is that?', said mother from inside the room, 'if anything more happens I shall go stark-staring raving mad', which upset poor Miss Permin greatly. She told us, later.

Mother's Unwavering Dislike of the Bible; Her Inability to Join Any Religious Group

Altho she insisted she liked the personality of Christ, as a man, & altho she *sometimes* (but mostly not) said she had religious feeling, she was unwavering in her dislike of any portion of the Bible. Sometimes (admiring it as literature) I would want to read her something from the Proverbs, or the Psalms, or the Song of Solomon[138]—or even from the New Testament. But she would *never* brook it. 'Be a good fellow & don't read to me from that awful depressing book.' She was truly fond of Mrs McGee, & at times maybe somewhat influenced by Mrs McGee's catholicism. Mother would say 'If I had to join any church, I think it would be easiest for me to join the catholic church. I like the way Mrs McGee is willing to sit in church beside any dirty old man. But I'm afraid I could never bring myself to say I believed in the things they would want me to.' At the 1st Kilalla, after father left (1889?)[139] & mother was rather desperate (how to earn for me & her), she would have liked to find some solace in religion & church, if she might. There was some curate, or someone from the church, who called on her & talked religion with her. All was well, until he suddenly knelt down beside her & said, 'Let us pray'. It seemed silly to her. (Thank goodness for that.)

Walt Whitman a Red Rag to a Bull

Yet once the church stood her in good stead. On the 1904 Ada Crossley tour mother gave a copy of Walt Whitman's 'Leaves of Grass' to (Uncle Jim's daughter) Violet,[140] whom mother thought the most book-loving of my

---

137. Adolf Edward Sigismund de Meyer (1868–1949), photographer and piano pupil of Grainger's.

138. In 1899, Grainger started to experiment with applications of speech rhythms to music in his *Love Verses from 'The Song of Solomon'* (scored in 1931 for soloists, chorus, and a variety of chamber orchestra and keyboard combinations).

139. Correctly, 1890.

140. Violet Aldridge (b. 1884) was one of Grainger's favourite cousins.

cousins. When Mrs Zebina Lane saw the book she delivered herself of a great tirade about giving such a book to a young girl. At the same time she asked mother to go to church with her to hear a preacher she specially admired & followed. When they got there, his sermon was on Walt Whitman: 'This great man, almost as inspired as the bible itself'. Nothing more said against Walt by Mrs Lane. In the first year in London, we met the mother & family of Onslow Orchard, father's friend in Perth, W.A., who sang in my try-thru choir in Hornton Street, Kensington.[141] (He always sang a fraction before each beat. When I told him, he said he knew it, but couldn't cure himself of it. How can a person be unable to cure himself of a defect he knows of?) There one afternoon, mother spoke about her devotion to Walt Whitman. Mrs Orchard drew herself up, grew very stern & said: '*Now* I know what your tastes are!' (I remembered that when I refused to recommend her son, Arundel Orchard, for the post in Hobart, 1935.[142] I would always revenge on a family any slight to my mother.)[143]

Mother's Artistic Judgements Formed on Her Own, without Me

Altho we were so close to each other, & our artistic life so shared, yet her artistic judgements were always formed on her own, without influence from me. Indeed, there might be said to be always some cleavage between our artistic opinions, especially about music. Mother's love of the deeply expressive was greater than mine—she somewhat lacking my love of the wild & weird. For instance, I never (after my first hearing of him, in Frankfurt, when he was 20, playing Tchaikovsky's 1st Concerto) particularly admired what Gabrilowitsch[144] did. But when mother heard him, with his own Detroit strings, do a chamber work (of Schubert's?) at some music festival[145] (Mrs Coolidge's, at which I played the Eichheim oriental pieces[146] & on 2 pianos with Selim Palmgren?[147]) she said to me, 'there must be something really about him—

---

141. I.e., in 1902.

142. Arundel Orchard (1867–1961) was director of the New South Wales State Conservatorium from 1923 to 1935, when he moved to become Head of Music Studies at the University of Tasmania in Hobart.

143. A variant of the story appears in 'Grainger's Anecdotes', 423-95.

144. Ossip Gabrilovich (1878–1936), Russian pianist, who, like Grainger, settled in the United States in 1914. He was conductor of the Detroit Symphony Orchestra (1916–36).

145. Probably a Berkshire Festival of Chamber Music concert on 1 October 1921, in Pittsfield, MA.

146. *Oriental Impressions*, by American composer Henry Eichheim (1870–1942).

147. (1878–1951), Finnish pianist and composer.

some deeply musical influence that he exerts—[to] make those men with him play so exquisitely—to get such a perfect performance', & I had the impression that at that festival she admired what G. did more than what I did. And mother didn't follow me at all in my dislike of Beethoven. And when she heard my English Dance for the first time (Beecham, Palladium, 1911)[148] with Delius's 'Walk to the Paradise Garden'[149] on the same program, she was more touched by his piece than by mine (she loved his use of the harp in it). She did not lose herself (her cool judgement) [because] I was involved in a concert. She put art above her love for her son. Sargent[150] brought Gabriel Fauré & the Capet string quartet[151] over from Paris to play, in Sargent's studio, before an audience of dowagers, duchesses & rich Jews, Fauré's works for piano & strings. I was away (would it have been around 1908?) in the provinces, playing. But mother went and was bowled over by the beauty of the Faurés. She didn't know that I was already a Fauré worshipper (I have always considered him a greater chamber writer, a more perfect classicist, than Brahms) & when I came home from the north she told me her admiration for Fauré with diffidence, thinking I might scoff at it. Likewise in Christchurch, New Zealand. While I toured with Ada[152] & her company in smaller towns, mother stayed on in Christchurch. She discovered that delicious little museum,[153] gathered together by someone with a German name, quite near that nice boarding [house] at which we stayed. Up to that time neither mother nor I were aware of native art—African or Polynesian beadwork, etc. When I got back to Christchurch I accidentally found the same museum & suffered the birth of a new taste, a new artistic life, on seeing these same things that had ravished mother so much—unknown to me. When I came home & told her of the life-changing experience I had had at the museum, she confided that she had felt the same thrill at the self-same things, but had been shy to tell me, fearing I would deem her taste childish. Her enthusiasm for the Irish writer Stephens[154] was acquired on her own, & her liking for 'The Crock of Gold', which latter I have still never read.

148. Grainger refers to Beecham's 18 February 1912 concert at the London Palladium.

149. Entr'acte from Delius's opera, *A Village Romeo and Juliet*.

150. John Singer Sargent (1856–1925), American painter resident in Chelsea, a patron of Grainger during his London years.

151. Led by French violinist Lucien Capet (1873–1928).

152. Ada Crossley (1871–1929), Australian-born contralto, in whose party Grainger toured Australasia in 1903–4 and 1908–9.

153. The Graingers' visits to this museum occurred in early 1909. For another recollection of this museum, see essay 81.

154. Grainger here refers to the mention of Stephens in the earlier section of this essay entitled, 'Mother's Matchless Devotion to the Arts'.

Mother's Lack of Prudery & Hyper-Decency (Unlike Her Mother)

Mother's complete lack of prudery & hyper-decency was not at all a matter of boldness, emancipation or modernism on her part. It stemmed from her complete un-preoccupation with the thoughts & interests (sexual, etc.) that lead most people to be either shy or ribald, as the case might be. She just *didn't think* about such subjects. So she was always saying things (as children do) that sound awfully funny & surprising to those whose thought continually cruises around biological subjects. Some of these funny-seeming sayings are recorded elsewhere. But where her awareness was aroused, of biological subjects, she was reticent rather than free-spoken. Thus, when she found she was going to have a child, she never said a word to any of her kin about the expected event. And thru-out her whole life she never confided the fact of having been [in Danish] infected with the 'Spanish disease' by my father [in English] to anybody but me & her doctors. That none of her kin were ever told of this fact during her lifetime made for a lack of understanding, on their part, for mother's willingness to part from father when I was seven. She had a horror of being ill, & hated the thought that any of her dear ones should know of her misfortune. Possibly also she didn't wish to broadcast anything likely to create a dislike for my father in the Aldridge ranks. Mother was entirely forgiving, in her nature—altho quite capable of speaking bitterly & drastically about things, at the time they happened, to the chief person or persons concerned. But she was naturally un-prudish in her habits—[in Danish] like my wife, it always gave her a little pleasure to sneak from her bedroom to the bathroom with a night pot, or to sneak out half-dressed into the corridor (between the bedrooms). [In English] She was a person to whom accidents could happen—bits of clothing could become untied & the like. Not that she would feel comfortable in such accidents; but her forebodings anent possible accidents were not enough to lead her to strictly take the steps needful to prevent them. In other words, she had a gay & free way in life. In all this she was so unlike her mother, she said; for her mother was never seen going to the closet, & would (evidently) wait hours rather than be seen going. Nor would it have been possible to talk freely on intimate subjects with her mother—as it was with my mother, to whom it was easy to talk on any subject, even if she wasn't always particularly keen to hear one talk—not because she was shy or reticent, but because (as I said before) she was not biologically inquisitive. [In Danish] I don't know when or why I began to walk around naked in her presence, for it seems to me that it began long before I heard the word 'nudism'. I think that it appeared quite natural to her (as it did to me) that a son should be nude in front of his mother. I find no particular virtue in the latter point of view (that a mother should not be nude in front of her son); I only claim that that was the way it was between us. [In English] Both mother & her grandmother agreed in considering her mother a little straightlaced & forbidding, & mother's grandmother would sometimes wink at my mother when my mother's mother was around, as if to say, 'We are birds of a feather'. As for me, I never sensed that my grandmother was either prudish or straightlaced or forbidding. I felt very much at ease with her & would call her gentle, retiring, delicately proud, rather than straightlaced. But at any rate, there is some life-dodging instinct at work in all of us (grandmother, mother, me). We are not part of the great army of breeders, family-builders, & society-bulwarks. We are, rather, the 'sports' by which Darwinian nature effects its changes.

Mother's Possible Severity with Me & Her Piano Pupils

One of the Husband girls spoke to Ella about my mother being severe with her piano pupils—liable to rap them over the knuckles with a ruler, & such. But my impression is that that was the custom in piano teaching, at the time. Other Australians have said to me (of late years) that they were sorry for me as a little boy, because I was always so dressed up, with 'Lord Fauntleroy' collar & gloves,[155] & therefore unable to play as other boys. But I didn't want to play with other boys. I said something to my mother like this: 'Must I play that game (cricket)? I get so cold, waiting for the ball to come my way, & when it does, I miss it. Now when I'm drawing & painting, I'm doing something nice all the time.' I suppose I was hit over the knuckles, too, if I held my hand 'wrong'. But, goodness gracious! A little boy is a small devil & should be tail-twisted all the time & treated to pain, cruelty, wilfulness. There was always a lot of talk of my being the living spit of 'Bubbles', Pears Soap advertisement; & that I was just like 'Little Lord Fauntleroy'. It all seemed quite natural to me & the gloves & the Eton collar didn't sissify me, that I know of. The spears & shield (garden sticks & rubbish box lids) game was not sissified,[156] nor that other game I played with Bede (1st Kilalla), each armed with sharp-cutting, blood-bringing shreds of bamboo (from worn-out Japanese blinds), seeing who could stand the most blows—first one, then the other,

---

155. For photographs of Grainger in such boyhood poses, see Bird, *Percy Grainger*, illustration 1; and Dorum, *Percy Grainger: The Man Behind the Music*, between pp. 16 and 17.
156. Such a game is recalled by one of Grainger's childhood friends, Ruth Curtain, in Gillies and Pear, *Portrait of Percy Grainger*, 10–12.

passively taking 5 or 10 blows at a time.[157] There is no doubt that mother's ideal was that I should be an art-man & a manly man at the same time—& that is why she didn't interfere in the deadly spears & shields game, until Uncle Jim pointed out how frightfully dangerous it was.

Mother's Daringness

While I was a young boy (up to the time of mother's terrible headaches at Sofiero, Rathmines Road, Auburn[158]) mother was still very daring & athletic. I always cherish a vision of her being thrown off a horse, at Clare, S.A. (when I was about 7), & her getting up off the ground, so bright & pleased to be thrown. At the 1st Kilalla, when she was getting after a tarantula, high on my bedroom wall, with a cricket bat, she fell off the washing stand (marble top) onto a bed post, or onto the marble top, & gave herself a bruise as big as a plate. If she cut her finger she would act so funnily—all thru life. She'd dramatise it so, 'Now I've cut my finger to the bone' & she'd hold the other hand over it, so I couldn't see the hurt. Then when she'd remove the other hand, it might be nothing but a scratch or very shallow cut—in which case she'd laugh so heartily over it. Always lots of fun, exaggeration—making the most of everything! But when those terrible neuralgic headaches came (when I was about 10, at Auburn) it seemed to knock the athleticness out of her. In Frankfurt, of course, she adored bicycling & took great risks—asking me to take her handle bar (as I bicycled alongside) & pull her faster than she could ride by herself. She ended up on a heap of sharp stones that way, once. But after she fell on the Glatteis,[159] on a footpath, hurt her spine & was for months on iced pipes, there was no more athletic fun for her. She was told it was all part of the [in Danish] Spanish sickness [in English] she'd got from my father, about which, in those days, folk talked with the darkest forebodings. If one was [in German] dissolute [in Danish] with women [in English] one got [in German] spine marrow disease.[160] [In English] If one had [in Danish] Spanish sickness [in English] one could expect to go mad, or blind, get paralysed. And mother feared that any of those would happen. 'What will you do if I go out of my mind? Will you visit me in the asylum? What will you do if I go blind? Will you be kind to me?'

157. This game with Grainger's older friend Adam Bede also features in Grainger's account of his penchant for flagellation (essay 59).
158. I.e., 1893–94.
159. Black ice (in German).
160. Rückenmarksleiden.

Did Mother Have a Touch of Hypochondria?

I think some people (who, of course, knew nothing of the [in Danish] Spanish sickness) [in English] thought mother hypochondriacal. But her doctors never seemed to think so, altho one of them, in Australia, in the early days (when I was a baby) wasn't sure whether she had the [in Danish] Spanish sickness [in English] or not. Her case was so muddled, in the first year. I think she was self-dramatising, prone to exaggerate, rather than hypochondriacal. She had such a hatred of illness, & of being ill. And I don't think one who told the facts of her illness to no one but me & her doctors can be called hypochondriacal. Even Fornander (who had [in Danish] Spanish sickness [in English] himself), who massage-treated her in Frankfurt, 1899, had no inkling that she had [in Danish] Spanish sickness. [In English]

Mother's Gaiety, Merry Voice, Lively Movements

My anxiety about her sufferings (bodily & soulful), & my sense of guilt in having failed her in loyalty & lovingness, make me prone to over-emphasise her sorrows, ailments & nervous conditions, perhaps. At all times, the main thing about her was her gaiety, her jollity, her ability to come out of suspicion & regain trustingness, her forgivingness & grudgelessness, her eagerness. The moment she would come into a house, a room, a gathering, one could hear her merry voice—so different from most grown-up voices! 'Is Percy here?' Even long after her back got bad & she found walking a trial, she still had such lively movements—crossing a street, or whatever it was. I couldn't see her in action without chuckling. And she could laugh so heartily.

Mother's Funny Sayings, Quotations

As a heritage of her girlhood, Adelaide days (possibly an echo of the way her brother Ted carried on—she & he were the most artistic ones in the family; there is a sweet drawing by Uncle Ted in the Museum), when the whole Aldridge family seemed keen on the theatre, light operas & other shows (her father engaged entertainment artists for a time), she had always plenty of quotations from plays & shows, & other jolly sayings, such as 'T E, tea, Jane Mould'; 'For he was such a careful man' (this addressed to me, of course).

Some of these are recorded elsewhere.[161] 'For I am tired & sleepy too', if I yawned or got lifeless.

Mother's Ability to Carry Thru Drastic Diet-Regimes

The way she stuck to her green apple & peanut regime, towards the end, showed ability to carry thru drastic resolves. This, & kindred evidences of desperate determination, suggests a type of character capable of embracing, & carrying thru, the suicide plan. It was suggested that she got giddy & just fell out of the window in Mrs Sawyer's office room.[162] But I have no doubt myself that it was suicide.

Mother's Possible Reasons for Suicide

1. Feeling that her mind & self-control were going (she complained of hallucinations), she dreaded a future in which she would be in a nurse's hands, in which she should be a burden to me, in which her wilfulness would come to an end.
2. From the time those friends thought us capable of [in Danish] shared incestuous life [in English], she saw no future for our together-life: 'Everything we do will be viewed with suspicion'. And when, a day or so before she died, I wired her from Los Angeles, 'Longing to hold you in my arms'[163] she saw confirmation of her fears that I, or she, would continually do things that would arouse suspicion.
3. The spectacle of several women friends behaving hysterically about me, & the fact that the sweetheart I loved (Bertha Knowles[164]) refused to marry me at any price (when mother begged her to do so) may have convinced mother that no satisfactory sex life could exist for me while she lived—this thought that others entertained so glibly may have come to roost with her. So she may have thought it needful to 'clear the decks' for my normal life by getting herself out of the way. That is just the kind of thing she was capable of: die that I might live.
4. Despair in finally realising that I was not loyal or devoted to her; when she asked me questions about my wishes for the future, I gave listless answers. Yes, I was very much in love with Bertha, yet I didn't know whether marriage was the best thing for us all—Bertha & I having been thru so much together. Yet I could not say that I *didn't* want marriage, or that all I wanted was our (mother's & my) together-life. I was a spectre of failure. These various possibilities will be treated more fully in the life-story.

161. See, e.g., essay 2.
162. The New York office of Grainger's concert agent Antonia Sawyer (1863–1941).
163. Grainger worried about the wording of this telegram for the rest of his life. See Gillies and Pear, eds., *The All-Round Man*, 52.
164. Lotta Hough.

Equally Fond of Men & Women

Due to mother's strongly platonic nature, I think it may be said that she was equally fond of men & women. When I started falling in love & spoke with much earnestness of my feelings, mother said, 'You're not the only person who has been in love. You always talk as if I'd never experienced anything like what you have. I've been very fond of men; but I don't make an awful song about it.' She could be very happy, talking with a comradely man like Frederic Austin,[165] who was a charming companion, relating the love overtures made to him when he sang in Germany. Mother always loved Cyril & Roger. But I don't think she was much impressed by what are called manly men. Mischke she loved; but he *really was* manly, not just called. Mother was not a 'woman's woman', talking intimacies with women she wouldn't with men. But she was very happy with her women friends Mrs McGee, Mrs Devlin,[166] Mrs Freeman, Beryl Freeman,[167] Mrs Wodehouse, Miss Permin, Miss Du Cane, etc.); in fact, her fondness for her women friends might be called her undoing. For even of those, who had thought such terrible things about her & me at the end of her life, she said: 'It's funny, but in spite of all that's happened I feel happier when they are around me'. Mother may have had love thrills & sex interests in her life, but I think it was in the main as Fornander said: [in German] 'No! Such a woman cannot be called sensuous. Loving rather than sensuous.' [In English] The chief impression I always had was of mother's *friendliness*, which colored her whole life—with men, with women, with servants, with strangers, with artists thru their art-works. Whatever sex stirs she had were certainly not allowed to run counter to her friendliness with very many different people.

Mother Championed the 'Under Dogs' amongst Her Friends

Whichever friend was set-upon, talked against, by her other friends, or by the world in general, she would be apt to favor. Thus, when her late-in-life friends talked against Mrs Simons (in particular, what an awful liar she was)

---

165. (1872–1952), English singer and composer, occasional performing associate of Grainger's.
166. Mrs. Adolph Devlin (Mary Hepburn), mother of the soprano Lilian Devlin (later Mrs. Albert Rawlinson). As with Rose Grainger, Mrs. Devlin had devoted herself to promoting her daughter's career in Melbourne and later in London. Her daughter also appears to have studied briefly in Frankfurt.
167. Mrs. Haidie Freeman and her daughter, the soprano Beryl Freeman, were Australian friends in London.

mother stuck up for her. 'I don't think she means any harm, even if she does exaggerate a bit'. 'The only thing I mind about her is that she will take my arm when we are crossing streets. I feel so much safer when I am left to myself.' Likewise when Alfhild[168] started talking against Ingerid[169] to mother (saying 'she's a gypsy') it only made mother like Ingerid much better than she had before. And when mother saw how poisonously the other women felt & talked about Louise[170] (in the last 9 months of her life) it made mother turn to Louise & urge her very strongly to marry me. There is no doubt that mother had her share of that inborn British propensity for 'the balance of power'.

Having dealt with several of her most outstanding qualities in the abstract, I will now draw a very brief sketch of the main outlines of mother's life, before passing on to a more detailed description of the same.

Brief Sketch of the Main Outlines of Rose Grainger's Life

Mother, like Aunty Clara (see 'Aldridge Family History' by Clara Aldridge), seems to have felt that my grandmother (mother's mother) had rather a hard time with my grandfather (mother's father). Altho he was unfailing in his devotion to his wife ('never looked at another woman'), altho he was a hard worker & a good provider, he was trying with his bossiness ('George is a slave-driver', said grandmother's mother), his drinking, his horse-whipping of his sons, his willingness to listen to stories against his sons, his vehemence. Grandmother cooked in the hotel kitchen (getting varicose veins from standing on her feet so much), scrubbed the floors & stairs (later helped by Uncle Jim), yet managed to live a rich family life with her brood of 9 children—half of them born in bigamy, before my grandfather's last wife died (see Aunty Clara on this[171]). There was lots of reading aloud (lots of it heady, romantic, love-provoking stuff, such as Byron, Tennyson) & the brothers seem to have been keen to help their sisters to music. (Read elsewhere of the piano intended for the elder sisters, but actually going to Rose (my

168. Alfhild Sandby.
169. Karen Holten.
170. Lotta Hough.
171. See 'George Sydney Aldridge (Uncle George) & Miss Cornish (P. G.'s grandmother on her bigamy)', in 'Aunty Clara's Aldridge History', T181-10, section 22, probably dating from 1926 (Grainger Museum, Melbourne).

mother) because she had secretly prepared herself to play a piece on it when it came.)

Jan. 5 1947, Men[l]o Park, Calif.—Jan. 9 1947, San Franc[isco].

Source: 'Bird's-Eye View of the Together-Life of Rose Grainger and Percy Grainger', 399-1 to 399-40 (complete) (Grainger Museum, Melbourne).

4

FRIENDS

21 [Dr Henry O'Hara] (1933)

Dr O'Hara had a thick Irish brogue, the kind 'that you could cut with a knife'. He tween-larded ((interlarded)) his speech with lots of meaningless tags of speech, such as 'D'ye see, d'ye see?', that arose out of the heat of his urgefullness. He had studied leech-craft ((medicine)) & cut-cure-craft ((surgery)) at Dublin All-School ((University)), I think, & at the time of my birth & afterwards was rated to be the most bright-shining ((brilliant)) cut-leech in Melbourne, or wellnigh so. When I was a little boy he was hurry-called out of Melbourne by a rich farmer or squatter to cut-leech ((operate)) [on] his wife, & after doing his jobs fightwinsomely ((successfully)) O'Hara put his fee at £1,000 (or was it £5,000?), which seemed a stiff price in those days. The squatter said, 'That seems a bit stiff, doesn't it?' But O'Hara stuck to his fee, telling the squatter, 'I've saved yr wife's life, haven't I? We doctors have to earn from the rich in order to give to the poor.' Mother said that O'Hara treated lots of poor folk for nothing, was wondrously thotfull & tender towards them & was greatly beloved by such. Many years later (when we were in Germany, 1894–1900?[1]) O'Hara was drawn into some wed-endment ((divorce)) case as a witness, being knight-likely keen to help the woman who was sueing for wed-endment, she being a friend of his, but no sweetheart—at least that was his story. Gavan Duffy[2] (another Irishman & a hard-living man) was the barrister [on] behalf of the sued-man ((defendant)) & at a moment when O'Hara was out of the court, he turned some

---

1. Correctly, 1895–1901.
2. A well-known Irish legal–political family in Melbourne. Grainger perhaps refers to John Gavan Duffy (1844–1917), son of an early premier of Victoria.

guilty-casting words upon O'Hara's rushing-to-the-aid of his woman friend, hinting that there was more than friendship in it & going so far as to say that O'Hara's plan was not in the witness box but in the act-part ((role)) of the sued-man ((defendant)). O'Hara knew nothing of all this until a friend told him of it. O'Hara went out to buy a newspaper, redd ((read)) the scaithfull [scathing] word-chain ((sentence)) in it & as he stood there in the street, he suddenly raised his eye to see Duffy a few paces off. He rushed up to him, shouting: 'Put up your hands, you dirty dog!', or suchlike words. Duffy was a fun-job ((amateur)) boxing olive-winner [champion] (or *had* been, shortly before) tho a smaller man than O'Hara. The two set to & the outcome might have been worse if Duffy had not slipped on a piece of banana peel early in the brawl. I forget whether Duffy took any law-some ((legal)) steps. At any rate O'Hara was the hero of the hour & I forget now how many hundreds or thousands of wire-sendments ((telegrams)) he got from old cure-finders.

Mother said the thing that befunnied ((amused)) her about the Gavan Duffy–O'Hara fight was that O'Hara had always called himself a coward & said he would run away from almost any man rather than fight him. Some time after his first wife's death[3] O'Hara had got deep into money troubles, having lots of debts—likely caused by race-course losses. So he made no bones of the fact that he was looking around for a wife with money. He told of calling on [ ],[4] a rich man, & asking for the daughter's hand. The father seemed to well-deem O'Hara's suit until O'Hara named his debts & asked how much money would go with the girl (which would not seem a shamefull askment to his straightforward Irish mind). The father flew into a rage, calling O'Hara a scoundrel, & telling him to get out before he kicked him down the stairs. 'What did you do?' the listeners asked O'Hara. 'I made off as quick as my legs would carry me', O'Hara answered. Mother thot this story, this owning up of O'Hara to his worldly & cowardly streaks—very type-true of O'Hara, & very Irish in its straightforwardness & not-goody-goodyness. (Nov. 7)[5]

. . . One day, shortly before we left for Germany (I was 11 or 12) Mother & I had been guesting him in Collins Street, Melbourne, & I had greatly joy-felt ((enjoyed)) boxing with Clive (his son) & had worked myself up into a great state of up-het-ment ((excitement)), so that when mother forth-told our leaving in the evening I would not, could not, heed, but kept dashing about madly in the hall, while mother & Dr O'Hara waited in vain for me at the

---

3. See 'Mother's Wilfulness' in essay 20.
4. Left blank by Grainger.
5. Grainger added this paragraph on 7 November 1933.

front door. In the midst of all my dashing his words to mother fell chillingly on my ears: 'That boy's love of pleasure will be his undoing'—words that my life have proved true enough.

L'Avenir, Atlantic, Oct. 8, 1933

Source: Untitled section, in 'The Aldridge-Grainger-Ström Saga', W37-39 to 37-41 (with additional paragraph of 7 November 1933, W37-40; Grainger Museum, Melbourne).

22   Dr Hamilton Russell Called Me 'A Tiger for Work' (1953)

After my trip to Australia in 1924, to see my mother's kin (no concerts), Dr Russell & I were on the S.S. 'Niagara' together, from Sydney to San Francisco (he was so impressed with the young women's string-&-piano group at the Clinton Cafeteria,[6] San Francisco). He was part of a medical congress, all travelling on the 'Niagara', bound for the Mayo Clinic,[7] among other places. Dr Russell had found out a new, simpler, way of treating hernia, & was to lecture about it. Sir Elliot Smith, the Australian (author of 'The Diffusion of Culture'[8]) was part of the delegation, or travelling with them, & I relished talking with him no end. I asked him what was the racial make-up of the modern European Jew, & he said, 'The Jew is no different to any other broadskull'. [In Danish] Dr Russell and I shared a cabin on the 'Niagara'. One day, I did something to myself, on the upper berth, early in the morning. My old friend did not see what I did but he had an inkling. Later on, he asked me if I had done something, and I admitted it. [In English] 'That gave me great pleasure' [in Danish] he said.[9] Before that, when I lived with him at Cliveden Mansions,[10] I had wanted to show him how my self-lashing led to the climax. I kept lashing myself, but without any result. He left the room for a moment, and when he came back, I was still lying there lashing myself without success.

6. At the time, the world's largest cafeteria.
7. In Rochester, MN. During the 1950s, Grainger would undergo surgery there for cancer.
8. Sir Grafton Elliot Smith (1871–1937), anatomist, anthropologist, and Egyptologist. His *The Diffusion of Culture* was published in 1933.
9. Grainger described this event in similar terms but greater detail in 'The Aldridge-Grainger-Ström Saga', W37-207, dated 18 December 1933.
10. I.e., during Grainger's 1924 visit to Melbourne, although elsewhere, in 'The Aldridge-Grainger-Ström Saga', W37-207, he places this flagellantic episode during his 1926 visit to Melbourne. Cliveden Mansions, on the site of the current Hilton Hotel in Wellington Parade, East Melbourne, had been reconstructed by Grainger's father. See essay 5.

[In English] 'Are you having a bad time?', he asked. He had confided to me that he felt love for young men. I asked him whether he had ever done love acts on them. 'Of course not,' he said. 'But it has made my relations with my students (at the university?) so pleasant.' And he told me how much he liked many of the students & what fine young fellows they were. 'Of course, if they are going home to some English university I have to advise them to behave a little differently to what they do here.[11] For instance, they mustn't talk to a professor in England with their hands in their pockets.' I said, 'I think it a great shame that Australians should be induced to conform to stick-in-the-mud English standards of behaviour. The Australians should force their superior Australian standards of behaviour on the English.' 'You do talk idiotically at times.'

On the 'Niagara' I was very busy clean-writing the full score of 'The Warriors'[12]—getting it ready for publication (by B. Schott's Söhne, Mainz).[13] I suppose I began work before (or just after) breakfast & wrote all day till about 11.00 at night—as usual. And I think I took no midday meal—in order to have more time on the scorings. 'I must say: You are a tiger for work', said Dr Russell. Towards the end of his delegation-journeys in USA he landed in Detroit, just when I was to conduct 'Colonial Song'[14] & 'Shepherd's Hey'[15] there with Gabrielovitsch's[16] orchestra (or perhaps Dr Russell arranged to be in Detroit in order to hear my numbers).[17] He did not praise my pieces, but said only, 'the orchestra in Melbourne will never be able to do those things', with which I disagreed. Two years later, in Melbourne (1926), after I had presented 'The Warriors', 'Colonial Song', 'Shepherd's Hey', etc., there,[18] I reminded Dr Russell of our Detroit conversation & added, 'and the Melbourne orchestra has done those pieces'. 'Well, *did* they?', said Dr Russell, meaning: can such a bad performance be considered a performance at all? Do all friends talk like that to each other, or is it only to me such things are said?

Aug. 13, 1953

11. In Melbourne.
12. Grainger's 'music to an imaginary ballet', for large orchestra and pianos (1913–16).
13. The 'compressed full score' was published in 1926.
14. (1911), the first of Grainger's 'Sentimentals', published in at least seven different scorings.
15. (1908–13), one of Grainger's most famous settings of an English folk tune.
16. Ossip Gabrilovich.
17. On 28 November 1924, Grainger conducted these works with the Detroit Symphony Orchestra and also played the Grieg Piano Concerto, under Gabrilovich's direction.
18. 26 October 1926, in a concert of the University (of Melbourne) Symphony Orchestra, conducted by Bernard Heinze.

Source: 'Dr Hamilton Russell Called Me "A Tiger for Work". Comment on My Orchestral Pieces in Melbourne, 1926. Our Trip on S.S. "Niagara", 1924. Sir Elliot Smith', in 'Grainger's Anecdotes', 423-47 (Grainger Museum, Melbourne).

✈ 23   A Day of Motoring with Dr Russell (1953)

I think it was in 1926 that Dr Russell took me for a day's motoring. A German called Lindt (or some such name) had a house, or room, or crow's nest, built high up on a gum tree. He had lived in the South Seas & had lots of photos of natives, native houses & the like. Of course I was much interested in these, & Lindt wanted me to see them. But Dr Russell was keen to get on. I said how much I would like to go to the South Seas, hear the music, etc. 'But if you do, you mustn't be impatient like yr friend here. Or you won't get anything out of it.'

Late in the afternoon[19] Dr Russell stopped before a house, out in the country, & said, 'There lives a woman I have been in love with for 16 years. But I cannot make up my mind to ask her to marry me because I am not sure I could rise to the occasion on the bridal night.' I said something like, 'If she has waited for 16 years I don't suppose she would be fussy about waiting a little longer too.' I think Dr Russell always underrated his stamina. He came out to Australia (about 1888 or 1889)[20] because he was consumptive.[21] About 1909 he told me that he did not see how he could live more than another 4 or 5 years. But his consumptiveness did not kill him, but a motor accident around 1931–32,[22] when his leg stiffness, from arthritis, made him unable to prevent his car crashing into a telegraph pole, just near Cliveden Mansions. (The pleasant Australian smells the thoughts of such places as Cliveden Mansions, Dr O'Hara's home,[23] Richmond,[24] Claremont[25] & the Husbands' old house[26] conjure up!)

Århus Kommunehospital, Aug. 13, 1953

19. Grainger also tells this story in the 'The Aldridge-Grainger-Ström Saga', W37-207, dated 18 December 1933, but places the event during his 1908–9 Melbourne visit.
20. Correctly, 1890.
21. I.e., suffered from tuberculosis.
22. Correctly, 1933.
23. 'Lansdowne' in Brighton.
24. Probably Richmond Park in South Australia, where Grainger's Uncle Jim lived.
25. Home of Grainger's Aunt Clara, in Kensington, South Australia.
26. On Riversdale Road, Hawthorn, Victoria.

Source: 'A Day of Motoring with Dr Russell. Lindt's House up the Tree. Dr Russell & His Sweetheart', in 'Grainger's Anecdotes', 423-48 (Grainger Museum, Melbourne).

⋙ 24   Karl Klimsch's Purse of Money, for Mother to Get Well On (1945)

I have written above (see [ ])[27] that mother's hard bout of illness at Frau Orth's (1901–1902)[28] followed upon a fall on an ice-slippery street. But I think I was wrong there. I think the fall happened at Fraulein Schön's Pension,[29] & not long before our trip to Italy around year 1899.[30] For I seem to see clearly mother lying in bed at Pension Schön's, after the fall, & that old Klimsch, Dr Mischke & Sigurd Fornander all went to see her as she lay ill. If I mistake not, Mischke & Fornander called on the same day, & mother got a strong mind-dent [impression] of the otherhood [difference] between the 2 men: Mischke was all tenderness & lovingness while Fornander, mother said, was 'nice, but selfish'. Klimsch, of course, was sheer goodness, helpfulness, kindliness. He laid a purse of money on the bed saying: 'For Percy's sake alone, you must get well as quickly as you can. What you want is an utter change, away from the scene of your work, in a warm climate. Go to San Remo[31] & stay there until you feel well. Here is money to pay for the trip. But if you take it, it is with this understanding: that you never pay it back & never be-name the gift again.' But before he came to the gift part of his talk Klimsch was less tactful. He said, 'My dear Mrs Grainger, the weakness of age, the blows of ill-health, come to us all, sooner or later. When it comes, we just have to be bide-fain ((patient)).' Mother much took him aback by snapping out of her sick-mood & saying briskly, 'You don't think I'm going to remain a permanent invalid, do you? Percy can't have a cripple on his hands.' Dear old Klimsch, soft-hearted & with-feelingsome as he was, was always being aback-taken by somebody or something. In 1923 (at the tea-table, with his breed-group [family] around him) he told me that he wrote sundry writs to the Frankfurt papers—& they wishing he wouldn't gabble about the war to a foreigner[32]—during the war, saying that the things they were print-

27. Left blank by Grainger. He probably refers to the immediately preceding sections, 384-62, 63, 65.
28. Where the Graingers lodged, probably in 1900–1901.
29. Where the Graingers lodged in 1898–99.
30. Correctly, 1900.
31. In Italy, 30 kilometres east of Monaco. The Graingers did then visit San Remo.
32. Text of this later insertion partly illegible.

ing about England & the English were not true, that the English were a noble people, and so on. 'The most out-of-the-run ((extraordinary)) thing about it all was that they never printed one of my send-writs!' Of course, Mr Klimsch was getting a trifle old-feeble by that time (1923).[33] But he was always much the same: meaning wonderfully well, but not really understanding men & their heart-stirs—or maybe we should say, their nerve-stirs. Myself, I underwent a lot because of Klimsch's tactlessness, hot speech & his running off at an angle of his own thought-hatching, in my teens—of which more elsewhere. But mother didn't. She always knew what he had at heart, & that was always goodness & wellwishingness. Heart-stir was everything to mother, & she had the gift to guess what it was, from time-spot to time-spot, inside a man. So mother, as she lay there in bed, at Pension Schön, took his purse with a full heart & with a will to fulfill Kilmsch's wish, that she regain her health.

[on train] Buffalo to Meadville, & Meadville, Pa., Nov. 7, 1945

Source: 'Karl Klimsch's Purse of Money, for Mother to Get Well On', in 'Ere-I-Forget', 384-66 (Grainger Museum, Melbourne).

25   The English Are Fickle Friends, Tho Never Vicious in Their Fickleness (1954)

I find the English—tho so warm & enthusiastic at the beginning of a friendship—fickle as time goes on. They never become vicious to their old friends, but one can see that the old glamor has wholly vanished after many years. Ask Cyril about his old friends & he hardly knows whom you are talking about—the man in Manchester, for instance, who embezzled money. Or speak about Austin & you get from Cyril: 'He's so awfully pompous'. Balfour Gardiner was mad about Bax[34] at the time of the Balfour Gardiner Concerts[35]—resentful that Balfour's & my short pieces had more success than longer works by Bax & Holst. But towards the end of his life Balfour had nothing but bad to say about Bax: 'He's always talking about the royal children disporting themselves on the lawn'. Or, 'Bax is terribly ambitious'. Or, 'I can't bear Bax's

---

33. Grainger spent most of the first six months of 1923 in Frankfurt. By this time, Klimsch was in his early eighties.
34. Arnold Bax (1883–1953), composer, later Master of the King's Music.
35. Concerts of 1912–13, sponsored by Gardiner. See, further, essay 101.

music'. But around 1910 everything that Bax did was right. If I asked Balfour a question re (un-tuneful) percussion (such as 'what is the difference between a side-drum & a snare-drum?'), Balfour would say, 'We must ask Arnold. He is splendid about everything to do with percussion.' At the time of his concerts he was so wrapped up in Fred Austin's work—the Symphony for instance. Every time one met Balfour, then, he had something to say about how Fred was getting on with his Symphony—as if it were an event of national importance.[36] But around 1948 he spoke most coldly about Austin's really stunning 'The Sea-Venturers'[37]—'a noisy, bombastic piece'. And he was always talking of 'stupid old Fred'. But in his last years Balfour was mad about Denis Blood's[38] music, as he had been mad about Cyril's, Austin's, Bax's, my music in the old days. Around 1905 he proposed to himself [that he] copy out the full score of my 'The Wraith of Odin,'[39] so he could have a copy of it for himself (I don't remember whether he actually copied it out, or not). As for me, it was clear to me that I had shot my bolt with Balfour long ago. He did not break with me, he did not say he didn't want to see me. But he was most emphatic about not wanting to hear my music, or any music. Yet he was always talking about Denis Blood's music & saying things like: 'The young men compose with much greater ease than we did'. I don't think it was true that Balfour lost his interest in music. He only lost his interest in his *own* music & in the music of his friends. He saw nothing in music later than 1920–1925. And older music, such as Bach, I don't think he ever had liked. But Tchaikovsky I think he still liked & was very critical about the unfeeling ways the younger conductors played Tchaikovsky. I don't think Cyril really cares to hear my music any more & altho he still is loving & well-wishing as of yore yet he always seems relieved when he hears one is going to catch an early train. Fred Austin, however, always seemed glad to see one & when he heard me run thru my *Lincolnshire Posy* with the Royal Air Force band at Uxbridge he was most enthusiastic, amazed at its originality. He couldn't have been nicer, or 'younger', in spirit.

Source: 'The English Are Fickle Friends, Tho Never Vicious in Their Fickleness', in 'Grainger's Anecdotes', 423-102, dated 6 November 1954 (Grainger Museum, Melbourne).

36. Austin's Symphony in E major was given its first performance at the last of the Balfour Gardiner concerts, on 18 March 1913.
37. (1934), first performed in 1936.
38. (b. 1917), during the early to mid-1940s, Balfour Gardiner's musical colleague, living at Fontmell Magna in Dorset.
39. To words of Longfellow, for choruses and orchestra (1903).

➤ 26   My First Meeting with Cyril Scott (1944)

When mother & I at-came ((arrived)) in Frankfurt it was between Cyril Scott's first & twaid ((second)) bouts there. The Klimsch breed-group ((family)) raved about the sweet & gifted little boy he had been on his first stay. (They were less keen about the more swollen-headed, know-all-y teen-youth of the twaid stay.) So Butzie Klimsch[40] (the daughter, a year or so older than Cyril) was very keen to bring us together. This happened on the stairs of the Klimsch home. Cyril acted bored at meeting me, so Butzie, to boost me, or just to make talk, said, 'Percy has just written a Piano Concerto'. So Cyril tossed me this ask-ment ((question)), more or less over his shoulder: 'Do you know anything about musical form?' I said, 'No'. 'Then you can't call it a concerto.' So much for meeting number one! Cyril has since always talked of this early concerto[41] (there was only one movement, I think) as in Handelian style. But I think it is more Mozart-like, as well it might be, for I was working at Mozart concertos then. I guess it is this sort of straight talk of Cyril's that turns folk against him—charming & on-draw-some ((attractive)) as he is. I always felt his North-English truthfulness & rudeness a skill for getting under folk's skin—at bottom, a kind of lovingness. His whole art, his whole who-th ((personality)) is just lovingness.[42]

(Canton, Ohio, Oct. 24, 1944)

Source: 'My First Meeting with Cyril Scott ("Do You Know Anything about Sonata Form")', in 'Ere-I-Forget', 384-3 (Grainger Museum, Melbourne).

➤ 27   Walter Creighton & Cyril Scott (1944)

When Walter Creighton[43] boarded with mother & me at 31A King's Road (Chelsea, London) (around 1909–1911, maybe) he told me that he & Cyril were walking in the Promenade (old town walls, razed & turned into a pomp-walk) in Frankfurt am Main, sometime not far from 1900, & that he,

40. Pauline 'Butzie' Schumacher (ca. 1878–ca. 1970). See her recollection of Grainger's Frankfurt years in Gillies and Pear, *Portrait of Percy Grainger*, 27–28.
41. 'Klavier Concerto', composed March–April 1896, with dedication to his mother.
42. For Scott's early recollections of Grainger, see Gillies and Pear, *Portrait of Percy Grainger*, 23–27.
43. (1878–1958), English singer, actor, and events manager.

Creighton, was talking a lot & that Cyril didn't seem to be paying much heed to it. So he said to Cyril, 'Are you listening to what I'm saying?', to which Cyril answered, 'Go on with your childish prattle! Your babbling helps me to think'. This sounds as if flawlessly called-to-mind ((remembered)) & just what Cyril *would* have said at that time, when he was always very uppish & liked to be rude in a graceful way. (It is of-a-piece with what Cyril said to me at our first meeting. See 384-3.)[44] One can see them both: both somewhat foppish—Cyril with eye-striking Stefan George[45] high collar & big tie, throwing his body nervously from side to side (with faked calm) & flourishing a handsome stick; Creighton more groovishly a gentleman, not willing to step into the realm of the queer in order to be eye-striking, yet fain to strike the eye all the same (the less gifted man isn't willing to pay so high a price as the over-soul ((genius))).

Source: 'Walter Creighton & Cyril Scott ("Go On with Your Childish Prattle")', in 'Ere-I-Forget', 384-1, undated (probably 24 October 1944; Grainger Museum, Melbourne).

➤ 28   Walter Creighton on Roger Quilter's Hide-Fain-th ((Secretiveness)) (1944)

When Walter Creighton (the son of a Bishop of London[46]) boarded with mother & me he told mother how aback-taken ((surprised)) he was to find out that Roger was *such* a close friend of mother's & mine. He knew we were all friends, of course, but not that we were such *out-singled* ((special)) friends. He said that was Roger all over—to hide from one close friend his close friendship with another. When Creighton stayed with us he saw, of course, how Roger came & dined with mother, or mother & me (if I were home), once a week (Thursday, I think). And Creighton also learnt from the things mother & I said about Roger how well we knew him—that is to say, up to a point: Does anyone really know anything about Roger, beyond that he is an over-soul, that he is angel-likely kind, that he is shy & shrinking as well as warm & fury-feel-thy ((passionate))? Why is Roger so painfully hide-fain ((secretive))—he who likely has nothing to hide that hurts? Maybe he got early

44. 'My First Meeting with Cyril Scott', essay 26, preceding.
45. (1868–1933), German poet and friend of Scott.
46. Mandell Creighton (1843–1901), Bishop of London from 1897.

mind-dints ((impressions)) of women's love-begrudgingness, or of the love-begrudgingness of friends. (Does 384-4 have a bearing on this?)[47]

Source: 'Walter Creighton on Roger Quilter's Hide-Fain-th ((Secretiveness))', in 'Ere-I-Forget', 384-2, undated (probably 24 October 1944; Grainger Museum, Melbourne).

⤳ 29   Roger Quilter Failed Me at Harrogate (1944)

I think it was the summer of 1929 (when Ella & I honeyed-mooned in Europe for 6 or 9 months) I plotted and carried-out the Festival of British Music at Harrogate,[48] pledging Cameron[49] would get my tone-wright friends to come & time-beat [conduct] (or listen to) their tone-works, if Basil Cameron would furnish the rest. Balfour would not join in, of course, but Cyril, Roger, Bax, (Austin?) & others came. Cyril 'stole the show' (to have him do which was my main aim in plotting the whole business), playing his piano pieces (they asked him to play them again on the last day) as well as his Piano Concerto[50] & having his 'Rima'[51] (did he time-beat this?) sung. In the midst of this mildly pleasing togetherness of tone-wrights I suddenly got the be-shaming postcard, whither-written ((addressed)) to 'Herr P.G.', which called me a white-livered pro-German & bade me begone, back to USA, where I belonged[52] (this postcard is in the Grainger Museum). Of course I was frightened—frightened of being struck, or beshamed, during the next tone-show—so cast about for someone to beshield me. Roger seemed my best choice, because of his tallness, his handsomeness, his moneyedness & his well-seen-ness. So I said to Roger: 'I want to ask you to do me a great favor, tho I won't tell you why, as yet. I am afraid of somebody or something—I have had a defamatory anonymous postcard—& I want to ask you to protect me. Will you sit in our box with us tonight?' But Roger stammered something about having pledged to sit with friends, & wouldn't. Of course, nothing happened

47. 'Roger Quilter Failed Me at Harrogate', essay 29, immediately following.
48. 24–26 July 1929.
49. Basil Cameron (1884–1975), English conductor, to 1930 mainly in British provincial cities.
50. (1913–14), first performed in 1915.
51. 'Rima's Call to the Birds', for soprano and orchestra, eventually completed in 1933.
52. Because of his departure to the United States in 1914 and his vacillating commitment to the war effort until 1917.

to me (writers of un-signed postcards are not deed-doers, as a rule) at the tone-show, tho my guilt-awareness led me to deem a man who sat in the back of our box out-singledly dark-mooded & foe-ful-seeming. Sheer mind-mirage on my part, no doubt. It is just as well that one is able to brazen-things-out unholpen, however much of a coward one feels oneself to be, in such a pass. For one is unlikely to get be-shieldment even from one's dearest friends, when one thinks one needs it. Ella was there, & she says she is my 'henchman'. She sometimes says her hands itch to get onto some man who has riled her (hero-race women seem more apt to wont to get their hands onto men than onto women), & I dare say she wouldn't make a bad job of disheartening a man who onslaughted [*sic*] her man. Hurrah for brave women! Both the women I have lived my life with (mother, & Ella) have been brave, beshielding women. I feel brave (at least, more-rather-than-less so) in Ella's at-ness.

[on train] Nov. 6., 1944

Source: 'Roger Quilter Failed Me at Harrogate', in 'Ere-I-Forget', 384-4 (Grainger Museum, Melbourne).

➤ 30   Balfour Gardiner Disliked What He Considered Political Falsification in Busoni & Harold Bauer (1953)

Balfour Gardiner (that noble soul & *genuine patriot*) could not brook seeing artists curry favor by means of political falsification. He despised Busoni[53] (who everyone knew was strongly pro-German) for turning up in England after the 1st German war with 'Légion d'honneur' printed after his name on his visiting card. Balfour was also disgusted with Harold Bauer[54] for talking so very English ('We English' & that sort of thing) once when they met—when Bauer in reality was just one of those international musicians. Not that Balfour was in the least chauvinistically British or ever took majority-mood attitudes about wartime behavior. He once said that I should be knighted for what I had done for British music—playing it, conducting it, teaching it. When I explained that I (as an American citizen) would not be permitted to accept a British title, Balfour burst out with his usual disgusted shout: 'How dreadful!' Balfour was *the real thing always*. Official angles, arbitrary controls,

---

53. (1866–1924), Italian pianist and composer, resident in Berlin from 1894 to 1912. See essay 106.
54. (1873–1951), British-born American pianist.

meant nothing to him. As regards my nationality[55] & my wartime behaviour, Balfour thought of me as I felt in my heart.

Århus Kommunehospital, Aug. 12, 1953.

Source: 'Balfour Gardiner Disliked What He Considered Political Falsification in Busoni & Harold Bauer. A Title for P. G.', in 'Grainger's Anecdotes', 423-44 (Grainger Museum, Melbourne).

31   Balfour Gardiner with Me in Norway, 1922 (1953)

After mother's death (Ap. 30, 1922) Balfour arranged to come to Norway to do part of my Norwegian concert tour with me (Sept. 1922).[56] He was the only one of my friends who went anywhere to be with me, after mother's death. When I arrived in Kristiania[57] (after folksong collecting in Jutland with Evald Tang Kristensen,[58] Aug. 1922) I must have being staying at the Grand Hotel (why I don't know). There, one day, I ran into Balfour, who didn't know I was in Kristiania & who had just been staying some days with Fred & Jelka Delius at Lesja.[59] When he saw me (for the first time for 8 years) he threw up his arms in despairing surprise & said, 'How young'. I had promised to go to the American consul's house that evening. I induced Balfour to go, too, rather against his will. The consul's wife was a typical American, full of questions the answers to which meant nothing to her. Introduced [to] Balfour as a composer & she asked him, 'What style of music do you write, Mr Gardiner?' Balfour squirmed for a moment, & then answered: 'Oh, the style of 1902, I suppose'. The consul's wife knew about 'Country Gardens'[60] & asked me to play it, which I did. Balfour had not heard C.G. When I came to where the bass is fragmentary (because the left hand is looking after the tenor voice, too)[61] Balfour jumped up & said 'how awful', much to the embarrassment of the consul's wife, who had no conception, of course, of the outspokenness of

---

55. Grainger became a citizen of the United States in 1918.
56. Balfour Gardiner also accompanied Grainger on a walking tour in Norway in the summer of 1939. See essay 101.
57. Oslo.
58. (1843–1929), Danish ethnologist and teacher.
59. Lesjaskog, about 150 kilometres southwest of Trondheim, where the Deliuses owned a mountain chalet.
60. (1918–19), Grainger's most popular work, setting of an English Morris Dance tune.
61. Grainger somewhat inaccurately sketched the left hand of bar 39 of the piece.

composers to each other. Balfour explained that all such fragmentary, incomplete voices (the continuations of which are imagined but never heard) were the bane of piano music. Balfour had to go somewhere for a few days & then joined me on my tour, meeting me at Moss, or Fredrikshald,[62] or somewhere there. We were out walking in the country, near one of those towns, when we heard delicious sounds of modern music (seemingly being composed under our ears—phrases being repeated & repeated, as happens when composing) from a some-way-off house, with gardens or fields in between. I wonder who it was composing there. Balfour's non-adjustment to the hours of the hotels & of my concerts was epic. My concerts began at 8.00 & the hotel dinner was on about 6.30. But Balfour could not eat before 8.00, so in each hotel he had to make special arrangements for a girl to serve him dinner at 8.00. Therefore, also, he could not turn up at my concert until it was 3-quarters over. Every time he said, 'I am sorry I was late for yr concert, Percy'. He was scandalized when I told him that I tmpe tljf[63] on the platform, especially in loud passages. We were photographed together in one of the towns—an excellent photo of Balfour.

Balfour was very distressed to see the nice new houses wherever we went—with clever accommodation of roofs. He said, 'It is very depressing to come to Norway & to find that they are doing everything more cleverly than I am doing it [in] Fontmell'.[64] He also said, 'I pride myself on selecting nice tweeds for my clothes. But every dock laborer in Norway has just as good tweeds.' That is why English people feel happy in Spain & Italy—they feel superior there. On the other hand, they don't like it in Scandinavia, because there they are not able to feel superior. (In Frankfurt, 1899, Sandby used to say, 'What is all this [in Danish] superiority in the English—what the devil have they done that they should feel so superior, all the time?' [In English] When we got to the town before Arendal (going west)[65] I told Balfour I wanted to trot the distance. He took a carriage & I trotted alongside. I think it was in Arendal, the next day, that Balfour & I took a long walk, to [ ][66] Kirke & back. I suppose I had been chatting too much, all day. As we turned to go home I asked Balfour what he thought about 'the immortality of the soul', or 'life after death', or some such nonsense. He said, 'Not another word, Percy. Not another word until we get back to Arendal.' He was a sweet companion. I could have been happy spending part of each year with him, joining

62. Halden, 100 kilometres south of Oslo. Grainger performed in Moss on 11 September and in Fredrikshald (Halden) on 14 September.
63. Grainger code words, perhaps meaning 'break wind'. See the Introduction.
64. Fontmell Hill, Dorset, where Gardiner would design and build his own house in 1928.
65. Grainger performed in Tvedestrand on 20 September and in Arendal on 21 September.
66. Left blank by Grainger.

with him in concert-giving & other musical policies & hearing his detailed criticisms on my, & other, music.

He decided that he was going to leave my tour at about Flekkefjord[67]— taking the post boat all the way back to Kristiania, train from there to Hamburg & Calais, & the boat to Dover. I explained to him that if he stayed with me to Bergen (about 2 days more)[68] he would get a much better boat to Scotland & be home much quicker. But he was not to be moved from his resolve. As he stood on the boat at Flekkefjord (the post boat taking him to Kristiania) & I stood on the quay, the tears came to his eyes & he said, 'I am sorry to leave you Percy'. He had done well by me, as he did by so many people in his life of endless benevolence. At the time of this tour he was still interested in composing, playing his latest works & willing to take advice. I urged him to lengthen a middle section in his masterly 'Michaelchurch',[69] & he did so, & wrote me responsively about it. His muse had not left him, as he put it, later on: 'My muse left me at Ashampstead'.[70] Balfour was a strangely queer mixture of not-to-be-expected-together things: heroic deedfulness, male harshness, womanly feelingfulness, fickleness, selfishness, endless benevolence, distressing self-criticism, unique politeness, secretiveness, downrightness, compassion, surging enthusiasm (such as one hears in parts of 'News from Whydah').[71]

Århus, Aug 17, 1953

Source: 'Balfour Gardiner with Me in Norway, 1922', in 'Grainger's Anecdotes', 423-80 (Grainger Museum, Melbourne).

➤ 32   Mrs L[owrey] and My Early London Days (1945)

Mother & I first set eyes on London (& England) on 'Mafeking Night',[72] [17 May],[73] 1900. We then spent a few days in London & a few weeks in Glasgow. I did my 3 days' tramp in Argyleshire (Garelochhead, Loch Foyle, Inverchorachan, Dalmally, Ben Cruachan, Glen Ryan, Loch Nell, Kilmelford,

---

67. About 100 kilometres southeast of Stavanger.
68. Grainger performed in Bergen on 1 October.
69. (1920–23), for piano, and dedicated to Percy Grainger.
70. Berkshire village, where Gardiner spent much time between 1911 and the late 1920s.
71. (1911), ballad for chorus and orchestra, dedicated to Bax, premièred at the first Balfour Gardiner concert in London on 13 March 1912.
72. Final day of the seven-month siege in the Boer War.
73. Grainger left this date space blank.

Ardrisheag[74]), on which I mind-birthed the tune of 'Walking Tune'.[75] We went back to Frankfurt & I started *Hillsong I* (swayed by bagpipes heard in Scotland & Egyptian pipes heard at Paris World Fair, 1900[76]) & *English Dance*. The summer of 1902[77] we settled in London, lured there by (Australian) Miss Devlin (singer, daughter of my mother's old friend in Melbourne, Mrs Devlin) [who] job-hired me to play singles ((solos)) at her first London song-show ((recital)).[78] (What a pretty blooming, sweet-heart-typed Australian girl! But mind-twisted against man, I think, by her mother, who had picked up sex-pox from her husband.)[79] Meseems I met Mrs L[owrey][80] that same summer (unless it was 1901 we settled in London). At any rate, it was the summer of 1902 we spent at Waddesdon, Bucks, where I took mother [on] long rides in her bath chair (16 miles a day) & worked on *Hillsong I*; & by that time I'd met Mrs L. Mrs L. was between 38 & 48, I guess, tallish, half-Irish & half-Polish, I think she said, with somewhat gaunt, big-boned face, teeth showing, thinnish lips, greenish eyes, dark hair, a stunning body-shape with plenty of bosom. Paired with a keen love of music, & a nose for art all-round, was a lot of old-fangledness in her—a longing to run a tone-art 'salon', a yearning to shine in the pomp-world ((society)), a craze for titled or gifted one-bodies [individuals], a firm belief in sex-fiery-fain-th ((passion)). All this seemed so strange & old-fangled to me, side-matched with my mother's Plato-love for all things & her gain-unseeking worship of tone-art, book-art, & the like. But I will not say that Mrs L's thrill-seeking, high-colored views of sex-love, money, art & the pomp-world were not real-felt in her. But she seemed to me as most pomp-world-tainted English-women would seem to most 'pukka' Australians: a bit shallow & strangely full of make-believe. She put lots of thought into her clothes, into the house-gearing ((furnishing)) of Rossetti House, Cheyne Walk, Chelsea, which she re-dubbed 'Queen's House' (or was it t'other way round? It had belonged to Rossetti,[81] hadn't it? And some English queen was said to have had something to do with it). She was hell-bent to make her mark in the pomp-world & therefore got her grappling

---

74. Ardrishaig, near Lochgilphead.
75. Composed for wind quintet (1904), later arranged by Grainger for piano solo, piano duet, and symphonic wind band.
76. Grainger had visited this Exhibition shortly before coming to Britain. In an extended programme note on *Hillsong I* of September 1949, Grainger described these instruments as 'extremely nasal Egyptian double-reeds'.
77. Correctly, 1901.
78. On 11 June 1901 at St. James's Hall.
79. See essay 34, following.
80. Grainger certainly knew Lilith Lowrey by 14 February 1902, when he played at one of her 'At Homes' in Chelsea.
81. Dante Gabriel Rossetti (1828–82), Pre-Raphaelite artist.

hooks into me—for a gifted young art-man in tow is deemed a useful art-key to the pomp-world door. Of course, my only wish was to be left alone to my art-duties: to mind-birth tone-works to the glory of my birth-land & of my blue-eyed race. I hated playing the piano, had no wish to shine in any kind of worldly world, not even to earn money. At the same time, I was scared of not being able to earn, & I hated to be a bad son, unable to look after my beloved mother as I should. Mrs L. asked to hear my tone-works, & when I played her my 'fast Song of Solomon'[82] she fainted just at the end. I thought it a put-up job (a feint rather than a faint), done to flatter me—to make me think she felt my tone-powers were more than mankindy strength could bear. I felt so silly, trying to bring her out of her faint. Of course, I was a cold clam—for I had strong feelings about pureness (freshness, unfakedness, heart-kindledness) in sex & love, tho I had no ought-code ((morality)) to hold me back from unlaw-hallowed sex. So I guess Mrs L. grew hurry-itchy ((impatient)) about me. So one evening, driving home to Queen's House in a taxi from some party, she told me that if I didn't become her lover she would do nothing more for me. [In Danish] I had no such inclination; on the other hand, I had nothing against [playing] the role of a male whore. But I feared the riskiness of the matter and her husband's attitude to it. [In English] A scandal wouldn't help my job-life either! Mrs L. told me that her husband[83] took no stock in her sex-life; didn't care what she did. [In Danish] So I went to bed with her the same night (as her declaration of war [occurred] that I must be her lover [in English] or else). [In Danish] I had never before slept with a woman, nor had I ever reached a sexual climax while awake. I had often had 'wet dreams' but never reached this kind of gratification in a state of wakefulness. In Frankfurt, from the times at Grünburgweg[84] until our departure from Frankfurt in 1901 or 1902, I had pushed the toilet-brush handle up my arsehole, pressed my naked flesh against hot stove tiles, or similar [things], everything giving me a beneficial excitement, but without any sexual climax, no juice-spurting. Protracted rubbing of my cock (until it became half blue-coloured from swelling up), one night in Balfour Gardiner's house in Michael Deever (Hants?),[85] had no better effect. I considered myself to be sexually useless—but was not unhappy about it. My lustful sadistic dreams and my self-inflicted pains were good enough for me. Ejaculation and feelings of [sexual] satisfaction did not

---

82. Sketched in 1899–1900, involving early experimentation with irregular metres and rhythms.
83. Frank Lowrey, a businessman who had made (and then lost) his money through mining in South Africa. Grainger devoted a one-page entry to him, 'Mr L', in 'Ere-I-Forget', 384-23, dated 26 May 1945.
84. I.e., about 1896–97.
85. Perhaps 'Moody's Down', at Sutton Scotney in Hampshire, where Balfour Gardiner's father lived.

attract me strongly. Imagine my surprise when, as I fucked Mrs L., I sensed within me an overpowering landslide, which seemed to start in my toes and reached its completion in my head! I thought I was about to die. If I remember correctly, I only experienced fear of death. I don't think that any joy entered into it. But the act of fucking had awakened my sex mechanism. And when I got home the same night, altogether dissatisfied with the sexual act, I rubbed my cock very hard and reached ejaculation soon in a mood of heavenly joy. [In English] I had just come across Bernarr MacFadden's Health magazine 'Physical Culture',[86] which's meat-loathing theme-writ stirred me greatly. [In Danish] I was even more taken with pictures of MacFadden's 3 or 4 young daughters in bathing costumes. Everything athletic, pure, youthful stimulated my sexual imagination, in the same way as everything that was sentimental, unclean, mature and worldly-wise had the opposite effect. I put up the swimsuit pictures in front of me and sacrificed (so to say) on their altar.

The fear of death experienced during my first fucking of Mrs L. disappeared, of course, when the sex act with her was repeated, and my duties as her male whore became lighter in that respect. But I did not find any proper joy in our common sexual activities. Very soon after the first time, she invited me to a weekend at The Compleat Angler Inn, Maidenhead, and another time to Burnham Beeches, on the River Thames. [In English] These outings I will treat of by themselves,[87] as I also will of a trip to Dieppe[88] (where I met Everard Feilding[89] & Jacques Blanche,[90] both for the first time) & of the tone-forth-playments at her house in London. But of the Dieppe trip I must say this here: [in Danish] after the first fuck with her (or one of the first fucks)—or, perhaps as a consequence of the manual rubbing of my cock, which I did around this same time—a liquid started seeping from my penis. I did not know what it meant: was it only an inflammation after an unusual activity, or was it dripping sickness [gonorrhoea] or syphilis—which she had told me her husband was suffering from? [In English] It was at Waddesdon that I noted the ailment [in Danish] (we must already have been at Waddesdon when our first fucking occurred) [in English] & I went in to our London leech-friend Dr Fenner (Dr Russell's sister's husband) as soon as I could. [In Danish] But he could not tell whether the seeping was simply a result of overexertion, or whether it was dripping sickness. In any case, he said, my penis needed a complete rest. [In English] But I was booked to go with Mrs L. to Dieppe that

86. Started in 1898 by the American physical culturist Bernarr MacFadden (1868–1955).
87. 'Ere-I-Forget', 384-21 and 384-22[a].
88. 'Ere-I-Forget', 384-20.
89. (1867–1936), British lawyer and founder, with Lilith Lowrey, of the Queen's House Manuscript Music Society, which gave early performances of some of Grainger's compositions.
90. Jacques-Émile Blanche (1861–1942), French painter; in 1906, he painted a portrait of Grainger.

same evening—had, in fact, seen Dr Fenner in London on my way from Waddesdon to the New Haven (New Haven—Dieppe boat) train, at the gates for which I met Mrs L. I tried to tell her that the trip would be no use, [in Danish] that I had a sexual disease. [In English] But she swept all that aside & we betrod the train (from London to New Haven) together. In the train I told her of my ailment, [in Danish] whereupon she accused me of having slept with a whore after our last being together. 'But I have never in my life been with a whore, and I have never in my life had sexual intercourse with anybody but you!' [In English] That made her wild-angry, for she thought I was lying. 'If you have had [in Danish] no sexual experience, [in English] how is it that you can talk so easily about [in Danish] sexual matters?', [in English] she asked. 'You don't talk like an inexperienced boy.' I answered that I had always read a lot, & talked a lot, about everything, but I still don't think she believed me, just as she didn't when I got back from Australia, New Zealand & S. Africa in 1904.[91]

When we got to Dieppe [in 1902] she wouldn't take no; [in Danish] I had to fuck her right away. And I did, that night and throughout the week, although my penis was quite sore. If it was true what I said (she remarked) that I had not been with a whore, and if the seeping from the penis only came from overexertion, fucking could not cause the penis all that much harm. Dr Fenner had given me Condy's Fluid[92] to inject, mixed with water, into my penis. Once I forgot the water, and the unmixed C's F. was quite burning. The seeping from the penis continued for some years (through my whole first Australian tour) and stopped only when I fell in love with Karen, about April, 1906. [In English] It didn't stop before, I guess, because my everlasting [in Danish] sexual self-help (about every other day, after the fucking with Mrs L. [started]) [in English] didn't give it a chance to get well-rested up. [In Danish] All the same, what bliss self-help is, for man or woman! What unique ecstasies! What liberation! What protection from dangerous and exasperating diseases! What independence from women and marriage!

One evening, at Mrs L.'s in Chelsea, her husband came home after I had fucked her. [In English] What a grand, loveable man! How handsome! How kindly & how art-loving! He looked at me with mild eyes. Maybe he was thankful I had taken over Mrs L. Or maybe he was glad to see some man *get* something out of her, instead of always *giving* her. I will write of him (& his gift to me of Walter Scott's 'Minstrelsy of the Scottish Border'[93]—a life-long life-brightener) by itselfedly. Here I will merely say what a lot I owe in art-joys

91. 'Ere-I-Forget', 384-22[b].

92. A disinfectant.

93. Grainger's library contained 1839 and 1887 editions of this work by Scott (1771–1832).

to Mrs L. & her art-loving friends: Border Ballads from her husband; at Dieppe, Everard Feilding (& thru him the English Competition Festivals at Brigg & Frome,[94] my first hearing of a sax-reed, my friendship with the Elweses,[95] my gathering of English Folksongs at Brigg, the 1st-forth-printing of my sing-host [choral] pieces[96]) & Jacques Blanche (a joy-giving art-friend, thru whom I got to first know Debussy's tonery ((music)) & whose theme-writ ((article)) on me & my tonery is likely still the best,[97] & whose paintings of George Moore[98] & me hang in my past-palace ((museum)), and, in a more round-about way, my meeting with Busoni at Mrs Matesdorf's (a friend of Mrs L.'s) in the spring of ?1903.

Mrs L. talked a lot of her last lover, a Polish piano-player whose name I cannot now recall. She doted on his playing as she (rightly) didn't on mine. She dwelt on his playing of Chopin's Barcarolle[99] & she reded [advised] me to learn it, as a piece that might suit me. And she was right; it did. Mrs L. often showed real taste, real insight. But what she liked to tell of her Polish lover was his fiery-moodedness ((passionateness)) [in Danish] and his lustfulness. He kissed her all over her body, she told me. [In English] (I stored that up in my mind as a good line to take.) [In Danish] About me she could have said that I licked her pussy [in English] (another good line to take into one's stock-in-trade, I thot), [in Danish] but I did that only upon her urgent request. She absolutely would not go without that, and why should she? [In English] In love, ways & means get further than moods & feelings; or should, in my deemth [opinion]. [In Danish] She certainly licked me too (the cock), I think; but without result. I have never in my life ejaculated while being licked—although I could well do it [in English] if more workers were put on to the job; [in Danish] if 2 bit my nipples and one lashed me on the bum (while the first sucked).

[In English] Mother was not against my love-serve-job with Mrs L., for mother was wholly open-minded about both love & business. But she herself didn't want to see too much of Mrs L.—she was afraid she might not get on

---

94. In Lincolnshire and Somerset, respectively. Grainger first attended these musical competitions in 1905.
95. Gervase Elwes (1866–1921), singer, and Winefride Elwes (1868–1959), an organizer of the North Lincolnshire Musical Competitions and sister of Everard Feilding.
96. Grainger probably refers to *The Hunter in his Career* and *Two Welsh Fighting Songs*, both published in choral arrangements (and variously including instruments) in 1904, preceding the regular publication of his works by seven years.
97. This article has not been identified. Blanche, however, wrote about Grainger on several occasions in his *Portraits of a Lifetime*, trans. and ed. Walter Clement (London: J. M. Dent, 1937).
98. (1852–1933), Irish writer, whom Grainger came to know personally in about 1911.
99. In F sharp (1845–46).

with her. Mrs L. was not cosy to get along with. She was what might be called tense. It seemed to me that she took needlessly hard & trying views of things (hard & trying to herself) because she clung to old-fangled & worn-out deemths & ought-slants [principles]. Sandby[100] could not abide her & she grumbled greatly at his 'boorishness'. Cyril & Roger (like the mild Englishmen they were) seemed to get on smoothly with her. Of Mrs L.'s high-jinks with me in Berlin (about July 1903 or 1904) I will tell by-itself-ly.[101] Right after that came my 1st tour in Australia, a.s.o. [etc.], with Ada Crossley (about 300 tone-shows) which ended up in South Africa. Mother (who, to save money, went straight on from Cape Town to England, while we toured S. Africa), Roger & Mrs L. met me at Plymouth or Southampton; of which meeting I write by-itself-ly.[102] I was 'true' to Mrs L. on the whole tour, not because I was in love with her, but because I was afraid to have love-bouts. All the same, I crept riskily near the border of love-bouts a few times on that tour. Still, I never crossed the border. When I got back & Mrs L. asked me what love-bouts I had had, & I said, 'none', she was wild-angry again, for she thot I was lying. I guess that she had never known a young man so life-afraid and so bide-willing ((patient)) as I. Mother's & father's sex-pox & my fear of scandal ruining my power to earn both kept me steadily scared. I guess it was my mother's plan to let me stay scared until I was money-fit to take up love.

Mother was not against my love-serve-job with Mrs L., but after a time (say on our back-coming to England, 1904 or 1905) she began to feel I was wasting too much time on it. Or maybe she thot I was not getting any real happiness (which I wasn't, not any), nor much business out of it. So mother wrote me, 'perhaps this *very great* friendship with Mrs L. should gradually come to an end' (mother always worded things very mildly). It did, but not thru any mind-made-upness, or show-downs on my part. Mrs L. (who never had really trusted me or believed what I told her) seemed to trust me less & less, & to veer away from me. Her husband was losing (or had lost) his money, & at last he killed himself. I think Mrs L. (who had suckled big dreams for herself) just settled back into wretchedness & down-heartedness. And in that mood she felt no urge to seek me. I had been part of her high-priced life, part of her wickedness & high hopes. Maybe she felt she had done with all that; that it was no use beating a dead horse. If so, she never understood my heartstirs. I, who had no wish to be her lover, would have been glad to be her friend. I, who hated & loathed the pomp-world in which she had

100. Herman Sandby. He visited London frequently during the Graingers' earlier years there.
101. During July 1903. See essay 33.
102. 'Ere-I-Forget', 384-22[b].

been so eager to shine, would have felt quite cosy & at home in any drab world of fight-loss into which she had sunk. But she dropped me & I was too busy, too harassed with lesson-giving and tone-shows (or else too dream-filled with tone-birthing thots) to take heed of it—in other words, I was too don't-care-ish, as always. Since I don't care much for my own 'life', it is hard for me to cough up much keenness about anyone's 'life'. Yet I would have truly liked to share art-haps with Mrs L. & it would have made me deeply happy if she (who had sensed some sort of light in me) could have lived to hear my tone-works forth-sounded. But no. Her health slumped. One day she came to see me (or mother went to see her) & Mrs L. was taken sick, and puked. Mother said what came up was like little berries, dry & round & small. Mother told me that she thot Mrs L. must be gravely ill. Soon after, she died of cancer. It seems to me she didn't want to be seen by me, toward the end. She had sent me a colored photo of herself, & a watercolor painting of Queen's House (or Rossetti House), where the first forth-soundments of my tone-works (& some of Cyril's & Roger's) had taken place. No doubt she wished to live on bright & wish-worthy ((desirable)) in my call-to-mindments [reminiscences]! It is deeply touching how women wish to add to the happiness & brightness & be-drunkenness of life; not seeming to sense that the sadness & heartbreaking doom-play of life is closer & dearer to men's hearts—at least to the hearts of high-born men. Tho I am cut out to be a greedily-loving husband, I was not cut out to be a pomp-life woman's lover. I was not gifted to serve. Yet I would have been happy to be a friend. And had Mrs L. been able to live long enough, I would have joy-quaffed more to up-bear her with money than, as a young man, I had joy-quaffed seeking gains at her hands, or business thru her plans. Mrs L. played up her Irish side a lot—her Irish blood, her green eyes. Just about when I met her first I was setting the Irish Tune from Co. Derry for mixed sing-host [chorus]. I asked her if she thought my setting Irish in mood—which I deemed it to be; I being so Irish-fain, so mindswayed by my Irish-Australian friends. I was aback-taken when she answered, 'Not at all; it seems to me thoroly English'. There is not much get-together between the pomp-world (or would-be pomp-world) & the yeoman.

Train, Maine, May 24,'45

Source: 'Mrs L[owrey] and My Early London Days', in 'Ere-I-Forget', 384-19 (Grainger Museum, Melbourne).

➤ 33   Frau Kwast-Hiller, Evchen, Mrs Lowrey in Berlin (1953)

I had always been fond of Frau Kwast-Hiller—the daughter of Ferdinand Hiller,[103] the wife of my piano teacher in Frankfurt James Kwast, the mother of Mimi, my first sweetheart. Even when I was in love with Mimi I was apt to take the mother's side, when they disagreed. At the time that I spent about 2 weeks in Berlin, studying with Busoni (see 423–42[104]) around 1904,[105] Frau Kwast-Hiller had a boarding house at [Leitzen Burgerstrasse].[106] So I boarded there, Mimi (married to Hans Pfitzner since about 1898) being out of the way, Frau K-H would have liked to see me fall in love with her blond, heroic, younger daughter Evchen (just as, about 20 years later, when she was living in Stuttgart, she tried to interest me in Mimi's daughter, Agi).

But Mrs Lowrey (having, I suppose, cooked up the whole Busoni business with Mrs Matesdorf (see 423–42)) turned up in Berlin. I was spending an evening with Mrs Lowrey at her hotel when someone of the hotel knocked at her door, saying that she could not have a male guest after 11 at night. Mrs L. said that I was her nephew, but that didn't help of course. The hotel man explained that they had to be very strict in this matter, [in Danish] because of the police. [In English] So I asked Mrs K-H. if Mrs L. could have a room in Mrs K-H's boarding house. Mrs K-H was torn between 2 urges—to earn a little money having Mrs L. in her boarding house, & her plans for Evchen. She decided in favor of Mrs L. But she was half angry with me, all the same; also half appreciative of a ruthless streak in me. That is why she wrote on the book of Goethe she gave me at the time: [in German] 'You naughty boy, I would not have thought you up to that'. [In Danish] As to Mrs. L., she was no temptation for me. I felt it an unpleasant duty to have to submit to Mrs. L.'s will. I was just unhappy that she turned up in Berlin. [In English] Somehow she got in touch with the Busonis & went there to tea, & Busoni was nice to her & spoke affectionately of me & hopefully of my career—so Mrs L. told me. None of those things (society ladies, famous virtuosos, seamy relationships) pleased me in the least. What I wanted was only to work hard & write great music for the honor of Australia.

Århus, Aug. 12,'53

---

103. (1811–1885), German conductor, teacher, and composer.
104. 'Busoni and P. G.', essay 106.
105. In July 1903.
106. Left blank by Grainger.

Source: 'Frau Kwast-Hiller, Evchen, Mrs Lowrey in Berlin', in 'Grainger's Anecdotes', 423-43 (Grainger Museum, Melbourne).

➤ 34   Miss Devlin's Sweet Australian Ways (1953)

What brought mother & me to London in 1902[107] was an engagement from Miss Devlin, who had been studying singing, for me to play some numbers at Miss Devlin's concert in London that summer.[108] Her mother had caught syphilis from the mother's husband. (Once, when my mother asked Mrs D what her husband had done for her—meaning what had he done financially, or in some other practical, helpful way—Mrs D pulled up her skirts, showing syphilitic sores on her legs & said, 'This is what he did for me'.) Miss Devlin was as lovely as an angel from heaven—tall, fleshy, blond & with the loveliest loving look in her face & the sweetest soft-hearted Australian ways. Once she talked so romantically about a table that figured in some French or Italian opera. The lovers had eaten off the table, made love on it, etc., & now it was to be thrown on the rubbish heap. I have seldom heard a young woman talk so devotedly about love. But I suppose her mother's experience with her mother's husband, & the way the mother talked of the curse a bad man can be to a woman, steered Miss Devlin into being a breathtaking old maid. I cannot remember how Miss Devlin sang, but I seem to remember hollow, flue-like sounds. What matter? It ought to be easy to sit & watch an angel from heaven utter flue-like sounds. What low-born swine people must be to applaud smart-alecky ugly-looking musicians of the lower races & at the same time cold-shoulder a vision of Australian beauty like Miss Devlin. (What part did the Irish father play in this Australian beauty? Perhaps he deserves as much praise as the mother, after all. For Miss Devlin's beauty was not unlike the ½-Irish beauty of Uncle Charlie's Elsie.)[109] At any rate I am thankful that my career in London was started, not by some professional crank-turning, but by an Australian, & by one of the loveliest visions of womanhood I ever clapped my eyes on.[110]

Århus, Aug. 10, 1953

Source: 'Miss Devlin's Sweet Australian Ways', in 'Grainger's Anecdotes', 423–34 (Grainger Museum, Melbourne).

107. Correctly, 1901. See also essay 79.
108. Devlin's 11 June concert at St. James's Hall involved five artists, including Grainger and Ada Crossley. He played solo works by Bach-Liszt, Chopin, and Liszt.
109. Elsie von der Dippe (later Dieppe; 1883–1935), by Charles Aldridge's Irish first wife, Annie Cairns (ca. 1860–1938).
110. Grainger also played as an associate artist in Lilian Devlin's Bechstein Hall (now Wigmore Hall) concert of 3 June 1902.

35   Jacques Jacobs on First Ada Crossley Tour (1953)

J. J., like most Dutch musicians, was an excellent musician. On our about 300 concerts of the 1st Ada Crossley tour (Australia, New Zealand, South Africa)[111] I never heard him have a slip of memory—perhaps I never heard him make a slip of any kind. He was the leader (conductor-violinist) of the Trocadero band (restaurant) in London.[112] I suppose he had stood there, in front of a non-critical, non-frightening audience, doing all his pieces a 100 times. Very good for the nerves. But he also played long pieces (such as that long violin piece of Saint-Saëns [ ][113]) equally well. There was no getting ahead of him, or getting up to him, for me. He was the darling of the audiences. He used to show us how to be sure of getting an encore: to let the bow stick out (in the sight of the audience) from the door when he went off the stage after playing. If the bow was not seen the applause was apt to stop. As long as the bow was seen the applause was apt to keep on. Jacques Jacobs & I opened the program with a movement of a sonata—usually Grieg's C minor, last movement.[114] We would play billiards together in the hotel till 7.55, then dash into evening clothes & be at the hall ready to open the program at 8.00. He was immensely strong—the story was that Sandau[115] had wanted to train him up to be a strong man star. He always had to be showing his muscles. In the early days of the tour I was always struggling [wrestling] with him, which he evidently didn't like, for he would turn cruel to me. So I gave up that line.

At that time I was keen to learn something about wind instruments, having recently finished *Hillsong I*, for piccolo, 6 oboes, 6 English horns, 6 bassoons, double bassoon. (Strings I have learned something about already, thru my association with Sandby, & thru scraping round myself on Sandby's cello.) I think I must have had my old pre-Boehm-system clarinet with me on that Ada Crossley tour. Sure it is that I brought a penny whistle & annoyed everybody by trying to play it. I never had a grain of talent for playing any instrument. J.J. could not see me struggling with the penny whistle without want-

---

111. Between 24 September 1903 and 26 March 1904.
112. Evidence of Jacobs' performing talents can be heard in a two-minute extract from the third movement of Mendelssohn's Violin Concerto, recorded on 5 April 1899 at the new Maiden Lane studios of the English Gramophone Company (Berliner 7917 (1850)), reissued in 1997 in the first volume of EMI's *Centenary Edition: 100 Years of Great Music* (7243 5 66183 2 9). The Trocadero Orchestra also featured in the earliest turn-of-the-century recordings of the company.
113. Grainger left a space here, intending to add in the work's name.
114. No. 3 (1886–87).
115. Eugen Sandow (1867–1925), an early exponent of bodybuilding.

ing to show me how much better he could do it, & I could not watch him play it without wanting to snatch it away from him. So it became a game of snatch, & once the penny whistle broke while we both had hold of it & my hand was cut, perhaps his too. Tho we started out quite friendlily [*sic*] we had gradually become somewhat hostile as the tour progressed (at least, I disliked him). One day, playing shuffle board, with J.J. & me as opponents in a 4-man game, one of us was holding his mallet on the deck to show his partner what to aim at. One of us (J.J. or I, I cannot remember which) protested that this was unfair, & tried to push the other one away. Somehow we found ourselves in a wrestling embrace (J.J. thought I began, I thought he did) & the struggle began. I saw that I must do something quickly. J.J. was vastly stronger than me up above, but perhaps no stronger than I in the legs & certainly less quick. With a violent effort I legged him off-balance & we both thudded to the ground, he on his back, I on top of him. By this time I was scared stiff & had no wish to fight on. Neither had he, and he merely said (still on his back), 'You must be out of your mind', & we both got up, helped by would-be separaters. In our struggle one of us had stepped on the mallet & it had flown up & cut the captain's eye-brow, which had to be sewn up by the ship's doctor. The funny thing was that Captain Pidgeon was overjoyed at the whole incident (in spite of having his eye-brow cut) as he loathed J.J.

About 4 years ago (thus about 1949) I was in a train in USA, going to New York from somewhere. There were 2 men in the day coach with me, one of them grumbling on-keepingly about something in the entertainment life or show business. He suddenly recognised me, & this was J.J. We were to meet in New York sometime, but his wife was ill & it was put off. At the time of our tour together (with Ada Crossley) J.J. was a horrible womanizer. Several times a day, with different women. When his room was next to mine, in a hotel, sounds of hard breathing would often be heard thru the connecting door ([in Danish] I suppose that he put the women up against the door). [In English] He seemed to hit the Australian women in the right place. When (later) I told Everard Feilding what a fine time J.J. had had in Australia Everard said, 'But I should object very much to leading the life of a stallion'.

Århus Kommunehospital, Aug. 17, 1953

Source: 'Jacques Jacobs on First Ada Crossley Tour', in 'Grainger's Anecdotes', 423-74 (Grainger Museum, Melbourne).

⤳ 36   Eliza Wedgewood, Out to Buy Old Furniture
from Folksingers (1953)

The name 'Eliza Wedgewood'[116] was always on the von Glehns' lips. She lived just near the Elchos',[117] in Gloucestershire. She wanted to collect folksongs with me, so she rounded up a lot of folksongsinging old men & women, & wrote down the texts of their songs.[118] I was to come along & phonograph their singing, & did so. When I arrived I was not put up at Miss Wedgewood's (where the folksingers sang to me) as I had expected to be, but was [in Danish] 'whisked away' [in English] to the Elchos' grand house, & thus could be relied upon to entertain H. G. Wells,[119] Arthur Balfour, etc., in the evenings. Arthur Balfour[120] (always very sweet to me) liked to hear the folksingers sing to me, & spent quite a time listening, & got into real talkative relations with the singers. An old man was singing about birds (was it 'And the blackbird & the thrush sat on every green bush, & the milkmaid sat milking her cow'?) & he asked A. Balfour if he ever got up at 4 or 5 in the morning to hear some particular bird singing, & A. B. admitted he hadn't. Miss Wedgewood wanted to combine old-furniture-collecting with folksong-gathering. 'And now Mrs [ ],[121] if you ever want to sell that chest-of-drawers over there, you just think of me.' 'O no, ma'am, I never don't want to part with that. It was my mother's, it was, & I hope to keep it as long as I live.' I believe this was the same old woman[122] who said of her 'Polly Oliver' song: 'A nice, proper song, & a happier world it would be if more people did like Polly Oliver' (that is: shoot their lover, if false to them). Why fussy & rather go-getting women like Eliza Wedgewood (who use their fairly-well-born-ness to further quite greedy & businesslike aims) are so featured, admired & talked about I will never understand.

Århus Kommunehospital, Aug. 13, 1953

Source: 'Eliza Wedgewood, Out to Buy Old Furniture from Folksingers', in 'Grainger's Anecdotes', 423-52 (Grainger Museum, Melbourne).

116. (1859–1947), of the porcelain manufacturing family, was, at this time, secretary to the Elchos; see following. She was close to John Singer Sargent and his Chelsea set in the pre-War years and was painted on several occasions by Sargent.
117. Lady Mary Elcho (1861–1937) and her husband, Viscount Elcho, Hugo Richard.
118. Between 1907 and 1909, Wedgewood collected over sixty songs with Grainger in Gloucestershire.
119. (1866–1946), English novelist. On 4 April 1908, he joined Grainger on one of his 'folk-song hunts' in Gloucestershire.
120. See 'Mother's Matchless Devotion to the Arts', in essay 20.
121. Left blank by Grainger.
122. Mrs. Packer of Winchcombe Workhouse.

➤ 37   Sargent's and His Set's Set-of-Mind toward My Betrothal to Margot (1944)

Rathbone's[123] mood on hearing of my betrothal to Margot,[124] was that of being frankly disheartened. And that is not so aback-taking. He loved me very much indeed, & he doted on his daughter,[125] & she sure-enough was aflame for my art if not more than that. He may have set his heart on our (his daughter & me) being spliced. At any rate, he was no outsingled friend of the Harrisons. So there was nothing strange about his stand. But Peter Harrison (Margot's father)[126] was one of Sargent's best friends, & what could be sweeter than the coming together of Harrison's lovely daughter with me—Sargent's outsingled boon-taker ((protégé))? Sargent was quoted as saying something about Margot not being a very suitable match for me. On the top-layer ((surface)) it seemed queer. But maybe Sargent saw deeper, maybe he sensed the unsunderable life-line that tied mother & me together. Or maybe Sargent didn't like wedlock for art-men; not having wed himself, & having spoken to me rather dolefully about Wilfred von Glehn's coming wedlock. Or maybe he had seen (or heard of) girlhood traits in Margot that did not, in his eyes, spell wed-worthiness—at least for one like myself. Be that as it may, the whole Sargent 'set' did not seem to thrill to the thought of this Harrison-Grainger wedlock. Maybe the whole thing, with them all, was just part of English-speaking nay-worship. Better no than yes. For a kindred showing cropped up when my toneworks (sing-band, string-&-wind-band) began to be forth-played (see 384-15[127]). As for Margot & me: it was lucky for us that both our being-types were tuned to love & didn't pick up any love-nay-sayment from the folks & deemths [opinions] around us. We lost each other it is true. But no unloving or quarrelling word passed between us. Our poor thwarted love-bout can stand as a sample of sweet English mildness & greedlessness.

(Nov. 19, 1944)

Source: 'Sargent's and His Set's Set-of-Mind toward My Betrothal to Margot', in 'Ere-I-Forget', 384-14 (Grainger Museum, Melbourne).

123. William Rathbone (1849–1919), English businessman and keen patron of Grainger in his earlier London years. See essay 72.
124. Margot Harrison. See essay 20.
125. Elena Rathbone. See essay 20.
126. (1866–1937), English painter.
127. 'Sargent, Rathbone, Other Friends Cool to Forth-Soundments of My Toneworks', in 'Ere-I-Forget', 384-15, dated 19 November 1944. That section ended: 'Are the English such snobs, such "holier-than-thous" that they cannot joy-quaff an artwork if the folkhost joy-quaffs it too? Or are they so helpfain & bestowsome that they join the fight only until the fight is won? They will not gloat with one, it seems. I give it up.'

5

WIFE

38   On Board the 'Aorangi' (1927)

Every weighty soul-hap is partly shaped & colored by the soul-mood or state-of-mind that went before it. When I got on board the lovely motor-ship 'Aorangi' at Sydney, Nov. 19, 1926, I was weary & down-hearted almost to the point of self-killing ((suicide)). Often, on the trip, I looked over the gunwale & wondered whether it were not best to leap & end my joy-less life—joy-less since my beloved mother's death, & weighed down with the knowledge of my dark soul-guilt. For over 4 years I had had no real opening of my heart, no real thought-unbosoming to anyone, had kissed no woman (but my near kin) nor sought woman in any way. My whole world-of-feeling had been shut down tight. It was right so, it was my duty. But an artist is not a hermit, & an artist living like a hermit is under a terrible strain. I was leaving Australia in great loneliness, out of touch with my fellows. I was understanding the unfulfilled-ness of my darling mother's early life in Australia, her delight at leaving for Europe in 1895. True, I had had wonderful days with my beloved Aunty Clara & Uncle Frank, with my fine Uncle Charlie, & with other dear kin & old friends. But none of it fed my own selfish innermost joy-life—none of it brought me the fuel so utterly needful to the life-engine of an artist. A ray of sunny hope had come to me from my dear sweet little uncle's-daughter ((female cousin)) Babs;[1] she had shown such kindliness & fond-show ((affection)) to me in word & deed that I had said to her: 'Dear little Babs, because of your kindliness to me I don't think I shall ever feel quite so wretched again.

---

1. Margaret Daisy Aldridge ('Babs'), born in the late 1880s, daughter of Grainger's Uncle Jim and Aunty Sarah.

You have made me feel that I can hope for happiness once more'—a foretell-ment ((prophecy)) soon to be fulfilled.

Of course, I had had the mind-fulfilment ((satisfaction)) of forth-handing ((presenting)) my biggest & best tone-works ((musical compositions)) to the publics of my birth-land & of seeing my try-deeds ((efforts)) met everywhere with friendliness, kindliness & mild-moodedness ((toleration)).[2] I think the Australian public felt a liking for me; maybe even a pride in me. But I do not think they had any natural inkling of 'what it was all about'. They were unused to the inward-turnedness ((introspectiveness)), painfulness & hard-drivenness of a begetsome ((creative)) artist. I guess ((suppose)) that the wistfulness of the 'Colonial Song' seemed a bit strange & and uncalled-for to them, for instance. 'Dear old Perks, but why is it (the 'Colonial Song') so sad? Isn't Australia a prosperous country?'; as a dear uncle's-daughter ((female cousin)) put it to me, typically. Also I had lived away from Australia too long to be able to under-stand them, their needs, their aims—or what they felt to be their needs, their aims. I felt I had been kicking again & again into unwithstanding ((non-resist-ing)) space—always a wearing act. So when I boarded the 'Aorangi' at Sydney the soil of my being was ready to fain-take ((receive)) the seed of life-giving happiness—it had lain drearily fallow long enough, it had been furroughed [sic] by the ploughshare darkmoodedness deeply enough.

We came to Auckland, Nov. 23, & we leisure-farers ((travellers)) had to interview the New Zealand folk-intake-wardens ((emigration [sic] officials)) in order to get our landing cards. 'S—', I heard sweet-voicedly behind me & looked around, mind-stirred ((interested)) by the Swedish name. My eyes met a vision of angelic loveliness; a face akin to that spirit-lit one of the young bride that had bewitched my mother & me in a Stockholm-Copenhagen train in 1913—a face akin to my darling mother's in its sunniness, joyousness, squareness, balancedness; I got a mind-print ((impression)) of Viking limbs (great manlike broad shoulders, Greek-like flowing, muscle-rich arms & legs like Amanda Dahlbö's) wedded to saintlike purity, womanly tenderness & grace—a being with a halo all round her. On the more worldly side I said to myself: 'An aristocrat if ever there was one' (which saying I now, after 2 months' close life with her in Pevensey,[3] underwrite with my heart's blood). Yet I did nought [to] get to know her. It was my life-tecnic [sic] to steer clear of women; besides, this one seemed to me so utterly *above me* in every way (&

2. See essay 80.
3. In England, on the Sussex coast. Ella Ström owned a house there, called Lilla Vrån, reportedly given to her by a former lover, the British parliamentarian, Frederick Leverton Harris (1864–1926). See essays 41 and 42.

seems so, still more, today); she seemed a rapt soaring thing of heaven, not a fellow-dweller of my poor dreary, drudging earth.

So my days went on without her (I sleeping away the days, reading away the days with Houston Stewart Chamberlain's enthralling book 'Die Grund-lagen des 19ten Jahrhunderts',[4] given to me by my grand new friend & fellow-speech-molder Robert Atkinson[5] in Hobart); tho I did not escape teas-ing glimpses of her loveliness from afar. Between Fiji & Honolulu I began to work-out ((practise)) for my Honolulu concert of Dec. 3.[6] While playing in the music-room I heard & saw her clicking on her type-writer there one day. I tried to take no stock in it. A day or so later, as I worked at the piano, she came up to me & asked me if I would help her with some chords on her ban-jolele.[7] I said I would be delighted to do so & she asked me if 11 o'clock in the music room, next day, would suit me, to which I said 'yes'. Carefully shaved and better dressed than my wont I awaited her next day. She came late & said: 'I have made such a stupid mistake. I thot you were the leader of the band; but now I have found out who you are & hope you'll forgive my having asked you to help me with my banjolele.' 'But why not?' I answered; 'I should be de-lighted to help you in any way I can. I am very fond of the ukulele, tho I don't know much about it, I'm afraid.' 'Oh no; I wouldn't think of it; and besides, my strings are broken & I have no others.' And with that the vision faded away. (It is my wont to easily think ill of women, to look-for ((expect)) in them [in German] 'the continual mendacity' [in English] of which Otto Weininger writes in 'Geschlecht und Chara[k]ter', to be-doubt ((suspect)) them for all kinds of shams & social nonsense. My angel word-sounded ((pro-nounced)) 'banjolele' in her Swedish way, turning it into 'banyolele'. I, like a fool, thot she was saying 'bandolero', which I, in my wonted boundless un-knowledge ((ignorance)), took to be the name of a Spanish or Italian tone-tool ((musical instrument)).[8] Bedoubtingly, as is my wont, I thot she was but 'putting on side', & asked myself: 'Why does she call a common–or–garden ukulele by the hi-faluting name of bandolero?' It was only 9 months later, at Pevensey, when I heard her word-sound ((pronounce)) the word again—& was by that time aware of her Swedish 'j's—that I real-saw ((realized)) my mis-take & knew her as guiltless of that sham as of all others.)

4. *The Foundations of the Nineteenth Century* (1899), by Chamberlain (1855–1927), the English-born precursor of Nazism and son-in-law of Richard Wagner.

5. (1872–1950), Yorkshire-born accountant, music critic, and linguist, whom Grainger had met while in Hobart in August 1926.

6. A midday solo piano recital at the Hawaii Theatre in Honolulu.

7. Banjulele, a cross between a banjo and a ukulele.

8. Grainger was perhaps thinking of the Latin American lute, the bandola.

I felt this fruitless, bootless fading-out of my angel vision as one more slap in my face. I wrote down my regret under the title 'P. G. Unlucky with Swedes' in the sketches for 'My Mother's and My Life' (see No. [94]) one evening (Tuesday, Nov. 30)[9] in the writing room, & Helen[10] happened to come in just as I had ended writing it, or soon after. She said, 'As usual; always hard at work', or something of that kind; adding that she did not wish to disturb me, had only come for something that she had left there, and so on. I swung round, asked her not to go, & we talked hard for an hour or so, opening up our hearts somewhat, it seemed to me. She told me she wrote rimes [poems] in Swedish & English, & painted tiles. I guess I spoke to her of my life's-work, of my tone-art ((music)) & of the book of my mother's & my life I was writing. I told her my tragedy & of my empty years since. No doubt she gave me a mind-picture ((impression)) of her own hardships. I talked harshly of women, calling them lazy & unwilling to solve their problems, & she rounded on me quickly, setting me right, & saying I could have no idea of the economic worries & trials most women in Europe had been thru since the war. What she said touched me & woke my trust. Then & there was born my eagerness to be her shield & weapon. The wish welled up in me to show her what I had written of her & her loveliness under the title 'P. G. Unlucky with Swedes' and I handed her my hand-writ ((manuscript)), asking her not to be hurt by my respectless ((disrespectful)) wording—'she-Swedes' & the like. She took it natural and straight, as she always takes all things, & our talk rushed along crowdedly, myself (at least) in a sweat of mind-heat ((excitement)). I also showed her what I had written that same evening (Nov. 30) in the book of mother's & my life under the title 'P. G's Powers during Australian Tour of 1926' (No. [96]).[11] (It is mind-stirring to note what I added the next day, Dec. 1, to the above writ—the part beginning, 'But one thing must never be forgotten', a.s.o.[12] This shows how the talk with Helen in the writing-room—the evening of Nov. 30—had brought to life all my memories of Scandinavia, my love for it, & a wish to put my right-deeming of Scandinavia on record.) When she left me I was aware of a keen rapture, of a rush of hope, of a gush of sudden strength within me.

9. Grainger's section on 'P. G. Unlucky with Swedes' began: 'Those that know the tale of my come-to-nought undertakings with Miss Ahrén in Göteborg, round 1904, will see the kinship between that & the following.' He then recounted the meeting with Ella Ström in much the same terms as in this 'Love-Life' recollection.
10. Ella Ström.
11. Essay 80.
12. See the final paragraph of essay 80.

Source: From 'On Board the "Aorangi" (Nov. 19–Dec. 9, 1926)' ('My Fore-mood', 'In Auckland Harbor', 'I First See Helen', 'The Banjolele & the Bandleader', " 'No luck with Swedes' ", 'Talk in Writing-Room'), in 'The Love-Life of Helen and Paris', pp. 2–5, dated 4 November 1927 (Grainger Museum, Melbourne).

39   The Nordic Nature of My Love for Her (1927)

I have been a worshipper of the fair race ever since my boyhood days, yet the thrill I got from Helen's special type of loveliness might not have been so deep and strong if my mind had not been stiffened in Nordicness by the books I have read of late years.[13] She stood before me as a very goddess of the breed I held holy above all other things in this world—it was as if that race I so adored had taken on flesh & blood before my eyes so that I might worship & honor it in a single person, so that I might clasp it to me in the guise of a living body. Every romantic thought of my life seemed to rise out of dim memories & rush towards her for fulfilment. Here was she with whom I would like to live in a cave, she with whom I would fain sail stormy seas in a small fishing-boat, my fellow-tramp with whom I might scale high-lands & tread endless deserts, the listening ear I would long to charm with my tone-craft ((music)), the fellow soldier with whom I would boldly face life's battles. For wherever she went, whenever I saw her, a voice said within me: 'There goes your wife'—my wife, that I seemed to have known always, seemed to have lost, somehow, & now found again; with whom it was so natural to talk, so soul-quieting to be. It could never have seemed seemly to think of anything between me & her that did not make for the honor of our both-some ((mutual)) race; any act of single selfishness on my part would seem hateful to me & traitorous to our blood-oneness. I felt as if I were a folk-errander ((ambassador)) of the Anglosaxon branch of the Nordic race to her who seemed the summing up of all the loveliness, sweetness & giftedness of the Scandinavian branch. I wished to show the older, purer branch, as flowering in her, that our outland branch had lost nothing of courtliness, knightliness & nobility in its wanderings in Australia & America. I wanted her to pluck & smell the fresh, pure Nordic scent in me as I did in her; I did not want to lag behind her in high-mindedness, gentleness, politeness & manliness; I felt on my mettle, eager to do my very best in all ways. These highborn urges were heightened by

13. Especially the books by American 'Nordicists', Lothrop Stoddard and Madison Grant, published between the mid-1910s and mid-1920s. See their entries in Bruce Clunies Ross, ed., *Percy Grainger's Library* (Melbourne: University of Melbourne, 1990).

things I happened to read in H.S. Chamberlain's aforesaid book those days, where he writes of [in German] 'the Teutonic fidelity, a fidelity as there never was before in the world'. 'The fidelity which the Teuton woman developed towards *her self-chosen man* was limitless and life-long.' [In English] And where he writes of Byron: [in German] 'Towards women he felt chivalrous, [in] what we immediately recognize as a beautiful, truly Teutonic way.' [In English] As I read these & kindred sayings the eager blush rose to my cheeks: could it be that I was going to be less true, less loyal to Helen than Tacitus wrote of the old Teutons as being?[14] Was she not my 'selbsterwählte Herrin' (self-chosen mistress)? Was I going to lag behind Byron in knightliness? I swore to myself that I would answer the noble trumpet-call of that book; that I, in my love for Helen, would be second to none in Nordic manliness & tenderness.

Source: From 'On Board the "Aorangi" (Nov. 19–Dec. 9, 1926)' ('The Nordic Nature of My Love for Her'; 'How H.S. Chamberlain's Book Swayed My Thots'), in 'The Love-Life of Helen and Paris', pp. 8–9, dated 4–5 November 1927 (Grainger Museum, Melbourne).

40   My Joy in Forming a Two-Some with Her (1927)

If I have not written much of the lustfulness her loveliness aroused in me it is because I take that for granted. It stands to reason that I, whose lusts are stirred everlastingly by almost everything in life, should be hotly fired by such a bewitching, teasing dream of beauty as she. Let it not be doubted! But I am moved more to write of the feelings that were new to me, that I had never felt before, or never to the same degree—for instance, the pride of forming a two-some ((couple)) with her. What bliss, to stand side by side with her, to walk side by side with her, thinking: 'I have found my jewel, I have picked my crown. Do not all folk envy us as we stand or walk; 2 perfect Nordics, 2 fellow artists, 2 fellow outlaws, 2 sex-lawless ones, equally strong, equally gay, equally wild, equally finely bred, something about us apart & aloof from the careful world of public-opinion-fearing, money-hungry, respectability-mongering, middle-class, lower-race bastards that ring us around? All my life I have dreamt, thought & talked of the ideal woman—she who is so nearly a man, yet so utterly a woman; here she is, take stock of her! All my life I have dwelt on the joyousness of free-love, the life-bettering boons of sex-lawlessness—behold now how it looks & laughs! This is she I pick from all the

14. Cornelius Tacitus (ca. AD 56–ca. 120) in Books I–III of his *Annals*.

world—my playmate, my soldier-sister, my fellow-sailor, my little sunflower-daughter.' Pride, more than any other feeling, I felt in her—and pride makes up such a very big part of my nature ('Of course you are a proud nature, with that nose', she said). *Pride of race above all else.* My feelings for my race—for the Nordic race—are deeper & stronger than my feelings for myself. I lose myself in my race as god-loving men lose themselves in the thought of god. My art is only my top-layer ((surface)); but my race is at the very heart of me. No old-time Hebrew felt more fiercely for his race than I do for mine. And Helen is the very vestal virgin of that race; the hallowed priestess of that breed-above-breeds; inside the bounds of her soft skin are gathered together all these hidden holy heritages, these no-where-else-found spiritual finer-nesses, hearty hardier-hoods, higher heroisms, richer thought-worlds; they are hers to bequeath, hers to pass on to mankind for ever. O, to be the father of her children—children that could not fail to be whole-Nordics with 2 such begetters ((parents)). O, the soul-joy of seeing such traits as hers born again, to be the abettor of such re-birth! I, to whom fatherhood before had always seemed laugh-at-able ((ludicrous)), saw it now with rapture & thanksgiving. O, to be but the race-tool in the hand of this life-goddess!

While my darling wondrous mother was alive I was a tool in her higher hands. Since her death need has made me a leader, a chooser, a willer, a single-soul ((individualist)). But my type is not such. My type is to serve, to help, to shield, to understand, to overset ((translate)); to show a dog-like, soldierly loy-alty [in German] to my 'self-chosen mistress'. [In English] I am content; I have found her.

Source: From 'On Board the "Aorangi" (Nov. 19–Dec. 9, 1926)' ('My Joy in Forming a Two-Some with Her; My Pride in Her', 'My Feeling for My Race; Helen Seen as Race-Priestess, as Mother of Nordic Children', 'My Type Is to Serve'), in 'The Love-Life of Helen and Paris', pp. 11–12, dated 5 November 1927 (Grainger Museum, Melbourne).

41   Pevensey (1928)

So it was only natural that I soon found myself cuddled up beside Helen[15] on that trainseat[16] as a child might be cuddled up, not caring whether my weight was heavy upon her or not, eager only to be close to her in a drowsy closeness,

15. Ella Ström.
16. On the evening of 7 August 1927, traveling from Southampton to Pevensey, via Brighton and Eastbourne, in England.

blissful in feeling *at rest*, like a boat in harbour with furled sails. Of what avail were Helen's Viking limbs, bold eyes & thrillseeking womanly nature if she was not to be the sheltering cradle for my tender, timid, doom-sensing artist-soul? (Is a woman's body not full of pillows, hollows & nests—restful blind-alleys—goals for the weary wandering he-some seed of soul, mind & body?) So, in that darling train, the unrealness of the last 6 wretched selfstrong, self-swayed, selfenough years[17] melted away from me magicly, bit by bit, until I at last felt myself at home in my own proper land again; screened & sheltered by the wings of a strong & lovely goddess.

How unbelievably heavenly to lie there let-happensomely ((passively)) in Helen's blessed arms, hearing her prattle so naturally, so self-revealingly of herself—[in Danish] how the *whanganuimate* [vaginal blood[18]] had visited her there in S'hampton, so that she felt irritable; that blood had run down along the veins so that the stockings became bloody and she had to hurry back to the hotel in order to change her stockings—[in English] how loafers loung-ing in the S'hampton streets had stared cheekily at her & her big legs, how she hated such staring & felt tempted to pull her skirts up & give them more to stare at, how she felt tempted to give them a stab or two with her sharp tongue, & the like.

After 8 months of waiting[19] for the sexmate (whom one's whole nature recognized at once as one's wife), after a thousand lustful mindpicturings of her, after scores of selfhelp-sexacts undertaken with thots of her for fuel— would one not guess that those hours there in the trains mostly by ourselves, from 5 to midnight, would have been lustful fiery ones & that the first kisses would be forever remembered? Nature is not so simple. I can record only that those hours were mainly restful rather than lustful (tho blended of both, of course) & that I have no special memory of any first kiss—tho at the Southampton hotel, or there in the train, must have happened the first real kisses of our love-life. I only know that I cared nothing where we were going to, cared nothing whether the train stopped or started (except that I wished our traintrip to go on for ever—& this in spite of the fact that a fuller freedom for lovemaking awaited us, I hoped, at our journey's end). Nor do I remember what clothes she wore, beyond a vague mindprint ((impression)) of some-

17. I.e., since the death of his mother.
18. I.e., menstruation. 'Whanganui' and following words ('momoe', 'ure', 'tara') of supposedly Maori or Scandinavian origin are part of Grainger's 'private' sexual language. For an introduc-tion to this language, see Dreyfus, ed., *The Farthest North of Humanness*, xxiv.
19. Grainger had last seen Ella Ström in New York on 23 December 1926, when he had seen her off on her ship to Europe.

thing lightcolored. [In Danish] Nor was I impatient because she suffered from *whanganuimate*. [In English] There was no hurry for any special form of joy. To be with Helen, in any way, in any place, was bliss enough. At her side, or in her arms, or merely looking at her or hearing her talk, I felt at home, at rest, at peace, will-less, full-fed ((satisfied)). I felt as a dog must feel when he refinds a beloved master after having been cruelly, blightingly sundered from him. I was in heaven, & I wanted this heavenliness to last as long as life lasted. This mood of restful soul-balm lasted thru the whole of my nearly two-months' stay with Helen—whether at Pevensey, London, New Haven, Grez,[20] Paris, or elsewhere.

> 'Home is the sailor, home from sea,
> And the hunter home from the hill.'[21]

ran thru my mind again & again as we sat & talked, close-hugged in that kindly train.

Of course it was nice for me to be able to give Helen a showing-off of my baggage-lugging when we changed trains at Brighton & Eastbourne. At about midnight we reached Pevensey & Westham railway station—a pitchblack night—& stood waiting quite a time while a taxi was brought to life by some friendly man at the station. I would have been well pleased to stand there waiting with Helen all night. A little later we landed at 'Lilla Vrån' itself (Helen's house), where I, rushing out heavily laden with grips into the inky darkness, stumbled over her gate-step & gave my knee a mighty lick (maybe this was the cause of that soreness in my left knee that I felt sundry months later?). As I sprawled there I thot of William the Conqueror's sprawl on the nearby sands of Hastings (that fatal Hasting that has played such a part in molding my Anglosaxon-loving, Norman-hating mind-life since childhood) long ago, & I wondered if my fall was an evil fate-token ((omen)). William had been able to grasp the yielding sands with both hands & turn out a quick-witted journalistic phrase that saved the day; but I could not do anything of that kind with the hard, skinscraping cement I fell on. So I said nothing. Now met us Electra,[22] a pretty youthful picture of sleepy welcome in a kimono, & I seem to hazily remember some food happily eaten in the kitchen.

I was taken aback & upheartened to see what a really lowly little home 'Lilla Vrån' was. I am earnest in my socialism, in my deeprooted feeling that

---

20. Where they visited Frederick and Jelka Delius.
21. From 'Requiem' in *Underwoods* (I.xxi), by Robert Louis Stevenson (1850–94). These two lines appear on Stevenson's tombstone.
22. Elsie (Elsa; 1909–1984), Ella Ström's daughter.

we ought to waste as little as possible upon needless 'things' & worthless 'comforts' as long as there are so many poor folk in the world that direly need help, in my feeling that life is better given over to thots, feelings, lusts, arts & bodysports than to a worldly keenness about belongings. True, Helen has written of 'Lilla Vrån' as being a 'workman's cottage', & that phrase had eased my mind somewhat. Still, Helen had lived long with the English upper classes, whose alarming & merciless hostesses are fond of saying of some carefully chosen & timewastingly fussed over countrified edition of their 'good taste': 'You see, it's really nothing but a hut with one sunflower in the backyard', always hoping that their subtly understanding guests will answer, 'But, my dear Gwen, it's a fairy palace with hanging gardens'. We all take *something* from the folk we live amongst & like, & I had qualms that the 'workman's cottage' might turn out, after all, to be the usual English masterpiece of taste & refinement (the nursing of which wastes 3-fourths of the owner's time), with maybe even a joykilling parlormaid in a white apron & cap. But the moment I clapped eyes on 'Lilla Vrån' I realized that all such fears were groundless, & saw that my angel had stayed a true Scandinavian (in spite of all her love for the English), given over to intilth ((culture)) but not to town-skill ((civilisation)), & that 'Lilla Vrån' could well be an artist's & socialist's abode-of-love where one never need to fear meeting 'the really *fine* things of life' (meaning the refinements based upon *wealth*, as against those deeper, more vulgar pleasures that any poor man may equally call his own). By letter Helen & I had wordwrestled as to whether I was to have Electra's bedroom (next to Helen's) or the attic bedroom a floor above. I had (wishhidingly) begged for the attic, shamming a dislike of turning E. out of her own room—in reality, however, hoping my words would not be heeded. So I was not taken aback when ushered into the coveted room, next to Helen's. [In Danish] I must have asked Helen whether I could sleep with her that night—[in English] but I can't recall it clearly. I can recall no details of that night, & very naturally so—for I was *living* just then, not *folksong gathering*!

But I can recall the sense of fulfilment with which I closed & locked her door on her & me. No doubt she was in bed already, having guested the bathroom before me. And no doubt I had made a thoro cleaning-up job of it myself in the bathroom, polishing myself up with true Anglosaxon puritanicalness & oldmaidishness. I am a clean-washing, tho not a 'clean-minded' lover. My puritanicalness ends, thank god, with the soap & water; for I have in sex neither the shyness nor the fieriness of the true puritan—that sexual fieriness of the Anglosaxon puritan that Isadora Duncan[23] does such justice to in her life-enriching masterpiece 'My Life'. It stands to reason that between such

23. (1877–1927), American dancer. *My Life* appeared in early 1928.

natural & yeaful ((positive, affirmative)) natures as Helen's & mine there could be no room for shyness or coyness, no fuss about nakedness, no hardship in making clear our sexual states & tastes & wishes at all moments. As for undressing, it seems to me we always stripped feverishly, roughly, unseeingly—like water-fond children hurrying to get into a swimming pool. But that was partly because we, being unwed, had a very bounded ((limited)) muchness ((amount)) of unhindered time with each other. But I am reaching too far ahead, now. [In Danish] It is likely that we began having *momoe* [coitus] during that first night, and that I (possibly in the morning) tried to use one of my 'French letters',[24] but [in English] then and later [in Danish] without success, of course. But I don't think we went to great lengths of *momoe* that first night. [In English] I never hasten where soul-joy is at stake, nor am I built for quick conquests. [In Danish] My *ure* [penis] is solidly built. [In English] When dear Dr Russell went over me (for vericasele?[25]) in 1904 or 1908 he was amazed to find me 'hung like a blacksmith'—those were his words. He said he had never before met an 'intellectual' of my build. Why force the issue, as Romeo did in Duncan's 'Life'? Why not side-step the stage she wordpaints as 'sheer torture', going straight, but warily & slowly, for the stage she wordpaints as 'heaven on earth'? [In Danish] On the other hand, it is quite certain that already on that first night I kissed her all over her body, [and] *momi*-ed for a long time on her *whanganui* [vagina]. [In English] Best of all, I remember the honeyed glow of our sandwiched bodies beneath the bed clothes, she on her back & I kneeling astride her with my head on her bosom or with my mouth close to her ear, chattering, chattering, chattering. Chattering too much, too soon, most so the next morning, as it turned out— for I was over-eager to broach & settle the matter & place of our next meeting, above all to hinder it from taking place in New York.

Source: From 'Pevensey', in 'The Love-Life of Helen and Paris', pp. 29–33, dated 'mid-April 1928' (Grainger Museum, Melbourne).

➤ 42   [Sex-Life] (1928)

I will try & wordpaint our sex-life first—since that was the strongest of all the many bonds between us; sex meaning more to Helen[26] & me than art or thot or religion or wealth or friendship ever could—more even than love itself. It

24. I.e., condoms.
25. Varicocele, varicose veins of the spermatic cord.
26. Ella Ström.

was not only because we were lovers & new-found lovers that sex ran upper-most in our being. Rank sex (as well as loving & tender sexlove) lay at the very root of her & my type at all times, flooded all our art & was the wellspring of any sway we held over folk thru art or any means whatever. Therefore (as long as our sex-fires burn) it is the sum of our whole life, meaning more to us than even health, wealth, goodness, honor & victory. I am taking it for granted that the reader has read the letters that passed between Helen & me up to the Pevensey guesting ((visit))[27] & therefore has a chance to know our tastes, types & feelings—has read my wordpicturements ((descriptions)) of Helen's beauty, is aware of her love-seeking, all-else-forgetting nature, knows that about nine-tenths of my sexstir is sex-cruelty & pain-worship ((sadism)), knows that both of us have been selfhelpers in sex for long years.[28] For such knowledge of us must go before what now comes.

[In Danish] Most of the time, *momoe* [coitus] took place early in the morning when I came from the hotel.[29] What heavenly bliss quietly to ascend the stairs and step into her room! The fact that she (the most beautiful woman of the world, life's dearest treasure) was still there, struck me as a miracle every time. That summer was quite chilly and wet, therefore our bed pleasures for the most part happened under the dunas—something that was new to me. It had the consequence that most of the complicated, refined sensuous games (which otherwise came to me naturally) in this instance were excluded. [In English] Thus we kept for the most part to an oldtime normalness of action that I would never have dreamed myself capable of. [In Danish] I have never been a Hercules in sexual matters; especially as a young man, I was quite weak, with a tendency to get tired or inflamed. In former times, I often had a feeling that my sexual parts were not fitted for *momoe*, that they did not 'swal-low-bum' [in English] (dovetail) [in Danish] well with the female parts—however much in love I otherwise was and however happy in my infatuation. My greatest sensitivity, the most reliable release of sexual excitement has al-ways been my nipples. When I practise self-help, I only need to tickle or

27. Grainger and Ella Ström had started corresponding even before she left the United States in December 1926. As an Appendix to 'The Love-Life of Helen and Paris', Grainger included an unsent letter of 9 April 1927, in which he outlined the reasons—sexual, racial, familial, business-related—why he might 'be destroyed by marriage'. He later ('Love-Life', p. 25, dated 6 November 1927) commented that this unsent letter was 'mean, unjust, maudlin, stupid', but that he did not resile from most of its opinions.

28. For a statement of Grainger's sexual intentions and hopes as he approached marriage, see his long letter to Ella Ström of 23 April 1928, reproduced in Gillies and Pear, eds., *The All-Round Man*, 94–100.

29. The Bay Hotel on Eastbourne Road in Pevensey, to which Grainger had moved during his Aug-ust 1927 visit to 'safeguard' Ella Ström's local reputation.

pinch or prick or burn my nipples to climax—without anything else at all. In former times, it was always my greatest joy when my nipples were bitten or pinched hard during *momoe*—most of the time I could not reach a climax unless my nipples were pinched so as to bleed. Often they were so injured by this treatment [in English] (so covered with scabs) [in Danish] that they could not be bitten again for a few days. But here, with Helen, it was altogether different—as if I were a completely different person with regard to sex! For the first time in all my life, I was a strong, normal person with regard to *momoe*; for the first time I did not need special treatment in order to reach the *parapara* climax [climax with semen] day after day. Even in Pevensey I was perhaps not a Hercules of sensuality in comparison with a thousand other, stronger men—but in comparison with my former self, I probably was one. Helen's enchanting beauty, her 'balsamic' nature, her positive view of life, her captivating *whanganui*—all this changed me into a new person, a persona I did not know myself!

No spot in the whole world could be so captivating as her *whanganui*. It was as if it had the sucking power of an octopus—it milked me like the most skilled milkmaid! Her *whanganui* is endowed with a spirit of generosity, a soul of hospitality, which does wonders! And that sucking power, that ability to transform and strengthen, flowed from Helen even when she was, or seemed to be, completely predominantly passive. She'd rather be ridden than ride herself. She never complained of anything in *momoe*; she never demanded anything in *momoe*. Apparently lazy in the sexual act, she exercised a power that seemed to be almost superhuman! It was with good reason that I had thought of her as a sex goddess. I never felt tired or inflamed after *momoe* with her—even when it lasted for several hours. Her inner flesh is at the same time soft and strong; it is as if it, in movements, structure and texture, pronounced the word [in English] 'Wellcome' [*sic*] [in Danish] a thousand, thousand happy times. We have all heard and read a great deal about 'post coitum omnia animalae triste',[30] but never did this proverb hold any truth for me when in Helen's arms. All glances, all acts, all turns in her were equally divine, enchanting, healing, happifying. Normally, at the beginning of *momoe*, I would spread myself on top of her as butter is spread on a sandwich—in order to warm her, as she did not have as much [in English] 'bear's warmth' (as self-heating powers are called in the Icelandic sagas) [in Danish] as I had. As soon as she appeared to be warm and cosy, I began to kiss or tickle or caress her body, and almost al-

---

30. Correctly, 'omne animal post coitum triste (est)' (Latin), or 'after sex every living being is sad', an anonymous post-Classical statement, sometimes incorrectly attributed to Aristotle.

ways to kiss and suck her beloved *whanganui*—often in the '69' position, with my *ure* [penis] parts wriggling over her face. She liked best to be tickled and sucked quite softly, with my tongue or my mouth, on her *tara* [clitoris]. Only, too often, my sucking was too hard or too wild; this certainly caused her to be more intensely roused, but was quite often followed by fatigue or pains. Because of these consequences, she asked me not to pinch her *tara* too strongly with tongue or mouth. It was often difficult for me to act as she requested—what I would have liked best was to eat her all up! When I had sloshed about in her *whanganui* with my mouth, Helen liked being kissed on her mouth immediately after so that she got the odour of her own inner juices (which my mouth brought to hers) in her nostrils. It was really only through her *tara* that she reached a full climax—with *momoe* in the *whanganui* it never happened, or almost never. She had always been like that, she said. All the same, she liked best *momoe* in the *whanganui*, although it did not bring her any climax. She never seemed unhappy or dissatisfied by her not coming to a climax in the *momoe*. [In English] 'It seems to leave me in a happier mood if I don't reach it. I don't want to feel too satisfied, too finished, with my sex.' (O woman; what unfathomable depths of tholesomeness [endurance], lissomeness [flexibility] & variety yr nature holds! Fullfed ((satisfied)) today with a certain man, his fads & his boundednesses ((limitations)); fullfed tomorrow with another man, a wholly othersome animal with t'otherwayround wonts & powers; finding the best of both of them; neither man ever coming to the end of you, O woman, O vast 'unknown quantity'.)

[In Danish] Sometimes my sucking, my *whanganui* kisses brought her to a climax (and that was perhaps the joy I valued most—to lead her to the goal in the intimate way; to feel almost smothered by her lustiness. If I had the choice between different forms of sex life, that is undoubtedly the one I would choose!); but often it was only the foreplay for the *momoe* itself. That, too, was something I welcomed—to breathe fresh air again, and to see her entire sweetness and beauty spread under my eyes. During the *momoe*, she almost invariably kept her eyes open, [in English] but like the eyes of one in a trance, unseeing, uncaring. [In Danish] When I pushed hard into her with my *ureroa* [erect penis], short, soft calls came from her half-open lips, and when the thrusts became faster and more forceful, they sounded as if from a [in English] victim on the rack. Helen was in these ways a living illustration of Swinburne's enthralling lines (in 'The Leper'[31]):

---

31. From first series of *Poems and Ballads* (1866), lines 59–62, by the English poet Algernon Charles Swinburne (1837–1909).

Felt her bright bosom, strained & bare,
Sigh under him, with short mad cries.
Out of her throat & sobbing mouth
And body broken up with love.

[In Danish] (Maybe it was mostly *surprise* these beloved sounds expressed; it was as if each *ureroa* thrust was bigger, more loveable, better than expected—that is the harmonious, positive nature my princess has!) [In English] It may be guessed what heavenly bliss these seemingly pain-laden cry-lets brought to the ears of a painworshipper like myself. To have the seemingness of giving pain, even without doing it; what a miracle of good luck! As our lusts burned fiercer, [in Danish] and my movements became more violent, she had a habit of holding her hands over her eyes (but without closing her eyes) or over her breasts—[in English] the last a thoroly joy-maddening gesture. [In Danish] When she approached the climax (which, as I said, failed to occur during *momoe*), it often happened that her fingers softly scratched her tummy or the region around it—[in English] clearly a leaving of her self-help wonts. [In Danish] With my own climaxes, I jumped out from her *whanganui* at the last moment and spurted my *parapara* [semen] over her breasts or her belly—after all, I had to rely on her not being made pregnant by me.

[In English] The sight of her little face, of her soft sweet breasts, of her amazon limbs & queenly body beneath me was a bedrunkening vision of flawless loveliness. And if my fires began to burn low I had only to seize her wrists, place them above her head, & look at the picture of her taut arms, strained breasts & beloved [in Danish] armpit hair [in English] to be spurred unwithstandably to keener lust. And when now & again she dropped her lethappensome ((passive)) holding & the octopus [in Danish] in her *whanganui* [in English] reached out for me with its tentacles [in Danish] it was as if all space consisted of a single irresistible force of attraction. [In English] It stands to reason that thru-out these sexjoys my mind was being fed with my wonted sexcruel thots & cravings. The sight of Helen's childlike, flowerlike, lilylike loveliness beneath me was neverfailingly being enhanced by mind picturements of tormenting & wastelaying that tender loveliness—whipping it, biting it, burning it. Yet I wrought no actual deeds of painworship ((sadism)) during the next 2 months except a *whakawhiu*[32] act (later written up) toward the end of my stay. It is not part of my loveplan to be a selfish painworshipper towards Helen; to risk wrecking her happiness or her trust in me, even in order to touch the deepest delights my being is capable of.

---

32. Probably meaning 'making a whipping'.

My dark angel must not cross the thresh-hold of our lovelife except at rare moments & in rare moods (if such happen) where I feel quite sure that he is truly welcome & guest bidden ((invited)).

[In Danish] On an average, *momoe* took place about once a day, but not quite regularly. [In English] Sweetest of all (to me) were those afternoon joys when I would suddenly clutch her & ask, 'Will you come upstairs with me?' What a frenzied undressing, all sweaty & heartthumping as we were; what rough fury, what flinging of limbs around, above, below; what heedlessness of ought save the ruthless lords of lust that rode & goaded us. After about a month of these daily sex feasts my sexstrength showed now & then signs of waning. Even then a touch or two of Helen's on my [in Danish] nipples [in English] would be enough to stoke my fires. [In Danish] But mostly, we did not even need that kind of rousing. [In English] It was my wish to test our bedrock normal sexpowers & instirs ((instincts)), unholpen by sexcraft or lustartfulness. (In the to-come [future], however, I am hoping we will score our toneworks with the full resources of the most lavish orchestra!) [In Danish] When I showed that kind of sexual fatigue or impotence, Helen was always a loving sister to me; never did she make any *demands* on me, never did she utter any reproach; [in English] her golden nature had unfailingly the helpful kindliness of a sweet mother to its cherished child. So utterly does Helen's beauty & sextype fullfeed ((satisfy)) my flesh that I could be wholly happy with her if our togetherness were based on flesh alone— if she were deaf & dumb, if she were an idiot in all but her lusts, if we were unable to share thots, even if we had no bond of fellowartistry—so wild & deep is the sex-bond. But I could also be wholly happy with her even if all sexacts were tabooed between us, even if I might never touch her except with my eyesight.

The life of talking with her, sharing her thots, watching her genius unfold, seeing her loveliness walk liltingly beside me—that too would be enough & more than enough. There is in Helen enough, & more than enough, to fill several kinds of lives-of-joy for me, & even the smallest crust of her precious life's loaf would be a wondrous soulfeast for my starving soul, worth giving up all else for. My mind swoons when it dwells on the thot that the full all-ness of this sungoddess, sex-priestess, race-errandress, artist, angel-heart may yet be mine to worship, serve, help, study, lay bare, pick apart, build up, strengthen, wear down, tease & gobble up. Is such richness possible on this poor earth? Can my life of long wretchedness really be born again into such a heaven of shadowless bliss?

(May 25, 1928)

Source: From 'Pevensey', in 'The Love-Life of Helen and Paris', pp. 38–42, dated November 1927 to 25 May 1928 (Grainger Museum, Melbourne).

⇒ 43   Ella's Rime-Piece 'In Search of Gold' (1937)

Her over-soulship [genius] is shown in the manifold *half meanings* in her rime-pieces [poems]. For more than any other thing, it was this over-soulship that I wedded her for—for the high right to live close to such a many-rooted, deeply-delving soul. The worthlessness of gold-lust may seem (at a first careless glance) the main meaning behind this rime-piece.[33] Yet it is hardly so. A mourning for sex-waste is one dim, tho main, meaning in it. Only a seeing soul-eye, living thru our timestretch of sex-naysayment [sexual denial], could put so much over-meaning into the girl's golden hair withering unseen. And then the half meaning of race: 'golden hair'. Such half meanings as: 'the golden hair of the pink-blue-gold race[34] is worth more than ore-y ((metal)) gold'; and 'this girl whom the miners knew naught of was a pink-blue-gold-racy girl'. The doom-thot of the over-lookedness of the noblest race is here hiddenly forth-hinted ((intimated)). These are the deep, dim thots of over-soulship that drew me to Ella—thots that she herself is not aware of, thot-goals she does not aim at, yet hits. She is so much over-full weighty in all her worths. This is what I worship. This is what I *saw at once* & pounced upon.

Train, Washington DC → N. York, March 31, '37

Source: 'Ella's Rime-Piece "In Search of Gold"', in 'Thots and Call-to-Mindments', pp. [16]–[17] (Grainger Museum, Melbourne).

⇒ 44   Read This If Ella Grainger or Percy Grainger Are Found Dead Covered with Whip Marks (1932)

I am a sadist & a flagellant—my highest sexual delight is to whip a beloved woman's body. Her screams, her struggles to evade the whip, the marks of the whip arising on her body, all give me a feeling of male power & exultation that swells my love & devotion towards my sweetheart a hundredfold & makes our love-life more intense & impulsive. To a lesser degree I enjoy being whipped myself (& before marriage used to whip myself every few weeks), be-

---

33. This poem, 'In Search of Gold', appears in Ella Grainger, *The Pavement Artist and Other Poems* (London: Hutchinson, n.d. [1940]), 28–30.
34. The Graingers' occasional phrase for 'Nordic race' because of its pink cheeks, blue eyes, and golden hair.

cause the smart of the whip on myself brings home to me the reality of the sex-cruelty I long to practice on my sweetheart.

Students of sex are familiar with all this & will understand that my sex-cruelty is not unlovingness, but the height of love; is not indifference, but a compassionate violation of my tenderness towards my beloved—a kind of brutal male reaction to the over-great sway exerted upon me (almost smothering me) by woman's exquisite, tantalizing, over-treat beauty (when she has it); least of all is my sadism anger, for I could not pleasurably whip a woman with a rough or unadmired nature. In other words, my sex-cruelty (strange as it may seem to those unfamiliar with the well-spring of sadism) is a form of worship & homage—a tribute to women's beauty, lovableness, tenderness, sweet-naturedness. Above all, it is the expression of my fierce sexual hunger and greed, which crowds every moment of my life.

My wife, with her deeply womanly nature (so rich in sex-divination & sex-tolerance) does not resent my sadistic love—for she is one of those angel-women to whom sex-satisfaction is as attractive as sex-frustration is repellent. Out of the generosity of her sex-love, out of the urgency of her sex-heat, she panders to both my flagellantic cravings—she lets me whip her & she whips me herself.

As far as we know, both our hearts are strong & we forsee, from our orgies, no accident to our health. Yet it is easy to imagine that the excitement of whipping orgies might cause a sudden heart-failure in either of us at any moment. Should either of us be found dead, covered with whip marks, embarrassing suspicions might fall upon the survivor. The purpose of this letter is to dispel such suspicions & to declare that any whip marks found on either of our bodies at any time are merely the result of a happy sadistic love-life willingly entered into by both parties—tho mainly made possible by the loving generosity of my wife's joy-bringing nature in response to my own greedy sex-nature.

We neither of us like the thot of possible tragedy, or expect it. But one thing I must say in closing: that such sex-happiness as we enjoy is cheap at any price—even if that price should turn out to be heart-failure, stroke, death, or what-not. It is no use living merely not to die—one should live to *really live* & Ella & I do.

Source: 'Read This If Ella Grainger or Percy Grainger Are Found Dead Covered with Whip Marks', dated 21 August 1932 (Grainger Museum, Melbourne).

6

SELF

45   [George Percy] (1933)

Mother said that the first thot she had when she saw me lying beside her was, 'He's like George'. I was called 'George Percy' because of my mother's out-standing fondness of her brother George (or because she thot I looked like him?) & because father wanted me to bear a typetrue Northumbrian name.[1] (I call-to-mind my father telling me that Percy was linked up ((connected)) with the Earl Percy of Northumberland[2] & that the name meant 'Pierce-Eye', one of the Northumbrian earls having had someone's eyes struck out.)[3]

Mother sometimes said to me that she wasn't aback-taken ((surprised)) that many women were willing to bear a new baby every year, for she thot giv-ing the breast to a baby 'the most delicious of all sensual sensations'. She spoke, too, of how much a little baby, with its mere gums, can pinch & hurt the nipple. (L'Avenir, Atlantic, off French Coast, Oct. 11, 1933.)

I don't think mother had the fun of nursing me long, for I gather that I was bottle-fed almost from the start. Maybe mother's store of milk gave out, or her ill-health arising out of her bearing-hurts [birth pains] put an end to it—for it soon was clear-shown ((evident)) that mother was somewhat torn inside. For months mother went about feeling wretched, having shivering fits, unable to stand or walk comfy-ly & with a sense of great weights dragging in-

---

1. Later addition of 22 October 1933, intended for around this point in the 'Saga': 'I used to hear something about my never having been holy-dipped ((baptized)) as a baby. But it seems dimly to me that I later heard that I was only nearly not holy-dipped—it had been forgotten, or some-thing. I would like to think that my father's god-naysayingness had forthgot ((produced)) some-thing senseful, or almost sense-full, along such lines.'
2. Probably referring to Earl Hugh Percy (1715–86), first Duke of Northumberland.
3. A sentence, now illegible, had been added here in pencil.

side her. At last, Dr [ ]⁴ sewed up the tears, with silver threads, I think, which were taken out after about half a year. The taking out of the threads was very nasty, mother said. This state of being torn, feverish, weak, cut-cured ((operated)) & being unable to walk or get around properly kept mother at home for a long time. At least, it seemed to have kept her at home in the evenings so that she went to no balls or parties. But father went all the more & mother joy-quaffed ((enjoyed)) hearing of all the fun he had & longed for the time when she would be well enough to go with him & share all these merrynesses. But when, after some months, mother was strong enough to go along with him, the fun he had word-painted to her became nothing but badtemper & fun-begrudingness on his part.⁵ Mother, of course, wanted to dance with handsome younger or youngish men, but if she did so father would get his back up saying, 'Who was that silly young pup I saw you dancing with? I thought you would be a help to me when you came out again. Why can't you dance with old Mitchell?'⁶ (or some other 'silly old contractor', as mother thot). Father wanted mother to help him on in his business links with buildmongers ((contractors)) & other power-wielders from whom he hoped orders & business might flow to him. (A mistaken view, to my mind, fight-winth ((success)) in one's job-life ((career)) growing out of work well done & out of nought else. The man who is highly-strung enough to do good work in an art or a craft is too easily put out & upset in the give & take of everyday life to make a pleasing rut-man ((acquaintance)) or man-friend in the eyes of common well-to-do folk, & the more they know him (or sense in-stirredly ((instinctively)) his feeling of his own over-mindedness, his feeling of their under-

---

4. Name not given by Grainger.
5. Later addition of 2 December 1933, at this point:

> That father's love-selfishness ((jealousy)) was not very deepgoing, however, peeps out of the following hap-tale ((anecdote)), sometimes told to me by mother. At some dinner, in the early wedded years, some friend of father's (Yates?, O'Hara?, I don't know who) had taken mother in to dinner & was seated over against father & father's dinner-mate at table. This friend lowered his voice in talking to mother during dinner & father's love-selfishness was at once aroused. 'What was that you were saying?', asked father briskly, leaning across the table. But mother's dinner-mate was ready-poised for this sally. With a graceful sweep of his hand round the table, he smilingly answered: 'I was just remarking to your wife what pleasant company, what delicious dishes, what pretty flowers are all assembled for our pleasure' (or: 'I was just remarking to your wife what a pleasant dinner we are enjoying—such entertaining company, such delicious dishes, such charming flowers.') Father laughed gaily enough & said, 'You old rascal, you!', or some such tease-word.

6. David Mitchell (1829–1916), Scottish-born stonemason and building contractor, with whom John Grainger collaborated in building the Princes Bridge in Melbourne. He was the father of the singer Nellie Melba.

mindedness) the less are they likely to throw the plums of business his way. We gifted ones do not seem likable to everyday honor-greedy ((pretentious)) & the less they know us the better it is for us in dealing with them. They can soon see that they sicken us with their witlessness & they hold our work-weighfullness ((criticalness)) against us—& why not. It is best for the art-man & the craftsman to be known to the crowd only by his work, for that is the bestseeming part of him in their eyes.)

Source: Untitled section, in 'The Aldridge-Grainger-Ström Saga', W37-42 to 37-45, dated 11 and 12 October 1933 (with later additions of 22 October and 2 December 1933; Grainger Museum, Melbourne).

⤳ 46   [For My Autobiography] (1902)

For lecture on training or a chief point to be proved in autobiography: on present system we allot to people much forced & artificial agony (such as learning in schools, toiling, & what is generally termed 'working') & as a counterpoise go thru a certain amount of forced & artificial pleasure, (so-called) holidays, picnics, etc. In civilised state [there would be] neither hateful toil nor forced pleasure, learning [would be] a joy, work a pleasure, athletics (with a view towards health) a recreation, in short, [there would be] no attempt to shut out the real things of existence. Why we have holidays at present is merely because we are dissatisfied with the average of days; the generality must be satisfying, pleasure or satisfaction as an exception is useless & barbaric.

Aug. 7, 1902

Source: Untitled passage, in 'Methods of Teaching and Other Things', from section 64 (p. [47]) (Grainger Museum, Melbourne).

⤳ 47   [Art and Craft] (1902)

No one was more conscious of how little an art-work taken purely from the craftsman's views tallied the vital cause of the same than W. W.[7] For instance (Sea-drift 2): 'Aware that before all my arrogant poems the real *Me* stands yet

---

7. Walt Whitman.

untouch'd, untold, altogether unreach'd', etc.[8] Yet no one so gloriously created art solely to express his own urge in more absolute candid sincerity. See: 'the best comfort of the whole business', etc. *L.O.G.* page 434, down to 'unerringly on record'.[9]

On the other hand, ignorance of the craft of art more than anything else binds one wholly to conventionality & makes it entirely impossible to handle the expressing materials so as to powerfully give out the feeling that w[ou]ld out, 'unstopp'd & unwarp'd by any infl[uence] outs[ide] the soul within me'.[10] [This] is the result of mastery over matter generally, & greatly the technical & ma[s]tering matter of artistic expression [*sic*].

Composers missing technique are for ever following the dictates of untamed technical possibilities instead of the instincts of their emotions.

Aug. 8, 1902

Source: Untitled passage, in 'Methods of Teaching and Other Things', from section 65 (pp. [47]–[48]) (Grainger Museum, Melbourne).

48   The London Gramophone Co. (Now 'His Master's Voice') & the Joseph Taylor Folksong Records (1932)

Sept 22, 1932

After gathering English folksongs in Lincolnshire, etc., in 1905, 1906, etc., certain singers stood out as out-of-the-way fine, & first amongst these was old Mr Joseph Taylor of Saxby-All-Saints, Lincs., aged about 75.[11] In order to have the art-wonts in his singing preserved for the future I arranged with

---

8. From section 2 of 'As I Ebb'd with the Ocean of Life', in 'Sea-Drift' (*Leaves of Grass*, 1891–2).
9. From 'A Backward Glance o'er Travel'd Roads' (1888), the prose epilogue to *Leaves of Grass*. The section reads:

> As fulfill'd, or partially fulfill'd, the best comfort of the whole business (after a small band of the dearest friends and upholders ever vouchsafed to man or cause—doubtless all the more faithful and uncompromising—this little phalanx!—for being so few) is that, unstopp'd and unwarp'd by any influence outside the soul within me, I have had my say entirely my own way, and put it unerringly on record—the value thereof to be decided by time.

10. See previous note.
11. Taylor was a bailiff from North Lincolnshire. During 1905–8, Grainger took down nearly fifty songs, or song variants, from him.

the London Gramophone Co. in 1907 for them to take some records of his singing, which they did.[12] Of course, I was paid nothing—& had no thot of being paid. Mr Taylor may have been paid something by them, but I hardly think so. I paid for Mr Taylor to travel from Brigg (Lincs.) to London & back, & he stayed with us at 31A King's Rd, Chelsea while in London. I always took the Taylor records very seriously, for as far as I know they were the only gramophone records of a genuine English folksinger made available to the public. When the records were taken the Gramophone Co. assured me that the master records (matrices) would never be destroyed. That was their obligation in the deal. In 1924, fearing that the Taylor records *might* be destroyed if there were no sale for them I ordered 14 or more complete sets to give to libraries, universities, etc., & to hold against the future, myself.

A few weeks ago I wrote to the Gramophone Co. (Hayes M'sex, England) telling them of my plan to put £1,000 or £2,000 into a trust fund, the yearly interest from which to be paid out in Joseph Taylor prizes (handled by the Competition Festivals?[13]) for the singers who best preserved the traditions of English folksinging as preserved in the Taylor records, & asking if the records would be on the market if I endowed such prizes.

Today I hear from the Gramophone Co. (Hayes), 'we regret to inform you that many of the master records to which you refer are no longer in existence'—but stating that 4 records are still available. 'By present-day standards the quality of recording & reproducing leaves much to be desired. For such a scheme as you have in mind we . . . [14] suggest that it might be worthwhile recording these folksongs with a present-day artiste such as John Goss[15] or Dole Smith,[16] who could be given the original recordings by Joseph Taylor to study beforehand. We think the tradition could be carried on in this way, with the immense advantage of modern recording.'

This is the typical Anglosaxon brutality towards art, treating art as subject to passing waves of fashion, & caring more for the material perfection of recording than for the deathless art recorded. This letter brings home to me all the bitterness I felt in England before the war at the treatment handed to

---

12. Grainger describes the Gramophone Co.'s collection of twelve songs sung by Taylor in his article, 'Collecting with the Phonograph', *Journal of the Folk-Song Society*, No. 12 (May 1908), partially reproduced in Teresa Balough, ed., *A Musical Genius from Australia* (Perth: University of Western Australia, 1982), 19–64 (23).

13. English county- or district-based folk-singing competitions.

14. Grainger's excision.

15. (1894–1953), English singer.

16. Perhaps Dale Smith.

Cyril Scott, myself & other geniuses (this English worship of the topical & the commonplace—oblivious to the rare & the lasting) & the effect this bitterness had on my war-actions.

Of course, I think that a man is part of his race & nation, & that his race & nation have a right to call on him for any sacrifice in war, even in a war he may not approve of personally. Of course, I think the Harrogate postcard (1929) was right when it said, 'You white-livered pro-German, what did you do for England in the Great War?'—in all except calling me a pro-German.[17]

I tried to avoid fighting for England because I hated the art-ignoring, genius-crushing, drink-loving, gambling mainstream of English life just as keenly as I loved & worshipped the small minority of rare English talents that inform English art & thot with tenderness & passion. I had no wish to sacrifice myself for a land (not my own, anyway) that sacrifices genius & works of genius so unregrettingly. I understood the wilfulness & uncaringness of the English towards genius & its works (the Joseph Taylor records, for instance), & I made up my mind to reply with my own kind of wilfulness. Not *willingly* (not if I could help it) would I sacrifice my genius (the bloom of the Australian desert) to a lot of suburban bad blood.

Source: 'The London Gramophone Co. (Now 'His Master's Voice') & the Joseph Taylor Folksong Records', in 'Sketches for My Book "The Life of My Mother & Her Son"', W35-89, dated 22 September 1932 (Grainger Museum, Melbourne).

➤ 49   Money Spent on Ideals, Friends, Etc., 1920–End 1923 (ca. 1924)

As a youth I was greatly struck with Cecil Rhodes'[18] saying: 'A man should *be able to afford* his ideals'. I believe in artists paying out of their own purse for the things they hold needful to artistic welfare. Also, I have always believed that the command of the Jewish religion, '10% to charity', is too low a rate of help-for-others. Better is the South-Sea-Island custom cited by R.L. Stevenson in 'A Footnote to History'[19]—'the obligations of a Samoan towards his kin & friends cease only when he can turn to them & say: "I have nothing more to give"'. No, I do not go as far as that. Believing that an idealist should

17. See essay 29.
18. (1853–1902), English-born financier and statesman.
19. Subtitled 'Eight Years of Trouble in Samoa' (1892). Grainger's quotation is not exact.

see to it that he will *be able to afford his ideals* in the future, as well as in the present, I feel that he should always save part of his earnings (say 25%?). But beyond that I feel he should spend *all the rest* on art, or science, on needy friends, on the ideals of gifted friends or fellow artists, & on charity. I have felt this many, many years. But the wish to provide for mother's health & security came before all else. Then my father's ill-health cost me a good deal at various times, & the world war, in various ways, cut into my earnings, so that it is only since 1919[20] that the realization of my ideals has come in sight. Before my darling's death I had begun to realize my ideal of spending part of my earnings on art & on friends & since her death still more so. I feel her heart would be with me in these matters, for she would think it generous of me, & she loved me to be generous. Personally I do not think such things 'generous' at all, but simply one's *absolute duty* as an artist & as a communist.

I do not set much store by 'personality'—by those things wherein one man differs from another. I love the *common ground of art*, the *common ground of humanity*. I love all those things that unite men together, the *craft of art* that binds artists to art, the thought of *one common future*, the thought that *culture* (the storing up & study of records of life & thought & skill) is *the surest form of deathlessness*. Be not surprised that my *gifts to art* are to *artistic friends* rather than to *artistic strangers*. There is more artistic admiration than personal liking at the bottom of my artistic friendships. Others helped (like Aunty Clara & Sigurd Fornander), were very close to my beloved mother or touched me by their loftiness or purity of soul. Soulfulness, feelingfulness, kindliness, skill; all these things make equal calls upon an artist, so it seems to me, for the on-march of artistic culture is along the path of purity, sympathy, inquisitiveness, universality.[21]

Source: 'Money Spent on Ideals, Friends, Etc., 1920–end 1923', in 'Sketches for My Book "The Life of My Mother & Her Son" ', W35-73, undated (probably mid-1924; Grainger Museum, Melbourne).

20. When Grainger was discharged from the U.S. Army and resumed regular concert life.
21. Grainger went on to list, in tabular form, his 'artistic spendings' during this period, including US$600 to support Evald Tang Kristensen's studies of Danish countryside life, $400 to publish musical works by Herman Sandby, costs of rehearsals of his own works in Frankfurt and Amsterdam, various costs relating to the publication of Delius's works and the Delius-Grainger concerts in the United States of April 1924, and the cost of an American rehearsal of his *Hillsong I* in July 1921; production costs of 'beloved mother's photos & book' (1922–23); and his 'human spendings', including support of Clara and Frank Aldridge, Sigurd Fornander, his concert agent Antonia Sawyer ('remembering great kindness, & to help out at hard time', $1,000), Frederick Morse ('remembering great kindness after beloved mother's death', $500), Alexander Lippay ('gifted conductor, Frankfurt', $40), Mimi Pfitzner ('for mountain cure for her sick son', $50), and Professor Bassermann's coal bill (Holland), as well as a five-pound donation to the Frankfurt Conservatory.

➤ 50   [The Centrality of Race] (1933)

Readers will have noted that I un-uplettingly speak of race, & many will think it a blemish that I view all one-bodies ((persons)) as race-full types or as swayed by raceful or landfolksome ((national)) sways. Some readers may have it on their tongue to ask me: Do you never see men as being lone-hand-some ((individualistic)) at heart, even if they show [as] landfolksome, class-ridden & training-swayed on their top layer. I must answer: No. I have never yet met any man or woman who had enough lone-hand-someness in her or him to be worth bothering about. All the men & women I have ever known were clearly the outcome of the raceful, or class-some, or time-stretchsome ((period-given)), or landfolksome ((national)), or god-worshipsome ((religious)), or mindtiltsome ((educational)), or weather-kindsome ((climatic)), or art-some ((artistic)) sways that have beaten down upon them. I was thrashing out this askment ((question)) with a Jew in Jacksonville, Florida, around 1920, and he put this askment to me: If an Italian or Jewish baby were to be brought up amongst Northlandsomeish [Scandinavian] farmers in Minnesota, would he grow up othersome in his heart-stirs, powers, gifts, judgements, manners, to the folk around him? I answered: Maybe not, but how are we ever to find out? When will we find Italians & Jews willing to try farming in Minnesota? Each race [is] still so careful not to allow itself to be caught in the roundringments ((circumstances)) type-true to other races. For these reasons (that I gave that time in Jacksonville) I do not look to come across true lone-handers ((individualists)) in our times. I lean towards believing that all races *might* show the same powers if given the same chances, & I believe hotly in giving all folk the same chances. But as this chance-for-all-dom ((democracy)) has not yet been opened up to the othersome ((different)) races of the world it is idle to look for outcomes ((results)) that could come only from such chances—being long offered, at that.

Source: Untitled section, in 'The Aldridge-Grainger-Ström Saga', W37-91, dated 'Nov. 4?, 1933' (Grainger Museum, Melbourne).

➤ 51   [Pure-Nordic Beauty] (1933)

The outward sign of greatness is beauty—beauty such as the Greeks had, beauty such as the Northmen, the Anglosaxons, the Irish (I am talking only of the white races; otherwise I would count the Negroes among the beauty-having races) have today. Ugly swine such as the French & the Germans (I mean, in the main; I know that a German here & there has the gift of beauty) should not only be ashamed of themselves for their loathesome beautylessness (the sickening shapes of their sculls, their unforgivable trend towards heavy bellies & light legs, the wild mis-even-weightedness ((unbalancedness)) of their part-against-part-metements ((proportions))) but should be twicely ashamed for even daring to make-believe that they, in their now-time state of ugliness, could ever hope to vie with us higher, lovelier races in point of world-leadership, art-giftedness, soultilth ((culture)). Let them sink back where they belong; in the dingy dungeon of mind-tilth ((education)). And all this tweenlandsome gracefulness came out of old Coope's old-time English hotel-door—green felt & brass knobs! But why should we mince matters? Must we Nordics go on *forever* shamming that we *do not know* that we are overmen in beauty, souldepth, spirit-powers? Must we stand by silently forever while the lower races (French, German, Jews) tell us they own powers & gifts that we know they don't? What gain is there to the world in these silent lies of us Nordics? If there is one thing I (as a one-body ((person))) never do, it is to overstate my case. All that I have abovesaid of the higher & lower races is understated, rather than overstated. But my awareness of full beauties (such as the bodily loveliness of the Nordic race, the soulful beauty of our soul-tunes, the frith-barelaying [nature-revealing] beauty of Turner, the life-mastering thot-loveliness of Walt Whitman & Edgar Lee Masters[22]) does not mean that I am blind to half-beauties. I can see that there is much beauty in Gauguin[23] (he is one of my art-sweethearts); but it is mixed with a lower-race ugliness that hinders it from reaching the pure & unalloyed beauty of the best Nordic art. I can see that there is bewitching beauty in Debussy—the beauty of frail tenderness, fleeting sadness, sweetsmelling calm (Debussy has been one of my life's art-loves; amongst other things I introduced his music into 8 lands[24]); but he does not rise to the peaks of Nordic grandness, Nordic understand[ing] of the all-life, the all-frith. There is art-beauty, craft-beauty, in Manet, but it is the beauty of a soul that does not crave the beauty of life, but only the beauty of things (art being, in this sense, a thing). When I come to worth-weigh the over-souls [geniuses] of largely-Nordic lands such as Germany the task becomes harder. It is clear to see that nearly-Nordic (if not quite Nordic) souls of Bach, Wagner & Brahms can, at times, rise to the full

22. (1869–1950), American writer. Grainger personally knew Masters, who dedicated his *Lee, A Dramatic Poem* to Grainger in 1926.
23. Paul Gauguin (1848–1903), French postimpressionist painter and writer. Grainger particularly admired Gauguin's autobiographical *Noa Noa* (1900).
24. Probably meaning Britain, South Africa, Australia, New Zealand, Holland, Denmark, Norway, and Sweden, in all of which Grainger performed during the earlier of his 'London' years.

heights of pure-Nordic beauty. It must be clear to all tone-understanding ears that the Air in Bach's D major room-music [chamber-music] Suite (no. 3) is lovely with full Nordic loveliness—but the bulk of the whole Suite is not; Bach not having a Nordic *standard* of loveliness to live up to. Likewise, it is clear-to-see that outsingled ((certain)) bit-pieces in Wagner (such as most of the Tristan Foreplay [Prelude] & the Good-Friday Tone-Piece[25]) are staggeringly lovely with full Nordic loveliness & oversoulship. But no *whole work* of Wagner's is kept-uply lovely thru-out as is 'The Song of the High Hills'[26] by Delius, the Battle of Brunanburh (8th yearhundredsome Old-English warpoem) or John Jenkins's First Fancy for Viols (in D).[27] It may even be asked if Wagner was even able to carry thru a single bit-piece with unflagging beauty—for there are clearly flaws in the Tristan Foreplay (the gappy, over-&-over-again-nesses of , dull bits (where the spirit-litness has sagged) in the Siegfried Idyll (harped-chord scamperings on the violins) & the Good-Friday Spell Tone-Piece—such saggings, flaggings of the beauty-sense as do not be-blemish the D major Viol Fancy (No. 1) of John Jenkins, the 1st Fancy & Air (G minor) for viols by William Lawes.[28]

There is nearly always a go-gettishness, a rough liveliness, in even the best German tone-art that causes Nordic beauty to fly out of the window. This is not so in the best of Grieg, nor in such Nordic masterpieces as César Franck's chorales for organ. I am forced to own up that there is always the highest type of kept-up beauty (evenweight ((balance)), calm, grandness—everything) in Gabriel Fauré's tone-art, which, while having all the frail, tender beauty that makes Debussy & Ravel so bewitching, also has the claim to full greatness & grandness that Debussy's & Ravel's tone-art lacks; & Fauré could not by any trick of talk-wrestlement ((argument)) be rated a Nordic. I own up to this weak spot (Fauré) in my talk-wrestlement.[29] But barring this out-countedness ((exception)) I stick to my first statement: that beauty is the test of race-some greatness & that the most Nordic races have the most flawless beauty and with it the most utter greatness. And if thinkers on this theme should come to twi-lean ((disagree)) as to the greatness or ungreatness of some of the best German tone-art I [ ][30] ((submit)) that it is because the more-or-less Nordic-

25. From *Parsifal*.
26. For chorus and orchestra (1911–12). See also essays 81 and 91.
27. In 1944, G. Schirmer (New York) published Grainger's edition of this five-part fantasy for modern stringed instruments, based on Arnold Dolmetsch's transcription of the original for viols.
28. Schirmer also published this Grainger-Dolmetsch edition in 1944.
29. Grainger produced piano editions for G. Schirmer of two Fauré songs ('Après un Rêve' and 'Nell') in Grainger's 'Free Settings of Favorite Melodies'.
30. Left blank by Grainger.

ness of the Germans (that of the German oversouls ((geniuses)) outchosenly ((especially)) so) is a moot point. In them the Nordic love of beauty is so strangely mixed with the un-Nordic fainth [fondness] of ugliness (think of all the go-getsome ((energetic)) tone-stretches ((passages)) that mar Bach, & still more so Brahms) that we don't know where we are (in my Australian childhood one of the most widely sung of folk-pleasesome ((popular)) songs was ''E dunno where 'e are'.[31] A joke of that time told of a clergyman seeing the title of this song on a weal-helpsome tone-feast tone-bill-of-fare ((program of a charity concert)) & forth-crying ((announcing)) it as follows: 'Mr Snooks will now sing a song entitled, er—er—"He doesn't know where he is" ').

Before leaving these race-side-matching ((race-comparing)) thots I would like to again state my main standpoint: that while mildmindness & fairness should be the cornerstones of Nordic worthweighment ((criticism)) (by which I mean that we should never draw back from giving quarter-beauty & half-beauty their due), it is our Nordic duty not to falter in worthsundering [distinguishing] part-beauty from full-beauty. An art-work that is only partly beautiful (such as a work that is craft-lovely without being soul-lovely, such as a work that is part-moodfully lovely without being all-moodfully lovely—without rising to all-sidedness, in other words) must never, from a Nordic standpoint, be allowed to vie with a work that is clearly wholly beautiful (lovely in its themes, in its mood, as well as in its handling; lovely in its form as well as in its feeling; lovely & spirit-lit *all thru*). We Nordic artmen must be strict in forcing thru this true weighing of art-worths & in dragging from the holy-pillars they wrongly bestand ((occupy)) such trifler-some, scatter-brained half-oversouls ((half-geniuses)) as Mozart & Beethoven; for if we do not, our world will never get a chance to hear art of our own greatness & book-art, poetry & tone-art will keep on forever being, as they are in the now-time ((at present)), cluttered up with trifling, skittish, shallow, unrounded-off, half-worked-out make-shifts-for-art.

The first step on the right path is to own up to our own greater beauty, wisdom, braininess, oversoulship & let those (of the lower races) as can, disprove it. Above all, let the artmen of the lower races *try*, at least, to rise to the higher standards of our Nordic art (it will do them no harm to 'snap out' of their lazy swollen-headedness, just for once) instead of everlastingly, halfwittedly jabbering & bragging about their own mainly merely fancied art-powers. But none of these things can come to pass until Nordics are willing to hear their own best tone-art, read their best book-art & rime-art [poetry]. But who shall bring them to do this? In the meantime, we cannot ask the artmen

31. Cockney music-hall song, probably from the early 1890s, by Fred Eplett.

of the lower races to judge our Nordic over-art for us, for Goethe was right when he said that a man can only judge of his own greatness—it is laugh-at-able ((absurd)) to think that the lower races can judge of artsome howths [qualities] that are too far above them for them to be able to see at all.

L'Avenir, Nov. 15, 1933

Source: Untitled section, in 'The Aldridge-Grainger-Ström Saga', W37-119 to 37-121 (Grainger Museum, Melbourne).

52   [A Flawlessly Nordic Way of Living] (1933)

I firmly believe that the Nordic races, if left to themselves (if allowed to live their own typetrue Nordic lives without [ ]³² ((interference)) from the lower races that swarm into the Nordic lands because they are greedy after the riches that Nordic hardworkingness has forth-brought—riches which the lazier not-Nordic races are unable to forth-bring on their own, because they are neither clever nor hardworking enough), if kept free from the betempting lure of not-Nordic lines of thot (the sex-lures of Paris & the South Seas, the sex-twisting art of Greece, Rome, India, the sex-upsetting mindsway come of living in lands where not-Nordic slavery, cruelness & chance-for-all-lessness warps our beginsome ((original)) trend of feeling), could at last birth a flawlessly Nordic way of living—a life in which all cruelness, unfairness, unhonestness, strong-feeding-off-weakdom, sponge-guestfulness ((parasitism)), all slavedriving of woman by man, all spoiling of the young by the old, all twisting of sex out of its mean-some ((normal)) birthful instirs, will be outlawed. I can mindpaint for myself the richness, the at-rest-setfulness, the pureness, the freshness, the goodness of such a life. But in order to birth for themselves such an angel-life the Nordics must get rid not only of all the lower races within their gates, but also of all wrong-codeful cocksucking bastards (or should I say [in Danish] 'cunt-licking bastards'?), [in English] like myself, whose mixed blood & mixed lifeslants unfailingly tend to undo the Nordicness of any life we come in touch with. It is true that I worship Nordic charm; but I worship it as a for-eigner worships, finding the pureness & untwistedness of Nordic wholesome-ness wholly nerve-tickling & aback-taking to my be-Greeked, be-Romed, be-

32. Left blank by Grainger.

de Saded,[33] be-savaged, be-heathened, be-arted mind. Mind; if I am a bastard Nordic, I am also a bastard not-Nordic, having wellsprings of Nordic pureness within me as well as gutters of not-Nordic bilge. But the point is: I am no less fond of the bilge than of the wellsprings. If Nordicness wishes to come into its full pure selfhood, it must get rid of bastards ([in Danish] bastards) [in English] like me—it must forbid Nordic English like my mother to mate with largely not-Nordic English like my father. (The race, before it can become worthy of itself, must war not without but within.)

It is hard to believe that I never dipped into Lempriere's Classical Dictionary in the Kilalla years[34]—years when I was so agog about Greece. Yet I must up-own ((admit)) that I cannot factfully *recall* reading Lempriere[35] then. My first clear call-to-mindment of Lempriere is of steeping myself in it in Frankfurt (when living in Grünburgweg[36]), at a time when I already knew of sexfacts & therefore found a great fillip in reading of the daughter who breastfed her father in prison, the maidens who were whipped on the altar of Venus, & the like. Yet what led me to the 'Aenead', if not Lempriere? So mother (or father, or someone) bot [bought] me Virgil's 'Aenead', because I was all-nosey about it, after reading Homer, & after hearing that the Aenead was a forward-carryment of the Odysseus [*sic*]. I was all in a stew to get the book & opened it with eagerness; but it proved a hopethwartment ((disappointment))—I simply could not read it thru—it might have been that the Aenead was given to me at Kilalla[37]—even before father left for England (1891?[38])—or it may have happened much later; it is can't-do-some ((impossible)) for me now to guess how long these childhood art-loves of mine lasted—[as the][39] Greek craze had quite faded away ere the Grettir craze[40] came on, or whether the [ ][41] ((various)) mindstirs stretched across each other in time, so that it is thinkable that I could be delighted to get the Virgil book even after my eyes had been opened to the greater glories of Grettir (as sidematched with the

33. I.e., influenced by French writer and sexual practitioner, the Marquis de Sade (1740–1814).
34. I.e., 1888–92, in Melbourne.
35. Grainger's library holds *A Classical Dictionary* (London: Routledge, n.d. [ca. 1879]) by John Lempriere (ca. 1765–1824).
36. I.e., about 1896–97.
37. Grainger's library (PA2/883:3) contains Alfred John Church's illustrated *Stories from Virgil* (London: Seeley, Jackson & Holliday, 1879), suggesting that Grainger thereby learned his first stories from the *Aeneid*, probably while still living in Melbourne.
38. Correctly, 1890.
39. Word(s) illegible.
40. Grainger's fascination with the character of Grettir the Strong and, more generally, with Icelandic sagas. Grainger elsewhere dates the start of the 'Grettir craze' to ca. 1892.
41. Left blank by Grainger.

Homer type of reading). It seems believable that I got the Flaxman[42] book-eyegays ((illustrations)) before father left for England, as they were just the sort of things he would be keen about & I must say, rightly.

Source: Untitled section, in 'The Aldridge-Grainger-Ström Saga', W37-141 to 37-143, dated 21 November 1933 (Grainger Museum, Melbourne).

⇀53   [The Truly Nordic Life] (1933)

Let this fact be swallowed & mass-treated ((digested)) that I, fated to be Australia's first oversoul-some tonebirther ((composer of genius)) (as far as I know), had to get my first soulwracking mind-prints ((impressions)) of tone-art (my chosen art, or, let us say, the art chosen for me by mother; at any rate, the art I was working at 2 hours a day) a few years later than my first great mindprints of book-art, shape-art, paint-art, pastlore & lust, simply because toneart in Australia was in the hands of twaddling Jews instead of in the hands of worthy men of our own race. We know that the Jews are very unlucky in being so ungifted in toneart—we know that altho the Jews are the most numberful of all the mindtilled ((educated)) races of Europe (races lacking mindtilth may birth lovelier toneart than mindtilled ones, yet it is only the mindtilled races who are able to write down their toneart so that it reaches the big world *with a name built on to it*, & thus is fame-ready) that they (in all European lands put together) have not been able (in the last 100 years) to tonebirth toneart that can be sidematched ((compared)), either in muchness or howth ((quantity or quality)) with the toneart forthbrought by non-Jews in a single land like England, or Norway, or France, whiches land-befolkment ((the population of which)) is much less number-full than that of the Jews in Europe. Or let us put it this way: more Jews are found earning their livings at toneart all over the world than any other race (likely Jews are earning 6 or 10 or 20 times more at toneart than any other single race); more Jews are fame-favored in toneart than any other race; yet the toneart birthed by all these Jewish tonearters all over the world is almost meaningless (in size & goodness) when we come to the highest flights of the art. The Jews are, it seems to me, a very wretched & pityworthy folk in toneart; & I, for one, would be mankindlily sorry for them if they were not dog-in-the-mangering the whole

---

42. John Flaxman (1755–1826), English neoclassical sculptor and draughtsman, particularly famed for his drawings of Homeric themes.

of toneart for us others. The Jews (being factfully in the saddle of toneart) as good as outlaw most of the world's noblest toneart, not because they are harshminded or forejudgeful ((prejudiced)) against it (the typetrue Jew hasn't got guts enough to be harshminded or forejudgeful against anything—these being evil heatkeenths [enthusiasms] of higher races), but because his own Jewish lowness & ungiftedness makes him truly (not shamly) blind to high gifts & howths—Goethe said, 'No man understands any greatness that is beyond his own'. So it is a case of the deaf leading the unhearing—for our Nordics *could* soul-hear (if they could only somehow be brot to believe in themselves enough to try to open their ears & eyes upon the already-happened sunrise of Nordic toneart) while the Jews are simply & hopelessly soul-deaf—after breedlinks ((generations)) of study, straining, & the holding of favored chances. Mind you, I am not saying that the Jew will never rise to the heights in toneart—for I am not one who firmly believes in raceful fore-fatedness or typechangelessness; I am not able to judge of what the Jews *might* do in a more cleverly-planned world than our now-time one. All I say is: let us Nordics, who have already proved our ableness to breed great oversouls, our ableness to forth-bring deathless art, stand-take ((insist)) that the Jews rise to our higher standards of artworths or leave artjobs to us who can do them nobly & at-rest-setfully. All the Jews do, as a rule, is to shame-shock ((scand-alise)) & de-evenweighten ((unbalance)) the world of art with their ungifted outputs—Epstein[43] & Schönberg, for samples. Then how is it (you may ask), if we Nordics are so good & the Jews are so bad at toneart, that the Jews sit cosily inside of the house of paid-for toneart, while we stand jobless & freezing outside? For a very simple reason: the Jews live up to their own Jewish standards loyally & unrankbrokenly; while we Nordics have not yet worked out our own standards of Nordic soul-tilth, but are trying lamely to fit ourselves into a [ ][44] ((system)) irish-stewed together of Jewish godworship, Roman law, Roman warwonts & roundsculled (I wordpoint ((allude)) here to the mean, greedy, rut-minded, swollen-headed, greedy-roundsculled or 'Alpine' racetype[45] that ruins the European mainland—whether in France, Germany, Russia, Italy, or in the Jewry) standputness [conservatism]—a system that does not fit our race-instirs, & never will fit them.

If we Nordics can work out a plan of life in which behestpowerfulness ((authoritiveness)), sale-gain ((profit)), slavedriving, brutalness (such as the

---

43. Probably referring to the sculptor Jacob Epstein (1880–1959).
44. Left blank by Grainger.
45. Grainger refers to the main European racial types, as commonly portrayed in between-the-wars literature: Nordics, Alpines, and Mediterraneans.

slaughtering of tame beasts for food, of men in war) & unkindness are outlawed—a plan of life in which sheer goodness, sheer beauty, sheer workwill-
ingness are worshipped for what they are (& not for the sale-gains or power-
sway they may roundaboutly or haphazardly bring with them)—we shall not
have any more trouble with Jews, or with whatever lower types there may be
within our own races. With the dawn of a justright ((perfectly)) worked-out
Nordic soul-tilth-dom ((culture))—awarely hand-pledged by our Nordic
landfolks ((nations)) as clearly & unmistakably as the setupment of mindtilth
[education], or the uprootment of murder or wifebeating, is handpledged by
our white man's townskillth ((civilisation))—the lower types (whether Jews or
the lower types in our own landfolks) will scamper away from our lands as rats
leave a sinking ship—as foreigners have been leaving America during 'this
thing'—the meansome American man's term from the now-time ((present))
bad times (('depression'—what Calvin Coolidge,[46] in one of his newspaper
writs, termed 'a slight trade retrogression')). We fine-type Nordics (I am not
saying that all Nordics are fine-typed—it will be one of the tasks of the near-
to-come to table-list & study-out the hows and the how-manys of this askment)—whether we are born in England, America, Ireland, The Northlands,
Australia, Russia, Germany, Holland, France, a.s.o.—have standard tastes &
cravings; we are alike in the sort of things we crave of ourselves, of others, of
life & of art—just as fine-type Jews have standard tastes & cravings. But while
the Jews are made (by the training given them by their birthgivers [parents] or
other kin) aware of Jewish standards & how to live up to them, we Nordics
waste much (if not all) of our lives in wondering and blundering—because
our standards & cravings are not table-listed ((tabulated)) or otherwise forth-
shown ((manifested)) to us. As far as our self-unaware instirs beable ((enable))
us to do so, we Nordics live Nordicly—that is, as far as our not-Nordic laws,
wonts, beliefs & mindsways allow us to.

If we Nordics could get to know the great art-works of our race (Grettir,
Beowulf, Kipling's poems, Walt Whitman, E. L. Masters, Norman Lindsay's[47]
paintings, the best Nordic toneart) maybe it would help us to lead a truly
Nordic life; but reading the Bible, or books about the Bible, Homer, Dante,
listening to Italian or Austrian tone-plays ((operas)), studying Greek & Latin,
& spending one's holiday (lifelong or otherwise) on the Riviera & in the

---

46. (1872–1933), Republican president of the United States between 1923 and 1929.
47. (1879–1969), Australian writer and artist. Grainger visited Lindsay in Sydney in the following
    year, 1934. In 1938, Lindsay presented Grainger with fourteen original etchings. In his essay of
    1943, 'The Specialist and the All-Round Man', Grainger held up Lindsay, along with Arnold
    Dolmetsch and Cyril Scott, as an exemplar of 'all-roundedness'. See Gillies and Clunies Ross,
    eds., *Grainger on Music*, 312–17.

South of France will not help us to lead a truly Nordic life. What is a truly Nordic life, as I see it?

1. to care as little as maybe for one's fate
2. to worship the frith ((nature)), in-reckoned all mankindsome feelings & instirs
3. to dream daydreams not drink-dreams
4. to care nothing for money, power, safeness, fame, comfyness, save as they are able to help the needy, forthsay truths, uphold beauty & goodness & help one to work hard
5. to ask no gain from one's gifts, one's work, one's ideas
6. to altar-slay ((sacrifice)) (if need be) one's health & wealth on the altar of lust, knowhunger ((inquisitiveness)), beenthrusomeness ((experience))
7. to trust all instirs, one's own or other folks'
8. to live for the race & for mankind, counting all other aims not-worth-while
9. to overwork, insofar as it beweels ((benefits)) forwardstridement ((progress)); to loafe, insofar as it furthers daydreaming, thereby beweels forwardstridement
10. to outlaw all hatred, fightlust, honorgreed ((ambition)), pompfaith, loveselfishness ((jealousy)), onebodysome ((personal)) feeling, fightwint[h]-worship ((worship of success)) as useless & upcluttersome leavings of the past
11. to honor no gifts or skills or work powers that ask a return, a gain, or sale-gain ((profit)) for what they give
12. to give to each man what he needs or wants, not what he earns
13. to distrust all forms of god-worship, right-codeth ((morality)), standputness ((conservativeness)), wont-boundness ((habitualness)) or thwartsome ((contrary)) to the unsetness ((irregularity)) & untrammeledness of the frith [nature]
14. to kill off the unfit, as soon as Nordic mankind is so far forwardstridden as to be sure that no killings are sought on greedy, selfish or hatefraught grounds
15. to set no pride in sloth or workbefreedness (always outcounted such loafing as is needed for fruitful day-dreaming)
16. to set no pride in hardship, rather than in ease
17. to honor art, knowlore & outtryth ((experimentation)), as long as they bring, thereby, no gain of power or ease to those following these mindstirs ((interests))
18. to set up mindtilthsome gear for the spreading of knowledge or selfawareness about Nordic racetype, feelings, howths, aims, standards—but to always be ready to fairly judge & worthweight the claims, deeds & howths of other races
19. to hinder the breeding of Nordics with other races (such as the mating of my mother with my father, with such bastard outcomes as myself) until the whole matter of racesome howths & ablenesses have been thoroly tested & bethot & befelt widespreadly by Nordics; to bend & change the Nordic views about breeding & tweenbreeding according to the proofs or near-proofs come at by ample outtryth ((experimentation)) & thotoutness
20. to plan against town living, as sundering mankind too far from the frith ((nature)); to plan country living as leading towards beauty, heroicness & goodness

21. to get rid of low jobs (such as butchering, deepdrainage), as forthbringsome of low types of mankind

22. to honor all yea-some hungers ((positive appetites)) & look askance at all nay-some dog-in-the-mangerness

23. to make far-sundered laws for breeding & sexlust—breeding to be viewed with its bearing on the race, sexlust to be freely viewed because of its linked-upness with soultilth, frithstirs & joyworship

24. to out-law from our Nordic lands all Jews & all other races that seem to us to upset or hinder the setupth ((establishment)) & unfoldment of flawless Nordic living, beauty, standards, art, soultilth, a.s.o. In thus getting rid of the lower races there should be no hurriedness, no harshness, no meanness. The thing should be done givewillingly, on the grandest scale thinkable. Nordics do not need easy weatherkinds or pampering roundringments—but maybe the lower races do; it is for them to say. In any case, set aside for the lower races the richest, finest, most wishworthy ((desirable)) landstretch in the land. If in America, set aside the whole of New York State, or the whole of California, or the whole of Texas, for the Jews—but see to it that they go there & stay there; at least, see to it that they don't darken the Nordic parts of our land with their ugly faces, nasty thots & foul body shapes. Overwhelm them with makeupments ((recompenses)) in money or goods for whatever they may lose thru being uprooted & outlawed. Give them long warning ahead. Do the thing gently & properly. The lower races will welcome whatever they can make out of the deal ((the outlawry)); on the other hand, no true Nordic should care how much he gives away to the lower races, since no true Nordic cares about power, money, ownership, ease, gains. Then let us set our house in order—kill off the sick, the nasty, the ugly, the lazy; honor those that are lovely to the eye, those that are gifted, learning, workfain, outfindsome, thotbirthful, artbirthful, kindly, knowlorefain. Let us tear out all the cancers that maim our beauty, our health, our goodness. And let sundry landstretches be given over to sundry outtryths: in one landstretch fruitfeeding will be outtried; in another grainfeeding; in another womanlessness, with buggery as sexwont; in another manlessness, with lesbianness as sexwont; in another utter freedom for murder & all other crimes, to see how it works out; in one landstretch only artgifted types will be allowed; in another no artfain types allowed; in another only sportskillsmen allowed; and so on. With sundry landstretches given over to sundry outtryths faring would be worthwhile, for there would be othersome modes of living to be seen in othersome places (instead of, as now, reading the same mass-sold ((syndicalized)) jokes in the newspapers over a vast mainland).

25. If, on the other hand, the Nordics find that they can live their own Nordic life, breed their own Nordic types, think their own Nordic thots & joy-quaff their own Nordic art in spite of having Jews & other lower races all round them, then there is no need to outlaw the Jews or other [non-]Nordic races. For my own

part, however, I must say this: I am able to do my own work in spite of the Jews; I am able to job-strive ((compete professionally)) against the Jews & get on all-right; but I cannot be *happy* when I see their ugly forms & faces. And I look upon happiness as the test of all things.

L'Avenir, Sund. Dec. 3, 1933

Source: Untitled section, in 'The Aldridge-Grainger-Ström Saga', W37-173 to 37-177 (Grainger Museum, Melbourne).

⟩ 54   The Thots I Think as I Grow Old (1937)

These are the thots I always think nowadays—now that I am nearly old,[48] near the time when it is likely I will die: I walk towards Denton, Cottier & Daniels (music store; Steinway agents) in Buffalo[49] (in order to get in as much piano practice as I may; when I am in the thick of concerts, I try to travel by night & practise by day: thus if I am headed for Duluth, Minn., from New York, I take a night train from New York to Buffalo, spend the day at D. C. & Ds in Buffalo practising, take a night train from Buffalo to Chicago, spend the day practising at Lyon & Healy's, Chicago,[50] take a night train from Chicago to Duluth) & I think: 'say that I come to Buffalo to practise like this once a season; I may come 5 times more, or 10 times more, or even 15 times more—but if 15 times more I will be 70, beyond the age when man, as a rule, writes masterpieces. If I come 5 times, 6 times, more, I will be as old as my mother when she died. Already I am older than she was when we came to New York. Yet how much younger I feel, & how much older I feel, than I think she felt then. Time is closing in on me, with my masterworks unwritten.' These are the thots I think, unless Ella is by me to dispel my gloom, or other nice mindstirs keep my thots off myself, my failures, my guilt.

Mar. 25, 1937

Source: 'The Thots I Think as I Grow Old', in 'Thots and Call-to-Mindments', p. [15] (Grainger Museum, Melbourne).

48. Grainger was fifty-four years old.
49. On Court Street.
50. Music firm on Jackson Boulevard, established in the 1860s.

⇒55   [Fraud with Food, Fraud with Hair] (1938)

All this[51] goes to show that our great fat white slobs are as gross, as coarse, as greedy, as swinish as they look—which (for sample) the Chinese & Japanese are not. This hoggish yearning for proteins—eggs, meats, nuts—& up-pepping spices![52] Can they never wait till they are hungry? This belief in fraud & trickery—fraud with food, fraud with hair. Why cannot Miss Leeds answer the boy:[53] 'You ought to be glad you come of a noble Celtic family that greys early. It is noble to reach for the grave before yr time. It is low to cling on to life with such zest!' We laugh at 'natives' who eat cow dung as cures, but what could be more filthy than tea-juice slopped over greased hair? And sulphur too! Thank god I always have plenty of monotony in all my serious music. Let food, music, sex, life test our hunger. Let all things be done to reward the stick-to-itive [persistent], deeply hungry man & to punish the man of shallow hunger, shallow zest. Let nothing be done to eke false hunger, but everything to sift the robust (hungry, lustful) man from the sissies. This is what I mean by Australian-ness.

July 18, 1938, Honolulu

Source: Untitled section, in 'Thots and Call-to-Mindments', p. [27] (Grainger Museum, Melbourne).

⇒56   Growing Nasty-Spoken as I Near My Sixties (1940)

By the time I am 60 I hope I will be quite sour-mouthed, when it is called for. I am working up for this as chances to whet my tongue come my way. On the way down to San Antonio the German first horn from Dallas joined my train & found me blue-print-writing the 1st Horn part of the Wind-Choir dishup

51. Grainger was commenting on three newspaper cuttings, reproduced on pp. [26] and [27]: Miriam Jackson, 'If Family Interest in Daily Fare Lags Then the "Same Old Thing" Won't Do', *Honolulu Advertiser*, 15 July 1938; another of apparently similar origin entitled, 'Relieve Menu Monotony with Delicious Dessert'; and Miss Leeds' personal advice column, dealing on that day with 'Graying in the Teens'. On several of the dessert recipes, Grainger has overwritten 'result: *muck*' or simply '*muck*'.

52. In an article, 'How I Became a Meat-Shunner', in the *American Vegetarian* (vol. 4 [1946], 4), Grainger explained how, from an early age, he had been concerned with the killing of animals. In 1924, he had committed to vegetarianism and had never since experienced a real cold. 'Now, at the age of 64, nothing seems to weary or discourage me; and I can work 16 hours a day, every day, and never want a change or a holiday.'

53. Miss Leeds's correspondent 'Joe' was only eighteen.

[arrangement] of my *Walking Tune*.[54] Meaning (I guess) to be jolly (but why sh[ou]ld he be jolly with me—a tone-birther—when he is only a horn-blower?), he said, 'I hope you'll write something that will be worth playing'. I said, 'It's usually considered so. But that's for me to say, whether it's worth-while, or not.' But he didn't understand me, or didn't want to seem to under-stand me. Nudging my ribs (as much to say, 'I'm yr friend', or 'you under-stand my little joke', I guess), he said, 'The horn part, I mean! I'm the horn player, you know.' Blindmeaning his nudging, I said, 'I know. But it's for me to judge whether what I'm writing is worthwhile or not. I'm not writing for other people's approval. I'm writing to please myself.' Silence. Afterwards, he was very much 'my man', running afar for me in 'Handel in the Strand', & quite red in the face with pleasedness, & again nudging me with well deemth ((approval)) at my loud playing of 'Handel'. All of which he would have done in any case, most likely.

He just likes me & my doings, in his uncouth German way. And I, in my cold-hearted, proud English way, cannot help my back arching against his well-meant heartiness. We are all queer sticks. We are riled with those who like us & would fain woo those who are deaf to us.

Just now, as I got into this train, after showing my ticket (St Louis to White Plains—the end of a White Plains–San Antonio–White Plains ticket) to the man at the day-coach door, I must have put it back wrongly into my pocket, so that it fell out as I was looking for a seat. When the ticket gatherer came round it was nowhere to be found. He started getting untholesome [im-patient], started raising his voice. I said, 'I would rather pay for another ticket to New York than have you get impatient'. 'You just look for that ticket thoroly & you'll find it' (in a loud voice). I said, 'don't raise your voice to me. I'd sooner pay for the ticket again than listen to you raise yr voice'. So he calmed down. In a little while he came back, the ticket having been found in the streamlined-chair car, where I went before finding this nearly empty old-style day coach. He said, 'You should take better care of your ticket', and so on. An hour later he came back & said, 'You were mighty lucky, to get yr ticket back like that'. I said (working up to my 60-year-old sour mouth), 'I don't care if I'm lucky or not. If I make mistakes, I'm quite willing to pay for them. What I don't want is, I don't want a lot of advice.' 'You mean, you've got plenty of money. Well, any man's lucky if he's got plenty of money.' 'I'm not saying whether I've got plenty of money or not. I don't care a straw about money. What I don't like is a lot of advice.' But is all this any good?

54. Scoring for 'wind choir of the symphony orchestra' (1940) of a tune originally conceived on Grainger's 1900 tour of the Scottish Highlands.

Later. He keeps coming back & talking to me, reding [advising] me to use 2 seats—spread my feet out, & otherwise shedding friendly, kindly talk. In fact, I seem to be the only one in the car that he does want to talk to. (That calls to mind, many years ago, when I was busy writing toneart [music] in a train, with a child hovering round, I overheard a woman say: 'That man never speaks to that child. But he's the only person in the train the child takes any stock in'.) Maybe the old man is just deaf, raised his voice because he's deaf, & didn't mind what I said to him, because he didn't rightly hear what I said. Or maybe he's just a friendly old man, liking to give good fatherly redes & not caring what he gets back.

Dec. 20, 1940

Source: 'Growing Nasty-Spoken as I Near My Sixties', in 'Deemths ((Opinions)) Book 1', section 4 (Grainger Museum, Melbourne).

57   Put-Upon Percy (1945)

Out of all my grumble-shouts ((protests)) about my wretched life as a folk-wise ((public)) piano-player, as a teacher (for I have loathed teaching even more than tone-show-giving), as a money-helper of kinsfolk & friends (for it does not suit my selfish self-hubbed being-type), it clearly hatches-out that I have been 'put-upon Percy'. And in the matter of being a 'loving son' (not in being a 'good son', for I always liked to behave well—that is deedfitly, help-fully, thoughtful-of-others—there is no hardship in that) I was out-singled-ly put-upon. For if there is anything I hate it is *needless love*, & I deem the love for a mother, [or] love of a husband for a wife needless.[55] The love of a mother for a child—while it is quite quite young—is all right. Life-needs crave it. But afterwards, as he becomes a youth & a grown man, it is just a silly time-lag, a time-mis-fit. But love of a son for a mother is pure non-sense, & would never be held by any mother other than by harsh boss-ment. When the son is very young the mother is just a kill-joy—however needful this joy-kill-ment may be (for sample, not letting her son play near a sheer-hill ((precipice))). Later on the mother (the best mother in the world) is just a drag-anchor.

As for mother's & my case, I want to do just-hood to it—it is very easy to get such a case twisted. My mother was a fair-to-see, clever, feeling-rich, spirit-lit being—a kind of oversoul [genius]. I worshipped her for her high how-ths

55. Grainger has here illegibly overwritten some further words.

((qualities)), for the fun it was to live with her. As a fellow-Australian, as a fellow-agin-the-law-man, as a fellow-art-man, I always *took her side*, in my own heart. This had nothing to do with love, or sonliness. Her puzzle-tasks, & my puzzle-tasks (or, let us say: hers because of the queerness of mine) took clear & merciless thinking. And both mother & I had the gift to think merci-lessly. Therefore, we made a good team.

It may be that most people are more all-round or many-sided than I am & that, because of that, they fit better into the give-&-take of life than I do. I *seem* to like walking, boating, bodily chores. But I guess that I couldn't have stood much of it, & that I have never really been cut out for an out-door life. I get a mighty thrill out of seeing the sea, the hills, the country. But one can hardly earn one's way out of such thrills. The things I like best in life (maybe it should say: the *only* things I love keenly) are: hearing my own tone-works & some other tone-works, & sex-madness (under which must be classed the books dealing with such sex-acts & sex-thoughts as kindle me[56]). Slightly less I like the following: reading books, seeing paintings, studying theed-speeches ((languages)). Friendship means something to me only if the friend births art-works that thrill me. Otherwise, I don't know what friendship means. Like-wise, with my kinsfolk: I care for them only if they show how-ths that strike me as art-typed. I have some feeling for Uncle Ted, because I worthprize his pencil drawing of the farm in Adelaide (was it Angas Street?). I had some lik-ing for Aunty Clara because she talked about her kin, not as a wontsome woman (not as a limb of rut-thinking mankind-as-it-is), but as a hap-lore-ist ((historian)).

I was happy with my mother because the art we shared (tone-art, reading-aloud, talk-life) filled my life with happiness. The other things that made up her life (her now-&-then-friendliness toward sundry folk, her wish to see me do well in life, & her great love for me) I did not care about—simply because love, friendship, well-off-ness are not things that happen to reach me. Her boss-ment of me made me angry at times, outsingledly when she slapped my face, or otherwise hurt my pride. Yet none of this wounded my soul, partly because I rather like boss-ment & selfishness in those I look up to, & partly because I am not a brave man who sets store in 'keeping his end up'. After all, she was a fellow art-lover, & she stood (like me) against the powers that be.

The puzzle-task before my mother & me was this: one cannot earn one's living merely by hearing one's toneworks forth-sounded, or by having sex-bouts of queer, un-rutworn types, or by joy-quaffing reading the Icelandic sagas & the Anglosaxon Chronicle. To earn one's living one must bend oneself

56. See essay 59.

to things that mind-stir more people than do the things I happen to like. So mother's task was clear: to keep me out of sex-acts that would land me in gaol or make me too shameful in the folk-eye to keep me pegging away at my hated piano, & to shape my fame so it would be bright enough to easy-make the forth-soundments of my toneworks that meant most of everything to me. To bring all this about I had to be foully 'put upon'—in that my time for tone-wrighting had to be narrowed with a view to earning, in that my sex-life had to be curbed. Since her death I have allowed myself to be further put-upon, in sundry ways. I choose to make Fornander[57] a mill-stone round my neck—but then: he has some hap-lore-sense [historical sense] like Aunty Clara.[58] The other ones that have cumbered me have either been art-men (over-souls), or a speech-betterer like Robert Atkinson.[59] I have willingly been 'put upon', both in my mother's time, & since, because [of] the branches of life (money, honor-slurs, dis-comfi-nesses of sundry sorts, such as dirty hotels & broken sleep) that don't happen to mean a thing to me. I have never bowed the knee, or tempered the wind, in those branches of life that are all-meaningful & life-giving to me. It is easy to see why most of my toneworks for strings-&-wind-band don't lure time-beaters [conductors]—works with undowithoutable organ parts & unwonted bell-work are a fruitless bother to them. But I like to hear organ with string-&-wind-band, so I keep on writing for it. When the hour strikes when I *do* hear a piece of mine forthsounded, I want to hear in it all the trappings that be-rich it for *my* ears. I cast all earning-ness, all fame, all fight-win aside in order to make my own one-body-some joy in the hearing as flawless as may be. So it stands to reason that I have to wait long to get my own choice hope-fulfillment: the forth-playment of a work, written only to please myself, forthsounded in a way to thoroughly please me.

Likewise in the matters of sex I have not been willing to put up with half-happinesses. I have not wanted children, or a breed-group ((family)) life. I have not been willing to blunt the keenness of my sex-joys in the rut-paths of wontsome wedlock. In my wedlock (as in my tone-birth life) I have had heav-enly happiness—nothing less, nothing else. I feel utterly at one with my wife in world-thoughts, art-stirs (outsingledly have I joy-quaffed her straight-forward tone-jobs for me) & sex-deemths. I have been wholly hope-fulfilled in even those sex-dreams least likely to be real-known. So I have not been 'put

57. Grainger had supported Fornander, at least since the early 1920s. See essay 49. Fornander died during this year, 1945.
58. Clara Aldridge had died during 1944.
59. The development of whose never-completed book, *Our Mothertongue*, Grainger was subsidising.

upon' in those things that are life & death to me. As to the things I do not real-feel; in them I have always been willing to be put upon.

[on train] Arizona, July 17, 1945

Source: 'Put-Upon Percy', in 'Ere-I-Forget', 384-33 (Grainger Museum, Melbourne).

58   The Things I Dislike (1954)

Almost everything. First of all foreigners, which means: all Europeans except the British, the Scandinavians & the Dutch. In other words, I hate all white men who gesticulate, shrug shoulders, who add 'expression' to their speech. I dislike many things in the 'white men' mentioned above (British, Scands, Dutch) but I do not utterly despise them. But if any of these white men mention a foreigner (such as Schiller, Einstein, Kreisler, Toscanini, Casals) all my happiness goes. I do not hate 'natives' (Negroes, Greenlanders, Filipinos, Japanese) as I do foreigners. But I might if I knew them better. All my happiness goes if rival musicians (Alban Berg, Aaron Copland, Prokoffieff [Prokofiev]) are mentioned. But I do not mind the 'great' composers being mentioned, except those whose music I especially hate: Haydn, Mozart, Beethoven. I am not jealous of living popular, or half-popular, composers such as Roy Anderson,[60] Cole Porter, Eric Coates.[61] In any case, I do not dislike any 'white-man' composer, even if I do not like his music. I dislike all fame, including my own. It was one of the many delightfulnesses of my wife, when I met her on the 'Aorangi' in 1926, that she didn't know who I was. I dislike everything about myself (my front face, my side face, my tiresome hair, the sound of my voice) except my compositions, my naked body, my 'blue-eyed English'.

I like the way many things (sandy earth, grey skies, children's faces & limbs) *look* in nature, but I hate the way they function: birth, death, self-confidence, sex-instincts, kill-lust, self-assertion, fawn-fainth, etc.). I could never be happy 'living close to nature'. I could never be happy as a farmer, a sailor, a fisherman, just as I cannot be happy as a performer. To know that audiences (which I hate) are looking at me disgusts & appalls me. I was happy in the army, because I was in a little back-water of the army, further away

60. Leroy Anderson (1908–75), American composer of popular music.
61. (1886–1957), English composer in eclectic styles.

from fighting & killing than any civilian, & also because my rank was low, & because fame-mongerers left me alone for the moment. I don't mind signing autographs, because it is such a lowly, plodding job & happens speechlessly. I hate all mention of my past ('I heard you in Boston 36 years ago', 'I knew your mother in New York').

I would have enjoyed playing the piano if I could have done it with even a reasonable amount of skill & accuracy. If I could have played with the facility of any of my advanced pupils (Kitty Eisdell,[62] Mrs Forrest,[63] Ralph Dobbs[64]) I would have loved to play the Schumann concerto, the G major Beethoven concerto, the 2 Chopin concertos, the Beethoven 'Emperor' concerto, 2 of the Rachmaninoff concertos.[65] And there are many pieces by Henry Cowell,[66] Cyril Scott, Debussy, Ravel, Schumann, Bach, Scarlatti I would have relished playing if I could have done it reasonably well. I do not hate the music of foreigners like I hate the foreigners themselves. Nor do I feel any difference between the music of Jews (Mendelssohn, Bizet, Gershwin), supposed-to-be-Jews (Delius, Rachmaninoff, Tchaikovsky, Wagner) & non-Jews. I am not fond of the orchestra (as a medium for my music) but I usually feel fairly at home (or wholly at home) in conducting orchestras. The same is true of bands. Chorus (a cappella, or with chamber music cooperation) I like best of all forms of music, but I usually feel very ill-at-ease & incapable when conducting choruses. Why all this is so, I don't know.

On the whole I have not liked my music-teachers or felt I learnt anything worthwhile from them. But this was not so as a young child. I cannot remember disliking practising while my mother sat beside me 2 hours a day ([aged] 6 to 10). I disliked my harmony lessons with Hertz[67] in Melbourne (aged 8?) & thought him an idiot. I loved Louis Pabst's playing of Bach & his teaching me Bach (age 10?),[68] but when he gave me pieces by Grieg & Chopin I lost confidence & interest. (I did not like his behavior to me when he & his wife & someone else played a Bach double-concerto at the Melbourne 'Risvegliato'.[69] I saw him & his sweet wife enter & I ran ahead & caught up with him, to greet him whom I loved. But he brushed me aside & took no notice of me because he was nervous about his pending performance

62. (1889–1971), née Parker, Australian pianist, student of Grainger's from 1909.
63. Grainger's student at Chicago Musical College, ca. 1920.
64. Grainger's student at Chicago Musical College in the mid–late 1920s.
65. Grainger did perform some of these concertos, including both the Schumann A minor and Beethoven G major concertos, during his London years.
66. (1897–1965), American composer and, in 1940–41, Grainger's 'musical secretary'.
67. Julius Herz, singing pedagogue and conductor of the Liedertafel Choir in Melbourne.
68. During 1892–94.
69. A concert series run by Pabst and his wife.

of the Bach concerto.) I disliked studying with James Kwast (1895–1902) & with Busoni, particularly the latter.[70]

I think that a great deal of my unhappiness in playing, teaching, rehearsing, etc. goes back to my bodily weakness. In my early years as a grown-up pianist I used to get worn out during my public appearances & feared I could not keep going to the end. Especially when playing concertos with orchestras I felt feeble & inadequate. As an old man all this sense of weakness (when playing) has left me. In teaching I felt unspeakably weary, as well as bored. But I could always compose all day without the least feeling of weakness & I always felt I could run & walk forever.

I suppose that most of my troubles in life lay in 'dealing with people'. Yet not in dealing with *all* people, for I always felt my mother was *right* (just clear-seeing, truth-speaking, generous, forgiving, help-fain) tho I was often riled by her tyrannic presentation of her point of view. Ella & I have always got on perfectly, because (there again) all her attitudes seem to [be] based on truth, generosity, joy-in-life & commonsense. I always enjoyed Evald Tang Kristensen, because he seemed to be exactly what a great man & cultural-custodian-of-the-race should be. Delius behaved like a genius always & I never had any trouble with him. Ella's kinswoman Elsie[71] seems to me human (free, relaxed, sweet-natured, intuitive) thru & thru, & so did my dear old Swedish friend Sigurd Fornander & my New Zealand friend Alfred Knox.[72] I have got on well with several old women (Aunty Clara, Sandby's mother, Mimi's mother, Ella's mother, Tant Ström,[73] Fru Jensen Post, Fru E. T. Kristensen) finding them quite un-mad & sweet company. Herman Sandby has always been a true friend with whom I was always at ease & happy. I got on well with all my old folksingers in England & Denmark & revered them as fearless, graceful, original, generous & amusing individuals. There has never been a shadow of disagreement between me & Burnett Cross[74] in all our work on the Free Music tone-tools [instruments], his imitation of folksingers ('Old William Taylor') & his copying of gramophone records. In all these cases (beginning with my mother, above) I have not felt overwhelmed with human folly or human stubbornness nor thwarted by mankind's inability to think & feel for human progress.

70. See essay 106.
71. Elsa Bristow.
72. Alfred J. Knocks (1849–1925), whom Grainger had come to know during his 1909 visit to New Zealand. See, further, essay 81.
73. Ella Ström's adopted mother.
74. (1914–96), American physicist and publisher. Cross worked with Grainger on these machines in the later 1940s and 1950s.

But these things (just mentioned) that I have not disliked make up only a tiny (almost non-existent) part of my life. Most of my life has been spent with dislikable or un-deal-with-able people who appear to me to have behaved like madmen, utterly oblivious to the future of mankind & their own well-being. That a sweet & well-meaning genius like Cyril Scott should be taken in by the Yogi business is utterly beyond me to grasp. That a great-hearted & gifted man like Balfour Gardiner should be so unhappy in his musical life as to leave works like his English Dance,[75] Philomela,[76] Dream-Tryst,[77] April[78] unperformed is sheer craziness. My sweethearts (most of them) appear to me quite as mad as the composers. That they should allow old-fangled morality to upset their sexual happiness seems unbelievable. Equally unbelievable is that parents will allow their sons to become soldiers & that children are willing to leave the parental home in order to start a new life with some sweetheart.

That people are so gross as to gorge themselves into fatness; that they develop bad habits like smoking & drinking; that nations allow the cleavage between themselves & their recent allies to degenerate into atom-bomb thoughts; that the greed of the middle classes is such as to force a kind of class-hatred on their working people; that thousands of people are continually employed raising, tending & slaughtering armies of animals; that music-lovers are so dominated by ambitions as to turn so lovely an art as music into a weapon in the class-wars; that parents can be so cruel as to sacrifice the happiness & health of their children to moral superstitions; that all Europeans except the Icelanders ruin their languages by a senseless & slavish preference for Greek & Latin words & roots; that home-makers prefer lawns to underbrush; that women (the unfunny ½ of the population) should set their pride in clothes, shoes, hairdos, that make them look exotic & laughable; that cities waste their money on symphony orchestras when large chamber music would suit their needs & resources much better; that all our lives are jeopardised by fast automobiles, fast trains, fast buses; that English-speakers (& copying them, the whole white man's world, eventually) admire white bread & despise the good brown breads; that tastiness is preferred to foodiness in foods; that most people prefer magazines to books; that even 'clever' people prefer sociability to work; that people believe in education but not in talent & genius; that people's selfworship is such that [they] are drawn to popular things & people, & not to those things that tear apart & let in light; for all these reasons people at large seem to me hate-worthy & association with them unbearably boring & a wicked waste of time. How can one put one's

75. (1904), for orchestra, dedicated to Grainger; first performed at the 1904 Queen's Hall Proms.
76. (1923), for tenor, women's voice, and orchestra; first performed on 4–5 May 1955.
77. (1902), for baritone and orchestra and composed afresh in 1909; apparently unperformed in either version.
78. (1911), for chorus and orchestra; first performed on 3 December 1913 in London.

finger on the cancer that creates all these evils? What is the central sin? Is it not that most people are too humble, too unpatriotic, too self-destructive? They would not inject foreign words into their language if they were proud of it. They would not overload their music programs with foreign music unless they undervalued their own music. The women would not dress funny & exotic unless they despised themselves for being sweet & straightforward. Nations would not go to war unless their disgusting modesty made them convinced of their inability to succeed peaceably. People would not be sexually moral unless they regarded all their natural inner stirs as foul & dangerous. In other words, religion is the ruination of life. All our dark & needless belief in sin stems from religion, while our disastrous ambitions stem from the fighting spirit of the Old Testament. The world of modern doctoring, modern machines, modern art, modern amorality would be just paradise if we could only shed the blight of religion. As long as men are religious, moral, ambitious, meat-eating & war-like I shall regard every moment spent with them as a shameful waste of time. And I shall welcome every calamity, defeat & loss-of-face that may befall them.

[on train] August 1, 1954 Chicago → N. York

It is true that in my life almost everything has happened as it shouldn't have. This is due to my having behaved badly to others, & others having behaved badly to me.

Take the case of Edgar Lee Masters. As soon as I saw 'Spoon River Anthology'[79] I knew him for the genius he was. And he recognised my genius all right. With each recognising the other's genius, here (one would think) the stage was set for perfect just-rightness of behaviour on both's part. Yet what happened? He wanted me to set the Spoon River tune; I wanted to set it. And I set it splendidly & he thought it splendid. It was published in a practical manner: for elastic scoring & also for piano solo.[80] And I programmed it continually, in both forms. And it became Ella's very best bells-show-off piece.[81] Here (one would think) he could hardly fail to earn a bit. But no. Today Spoon River is beginning to be done steadily by orchestras—maybe as much as Shepherd's Hey or Mock Morris. But not in Masters's time, despite my playing it so much. Here one cannot say that Masters failed to behave well to me, or I to him. The public was too slow to catch on during Masters's lifetime,

---

79. (1914–15), a series of epitaphs in free verse.
80. Grainger's American Folk-Music Settings Nos. 1–3, published by G. Schirmer (New York) as a piano solo in 1923 (No. 1), for elastic scoring in 1930 (No. 2), and for two pianos (four hands) in 1932 (No. 3). The original fiddle tune had been sent on to Grainger by Masters in ca. 1915.
81. I.e., for Ella Grainger in playing staff bells as part of the 'tuneful percussion' ensemble in this 'elastic' setting. For 'elastic scoring', see essay 76.

that was all. Then there was the case of the blind Negro pianist. (This was after mother's death & before I met Ella. So there was 'no female fingers in my woof of life'[82] involved in this case.) Masters invited me to dine with him, or spend the evening with him, in New York. I was looking forward to a 2-genius chat about his poems, or a 2-fold tongue-chastisement of life. But when I got there I found he wanted me to meet & hear a blind Negro pianist. Also that Masters was Chopin-mad & wanted me to play Chopin numbers I did not know, or couldn't remember. (One of the wretchedest things in my life has been being asked to play, 'standard repertory' piano pieces I had never learned or couldn't remember—with my wretched memory.) To meet & hear pianists (even if they are blind & Negro) is sheer agony to me. In this case, I suppose I behaved very badly. I shammed sickness & left Masters high & dry. Ella always behaved well to Masters—liked him, liked to hear him read his poems (which I didn't. I hate anything personal in art—the poet's voice, the composer's improvisation. I like art to be printed & be damned to you) & took me sometimes to the Hotel Chelsea (New York)[83] to see him. But I neglected him shamefully in his last years, when he was in the poets' home near Philadelphia.[84] I could so easily have gone there—it [was] so nearby! But I didn't (also I didn't know it was so nearby & get-at-able). And if I behaved badly to Masters, whom should I behave well to? I *quite* understood the size of his genius & no art ever meant more to me than his at times. After mother's death his novel *Children of the Market Place*[85] was a life-saving soul-cure, personally directed at me. It made me cry buckets, it brought me unbelievable relief. I don't suppose any man or woman in this wide world knew his after-Spoon-River-Anthology volumes (*The Great Valley*,[86] *Towards the Gulf, Starved Rock*,[87] *Eleanor Murray*,[88] *The Fate of the Jury*[89]) as well as I, or got as much out of them. His art was part of my *sentimental life*. Yet I couldn't behave well to him. Nor could I to Vachel Lindsay,[90] tho some of his poems (The Chinese Nightingale,[91] The Santa Fe Trail[92]) also were part of my inner

---

82. 'This man / Died woman-wise, a woman's offering, slain / Through female fingers in his woof of life' (Swinburne, *Atalanta in Calydon* [1865], lines 2303–5).

83. On West 23rd Street.

84. For a letter (28 March 1948) of Grainger to Masters, shortly before Masters's death in 1950, see Gillies and Pear, eds., *The All-Round Man*, 219–21.

85. (1922).

86. (1916).

87. (1919).

88. 'Elenor Murray', in Masters's *Domesday Book* (1920).

89. (1929).

90. (1879–1931), American poet.

91. In *The Chinese Nightingale, and Other Poems* (1917).

92. In *The Congo, and Other Poems* (1914).

soul-life & my recitation of them in the train (Vancouver to Albany, N.Y.[93]) helped me to woo Ella. Yet one evening (sometime before my marriage, about a year before he killed himself[94]) when I got home tired from a concert trip & the Morses said to me, 'You know that Vachel Lindsay is lecturing (or reading his poems) here tonight', I answered, 'I just can't drag myself to a public hall to be pounced upon by all sorts of people'. It was just about then that Vachel said to Masters (so Masters told me after Vachel's self-kill-ment), 'Even my best friends have deserted me'. If I was a bad friend to Vachel Lindsay & Masters, to whom should I have been a good friend?

If I was not to find comfort, after mother's self-kill-ment, from dearest friends such as Roger Quilter, Cyril Scott, where was I to look for comfort? (Balfour Gardiner, Roger Quilter,[95] were all to meet me in Frankfurt & spend some months there with me in 1923. I had their letters about what rooms to engage for them. But the French occupation of the Ruhr took place & my friends got cold feet.[96] Balfour, however, came to Norway to be with me there on my tour, Sept. 1922, & spent a few weeks with me.[97] So I never feel that he failed me after mother's death.) If such friends cannot be relied upon, why should I be considered a 'good risk'? If I cannot be relied upon, why should one expect them to behave well?

The fact is, none of us behave well—not Roger to his beloved mother, not I to my beloved mother, & (if the truth is to be told) not the beloved mothers to their beloved sons. It is hard to feel so guilty. But the fact is: we all behave badly—sooner or later, in one form or another. And it is idle to look for anything else. We are all wonderfully equipped to behave well & to behave badly, & wonderfully equipped to bear the knowledge of our bad behavior to those we love best & to bear with their bad behavior to us. The main thing in life is not loving & kindly behavior, nor loyalty, nor justness or happiness. The main thing is anything & everything that prods mankind forward on his path-of-betterment, his path of greater knowledge, greater power, greater insight, greater at-one-ness with mankind. I know that for my part there is no question of my behaving well & lovingly. I am too hounded by artistic duties, artistic, racial & linguistic mind-stirs. Not only *I* am not geared to behave well & lovingly as son, friend, sweetheart. Nobody is. All of mankind is steeped in idolatry, taboo-madness, self-unawareness. And it will be so as long as religion exists—that most fell of all human curses. Religious moralising

---

93. In December 1926.
94. Grainger's chronology is faulty here. He married in August 1928. Lindsay committed suicide in December 1931.
95. Grainger also entered here 'Cyril Scott', but then crossed it out.
96. See, further, essay 91.
97. See essay 31.

makes man afraid to see himself as he is (in all his cruel-lustfulness, his unfairness, his meanness). We should glory in our sins (as perhaps many criminals do?) & our virtues. All of them are bequeathed to us by our race, by our parents, our training & the privileges of life. It is our business to understand the queer patched-quilt (of 'good' & 'bad') that each one of us is. The first need is to realise that mankind as at present constituted is loathsome, unworthy, unfair & that it is useless to expect happiness, justice, shrewdness, companionship, good-taste from human beings as they are today. Before life can be 'fun' we will have to do a lot of work on mankind first. For almost every reaction, of mankind as a whole or of individuals as persons, is hopeless, blind, disgusting.

What is the central core of all these things in life that strike us as being revolting, joy-destroying, health-undermining, anger-provoking, genius-denying, wasteful, truth-perverting? Is it not *forcefulness*?

1. forcefulness in the form of emphaticness: using gestures, speaking with bold voices, the barking of animals, [in German] 'stately man'[98] [in English] type, 'standard forms' of languages, talking other people down, seeking jobs that carry authorit[at]iveness with them such as musical conductors, judges, educators, clergymen, soldiers, policemen.
2. forcefulness in the form of argument & persuasiveness; using one's brains to win over other people & their opinions.
3. the forcefulness of using weapons; for instance against animals (the man who uses a chair against a tiger in a circus act).
4. the forcefulness of speed, whereby the lives of many are endangered to give satisfaction to a few. No country can be called 'civilised' that allows trains, buses, airplanes to go more than (say) 10 or 15 miles per hour.
5. the forcefulness of skill & courage which enables
   (a) prizefighters & other brutes to earn big sums,
   (b) musical conductors & virtuoso soloists to gain powerful positions over less skilful & less courageous music-lovers.
6. the forcefulness of health & having doctors on one's side.
7. the forcefulness of 'biological' behavior, such as coquettishness in women, gloating over family feelings, washing clean linen in public, persecuting of 'perverts', suppression of obscenity & immorality & other innocent things.
8. forcefulness of herding, killing & eating animals.
9. the forcefulness of war, the respect for the officer class.
10. the forcefulness of upper-class protection, including stately houses, refined manners, unwritten laws, good class clothes.

98. 'stattlicher Mann'.

11. the forcefulness of grown-ups to children, of animal-lovers to their pets.
12. the forcefulness of university & other degrees.
13. the forcefulness of education in general: 'educated' people having the audacity to pretend to know unknowable things.
14. the forcefulness of religion—the most brutal & disastrous of all forcefulness, including the forcefulnesses that stem from it: censorship, exposing abuses, blackmail.

Against this formidable array of forcefulness—which confronts the weak freedom-lover at every turn—it is surprising that the non-forceful types (immoralists, rebels, amateurs, non-consistants [*sic*], lewd-mongers, beauty-worshippers) can survive at all & reap any happiness at all in life. The fact is: they can. The anti-moral libertine is just as kindly treated by women as the 'biological' family-raiser; the iconoclastic artistic genius is just as much welcomed in art as the degree-toting non-genius. But, of course, the libertine cannot 'claim' his women (as the moralist can) & the iconoclastic artistic genius has no 'standing' in his art. Not often. But why should one want to 'claim' women, or artistic standing, or anything else?

For my part, I am deeply thankful I have not been put in prison or ill-treated in a concentration camp. I am glad I have not been dragged into public, or national, scandal. I am thankful that none of my sweethearts have been vindictive to me (in spite of my unsatisfactoriness to them) & that 'professional' musicians have not ganged up on me more. The back of my soul is broken by the knowledge that I proved a bad son & I am bitterly ashamed of having had to change my nationality. I feel disgraced by my feebleness as a pianist (my poor fingerwork, my unreliable memory) & as a conductor (by that feeling of helplessness when I stand before a choir or orchestra). I hated the drudgery of teaching (except when teaching such sweet talents as Kitty Parker, Mrs Forrest). I have enjoyed every phase of my marriage, thanks to my wisdom in choosing a non-forceful, non-biological fellow-artist. ([In Danish] Marriage easily turns into a temple of lasciviousness.) [In English] And I have been unspeakably lucky in the vast joy I have drawn from the arts & from thoughts about theed-speeches ((languages)). I wonder whether any other composer has enjoyed other composers' music as keenly as I have. No-one has enjoyed reading aloud more than I have. I think I can claim to have deeply relished almost every type of music, including many works by those composers (Haydn, Beethoven, Mozart, Weber) I have inveighed against most. The following incomplete lists of my favorites[99] show how many types of

99. Cf. other lists of Grainger's favourites in music, art, and life from his later years: 'Questionnaire (1955)' (Gillies and Clunies Ross, eds., *Grainger on Music*, 373–76); letter to Cyril Scott, 10 and 11 December 1951 (Gillies and Pear, eds., *The All-Round Man*, 252–58); and essay 78.

music have brought ecstasy to me: Almost all records of African, Madagascan, Asiatic, South Sea musics.[100] Where'er she walks.[101] 'Golden Gate'.[102] Henry VIII Dances.[103] Bolero.[104] On the Steppes.[105] Thamar.[106] Bicycle built for 2.[107] Maude Valérie White.[108] D.G. Mason Scherzo.[109] Fauré Pavan & Ballade.[110] Siegfried Idyll. Albéniz. Dvořák's In der Natur.[111] Frederick Stock's[112] arr. of Bach Air in G Major. Gershwin Concerto, Rhapsody in Blue (heard on a band in Brooklyn), Love Walked In.[113] Gould's[114] orchestral arr. of 'I got rhythm'. Albéniz's El Albaicín, Jerez, El Puerto.[115] H. Duparc's[116] songs. J. des Prez's La Bernardina.[117] The 4-note Pavan. Dom Anselm Hughes's[118] discoveries. John Jenkins's 1st 5-part Fantasy. Antonio de Cabezón 'Prelude in Dorian Mode'.[119] The Ciciliano & Intermezzo from Cavalleria.[120] Much of Puccini & Stravinsky. Schönberg's 5 orchestral pieces.[121] Peasant dance in Vlatava.[122] Norwegian folksong, 'Frånar Ormen'.[123] Færøsk[124] & Danish folksongs. (Swiss) Martin's concerto for harp, harpsichord, piano &

100. Grainger's main collections were the *Musik des Orients* album (Carl Lindström, Berlin) and *African Records* (issued by The Gramophone Shop, New York), both from the early 1930s, and the recordings personally presented to him by Alfred J. Knocks (South Sea Islander music) in 1909.

101. Perhaps referring to 'Where'er you walk' from Handel's opera *Semele* (1744).

102. Possibly '(Mary at the) Golden Gate', Lincolnshire folk song.

103. Three Dances from the Music to *Henry VIII*, by Edward German (1862–1936).

104. Ravel's ballet, *Boléro* (1928).

105. *On the Steppes of Central Asia* (1880), by Alexander Borodin.

106. *Tamara* (1867–82), symphonic poem by Mily Balakirev. See essay 75. Grainger probably first heard the work in a 1912 London production of Diaghilev's Ballets Russes.

107. (1892), popular song by Harry Dacre (1860–1922).

108. (1855–1937), English songwriter.

109. Op. 22b, by Daniel Gregory Mason (1873–1953), American composer and academic.

110. Op. 50 and Op. 19, respectively.

111. *In Nature's Realm*, Op. 91 (1891).

112. Frederick (Friedrich) Stock (1872–1942), German-born conductor of the Chicago Symphony Orchestra (1905–42).

113. Grainger's solo-piano arrangement of Gershwin's 'Love Walked In' was published by the Gershwin Publishing Corp. (New York) in 1946.

114. Morton Gould (1913–96), American composer.

115. All from *Iberia* (1906–9), for piano solo.

116. Henri Duparc (1848–1933), French composer.

117. In 1934 (rev. 1939), Grainger made a transcription of this piece for violin, viola, and cello, intending it for his 'Chosen Gems' series for strings.

118. (1889–1974), English musicologist and historian, who collaborated with Grainger during the 1930s and 1940s in the *English Gothic Music* series.

119. Arranged by Grainger both for strings (1935) and for winds (1941).

120. The Siciliana and Intermezzo from Mascagni's *Cavalleria rusticana* (1890).

121. Op. 16 (1909).

122. Vltava (Moldau; 1874) from Smetana's *Má vlast*.

123. Norwegian heroic song, found in Landstad's 1853 collection of Norwegian folk songs. See essay 111.

124. Faeroe Islander.

strings.[125] Arthur Fickénscher's[126] 'From the 7th Realm',[127] 'Willowwood',[128] 'The Chamber Blue'.[129] Holst's 'Beni Mora' Suite.[130] V. Williams's English Folk-Song Suite.[131] Edouard Moullet Chansons pop. de Haute Normandie.[132] Henry Eichheim Oriental Pieces. The singing of my Lincolnshire folksingers, especially Dean of Hibaldstow,[133] Jos. Taylor,[134] Geo. Wray, George Gouldthorpe.[135] Countless works by my favorite composers Bach, Scarlatti, Schumann, Brahms, Wagner, Grieg, R. Strauss, Cyril Scott, Herman Sandby, Balfour Gardiner, Roger Quilter, Sparre Olsen,[136] Dag Wirén,[137] Debussy, Ravel, C. Franck, Balakirev, Tchaikovsky, Rachmaninoff.

On the whole, I dislike the orchestration or band-scoring of my own works, such as Shepherd's Hey, Spoon River. I feel ashamed when I hear them. Nevertheless, a few rehearsals or performances stand out as having swelled my chest with pride & satisfaction when I heard them (generally when conducted by someone other than myself):

> *English Dance*, Portland, Maine Symphony (Russell Ames Cook,[138] conducting) 1949.
>
> *Kipling choruses*, rehearsal by Sem Dresden[139] (Madrigal-Vereniging), Amsterdam, 1922.
>
> *Hillsong No. 2*, 24 woodwind, Arthur Williams,[140] Oberlin College, Ohio, 1951.
>
> *Hillsong No. 1*, large chamber music, Francis Resta,[141] West Point, N.Y., 1947.

125. *Petite symphonie concertante* (1945) by Frank Martin (1890–1974).
126. (1871–1954), American composer and pianist.
127. See essay 77.
128. Fickénscher composed both *Willowwood and Wellaway* (1925), for orchestra, and 'Willowwood', for voice, viola, optional bassoon, and piano. Grainger had heard the latter.
129. (ca. 1907–35), to words of W. Morris, for soloist, female chorus, and orchestra.
130. See essay 101.
131. (1923), for military band.
132. Collection of some fifty song arrangements (1890) by Édouard Moullé.
133. Mr. Deene of Hibaldstow, in Humberside. See Jane O'Brien, *The Grainger English Folk Song Collection* (Perth: University of Western Australia, 1985), indexes.
134. See essay 48.
135. Both singers from Brigg, Lincolnshire. See O'Brien, *The Grainger English Folk Song Collection*, indexes.
136. (1903–84), Norwegian violinist and composer, friend of Grainger from 1932. See essay 70.
137. (1905–83), Swedish composer. Grainger commented in 1949 of Wirén's Serenade for String Orchestra (1937) that there was 'no previous Swedish composition that rises to such heights of universal appeal' (Gillies and Clunies Ross, eds., *Grainger on Music*, 354).
138. (ca. 1888–ca. 1965). The concert took place on 24 May 1949.
139. (1881–1957), German-trained Dutch composer, director of the Amsterdam Conservatory (1924–37).
140. (1902–73), American bandmaster. The concert took place on 14 January 1951.
141. (1894–1968), Italian-born American clarinettist and West Point bandmaster (1934–57). The concert took place on 20 April 1947.

Bell Piece[142] try-thru, myself conducting, Overgard's[143] band, Detroit,
1951.

As I review my life as a whole (humanly & artistically) it seems nothing
but tragedy, futility, heart-break—due to my wickedness, pig-headedness,
cowardice, clumsiness, lack of skill. But I am (& always have been) kept
going by my interests. Tho my conscience tells me I should kill myself,
there is always some pending rehearsal, or something that anchors me to
life. These days, of course, it is my Free Music gins. These, like my marriage, 'entirely satisfy' (as Kipling makes his Indian Hillman say of the 1st
German War).

[on train] August 20, 1954, Chic.–N. York

Source: 'The Things I Dislike', in 'Grainger's Anecdotes', 423-87, dated 1 August and 20 August 1954
(Grainger Museum, Melbourne).

59   To Whoever Opens the Package Marked 'Do Not
Open until 10 Years after My Death' (1956)

by Percy Grainger (May 10, 1956)[144]

I fervently hope that whoever opens the package will regard my wishes *that
none of the contents of the package be destroyed*, but lodged with some medical
or historic or scientific society or library that may wish to investigate the nature & habits of creative Australians.[145]

For I attach enormous importance to flagellantism. I feel that flagellantism (like boxing, football & some other sports) is a means of turning hostile,

---

142. 'Ramble on Dowland's Now, O Now', first publicly performed on 9 April 1953 in Hollywood,
FL.

143. Bandmaster Graham T. Overgard.

144. Grainger wrote this explanatory note during the time that his friend Sir Eugene Goossens
(1893–1962), conductor of the Sydney Symphony Orchestra, was being investigated for having
brought over one thousand pornographic photographs into Australia. Goossens had been ques-
tioned on his arrival at Sydney Airport on 9 March 1956. He finally left the country, having admitted the offence, on 26 May 1956. The Graingers were, during this time, in Melbourne working on the exhibits of the Grainger Museum.

145. On leaving Australia for the last time, in June 1956, Grainger lodged this package, containing
photographic evidence of his sex life, in a Melbourne bank. Since the package's opening in 1971,
these photographs have been held in the libraries of The University of Melbourne.

harsh & destructive elements in man into *harmless channels*. Much of civilisation consists of turning hostility into playfulness. The fact that I have enjoyed whipping myself, or having myself whipped by woman, shows that my wish to whip woman does not (as far as I can see) arise out of the wish to humiliate or dominate woman. The photographs of myself whipped by myself in Kansas City[146] & the various photographs of my wife whipped by me[147] show that my flagellantism was not make-believe or puerility, but had the element of drasticness in it. Nevertheless, my flagellantism was never inhuman or uncontrolled. And the fact that neither my wife or any of my sweethearts resented my flagellantism suggests that it was not unduly harsh—no worse than the pains & hurts endured in football or other rough games. I have never met a woman who was flagellantically inclined herself. In my experience it is the woman's delight in seeing her lover happy & satisfied that makes her willing to submit to flagellantism.

I have always been potent sexually & never had any interest in homosexuality. My flagellantic orgies by myself were almost always followed by self-help (onanism) & my flagellantic orgies with my wife & sweethearts almost always followed by normal coitus. But normal coitus was always easy & satisfactory to me without flagellantism of any kind. So my flagellantism must (I think) be viewed as something complete in itself, & not as an aid to other activities.

To me it has always seemed that my flagellantism is connected with my love of beauty, my love of Greek statues & nakedness & my longing for something sharp & drastic—such as we hear in Tchaikovsky's music.[148] I have always disliked pornographic or indecent pictures, photos & literature. Indecent incidents occur in many of the flagellantic books I have enjoyed. In those cases, I have been bored by the indecent passages while thrilled by the flagellantic passages.

I think the happiest moment of my life was in 1910 in Amsterdam when I saw in a bookshop near the main post office flagellantic books openly displayed—such books as 'Sous le f[o]uet',[149] 'In Louisiana', 'White Women Slaves', 'Sadie Blackeyes', etc. It was a few days before my first recital in Holland[150] & I put the books aside—unread—until after my concert. I didn't wish to weaken myself before my concert. After the concert I read the books all night—the happiest night of my life, I suppose.

---

146. Dated 9 February 1933.
147. Apparently dating from late 1941 to 1943, mainly 10–11 January 1942.
148. See essay 61.
149. 'Under the Whip' (in French).
150. Grainger's first solo recital in Amsterdam was on 15 March 1910 at the Concertgebouw.

When I was about 6 my mother whipped me severely for kicking a cat around a room. At about the same age (or later?) I saw Mrs McGee take down Faerie McGee's drawers & spank her bare bottom.[151] The whipping episodes in 'Nicholas Nickleby'[152] & other books (not intended to be flagellantic) excited me terribly as a little boy & made me shiver as with severe cold. I knew nothing of sex before I was 12 (told by Desmond McGee) & had no idea why I shivered. At about the age of 11 I read of Japanese boys whipping, or beating, or hurting each other, to see who could stand most. So I tried this with my boy friend Bede[153]—a few years older than I. We whipped each other's legs with strips of bamboo from worn out Venetian blinds. Our legs bled. But no sexual stir was aroused.

By the way, in whipping woman, or being whipped myself, I never craved severe cruelty. My sadism was always tempered by moderateness. But in my early years in Frankfurt (1895–1898?), long before I practised any flagellantism, I had inhuman sadistic dreams. Best of all was to insert fish-hooks into a girl's (woman's) breast or nipples & pull her up by her nipples, so the fish-hook tore thru her breast or nipple thru the weight of the girl being lifted by the fish-hooks.[154]

I consider pornographic literature (for those that like it), flagellantic literature, etc., most important for the future of mankind—as a means of releasing tension & relieving the sexual fury proper in a vigorous male.[155] I have had more pleasure from badly written flagellantic books than from the world's best literature. Sex is better than art—goes deeper. Of all books, those not intended to present flagellantic appeal have excited me most: Lempriere's Classical Dictionary (Spartan maidens whipped naked on the altar of Venus), Mark Twain's 'A Yankee at the Court of King Arthur',[156] etc.

Source: 'To Whoever Opens the Package Marked "Do Not Open until 10 Years after My Death"' (Grainger Museum, Melbourne).

151. See, further, essay 8.
152. By Charles Dickens (1839). See, further, essay 62.
153. Adam Bede. See, also, essay 20.
154. See, also, essay 61.
155. Grainger compared English, French, Scandinavian, and German flagellantic literatures in his unpublished essay of May 1955, 'National Characteristics in Modern Flagellantic Literature' (Grainger Museum, Melbourne).
156. (1889).

The Albert Bridge, Adelaide, designed by Grainger's father, John, 1879 (Grainger Museum)

1

Rose Grainger and Percy Grainger, in Australia, ca. 1891
(Grainger Museum, Melbourne)

Grainger museum

The Story of Grettir the Strong

This is the book that had the
greatest influence on my
human & artistic life. Grettir
was to me what Christ is
to many Christians.
I read the story when 9 or 10
(or 11?) in Melbourne, but
not in this translation (which
became known to me in London
?1905 — 1912?). The translation
I read as a boy was part of a
book by Dasent: "Popular
Romances of the Middle Ages",
which book (the one I read from
as a boy) is in the Grainger
museum.
          Percy Grainger, Oct 1936

The cover of Grainger's copy of *The Story of Grettir the Strong*,
claimed by Grainger in 1936 as "the greatest influence on my
human & artistic life" (Grainger Museum)

3

Grainger's painting of Cronberg Castle, near Frankfurt, June 1896 (Grainger Museum)

Manuscript of Grainger's first "Klavierstück", October 1897 (Grainger Museum)

5

6
Anatomical drawing by Grainger, probably 1898 (Grainger Museum)

7
James Kwast, Grainger's piano teacher in Frankfurt, by Cosmo Rowe (Grainger Museum)

Grainger's first mistress, London socialite Lilith Lowrey,
by E. W. Histed (Grainger Museum)

8

Grainger, side view, ca. 1905, by Adolph de Meyer (Grainger Museum)

10

Grainger, in artist's smock,
ca. 1905, by Adolph de Meyer
(Grainger Museum)

11

U.S. Army bandsman Grainger,
with soprano saxophone, 1917
(Grainger Museum)

12
Grainger with Frederick
Delius, Frankfurt, April 1923
(Grainger Museum)

13
Grainger's wife, Ella Ström,
with her daughter Elsie (Elsa),
probably Pevensey, Sussex, late
1920s (Grainger Museum)

14

Grainger "self-beaten,
Kansas City, Feb. 9, 1933"
(Grainger Museum)

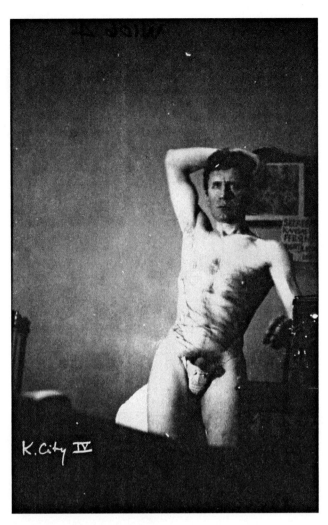

15

A selection of the
whips held in Grainger's
Museum in Melbourne
(Grainger Museum)

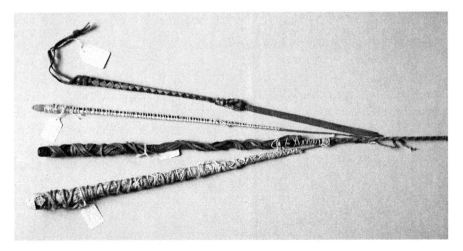

Photograph of full ensemble for the concert of 23 November 1935
in Wellington, New Zealand (Grainger Museum)

16

17

Grainger at the keyboard,
National Music Camp,
Interlochen, early 1940s
(Grainger Museum)

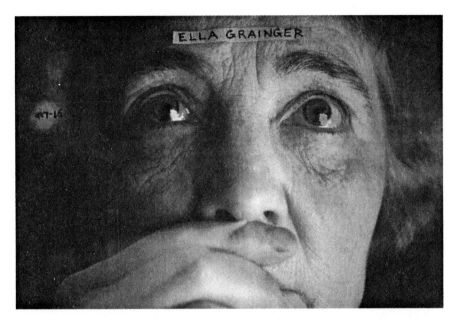

The eyes of Ella Grainger, from Grainger's photographic collection of artists' eyes, early 1950s (Grainger Museum)

18

19

The clothes of Grainger's friend, H. Balfour Gardiner, in the Grainger Museum, flanked by Ella and Percy Grainger, 1955–56 (Grainger Museum)

Grainger's interment, West Terrace Cemetery, Adelaide, 2 March 1961
(Grainger Museum)

20

PART II

The Musician

7

COMPOSER

➤ 60   [The Goal of My Art] (1922)

I can think of no qualities I would rather see in my compositions than
those I see in my darling mother's looks. For it is not the goal of my art to
express the deeps of the human heart, to unite mankind in universal feelings or to reveal mystic truths. It is the goal of my art to bear the stamp of
a distinct type, like a bright cactus flowering in the desert, to lift to the
world the clean face of a pure race. Dear mother had the quality of race
purity more overwhelmingly than anyone I can think of. She was not only
an ideal Nordic to look at; she seemed the very source & essence of all
Nordicness boiled down to a point of concentration. It is of precisely her
type of Anglosaxon beauty that one pictures the Roman Emperor saying:
'Angels, not Angles'. Her proportions, the graceful squareness of her
face—neither too heavy nor too light (George Moore wrote in Esther Wa-
ters:[1] 'Her face had the lovely prose of the Saxon'), the daintiness of her
ears, the radiance of her hair, the melodious curves of her strangely perfect
mouth; these things breathed an aristocracy of race, a freedom from all
basely-blended alien blood, a singleness of type wholly unique. Beside her
I (tho I have points of beauty rare in man) am a mulatto, with my crooked
mouth, my face too narrow at the base, my greener-tinged hair (lovely tho
it was in boyhood), my slightly squinting eyes (where hers are straight as a
die), my exaggerated nose. Not what *I* am does my art crave to voice so
much as what *she* was. The purity & radiance of vocal sound that I tried to

---

1. Novel of 1894.

touch in such a cappella writing as 'Morning Song in the Jungle'[2] is like her sunkissed hair & open-hearted pure eyes (see Chicago picture).[3]

The buoyant optimism of 'Marching Song of Democracy' is like her brave energetic mankind-loving nature & wholly unlike my timid, menschen-schen,[4] naturally gloomy type. The setting of 'Irish Tune from Co. Derry' is typically Aldridge, & shows not the taint of Grainger that is upon me as a man. 'Shepherd's Hey' for full orchestra (No. 16)[5] is an excellent expression of her skittish, somewhat teasing gaiety, to which nothing in me accurately cor-responds—as my gaiety is some much rougher & more sinister. The works that express *me* rather than her are those that are savage rather than gay, deso-late rather than poetic. Thus the Hillsongs are me rather than her (expressing the unabridged wildness & non-humanness of nature) & so is 'The Warriors' (in which the type of excitement is mainly sinister & sadistic) & perhaps 'Fa-ther & Daughter' also. These non-Aldridge-like works will not be found ded-icated to her.

Amsterdam, Dec. 24, 1922

Source: Untitled section, in 'Sketches for My Book "The Life of My Mother & Her Son"', W35-22 (Grainger Museum, Melbourne).

61   Notes on Whip-Lust (1948)

But I cannot give a true picture of my tone-art & of my art-life if I do not tell of the cruel-joy ((sadism)) that is one of the main stirs of my being. How can a true man, I ask, feel anything but cruel-fain towards lovely women (for no right-wise man could feel cruel-fain towards ugly, fat, heavy or harsh-natured women. Man's fiendishness is set aside for the sweet, the yielding, the sportive, the bright, the slight & girlish woman)? It is part of skittish woman's make-up to wish to run away (the he-horse has to sink his teeth into the neck of the mare to hold her still); what can man do to lovely woman but wish to tie her down, & having tied her down, wouldn't he be stupid if he—calling-to-mind her gigglings & laughters—did not punish her somewhat? It is true that man

2. Mixed-chorus Kipling setting, written as a present for Rose Grainger's birthday of 3 July 1905.
3. Grainger probably refers to a photograph by Koehne, Chicago, of 29 July 1920 (Picture 37 in the memorial volume, *Photos of Rose Grainger*).
4. 'Little man' (in German).
5. No. 16 of Grainger's British Folk-Music Settings series.

is be-laugh-worthy in his over-eagerness; it stands to reason that girls & women should giggle & laugh at him. But laughter can be quenched by whip-blows, & of what use is man's greater bodily strength if he cannot gain woman by it?

Did my cruel-joy (which shows itself both in wishing to give pain & to take it) arise from the whippings my mother gave me, from the earliest child-hood up to 14 or 15. Maybe it did. And if that is the case, I must feel doubly thankful to her for having given me my life's greatest boon. (For it is a priceless boon to feel cruel-fain towards women. Man feels maddened by his pent-uppness, & woman seems to understand that a rightwise man's cruel-fain-th is part of his hunger for women. Women, I think, feel kindlier to cruel-fain-ful men than to others, for they sense how dire is such a man's need of woman; whereas kindly, gentlemanly men just pass women by as if woman had claims on man, but man no claims on woman). I did not like being whipped as a boy, & it did not arouse any joyful stirs in me at the time. I took it for what it was: that I was a somewhat devilish boy whom a rightwise mother could deal with in no other way; & I also took it as a part of my mother's dire-deed-make-up. Let no-one now come with the talk that cruel-fain-th arises out of downtrod-denness & out of a wish to lift oneself into a better standing. For my standing was always top-hole all thru my childhood, & I never felt especially downtrod-den in any way. But Frankfurt, in my teens,[6] was full of buildings in which bust-ful women statues and foundations held aloft balconies; & the galleries, & books, & *Simplicissimus*,[7] ever full of pictures of naked women, some of which I copied in pencil. And I was be-flamed by the beauty & unget-at-ableness of girlhood & womanhood. If the whippings I had had were the only root of my cruel-fain-th, why did quite other forms of cruel-hood delight my inner eye? For one of the next outcome dream-sights of my mid & late teens was of sticking 2 fishhooks, slung on 4 pulleys, one into each of a woman's breasts, & then pulley-raise the fishhooks till the weight of the woman's body caused the fishhooks to rip thru the breast-flesh.[8] Rather, were not such stirs just an outcome of the vast wildness of my nature—the same wildness that made me walk from one 3rd storey window to another along a 2-inch strip of moulding on the house's outer wall, to scare old women below; the same wild-ness that led me to burn myself on hot stoves; the same wildness that fills my Hillsongs & English Dance?[9] Need we ever label such cruel-fain-ths as I have

6. I.e., 1895–1901.
7. A weekly satirical journal founded in 1896 in Munich.
8. Cf. essay 59.
9. All three of these works were commenced in the period 1899–1901.

word-painted as part of sex-wildness? Are they not just part of life-wildness—
that wildness that makes young men yearn to do fool-hardy acts, that makes
theeds [nations] worship war & murder-stories; that leads crowds to lynch.
That same stir that crams a whole rebirth into a crowded all-within-a-fifth-y
chord in Tchaikovsky, like a broken-bottle end into the rounded cap of which
the sun streams many-angled-ly until a bush fire is started.[10]

Segeltorp, Dec. 24, 1948

Source: 'Notes on Whip-Lust' (Grainger Museum, Melbourne).

62   What Is Behind My Music (1954)

Ella & I are bound for the Mayo Clinic (Rochester, Minn.) & the operation I
expect to have done there is one many have died from.[11] Yet I am less afraid of
this operation than I am of playing before an audience. So this bears out what I
have always thought: that I am more afraid of playing in public than of anything in the world. This fear may have started when I first played, at the age of
ten, & discovered how unreliable my memory was & how faulty my execution,
when scared by an audience. And it may have been made worse, around my
twenties, as I came to realise how much hinged upon my poor, faulty pianism.
All things seemed to combine to make performing in public the terror of my
life. As my British-Australian patriotism was fanned by the Kipling books my
father sent me when I was about 17,[12] & also fanned by the hatred of the British
shown by the Germans at the time of the Boer War, another factor was added to
make my piano playing seem a disgrace to me: every time I played any music
that was not British, American or Scandinavian I felt I was a traitor. This feeling
has lasted thruout my whole piano-playing life. When I play Grieg's *Ballade*[13] or
Cyril Scott's *Sonata*[14] I feel I am being sustained & sponsored by my racial an-
cestors. But when I play Chopin, or Tchaikovsky, or Bach, or even Debussy
sometimes, I feel that a hostile host [is] confounding me.

  Between 7 & 10 I read a lot of Homer, & phrases like 'the javelin crashed
thru the shield' were always on my inner lips. Later on (aged 10 to 12?), when

10 Grainger here quotes Tchaikovsky's Sixth ('Pathétique') Symphony, III.96–98.
11. This was Grainger's third operation for prostate cancer in five months.
12. The first of these books was Kipling's *The Jungle Book* sent in 1897.
13. Op. 24.
14. Op. 66.

I read the Icelandic sagas, the thought of a battleaxe hewing from the shoulder to waist gave me my greatest mental delights. In the meantime, I had found in Dickens (such a passage as Nicholas[15] striking the schoolmaster on the cheek with the cane, leaving a 'livid' streak) & in all sorts of stories (one about a boy of about 12 who ran away from home to join a circus & was [in Danish] whipped [in English] by the circus manager) fuel to fan the flames of my [in Danish] delight in cruelty and lashing. [In English] These passions were quite unconscious, & I had no idea what caused me to shake with [ ][16] when I read such descriptions. Much later (1910, in Holland) when I saw for the first time the extent of [in Danish] flagellantic [in English] literature, I had the greatest literary treat of my life. Since then, all other forms of literature seem to me footling. Each person must have *some subject* that fires him to madness. Whatever it is, to put up with less seems crazy.

Out of this world of war, violence, cruelhood & tragedy my longing to compose arose. Many children are cruel to animals, & many little boys harsh to little girls. But this fierceness wanes as they grow up. But I never grew up, in these respects, & fierceness is the keynote of my music in *The Only Son* (1946)[17] as in *Hillsongs I & II* (1902[18]–1907). Only in one particular did I change as I grew up—compassionateness was added to my delight in suffering & violence. As a little boy I saw nothing in the wounds of war (the shoulder axe-cloven to the waist) but sheer delight & innocent fun. But as a young man there was hardly a suggestion of any kind (a dance, a memory of the sea, any form of competition, all forms of wastefulness) that did not awaken some more or less agonised reaction. What is all this unrelieved misery for? I haven't the faintest idea. Is it because our era (with its myriads of young men doomed to flaming deaths in the sky & wholesale drownings in the sea—whether in submarine or submarined) needs to have its injustices to the young brought home by art? (Fancy young men being conscripted to fight at ages in which they are deemed too unripe to vote.) Is my 'Powers of Rome & the Christian Heart'[19] the only specifically conscientious objection music in existence?

[on train] New York—Rochester, Minn., Jan. 16 or 17, 1954

Source: 'What Is Behind My Music (A Hasty Account)', in 'Grainger's Anecdotes', 423-88 (Grainger Museum, Melbourne).

15. In *Nicholas Nickleby* (1839), where Nickleby beats Squeers.
16. Left blank by Grainger.
17. Grainger's last Kipling Setting (No. 21), composed between July 1945 and February 1947.
18. Correctly, 1901.
19. Grainger started this work in 1918 while in the U.S. Army, claiming its inspiration in the agony experienced by the early Christians as they confronted the power of ancient Rome.

➤ 63   Why 'My Wretched Tone-Life'?[20] (1953)

This is an attempt to make clear, in very brief & sketchy form, why any true account of my musical life must stress its wretchedness. Not because I, in myself, am a wretched creature, but merely because, in the realm of music I am 'a fish out of water'. I was not 'wretched' as a child, I was not wretched as a soldier (altho I am a pacifist) & I have not been in the least wretched as a husband. Why, then, have I been wretched in music? For the same reason that Grieg was, or Cyril Scott would be if he hadn't entrenched himself behind other interests. Because countries like Norway, England, Australia & America are stupid in their uptake of native musical genius. England is just as stupid about Maude Valérie White as she is about Cyril Scott.

At any given moment there is always one race (or group of races) that is clever, while others are stupid. It is quite clear that the English-speaking countries & those other countries that share their general outlook on life (Scandinavia, Holland) are the clever ones in our times. Whether thru the efforts of our successful races, or due to other causes, the changes that happen in world affairs & social customs suit our own temperaments. And (if a member of the successful races) by the time we have reached old age we are apt to find that current conditions suit our tastes & moralities better than conditions did in our youth. For instance, we are closer to nudism today than we were 60 years ago. Of course, within these general tendencies (affecting whole races or the whole of humanity) there are all kinds of half-measures. There are the clever people in the clever nations (Walt Whitman, Swinburne, Grieg), the stupid people in the clever nations, the clever people in the stupid nations, & the stupid people in the stupid nations. But even the cleverest people in the stupid nations are stupid as compared with the stupidest members of the clever nations.

Thus, the texts of Schubert's Müller Lieder & Winterreise cycles[21] are revoltingly stupid from an Australian standpoint. Tell any Australian that the man (in the cycles) complains that the girl jilts him, or is otherwise cold & unloving, & the Australian would say, 'Has he tried spending more money on the girl?' As far as I know (in spite of the welter of Walt Whitman texts set to music) no non-Australian has been bright enough to write music celebrating Democracy.[22] Nor has any non-Australian written a Thanksgiving Song dedi-

20 'My Wretched Tone-Life' was the title of Grainger's projected autobiography. His draft introduction to the book, written in July 1951, is reproduced in Gillies and Pear, *Portrait of Percy Grainger*, 206–8.

21. *Die schöne Müllerin* (1823) and *Winterreise* (1827), both to words of Wilhelm Müller.

22. Grainger's *Marching Song of Democracy* was composed between 1901 and 1917. See essay 106.

cated to all the women he has loved all thru life.[23] The English-speaking world
has produced 'Society for the Prevention of Cruelty to Animals' & 'At times
[*sic*] I feel I could turn & live with the animals. . . . Not one is respectable or
unhappy over the whole earth,'[24] but I doubt whether any non-Australian has
written a long musical work devoted to feelings about animals, as I have in my
'Kipling Jungle Book Cycle'. But that doesn't mean, necessarily, *that a single
Australian sees the importance of what I have done in this respect.* The Australians may be the world's most advanced people, yet they may have a blind
eye for musical values, just as the Norwegians (an equally advanced, or more
advanced nation) do.

I am not prepared to explain why the cleverest nations usually act with
outstanding stupidity towards their greatest geniuses (unless it be that clever
nations do not need geniuses, getting on quite well without being aware of
them. If this is not so—that clever nations do not need geniuses—what point
is there in an Englishman writing 'Lady Chatterley's Lover,'[25] in an Australian
writing 'The Age of Consent,'[26] if these books are banned in their countries-
of-origin?) All sorts of factors may enter in. Robert Burns[27] may have suc-
ceeded with Scottish people partly because his Scottish lingo caters to their
Scottishness. On the other hand Swinburne's Border Speech does not appeal
to English patriotism. So his superb riming [*sic*] skill, anti-morality & deep
philosophy runs largely to waste. Yet the deadly boredom of worldwide uni-
formity, which is the greatest bugbear of English-speaking worldwide prosperity, is well counter-balanced in Swinburne. 'Classical music' (having been neglected in our advanced countries for generations, 1700–1860, & after that
discovering one of the means by which the upstart classes pull themselves up
by our boots) having been allowed to degenerate into 'Southworship,' a
Nordic musician can earn a living only if he becomes a slave to the music of
the inferior (the 'stupid') nations, or if he is able write as-stupid-as-if-South
music, such as Elgar's 'Salut d'amour'.[28] It is a bitter pill for the pukka Australian to have to play the music of the inferior nations, lending his manliness
to garnish such namby pamby foreign music. A proper Australian musician
feels about playing 'enemy' music as an Australian feels about the immigra-

---

23. Grainger's *Thanksgiving Song* (ca. 1918–45), conceived in three movements, is only partly ex-
    tant. It included music inspired by or once dedicated to Margot Harrison, Karen Holten, Lotta
    Hough, and Ella Ström, probably amongst others.
24. From Walt Whitman's 'Song of Myself', 32.
25. (1928), by D. H. Lawrence.
26. (1938), by Norman Lindsay.
27. (1759–96), Scottish poet.
28. (1888), for many years Elgar's most frequently performed piece (in several arrangements).

tion of the colored races or the inferior European races into Australia. It is natural to an Australian more to be anti-salon & anti-boudoir. How can he ex-
cusably play Chopin's salon-ish & boudoir-ish music—however much he may
admire & revere Chopin's genius? The anti-socialistic prosperous classes of
our 'clever' countries like Mozart, because it conjures up in their imaginations
the satin-waistcoat waited-upon-ness of the pre-French Revolution. But Australia does not plan to restore pre-F. R. days, Australia being a do-your-own-
work country, like Scandinavia. So how can any Australian play Mozart without feeling deeply ashamed of himself? That is why I gave up playing
Haydn-Mozart-Beethoven as soon as I could. But such social & political con-
flicts make one's tone life wretched. But the chief source of wretchedness in
my pianistic life was the clumsiness of my fingers & the faultiness of my
memory. The very first time I played in public, when I was 10, my memory
played tricks on me & my fingers indulged in back-to-front inaccuracies that
have clung to me thru my 61 years of public playing. If I didn't practise 6–9
hours a day my memory was unreliable. If I did practise 6–9 hours a day my
fingers, etc., were too tired to play well. But while my heavy Nordic hand was
too clumsy to play Bach, Scarlatti, Mozart, Beethoven, Schubert really well
that same hand was superb in Brahms, Tchaikovsky, Cyril Scott Sonata &
Grieg *Slåtter*.[29] *But nobody wanted to hear such things.* So my pianistic career
had to be based on 'enemy' music, & on music I was constitutionally unable
to play well. And on music I felt a political traitor in performing.

It is hard to face an audience that you hate, playing music that you hate
or despise, also knowing you are unfit to play it. It is hard to sit there (in the
sight of hundreds or thousands) making horrible mistakes, fearing still worse
mistakes (fearing complete 'breaking down in public') & having to appear
confident & self-satisfied. I am an honest man. I hate to defraud the public, or
anyone else. Englishmen (unless they are Jews) cannot rise to brilliant careers
as pianists as we Australians can (Ernest Hutcheson,[30] George Boyle, myself,
Eileen Joyce[31]). I suppose the English are too noble. Our low-class Australian
class-background enables Australians to succeed where English fail—in my
case, to my lifelong wretchedness.

I have always enjoyed composing, & always composed easily. No
'wretchedness' there. But the whole emotional stir behind all my music (except some 4–5 light, bright numbers, mostly folk-music) is so utterly the op-

29. Op. 72, Norwegian Dances.
30. (1871–1951), Australian-born musician; during 1937–45, president of the Juilliard School of
    Music.
31. (1908–91), Australian pianist early encouraged by Grainger.

posite of what the public wants (anywhere in the world) that a blast of fiery unwillingness marks every composition I put forward. [It is] impossible to feel anything but wretched under such hostility.

My mother's family (Aldridge) viewed life adventurously. Two of my uncles were on telegraph-laying expeditions, from Adelaide to Darwin. Uncle Jim stopped run-away horses & had fisticuff fights with men in the parks. In my early childhood, the vast amount of reading aloud that was lavished on me left me with Homer as a favorite (phrases like 'the javelin crashed thru the shield' were constantly in my mind) around the age of 10 to be replaced by a lifelong preference for Icelandic sagas. (Now the battleaxe clove the enemy from the shoulder to the waist.) But whether it was Hector, or Beowulf or Grettir-the-Strong, the heroes all were self-sacrificial. I see no good in self-sacrifice today, tho I still see infinite good in heroism. For whatever reason, my music early settled down to being a celebration of heroic self-sacrifice. The first orchestral piece I planned was 'The Long Serpent' (Longfellow's Olaf Trygvason—who was drowned, of course).[32] Amongst folksongs it was always the tragic ones that appealed to me most (Bonny George Campbell rode out on a day, Home came his guid horse, but never came he.[33] And the waes o' my heart fa' in showers frae my e'e.[34] Willow Willow, Lord Maxwell's Goodnight, The 3 Ravens, The Twa Corbies. Death-Song for Hjalmar Thuren. Father & Daughter. Died for Love. 6 Dukes went afishin'. The Rival Brothers) while in Kipling (Jungle Book Cycle, Tiger Tiger, The Widow's Party, Danny Deever, We have fed our sea) & Swinburne (The Bride's Tragedy, A Reiver's Neck-Verse) it was always death, hanging, burning & other forms of disaster that inspired me most. All this seems to me to have come out of a Brahms influence, rooted in such things as the 'Edward' Ballads,[35] & the songs 'Verath'[36] & 'Es ritt [reit] der Herr von Falkenstein'.[37] A perfect literary example is the first story in Johan[n]es V. Jensen's 'Himmerlands-Historier'[38] (about the 2 Reitknechter & the consumptive girl). My settings of these types I call 'Knights

---

32. In his manuscript notes, 'Methods of Teaching and Other Things', in a passage written in late September 1902, Grainger described this intended work as 'The Saga of King Olaf', for chorus, solo voices, and orchestra. In 1898, he had sketched 'The Crew of the Long Serpent (Dragon)', a twelve-page 'seascape' for piano duet.
33. 'Bonnie George Campbell' was one of Grainger's *Songs of the North* setting of Scottish folk songs (1900). Correctly, ' . . . Bonnie George Campbell rode, out on a day. / He saddled, he bridled, and gallant rode he, / And hame came his guid horse, but never cam he. . . . '
34. From 'Auld Robin Gray' by Lady Anne Lindsay (1750–1825).
35. Grainger may be referring to either Brahms's Op. 10 or Op. 75 sets of Ballades.
36. 'Verrat', Fünf Lieder, Op. 105 No. 5.
37. Vier Gesänge, Op. 43 No. 4.
38. *Himmerland Stories* (1898–1910) by the Danish author (1873–1950).

mouldering in a ditch'. I have always mourned the deaths of young men. If it is true, what Cyril Scott asserts, that the genius is stirred by forebodings of events to come, there is ample justification for my 'Knights mouldering in a ditch' (Ein toter in dem Blumen lag)[39] mood. The wars were coming, with their heavy toll on young men. But none of this in me awoke an echo in any part of the public. They liked my 'The Warriors' (a celebration of the gay fighting man) as little as they liked my lament-like number ('The Twa Corbies'[40]). And I must say they liked Grieg's heroic 'Den Bergtekne'[41] equally little. I think that young men in their teens respond (at least to the foreword of) my Conscientious-Objector piece 'The Power of Rome & the Christian Heart'. But on the whole I think the entire musical world is entirely oblivious of the whole world of bitterness, resentment, iconoclasm & denunciation that lies behind my music. If they were aware of it I am not sure it would make any difference. One thing is certain: I will not leave any point unprotested if I live to write about it all.

Equally wretched (in the lack of acknowledgement of my efforts) has been the response to my *large chamber music* innovations, started about 1898 & based on influences from the Bach 'Passions' etc. The best example of these are 'Under en Bro',[42] 'Bold William Taylor', Hillsongs I & II, 'Green Bushes'. I can think of several reasons why the musical world does not take me seriously as a composer & does not give me credit for the many innovations that other composers (Cyril Scott, Delius, Gould, Gershwin, V. Williams) have taken from me & incorporated in their own music—irregular rhythms, wordless choralism, large chamber music, discordant harmony & closes, etc. I am a poor orchestrator, I lack melodious inspiration—tho I consider myself an expressive harmonist & an inspired counter-melody-writer I feel I am at my best in a cappella writing. Being naturally very shy & impatient, & easily discouraged, I am particularly ill-equipped to prove the worth of my innovations in performance. Sometimes I think my music might do better if I never took part in any performance of it in any way. My clumsiness (as musical thinker, as pianist, as conductor, as orchestrator) has always disastrously handicapped me.

If my music ever makes its mark, it will do so because of the intense tragic feeling behind it, because of my insight into racial qualities, because of my

39. The second-to-last line of Brahms's 'Verrat' [Betrayal], Op. 105 No. 5 (text by Karl von Lemcke). The poem's last two lines translate as: 'A dead man lay in the flowers / to the sorrow of a false woman' (in German).
40. 'The Two Ravens' (1903–9), with text from Walter Scott's *Minstrelsy*.
41. *Lost in the Hills*, Op. 32.
42. 'Under a Bridge' (1945–46), Danish Folk Music series No. 12.

compassionate sympathy with the tragedies of men,[43] & my bitter resentment at the needless cruelties & injustices of life—especially war.

Percy Grainger, July 3, 1953 [on train] Chic—N. York

In considering a composer's genius, & his recognition, it is most important to examine the geography of his inspiration. Brahms's inspiration was 'Des Knaben Wunderhorn'[44] (his sonatas & symphonies sound as if 'D.K.W.' stories lay behind them); thus more locally German than Bach's inspiration, which, amongst other things, was French, English & Italian. Wagner's inspiration was Hans von Wolzogen-ism (Frankish, Celtic, Scandinavian legends).[45] Ravel's inspiration was Spain & Debussy's was Ancient Greece. My geographical inspiration boils down to a small area in the North Sea, comprising the English-Scottish border (Twa Corbies, Bride's Tragedy, Lads of Wamphray, Lord Maxwell's Goodnight, Scotch Strathspey & Reel), Ireland (Co. Derry Air, Scotch S&R, Molly, the tune I set at Fred. Sandby's[46]) & the Faeroes (The Merry Wedding, The Rival Brothers, Death-Song for Hjalmar Thuren, Father & Daughter, Let's Dance Gay). Beyond this geography there are a few flights of inspiration. 'Under en Bro' is almost as good as my Faeroe settings. The 'English Dance' is one of my best pieces, & must be explained later. 'Hill-Songs I & II' are my very best, but they come really under Scottish inspiration. Some of my Lincolnshire folksong settings (Bold William Taylor, 6 Dukes, Brigg Fair) are pretty near the top, but it must be remembered that Lincolnshire is just as Scandinavian in origin as Ireland & Scotland. So my inspiration boils down to 'Scandinavians in their Western settlements' with peculiar concentration upon the Faeroe Islands. 'Father & D.' & 'Let's Dance Gay' are more inspired lively dance settings than 'Sir Eglamore' or 'Shepherd's Hey'. 'The Rival Brothers' & 'Death-Song for Hjalmar Thuren' reach depths not touched in my settings of English folksongs. Yet my 'English Dance' is a thoroly good piece, & my Kipling settings are a response to Englishness that stands high. But is not Kipling North-English? At least his lingo in 'The Seawife'[47] & 'The Last Rhyme of True Thomas'[48] is as much 'border', as Swin-

---

43. One illegible word follows here.
44. Anthology of old German folk poetry (1805–8) by Achim von Arnim and Clemens Brentano.
45. Hans von Wolzogen (1848–1938) was an assistant to Wagner and then for sixty years analyst and interpreter of his works and ideas.
46. Grainger visited Herman Sandby's brother, Frederick, in October 1904 in the Danish village of Sønderjaernløse. The tune was 'Colleen Dhas' (or 'The Valley Lay Smiling'), an Irish tune set by Grainger in 1904 and first performed by a chamber ensemble during his stay with Frederick Sandby.
47. First set by Grainger in 1898.
48. Not set by Grainger.

burne's ditto. The queer fact with the English is that Scandinavian looks & temperament may appear amongst them at any moment as (I presume) they do not in Normandie & other Norse settlements on the European Continent. From the standpoint of my inspiration England (as in my 'English Dance') appears sporadically for the good reason that first-class Scandinavian may appear at any moment in the English midst. Yet it appears doubtless in more mixed & muddled forms than it does in Ireland, the English-Scottish border, the Scottish Lowlands, Orkney & the Shetlands. My conventional reasoning tells me that Englishness is at its worst where it is most mixed with Norman-ness & Celtic-ness, & at its best where it is most mixed with Scandinavian-ness—as in the case of Swinburne, Kipling, Minstrelsy of the Scottish border. I take it to be a justifiable platitude that British greatness (in turn generals such as Monty[49] & Wellington, in Scottish & Northern-Irish shipbuilding, in North-English industry, in games such as golf, in words such as 'through-put', in foods such as porridge, in customs such as strikes & lockouts, in liberals such as Keir-Hardie,[50] in thinkers such as Malthus,[51] in Carnegie-ism[52]) largely originates in the 'western areas of Scandinavian settlement' that form the inspiration of my music & that my special concentration on the Faeroes is especially reasonable & justifiable. Because in Iceland & the Faeroes we get Scandinavianism purer & less disturbed than in England (where it is mixed with Roman-ness, Norman-ness, etc.) or in Norway, Sweden & Denmark, where it is partly spoiled by German, Dutch, British & other elements, seeping in with the Hansa League. For instance, in Icelandic the sharp English 'th' (þ) is still preserved (tho it has disappeared from Norwegian, Swedish & Danish) & in the Faeroe Islands the English double vowels (hä-er = hair, moa-oot = moat) are in full bloom. Thus if we want to study those elements that have given English & Scottish speech their main character, & those elements that have led to the great inventions & developments (steamboat, trains, Ford, pianola, strikes, lockouts, cooperative societies) thru which Britain & USA have changed the modern world, we will find that these elements very often have connecting roots to the areas that have inspired my music. One may say that my music is an effort to concentrate English-speaking thought & feeling upon those elements in the North Sea & in the British isles that are likely to prove useful to our theeds ((nations)) in the future, as they have been in the past. Kipling was a great genius in concentrating on the heroic (that is, the

---

49. Field-Marshal Bernard Law Montgomery (1887–1976)
50. James Kier Hardie (1856–1915), first leader of the Labour Party in the House of Commons.
51. Thomas Robert Malthus (1766–1834), English economist and demographer.
52. Andrew Carnegie (1835–1919), Scottish-born American industrialist and author of the essay 'The Gospel of Wealth' (1889).

Scandinavian) elements in the British world. But he didn't have the insight or the courage to separate the superior from the inferior elements in British life. The only hope for the English-speaking world is to realise the tragedy of their own mixed blood & to cleanse their own races by studying the inferiority of the dark-eyed, dark-haired elements & the superiority of the fair types. If this is not done the wonderful prosperity created by the fair types will become a plaything mischievously exploited by the dark types, as it is at present. If we cannot rise to Scandinavian heights of lovingness, truthful outspokenness, thrift & self-worship the prosperousness of our English-speaking world will all be for nothing. And what is the Scandinavian superiority (as we find it in Laxness,[53] J.V. Jensen, Thor Johnson,[54] Kipling, Swinburne, Delius, the Icelandic sagas, the Scottish & the Faeroe ballads) rooted in? The willingness to face the greatest possible sadness: (when my wife met me, I was the saddest man she could find. She was not afraid to take me on.) It is only Kipling's & Swinburne's *sad* poems that have any special value for me. My favorite of Swinburne's is 'The Jacobite's Exile'[55] (is it, indeed, not the poem of my own life?) What is the meaning behind all this? Does mankind need suffering more than all else? Must man's unforgivable inhumanity to animals (to be willing to kill & eat them) be cured by art? Will man's filthy appetite for war & competition (whether in the form of business or Olympic Games) cease only when man has been drenched in an artistic presentation of the sadness of life? I have no idea. I only know that great poets such as those I have mentioned have been able to squeeze the sorrows of life into their poems, & that such poems ('The Only Son', 'The Bride's Tragedy') inspired me to write some of my best music. And the worth of my music will never be guessed, or its value to mankind felt, until the approach to my music is consciously undertaken as a 'pilgrimage to sorrow'. Other composers have based the appeal of their music on broad formal effects & on orchestrational brilliance (contrasts of tone-colors) or on clever manipulations of intervals. I know nothing of all those things. I strive to make the voice-leading of my tone-strands touching & the effect of my harmonies agonized. As early as 1897 Knorr[56] said 'die Harmonien schielen' (the harmonies squint). My effort, even in those young days, was to wrench at the listener's heart with my chords. It is a subtle matter, & is not achieved by mere discordance. As Henry Cowell cleverly pointed out: when 6 trombones are made to play nothing but close-together discordant intervals (such as A flat, A natural, B flat, B natural, C, C sharp) they do not sound dis-

---

53. Halldór Kiljan Laxness (1902–98), Icelandic author.
54. Probably Thorsten Jonsson (1910–50), Swedish-born writer.
55. Correctly, 'A Jacobite's Exile'.
56. Iwan Knorr (1853–1916), Grainger's composition and theory teacher in Frankfurt.

cordant as music is not made agonizing merely by sharp discords any more than literature is made agonizing by crude events. It is the contrast between the sweet & the harsh ('I could have ridden the border round had Christie Graham been at my back'[57]) that is heart rending. Perhaps these assaults upon the tenderness of man's hearts (as we find them in tragic poetry & music based on the same) will play their part in weaning men from massed murder of mankind in war, & mass murder of animals for food. I do not know what other purpose such an artistic wallowing in sadness as that found in my art can have. There is no doubt that the sad & tragic poems (North-English, Scottish, Faeroe Island, Scandinavian) I worship really affect me *personally*. I cannot read my favorite type of Kipling or Swinburne poetry aloud without crying & losing control of my voice. Everything in my art is based on violently sentimental emotionalism & must be received on that basis to get anything out of it. The imitation of *wailing* is the concern of the voice-leadings that make up my harmonies. And that is the object of my Free Music: to provide wailing sounds of a subtlety, magnitude & refinement hitherto unknown in music. This wish to write the-music-of-grief has swayed me much, no doubt, in my choice of instruments & habits of scoring. The symphony orchestra (with its voluptuous strings, its harsh brass & very unequal tone-strengths of the various tone-families—more built for contrasts than for blends) is seldom poignant enough for my purposes. The wind-band is better. But the ideal (for my grief-stricken music) is large chamber music, where a harmonium can give background sounds & single strings can moan & single winds can wail with a greater edginess (sharpness of tonal line) than in more massed combinations, such as band or symphony orchestra.

Much of the wretchedness of my tone life has been occasioned by my unusual scoring habits—mostly rooted in the above preference for groupings—sometimes 8 single instruments, but often as many as 24 single instruments. Who can perform such works? No chamber music organisation has so many players & no symphony orchestra cares to use only ¼ or ⅛ of their group. So most of my best works (like 'Hill-Song I')[58] go unperformed, year after year. But I am sure that my scorings, if properly worked out, will have the qualities of intensity & drasticness that the music craves, & I have no willingness to descend to what I feel (more conventional scoring) is a lower level of expressiveness. The object of my music is not to entertain, but to agonise (to make mankind think of the agony of young men forced to kill each other against their will & all the other thwartments & torturings of the young). Perhaps,

---

57. Lines from 'Graeme and Bewick' in Scott's *Minstrelsy*, correctly: 'I durst hae ridden the Border through, / Had Christie Graeme been at my back'.
58. Originally scored by Grainger for 'room-music 22-some (or 23-some)'.

after some years, a certain proportion of music-lovers will want not only 1,000-times-repeated classics & entertainment-music & will want to hear something in a more tragic vein. I hope they will find it in the first Australian composer (myself), as well as in all sorts of other music (Bach, Wagner, Grieg, Balakirev, Sandby, C. Scott, C. Frank, Delius) from which I have drawn comfort & inspiration.

[on train] Chic. → Kansas City, P.A. Grainger, July 14, 1953

My art set out to celebrate the beauty of bravery. The lines of limbs on Greek vases that I delighted in as a little boy, the javelin crashing thru the shield, Grettir entering the ghost's grave to get the sword, these are all hymns to bravery. In fact, is there any beauty other than the beauty of bravery? The beautiful races (the Irish, the Norwegians) are just the brave races. And a race that never loses bravely, like the Jews, has *no* beauty, *ever* (I don't mean that Jews are cowards, far from it. But danger does not stupidly attract them, as it did me when I walked round the ledge of the house, window to window outside, on the 4th floor at Blumenstrasse).[59] If I was naturally brave then, what turned me into a coward? I haven't the faintest idea. I could put forward several explanations, but it would be mere guess-work. There was Weininger's theory: that the mother-type was brave because she sensed 'society' behind her, that the whore-type was cowardly because she sensed society was against her.[60] In my case it piled up. In 1895 the Germans were against everything in me that Australians would have approved of. In 1902 the English were against all sorts of views I had picked up in Germany (including awareness of the dangerousness & hostility of the Germans). Like the whore, I have always had the world sexually against me (with the possible exception of Scandinavia). By the time the 1914 German War began I had become a coward (or had I always been one?): not a very effective spectacle—a coward, a turn-coat, whose lifework was to celebrate in music beauty-born-of-bravery! No wonder no piece of mine (except 'Country Gardens') has 'caught on' since 1914. But that one exception is suspicious. I am quite willing to acknowledge myself a coward, & quite willing to ascribe my failure as a serious composer to my proven cowardice. But I am equally ready to weigh other considerations. As a child, there is no doubt that I worshipped bravery, & the beauty of bravery, with a burning devotion. And there is also no doubt that I have come to consider most bravery rather silly. Yet is it not true that my music disports the beauty of bravery & the speed & directness of bravery (no 'beating about the bush', but going straight to the point) as the music of V. Williams, Walton, Holst does not? The emotional background of

59. At Pension Pfaffin in Frankfurt, where the Graingers lived in 1895–6. See also essay 61.
60. See earlier discussion in essay 20.

'The Bride's Tragedy', 'Father & Daughter', 'English Dance', Hill-Songs, 'The Rival Brothers', seem to me drenched in the beauty-born-of-bravery in a way that V. W.'s London Symphony, Pastoral Symphony & Walton's exquisite meanderings are not. Most composers are pompous & celebrate power & success. In spite of all my shortcomings as a man & as a composer I will not admit my inferiority to the men (like Prokofieff [Prokofiev]) who are most famous today. I admit that there is a rooted difference between them & me. But I claim the differing is to my advantage. I claim that my qualities (& my defects) are those of superior genius, greater purity & a more intense inspiration. I expect that the greater worldliness & platitudinousness of my contemporaries will be eventually recognised for what it is & that my more passionate & tender qualities will get home & make their mark.

I have already admitted how my various systems of scoring prevent & mar performances of almost all my works. A badly played organ or harmonium part is enough to wreck any of my pieces. (And good organ & harmonium players, in my sense—studying the music as quartet players study a Beethoven 4-tet—hardly exist.) Never the less, I still consider my use of organ or harmonium for background harmony utterly justified & firmly believe it would produce more perfect tonal results than any other method in my music—if scrupulously carried out. There is no doubt that my instinct for tonal balance (a balance that would allow the prominent voices to emerge effortlessly without the conductor struggling with the sonorities) is often very faulty & that my lack of proper instinct in this particular may have to be replaced by curative method on the part of the conductor, or even by re-scoring of certain details. But I claim that in most cases my vision of a rich, complex & telling blend of sonorities is always present in the scoring & that a satisfactory solution of tonal balance is never far around the corner. I also believe that my vision of sonorities (even when obscure) is original & expressive enough to be worth the trouble of fussing & struggling with it.

PG, July 15,'53, KC[61] → St Paul

The best-sounding performance of my 'Children's March'[62] (which is scored for very big band) was given by a very small & very poor naval band very well trained by Storm Bull,[63] on Navy Pier, Chicago, early in the 2nd German War.[64] Being such a small band, each player had to pull his weight & show re-

---

61. Kansas City.
62. 'Over the Hills and Far Away' (1916–18), scored for military band (1919).
63. (b. 1913), American pianist and student of Grainger's at the Chicago Musical College in the late 1920s.
64. Probably on 27 July 1942, when Grainger also performed in the programme.

sponsibility. That is the main thing with my music, for it to sound well—that every tone-strand (part, voice) that makes up the harmonic texture is clearly heard in a harmonic sense. The harmony is what matters in my music—not the tone-color.

Because pieces of mine like 'Molly on the Shore', 'Father & Daughter', 'Mock Morris' made such a success in England that some of them became world-known it must not be assumed that my tone-life at that time (1909–1914) was less 'wretched' than it has been before or since. The wretchedness has always lain in lack of sympathy with the emotional background of my compositions. In Frankfurt my English composer-friends (Cyril Scott, Roger Quilter, Balfour Gardiner) always laughed when I played them a new composition. They did not laugh unsympathetically. But the originality & unexpectedness of my music struck them as funny. And the impression of funniness was stronger than the impression of heart-throbs or heart-break. Not Herman Sandby. When the others laughed, Sandby waited till the others had gone & said, 'I see nothing to laugh at in yr music'. He caught the heart-throbs or heart-break in my music & saw nothing funny in it. To the cool, conventional English nature my passionate & exaggerated nature seems comic. But Sandby has a very intense & passionate nature himself & he recognised similar qualities in me for what they were. Music-lovers are used to Italians & others feeling passionately about sex & writing passionate music about it. But they are not used to passionate & tragic music being written about hills, the sea, animals, racial characteristics & the deaths of young men. And as long as this basic lack of sympathy exists my tone-life will continue to be wretched—& the shallow success of a few tuneful snippets like 'Country Gardens' & 'Handel in the Strand' will not alter matters.

P.G., July 17, 1953, [on train] St Paul → Kansas City

Source: 'Why "My Wretched Tone-Life"?' in 'Grainger's Anecdotes', 423-89, dated 3–17 July 1953 (Grainger Museum, Melbourne).

64   Length (Size) in Tone-Art & Other Art (1935)

Size in itself is a kind of fair-hood ((beauty)). The mere bigness of an elephant, or of a great ocean-liner, is a joy in itself. A great roll of paper for newspaper printing fulfils something in man. And so in tone-art. We must praise the Germans, above all others, for having brot *size* into tone-art. How small are the form sizes of Dufay, Palestrina, Worcester Mediaeval Harmony,[65] Javanese Gamelan tone-art when sidematched [compared] with the 1st chorus in the Matthew Passion, with a Brahms symphony, or Strauss's 'Domestica'![66] The 1st real lull in R.S.'s 'Heldenleben'[67] would not be as soul fulfilling as it is if it didn't follow after a long outburst of force-forthputment![68] Only a great length of deedishness would crave such an after-rest. So a work lasting 1 hour can bring tonesome forth-filments of weariness & turnovers of mood that would not freethly ((naturally)) come into being in a short tonework. So sheer size has its great gift to give to tone-art.

Delius is German in his inborn leaning towards length. And my leaning towards shortness (that Ella rightly blames) is British—tho I was not as thusly British in my early works ('Hill-Song I', 'English D[ance]') as later. If one left tone-art in the hands of the English-speakers our nowtime great artworks would soon be whittled down to the shortness of Dufay & Dunstable. The Old English ((Anglosaxon)) Timekeepbook ((Chronicle)), the sagas, Walt Whitman & Edgar Lee Masters all show, however, that length is as at home in English-speaking oversouls [geniuses] as in those of other Germanic folks. It seems to be the mind-tilth-jilting laziness & unforwardpressingness of the cosier, wendelsea [Mediterranean] racesome & old-stoneage racial riffraff in the English that cannot grip hold of length, size, & gladtake it.

Source: 'Length (Size) in Tone-Art & Other Art', in 'Nordic English. Thots on Tone-Art', undated (probably mid-July 1935; Grainger Museum, Melbourne).

⤳ 65 The Strange Idea That I Compose for Piano & Then 'Arrange' for Strings, Orchestra, Etc. (1937)

This strange notion has grown up, unhindered by the fact that I have never composed direct for piano (except for things labelled clear 'transcriptions') & have dubbed my arrangements of my other compositions (for room [chamber] music, chorus, orchestra, etc.) 'dished-up for piano', to make it quite clear that they are only a 're-hash'. But it has not helped. The fact that I am a

---

65. Known to Grainger through Anselm Hughes's *Worcester Mediaeval Harmony of the Thirteenth and Fourteenth Centuries* (1928).
66. *Symphonia Domestica* (1902–3), by Richard Strauss.
67. Strauss's *Ein Heldenleben* (1897–98).
68. Extended *forte* passages (in Nordic English). Grainger is probably referring to the general pause and the start of the 'Critics' section, following the Hero's lengthy exposition.

pianist is enough to make everyone rush to the belief that I compose first for 'my instrument'. It is hard that this should happen just to me, the re-birther of Bach-like 'large chamber-music' & a hater of the piano. The climax was reached when a Boston critic (after my Boston orchestral concert with the People's Orchestra[69]) wrote: 'Mr Grainger is one of those composers like Moszkowsky,[70] who has a knack of writing popular piano pieces which afterwards appear in arrangements for all sorts of combinations', or words to that effect.

Nov. 29, 1937

Source: 'The Strange Idea That I Compose for Piano & Then "Arrange" for Strings, Orchestra, Etc.', in 'Nordic English. Thots on Tone-Art' (Grainger Museum, Melbourne).

➤ 66   'The Inuit' at La Crosse, Wis[consin] (1923)

Here at the home ([in] Spokane) of Greenwoods'[71] friends, the Geo. W. Burtons,[72] at La Crosse, Wis., I read again Kipling's 'Jungle Books' & they touch me as of yore. 'The Inuit'[73] makes me remember that I have left out my 'Inuit' setting from the sketch of my New York Room-Music programs for 1924–25.[74] The 'Inuit' chorus has never been well received anywhere, not by mother & my composer friends, & when given in London by Kennedy Scott[75] at Balf. Gardiner's concerts[76] proved a real fiasco & humiliation for me—K. Scott repeating it without a real encore demand by the public, who were lukewarm or cool. Noone seems to have sensed the depth of feeling out of which this little composition arose, & into which, thinking of it & playing it

69. The semiprofessional People's Symphony Orchestra was established in 1920 and wound up in 1936.
70. Moritz Moszkowski (1854–1925), German pianist and composer.
71. George Greenwood (1884–1952) and Victoria Greenwood, good friends of Grainger's who would in 1928 accompany Grainger and his wife on their honeymoon hiking trip.
72. (1858–1931).
73. For a cappella mixed chorus; composed in 1902, revised in 1907, and published by Schott & Co. in 1912.
74. Grainger's chamber-music concerts took place on 26 April and 3 May 1925 in the Little Theater of Carnegie Hall. The first concert included seven of Grainger's Kipling settings, but not 'The Inuit'.
75. Charles Kennedy Scott (1876–1965), English (mainly choral) conductor.
76. On 11 February 1913 at Queen's Hall, London. This was the work's official première, although it had been performed at an 'At Home' of Mrs. Lowrey's on 28 May 1903.

throws me afresh each time. It is sung too English-wise, too detached—whereas I intend it with Italian Caruso-like clinging legatissimo. The urge behind this poem is the very strongest & most pronounced root emotion of my life: the love of savagery, the belief that savages are sweeter & more peaceable & artistic than civilized people, the belief that primitiveness is purity & civilisation filthy corruption, the agony of seeing civilisation advance & pass its blighting hand over the wild. Not 'the survival of the fittest' but 'the survival of the fetidest'. And the rather mawkish Longfellowish sentimentality of this music is utterly true to my nature & pleasing to me at all times. I wish to say that I stand back of[77] 'The Inuit', the poem & the music & all it signifies, as wholeheartedly today as 20 years ago & that I regard it as one of the worthiest of my works. Altogether I attach much importance to my Kipling 'Jungle Book' settings, wish them not to be left out of schemes for presenting my works, & suggest the following grouping for a room-music concert, consisting of works for a small a cappella choir with & without room-music instrumental accompaniment:[78]

Source: ' "The Inuit" at La Crosse, Wis.', in 'Sketches for My Book "The Life of My Mother & Her Son" ', W35-68, dated 19 November 1923 (Grainger Museum, Melbourne).

⤳ 67   My Dealings with Stanford anent His 'Four Irish Dances' (1949?)

There is no doubt that Stanford[79] had some real love for me. My inborn weakness makes me a dish for old men. He asked me to look in & see him any & every Sunday morning when I could.[80] And I often did—seeing him writing piano music miles away from any piano; & didn't it sound like it too. One of these Sunday mornings, there he was dishing up his 'Four Irish Dances' for piano solo—easy grade, Sunday school stuff. (Shortly before I had heard him time-beat his '4 Irish Dances' on the orchestra he had composed them for.[81] I liked some of the music in them, but marvelled at his hopelessly dull scoring.

---

77. I.e., stand behind.
78. Grainger's manuscript appears not to provide the promised grouping.
79. Charles Villiers Stanford (1852–1924), Irish-born composer, conductor, and professor of music at the University of Cambridge from 1887 until his death.
80. Grainger is probably referring to the 1904–8 period in London.
81. (1903), unpublished.

Fancy such a muff at orchestration as he being allowed to teach it! It never fails.) I could not forbear saying that I thought such pieces should be pianised in a sparkling, show-off sort of way—even if they thereby became hard to play. So Stanford said: 'Very well. You do them. You're the man to do them'. And I did. And my dish-ups were published by Stainer & Bell (a firm in which Stanford had some money, or where he was the art-side storeman).[82] I asked no royalty, of course; & I played them on something like 300 concerts of the Ada Crossley English tour, about 1907–1908.[83] I also had slips printed, at my own expense, stating that the dances were published by Stainer & Bell & giving their address. These slips I laid on every seat of almost every concert of the tour. At the end of the tour I asked Stanford how the dish-ups had sold—for I wanted to know if my slip-laying tactics had borne any fruit. But he looked away & didn't answer me. Maybe he was ashamed to admit how badly they had done (in USA they never sold either), or maybe he thought I wanted to ask a share in the earnings. (The North Sea-dwellers, so long half starved, can never understand the loose give-willingness of an Australian.) Some 5 years later, just after I came to America, I wrote Stanford that J. Fischer & Bro. wanted to buy the USA rights of his 4 Irish Dances, both the original orchestral version & my piano arrangements, offering 200 pounds for the 2, I think. Stanford wrote back that he saw no reason why he should refuse—& didn't.[84] But his letter to me read sad, I thought, like a man writing to one who had deeply hope-thwarted him. And that I had done that, in being a turncoat,[85] goes without saying. Stanford had a simple Irish-Protestant British patriotism that comes out beautifully in his spine-chilling 'Songs of the Sea'.[86] He could say 'the man was a rebel' with a forcefulness that was surprising in one who had lived so long in temperate England ('where temperate winds of England blow the hurrying cloud'. Edgar Lee Masters, in 'The Autochthon'.[87])

(1949?)

Source: 'My Dealings with Stanford anent His "Four Irish Dances"', in 'Grainger's Anecdotes', 423-18 (Grainger Museum, Melbourne).

82. The four dances—'A March Jig', 'A Slow Dance', 'Leprechaun's Dance', and 'A Reel'—were originally published in 1907–8 by Houghton & Co., London, and later assigned to Stainer & Bell.
83. This provincial tour lasted from 15 October 1907 to 25 March 1908.
84. The rights in Grainger's piano arrangements were assigned to J. Fischer & Bro., New York, in 1916. The orchestral rights appear not to have been taken up.
85. I.e., for leaving England hurriedly at the start of the First World War.
86. Op. 91 (1904), for baritone, male chorus, and orchestra.
87. In Masters's *The Great Valley*.

➤68   Stanford Deemed My 'Irish Tune' Un-Irish & My 'Brigg Fair' Un-English. His Disapproval of Vaughan Williams's Norfolk Rhapsodies (1949?)

Stanford made it quite clear that he disliked my setting of 'Irish Tune', that he deemed it 'un-Irish'. 'It's Grieg my lad, not Irish'. Or was it of 'Brigg Fair',[88] he said: 'It's Grieg, my lad, not English'? Or was it my treatment of flat sevenths in 'Molly' that he was talking about? He said that the Irish way of treating flat sevenths (when they had shifting drones on the Irish bagpipes) was [music notation] not [music notation], the latter being Grieg. These Irish settings of mine had to be be-talked by me & Stanford, because I felt it 'called' for to ask him—as the editor of the Petrie Collection[89]—for his permission for me to forth-print my settings of Irish tunes in that collection. He gave me the green light, but it was clear that he disliked my barging in & setting Irish tunes—a realm in which he fain would have been the only king. (Not in any nasty way, of course.) In a kindred way he looked askance at Vaughan Williams's 'Norfolk Rhapsodies':[90] 'As if the English had any melodies worth making rhapsodies out of! Now with us in Ireland it's different.' It was part of Stanford's poor tone-man-ship that he (who lived thru the whole period of recognition of English folksong) was not able to real-see that the best types of English folksong (such as the Somerset 'Sheep-shearing Song' & Burstow's 'Duke of Marlborough'[91]) were a jump ahead of even Irish ones in close-to-the-soilness, old fangledness & lordliness.

At Stanford's 'At Homes' the only things I call-to-mind Stanford really *wanting* me to play were the Bach-Busoni Chorale-preludes & the Stanford 'Four Irish Dances' (see 423-18)[92] & Dante Rhapsodies (see 423-19).[93] Quite naturally. Stanford was a simple-minded, mean-natured but quite loveable

---

88. Tune collected at Brigg, Lincolnshire, in 1905 and arranged for tenor solo and a cappella mixed chorus in 1906.

89. *The Complete Collection of Irish Music as noted by George Petrie*, 3 vols., ed. Stanford, was published in 1902–5.

90. Vaughan Williams's three *Norfolk Rhapsodies* date from 1905 to 1906. Only the first was published.

91. Song collected by Lucy E. Broadwood from Henry Burstow of Horsham, Sussex. Grainger's *'The Duke of Marlborough' Fanfare* of 1939 was based on the tune.

92. Essay 67.

93. In this short passage from his 'Anecdotes' (423-19), Grainger recalled Stanford's (three) Dante Rhapsodies (Op. 92, 1904); Stanford's dedication of them to him; and his embarrassment at playing their 'dull, dry phrases' in concert.

natural Irishman. Such selfish natures are not bad—one knows where one has them. To me he was always wonderfully kind—getting me engagements & being really fond of me. But then, I was useful to him. Who else would have bothered with his dry 'Four Irish Dances' & miserably dull Dante Rhapsodies?

The worst thing about Stanford was the blend of good & bad tone-man in him—one minute his enthralling 'Lough Aruma' & (in spots) heavenly Requiem;[94] the next moment those awful Dante Rhapsodies! And such a man's redes [advice], in matters of tone-craft, would never be worth the having. If one looked into it, I fore-ween [predict] one would find that all English composers that came under his sway at all were much the worse for it. Except for his best moments, he was a 'professional man' (like a solicitor) rather than an artist. As a tone-man he was clearly a thrall to Germany-in-the-saddle-ness. One thing I forgive him—his spleen at my 'Irish Tune from Co. Derry' setting. It was only natural that he should deem his own setting (in one of the Irish Rhapsodies) the only law-hallowed one & view such settings as mine as interlopers & poacher tricks. But when I set the Irish Tune (1902) I did not know of his Irish Rhapsodies.

(1949?)

Source: 'Stanford Deemed My "Irish Tune" Un-Irish & My "Brigg Fair" Un-English. His Disapproval of Vaughan Williams's Norfolk Rhapsodies', in 'Grainger's Anecdotes', 423-17 (Grainger Museum, Melbourne).

69 Beecham's Cheek about 'Colonial Song' (1945)

Was it early in July, 1914, that Princesse de Polignac[95] gave a toneshow to guests in a house just by the corner of King's Road & Cheyne Walk, Chelsea (London),[96] for which she hired me to play on 2 pianos with her such French gems as 'L'Après-midi d'un faune',[97] Fauré's 'Pelléas et Mélisande' Suite—maybe also Debussy's 'Fêtes', 'Sirènes'?[98] That was the same time she said, 'War is already a fact. In France, all my officer friends are mobilised already.' I was witless enough not to believe her—yes, I believed her officer friends

94. Op. 63 (1897).
95. The American-born Winaretta Eugénie Singer (1865–1943).
96. Elsewhere ('Grainger's Anecdotes', 423-5), Grainger identifies that house, more plausibly, as being near the corner of King's Road and Oakley Street.
97. Debussy's orchestral Prélude (1892–94), arranged for two pianos (1895).
98. The final two of the three orchestral *Nocturnes* (1897–99).

[were] on a war-footing, but not that war would come. It was at that party (an afternoon one?) that Thomas Beecham[99] said to me: 'My dear Grainger, you have achieved the impossible: you have written the worst modern orchestral piece!' 'What is that?' I asked. 'Your Colonial Song.' 'I'm afraid it's not quite so distinguished as that', I said. He must have heard it at Balfour Gardiner's toneshows, a few months before.[100] It does not stand very high as a piece for string-&-wind-band, I up-own. But as a toneshow number for 2 single voices[101] & string-&-wind-band (for which set-up there are not many worth-while numbers, other than those in operas), it seems to me to fill a hole. And it was with 2 voices (Gervase Elwes, & was it Carry Tubb?[102]) that Beecham must have heard it at Balfour's toneshows. How very hard-hearted of such Englishmen as Beecham to feel no kindly stir towards the first big-frame voicing of a Colonial selfawareness in tonery by a Colonial! How little fore-seeing of the wars & haps to come! How ungifted of them! This I held against the tone-fond English at large—that they felt *no warmth* towards the Australian-ness of an Australian who had done so much for English folksong (making it world-liked. 'These are the best things that have come to us from England', Henry T. Finck[103] had already written in New York, about 2 years before I went to USA), & for English art-tonery (doing so many 'first forth-playments' [premières] of English toneworks in sundry lands) as I had. But against Beecham, for his cheek as a mere band-boss daring to worth-judge a work of mine, I felt nothing—nothing beyond sorrow that he didn't like it. After all, he had given the first forth-playment of any work of mine for strings-wind band anywhere (my 'English Dance' at the Coliseum, 1911[104]). There were lots of mistakes in the band parts, but Beecham—like all other band-bosses—caught none of them. I couldn't hear a rehearsal as I was playing in Belfast. But I got home for the toneshow, in which my work shaped poorly enough. It came just after Delius's 'The Walk to the Paradise Garden' which struck my mother by its lovely use of harp-sounds. Mother said that this E. D. [English Dance] forth-playment was a good shower-up of the howths [qualities] of the friends that heard it. The von Glehns were glum, &

99. (1879–1961), English conductor.
100. 25 February 1913 at London's Queen's Hall. In his 'Anecdotes' recollection (423-5), Grainger suggests it may have been at the 1914 Torquay Festival (on 16 April) that Beecham heard the piece.
101. Tenor and soprano.
102. Correctly, Carrie Tubb (b. 1876), who did certainly perform in the work at the 16 April 1914 concert.
103. (1854–1926), critic for the New York *Evening Post*.
104. 18 February 1912, at the Palladium, with Beecham conducting the Beecham Symphony Orchestra.

so were other non-oversoul friends. Balfour Gardiner took a very marked stand, which I will be-write elsewhere (see No. [ ][105]). But Cyril Scott & Willy Strecker,[106] who heard it together in the gallery, came down in flaming worth-prizement. 'You see,' said my mother, 'Cyril is the only *real* genius among them. He hears with his imagination, & the others only hear with their outer ears.' Then Beecham asked me to write dance-tonery for the Russian Ballet which led me to write 'The Warriors'.[107] He also asked me to become one of his steady opera band-bosses. I was thankful for his trust in me. But I couldn't trust a dark-eyed man. I didn't mistrust his well-meaningness—only his steadiness & manliness.

[on train] Kansas, July 18, '45

Source: 'Beecham's Cheek about "Colonial Song" ', in 'Ere-I-Forget', 384-39 (Grainger Museum, Melbourne).

⟶ 70   Balfour Gardiner's Criticisms of Sparre Olsen, Ravel, My 'Colonial Song' (1952)

Balfour Gardiner was mostly drastic & usually unusually original & aback-taking in his musical criticisms. He took to Sparre Olsen very much (who wouldn't?) as a man, so I showed Balfour some of Sparre's choruses, hoping Balfour might show them to Charles Kennedy Scott. But Balfour surprised me by saying, 'It's terribly poor stuff, isn't it? It's too bad that such a delightful chap should write such poor music'.

When Ravel's 'Gaspard de la Nuit' was new I played 'Ondines' & 'Le Gibet'[108] to Cyril & Balfour one evening—somewhere north of the park it seems to [me] it was (could it have been at Balfour's father's house?). Cyril, or I, or both of us, were praising 'Ondines', but Balfour said: 'That's all very well but that trickling water business has been done before in French music. But what Ravel does in "Le Gibet" is entirely new.'

When I first played Balfour my 'Colonial Song' he kept silence during the first [43][109] bars, which never leave E major. But when, in the [44th] bar, it

---

105. Left blank by Grainger. See essay 101.
106. (1884–1958), Grainger's publisher with Schott & Co. (London) from 1911.
107. Grainger's 'music to an imaginary ballet', for large orchestra and three pianos (1913–16).
108. The first two movements of *Gaspard de la Nuit* (1908).
109. Grainger left these and the following bar numbers blank.

modulates into G major Balfour lept out of his seat, shouting in a loud voice, 'Thank God for that'. He was also very funny about those trill-on-three-notes-like passages that occur in bars [50–51] which, by the way, I had clearly cribbed from Enesco's First Rumanian Rhapsody, just as I had clearly cribbed cadences from Enesco's Second Rumanian Rhapsody[110] in my 'Tribute to Foster'.[111] (I had recently been on tour in Holland with Mengelberg[112] & the Concertge-bouw orchestra, hearing Enesco delightfully conduct his enthralling pieces night after night.) Balfour said, 'How do you think your Australians will like those Hungarian [sic] immigrants?' He always referred to the trill-on-3-notes-like passages as 'your Hungarians'. And when he heard I was going to conduct my 'Colonial Song' at Sir Henry Wood's Promenade Concerts (with Gervase Elwes & Carrie Tubb singing the voice parts)[113] Balfour said, 'And do you think you will get much satisfaction out of that?' I said, 'I don't see why not'. But Balfour was right & I was wrong. I have never had any satisfaction out of the 'Colonial Song'.

Sept. 8, 1952, Up[p]sala.

Source: 'Balfour Gardiner's Criticisms of Sparre Olsen, Ravel, My "Colonial Song"', in 'Grainger's Anecdotes', 423-7 (Grainger Museum, Melbourne).

➤ 71   Grieg's Growing Fretfulness at My Tone-Works (1949/52)

When Lady Speyer said to Grieg at dinner the first time I met Grieg,[114] 'You should hear Percy play your compositions', Grieg answered, 'What instrument does he play?' Grieg didn't know I was a piano player when he asked Lady Speyer to ask me to meet him. She had asked him, 'Are there any people you would like me to invite to meet you, while you are in London?' (The Griegs were staying with the Speyers.) And Grieg had said, 'No, I am too tired'. (The

---

110. The two orchestral Rumanian Rhapsodies, Op. 11, of the Rumanian George Enescu (1881–1955), date from 1901.
111. Composed during 1913–16.
112. Willem Mengelberg (1871–1951), Dutch conductor from 1895 of the Concertgebouw Orchestra.
113. Grainger ended up conducting a new orchestral version of *Colonial Song* (with no voices) at the 18 August 1914 Promenade concert.
114. On 15 May 1906 at the home of Sir Edgar Speyer (1862–1932), banker, and Lady Leonora Speyer (1872–1956), musician and society hostess.

fact is, he was next door to dying.)[115] But later he said, 'Yes! There is a young composer from Australia I want to meet.' And he mentioned my name. Mrs Speyer said, 'I know Percy well'. The whole thing was started by Herman Sandby (unknown to me) showing some printed choruses of mine (which were they? Irish Tune from County Derry. The March of the Men of Harlech. The Camp. Brigg Fair. I'm 17 Come Sunday?) to Grieg when he met him in Copenhagen (was it 1904?). Like a bolt out of the blue I suddenly got a photo from Grieg & on it: 'Thanks for your splendid choruses'.[116] Now, had Grieg sent me this photo because he really wanted to (that sounds impossible) or had he been wheedled into it by Sandby. Sandby may have had the photo in readiness (he would do *anything* for me) & more or less railroaded Grieg into writing something nice on it—I don't know. But Grieg's asking Lady Speyer to get me to come & meet him (on my own, I would have run miles to *avoid* meeting Grieg. I hate meeting my gods) seems to argue that Grieg really felt some mind-stir in me. And that first evening he asked me to play my own compositions & his praise of whatever I did (Tulluchgoram?[117] Irish Tune? Burstow's 'Duke of Marlborough'? Brigg Fair? Did I sing 'Six Dukes'?) seemed to ring true enough. Of course, whatever mind-stir he felt in my own things was overshadowed by his aback-takenness & delight in hearing me play his op. 66 & op. 72[118] so wonderfully—for *that* I did. And at 'Troldhaugen' a year later, he asked me to play to his tone-friends Frants Beyer[119] & Julius Röntgen[120] my own things no less than his own op. 66 & op. 72 & the Bach C sharp minor Prelude & Fugue. Of *Irish Tune, Tulluchgoram*, & other samples of British folk music, Grieg said with happy wonderment: 'They are so strange, as if they came from China'. Then I brought out the orchestral score of *Green Bushes*,[121] which I had finished the summer before & honor-tokened ((dedicated)) to Grieg. The first time I played it I thought Grieg seemed pleased enough, & as for Röntgen (that noble & generous soul but clod-hoppery art-man), he was utterly bowled over, repeating again & again in a loud voice [in German] 'There's the up-and-coming man for you!' [In English] But the next time I played *Green Bushes* I thought I sensed an unbroken fretfulness in Grieg—fret-

---

115. Grieg died the following year.
116. Grainger had received this photograph in April 1905 and had written with thanks (and a photograph of himself) to Grieg on 14 April 1905.
117. Tullochgorum. Grainger refers to the Reel of his *Scotch Strathspey and Reel*, which is underpinned by 'The Reel of Tulloch'.
118. 19 Norwegian Folk Tunes and *Slåtter*, respectively.
119. (1851–1918), Norwegian folk culturist and neighbour of Grieg at Troldhaugen.
120. (1855–1932), German-born Dutch-resident musician.
121. A 'passacaglia on an English folksong'. This arrangement of 1905–6 was for small orchestra.

fulness that was still more marked when I played Debussy, Ravel, Cyril Scott &
Roger Quilter. And it seemed to me that this fretfulness spread to everything of
my own that I played. So I gave up playing my own stuff altogether; & when I
tone-wrought [composed] my chorus 'Soldier-Soldier'[122] down in the
Komponisten-Hytte, halfway down the 'Troldhaugen' rock,[123] I said nothing
about it & played nought of it to Grieg, in spite of his saying something (he
was always so sweet & tender) about 'sweet tones' (or 'strange tones') arising
from the bottom of the hill. So the evenings (at Troldhaugen, with Grieg) became nothing but painful tone chores for me—I eager to give the darling man
some tonal happiness before he died,[124] but feeling ill-geared to do so (as I
could not play the Chopin, Mozart, Beethoven pieces he asked for) & always
in terror that my gifted but unorthodox way of playing his pieces would pall
on him. He had already said (going down from Beyer's house to the boat in
pitch darkness), with regard to op. 66, [in Danish] 'You know, you don't follow
my intentions. But I like it like that—you are full of individuality.'[125] [In Eng-
lish] Of course, I felt crudely snubbed as a tone-wright [composer]. His words
on the photo sent before I knew him, his seeming enthusiasm over my compositions in London, had all led me to believe that this great over-soul [genius]
that I worshipped sensed a fellow in me. But it was a case of 'down-side'. Tho
no belittlement of my tonery crossed Grieg's lips in my hearing, still my sense
of Grieg's fretfulness at my tone works was borne out by those entries in his
day-books in which he speaks of [in German] 'Will you always roam
further?'[126] [In English] Having found in me a flawless forth-heralder of his op.
66 & op. 72 it went without saying that he would want to see me stick to pianism. But that he should view my tone-wrighting & folk-music gathering as

122. Kipling setting, originally of 1898–99, but resketched at Troldhaugen (2 August 1907), leading
    to a scoring for single voices and mixed chorus in 1908.
123. Grieg's 'composing hut', overlooking the fjord.
124. Grieg died a month later, on 4 September 1907.
125. In his diary, 'Doings & Sayings at the Griegs, Troldhaugen, 25.7.07–4.8.07' (Grainger Museum,
    Melbourne), under the entry for 31 July, Grainger recorded (in mixed languages), 'He [Grieg]
    rounds & says: "The joy to me is to hear your individual, unexpected renderings of these
    things. . . . But that pleases me—*when there is real personality*. Then I am liberal, very liberal; but
    if no personality: *No*." And he shook a threatening stick in the black air. He won't tell me, tho,
    what the things are that I do other than his intentions.'
126. 'Willst du immer weiter schweifen?'. Grainger learnt about Grieg's day-book entries for his 1907
    visit from David Monrad Johansen's book entitled, *Edvard Grieg* (Oslo, 1934), which Grainger
    formed into a press release, 'Grieg's Estimate of Percy Grainger' (Grainger Museum, Mel-
    bourne). Grieg's entry for 5 August 1907 read, in part: 'It seems to me that he [Grainger] will
    devote all his best powers to folk music, which I greatly regret, as it presupposes in him an un-
    dervaluation of his pianistic qualities—an undervaluation that is only too apparent.'

will-of-the-wisps, luring me away from my true path (pianism), was a bit hard to bear. How could I have played op. 66 & op. 72 as I did if I had not been a tone-wright & a student of folk music? These deemths of his no doubt colored Nina Grieg's[127] stand-take-ment towards my tonery noted in 423-11.[128]

Oct. 1949, revised 1952

Source: 'Grieg's Growing Fretfulness at My Tone-Works', in 'Grainger's Anecdotes', 423-10 (Grainger Museum, Melbourne).

72   Sargent & Rathbone Lost Interest in My Compositions When Publicly Performed (1953)

As long as my compositions were not publicly performed Rathbone & Sargent seemed to take a keen interest in them. Between 1904 & 1912 (1913–1914?) they were always engaging me to play (& shout out the prominent voices) such things as English Dance, Green Bushes, Father & Daughter to their friends, at their 'at homes', etc. There was always lively speculation as to how the orchestration, the guitars, etc., would sound. But when Beecham did 'English Dance' about 1911 [*sic*], when I did 'Father & Daughter'[129] at Balfour Gardiner's concerts about 1912,[130] & when I did 'Green Bushes'[131] at Wood's Queen's Hall Symphony concerts (about 1913),[132] I cannot remember Sargent or Rathbone being present, & I particularly remember that I got the impression that they never spoke to me of these performances.[133] There are several possible explanations for this silence on S's & R's part:

127. (1845–1935), Norwegian singer, cousin, and wife of Edvard Grieg.
128. 'Nina Grieg Deaf to Delius's and My Music', in 'Grainger's Anecdotes'.
129. For five male soloists, double mixed chorus, strings, brass, and percussion, with ad lib. mandolin and guitar bands (composed 1908–9), dedicated to John Singer Sargent.
130. 13 March 1912, at the Queen's Hall, London, conducted by Grainger.
131. Passacaglia on a Somerset folk-song, for small orchestra (composed 1905–6), dedicated to Karen Holten. It was later rescored for several larger ensembles.
132. 19 October 1912 at the Queen's Hall, conducted by Grainger.
133. Grainger could not complain of the response of their friend, Jacques-Émile Blanche, who wrote to Grainger (26 February 1913, in English, Grainger Museum, Melbourne) on the day after the Balfour Gardiner concert featuring performances of Grainger's *Hillsong I*, *Molly on the Shore*, and *Colonial Song*: 'The only, the *one* danger in your disposition, might be as to your indulging into some a trifle too *facile* effects in the way of big *ensemble*, just a little too *la[c]king*. I think you are at your best whenever you seem to dive in a vort [*sic*] of turmoil of superforced and intricate currents—Do give us a lot more!'

1. That they were bitterly disappointed in my orchestrations. Compositions heard often on the piano sometimes lack 'bite' when heard on the orchestra or the chorus. The piano is an ugly-toned instrument; but you can get close up to it, & it *is* trenchant.

2. That the works did not have the public success they had expected. This could be true of English Dance, Green Bushes, Hillsong II, Lord Maxwell's Goodnight, but surely not of Father & Daughter, Molly on the Shore, Mock Morris. ('Father & Daughter' was one of the most spontaneous successes I have ever witnessed in a concert hall.[134]) Perhaps they felt that my 'special instruments' (guitars in 'F[ather] & D[aughter]', xylophone & guitars in 'Scotch Strathspey & Reel') were a bit foolish in actual concerts. But the guitars in 'F & D' surely must be said to have made their mark.

3. That they felt that the public performance rubbed the bloom off the works. For years they had been almost their private property. Now they belonged to any music-lover that heard & liked them.

Århus Kommunehospital, Aug. 10, 1953

Source: 'Sargent & Rathbone Lost Interest in My Compositions When Publicly Performed', in 'Grainger's Anecdotes', 423-33 (Grainger Museum, Melbourne).

⟿ 73   Vaughan Williams's Praise of a Detail in 'Irish Tune from County Derry' (1953)

I forget when it was that Vaughan Williams joined the choral meetings (started in Hornton Street (Kensington)[135] to try thru my own & other composers' choruses. We started with composers (Roger, Cyril, Balfour, Sandby, myself) & a few amateurs (Henslow Orchard,[136] Alec Lane[137]). Later on (as I travelled more & was more seldom available in London) the meetings were called 'jamborees' by Everard Feilding, finally were held at Lady Winny's[138] or Mrs Colefax's,[139] & degenerated into a 'play-&-sing-for-

---

134. *The Times*'s critic reported: ' . . . the brilliance of the work lies in the way in which all the means are used to enforce and not to obscure the character of the song, and the audience were so stirred by it that it had to be repeated' ('Music: Mr Balfour Gardiner's Concert', 14 March 1912, p. 10).
135. Where the Graingers lived between May and October 1902.
136. Onslow Orchard, son of a family known to Grainger's father in Perth. See essay 20.
137. Australian student, then at the Royal College of Science.
138. Lady Winefride Elwes, lawyer, sister of Everard Feilding, and wife of the tenor Gervase Elwes.
139. Sibyl Colefax (1874–1950), artistic patron.

nothing' trying-out-ground for young musicians & foreign musicians—that wretched entertainment so dear to the English, where listeners who have paid nothing for the entertainment hear performances worth paying nothing to hear. But before it had degenerated into the 'jamboree' stage there were more or less regular meetings at one place (31A King's Road)[140] which Vaughan Williams took charge of when I was away. These must have been in time between 1909 (when we got back from Australia) & the Balfour Gardiner concerts.[141] At one of these meetings Vaughan Williams pointed to this bit in my 1902 'Irish Tune from County Derry' setting & said: 'That's as good as Bach'.

Århus, Aug. 11, 1953

Source: 'Vaughan Williams's Praise of a Detail in "Irish Tune from County Derry"—"As Good as Bach" ', in 'Grainger's Anecdotes', 423-40 (Grainger Museum, Melbourne).

74   Delius Hostile to Harmonium Parts in My Chamber-Music Scores (1953)

When I was in Frankfurt the same time as the Deliuses (1st ½ of 1923) they were living in the Dom Platz[142] & the sound of the organ drifted into their rooms. Delius was much against my use of the harmonium in large-chamber-music scores such as 'Hill-Song I'.[143] 'If you go on using the harmonium in all yr scores they will all sound like that organ droning away over there'. And he said something much more humiliating & probably quite unanswerable: 'Your use of the harmonium suggests that you cannot accommodate yr

140. Where the Graingers lived, with several breaks, between December 1907 and the summer of 1914.
141. I.e., March 1912.
142. Cathedral Square (in German).
143. In its revised scoring of 1921–22 for thirteen wind instruments, six strings, percussion, piano, and harmonium.

harmony-voices in your orchestral texture.' It is with me like it was with Wagner in the three-themes-at-once bit in the Meistersinger Prelude so well described by Tovey ('the classical effect of the harmony achieved by the modest chords in the woodwinds & horns').[144] If Wagner had 3 characteristic themes that had *to be heard prominently* at one & the same time, it stands to reason that he has to have some non-prominently-heard weaker-toned background instruments to play the harmonies for his 3 prominent themes. The 'modest' wood-wind & horns sufficed in his case, because they were weaker than the trumpets, massed strings & massed basses that were forth-sounding his prominent themes. But in my large-chamber-music scores I often want my prominent voices to be played by *single* instruments, not massed instruments (because of the greater edginess in the sound of single instruments). So I need a background instrument, to play the accompanying harmonies, that is weaker-toned than my prominent single instruments. In chamber music the harmonium seems to me perfect for this purpose; with orchestras, the pipe or electric organ. (Fancy that professional musicians have so deteriorated since Bach's time that they cannot hear that the harmonium, or reed organ, is the most essential of all chamber-music instruments. See Tovey's remarks '& here not even the finest harmonium would serve'. See [ ].)[145] Perhaps it is humiliating to have to admit that in much modern music (Wagner, Grainger, R. Strauss, perhaps even César Franck) the prominent tone-strands do not provide the harmony, which has to be added separately—quite different to Josquin, Palestrina & Bach, where the melodious tone-strands also provide the harmony.

Two things have changed since then:

1. the prominent voices have grown more prominent (think of the trumpets in 'Poem of Ecstasy')[146]
2. our sense of harmony-in-its-own-right has been born. Bach has exquisite harmonic moments, but much of his polyphony is non-expressive, whereas Cyril Scott's (& César Franck's) harmonies can be expressive for long stretches. Is it not a gain to have such expressive harmonies *plus* arrestingly prominent voices?

I have no doubt that it was the part-Jew in Delius (if it is true that he was part-Jew) that disliked the organ & harmonium as something Christian &

---

144. One of Tovey's analyses of this Prelude, although not exactly containing Grainger's quotation, is found in *Essays in Musical Analysis*, vol. 4 (London: Oxford University Press, 1937), 126–28.
145. The reference was left blank by Grainger.
146. Op. 54 (1905–8), by the Russian composer Aleksandr Skryabin (1871/2–1915).

puritan. Even if Delius was not ½-Jewish, he mixed with enough anti-Christians in his musical life to accept their anti-Christian hatred of the organ & the harmonium.

Århus, Aug. 15, 1953.

Source: 'Delius Hostile to Harmonium Parts in My Chamber-Music Scores', in 'Grainger's Anecdotes', 423-56 (Grainger Museum, Melbourne).

➤ 75   Mother Thought My Music Sounded Like Hymn-Tunes (1953)

I am glad to recall that when I first started to compose seriously in Frankfurt my mother thought that much of my music sounded like hymn-tunes. This is certainly true of early things like 'The Beaches of Lukannon', 'Tiger-Tiger', 'The Merchantmen',[147] & equally true of later things such as the tailpiece of the 'Thanksgiving Song'[148] & *To a Nordic Princess*. I suppose most musicians turn to classical music as an antidote to the churchiness of their childhood, or of their parents, or of their past. But I was not dragged to church against my will, & did not associate hymn-tunes, or other churchy music, with being bored. I heard the church music welling out of Saint Colomb's (in Glenferrie)[149] as we walked past, & I found it bright & glorious. One thing I like about church music: it seems to include both men & women & does not typify drunken men (like many opera arias seem to do) & does not suggest that mother's daughter has learnt dancing—as Mendelssohn's Spring Song, Elgar's elefantine Suite dedicated to the royal children,[150] Tchaikovsky's Sugar Plum Fairy, Sibelius's Valse Triste, & even Grieg's Anitra's Dance[151] all seem to do. One reason why things of mine like 'Molly' & 'Shepherd's Hey' are good is because they have so little gaiety & fun in them. Where other composers would have been jolly, in setting such dance-tunes, I have been sad or furious. My dance-settings are energetic rather than gay. They are more like Russian music than English music: they are sad like parts of Balakirev's 'Tamara' or fierce like the 'Trepak' in Tchaikovsky's

---

147. All initially composed by Grainger in 1898–1902 and so some of the earlier of his Kipling settings.
148. The conclusion of *The Power of Rome and the Christian Heart* (1918–45).
149. Now St. Columb's Anglican Church, Hawthorn, Melbourne.
150. *Nursery Suite* (1930), dedicated to Elizabeth, then Duchess of York, and her two children, Elizabeth and Margaret.
151. From Act IV of Grieg's *Peer Gynt* music (1874–75).

Nutcracker. [In Danish] I can well see that life will be bright and happy in the future. But I, with my dark nature, am grateful that I was allowed to live through a time that was dishonest, severe, grim and inhumane, a time in which young men were killed by the million. [In English] I can be the mouthpiece of such an age, as I could not be the mouthpiece of a happy, just & kindly age.

Århus, Aug. 15, 1953

Source: 'Mother Thought My Music Sounded Like Hymn-Tunes', in 'Grainger's Anecdotes', 423-57 (Grainger Museum, Melbourne).

76   Anent 'Elastic Scoring' (1929)

To Conductors and Those Forming, or in Charge of, Amateur Orchestras, High School & Music School Orchestras & Chamber Music Bodies[152]

In our age orchestras & orchestral conditions are changing. In a few years an otherwise-made-up orchestra may have replaced the conventional 'symphony orchestra'. Rather than such a mere replacement of an old form by a new, I, personally, would prefer to see several different kinds of orchestras (including the symphony orchestra) thriving side by side in friendly rivalry; none of them final as to make-up & with no hard-&-fast boundaries between them. In any case, let us hope that the new type or types of orchestra will be richer, warmer, more singing & feelingful, better balanced, less blatant and noisy than the present symphony orchestra. We can easily bring that about, if we will.

We might well look upon the present time as one well-suited to bold experimentation with orchestral & chamber-music sound-blends. Let us encourage all music-lovers, particularly young ones, to enter orchestras & other music bodies formed with the express purpose of trying new combinations of instruments. In such try-outs let us use copiously all instruments that our young people like best—such as saxophone, piano, celesta, xylophone, marimba, guitar, banjo, mandolin, ukulele, etc. Let us not snub budding music-lovers because they have chosen instruments unwritten for in 'classical' music. (Bach—who seemed so willing to write for all the then new & old in-

---

152. A much longer, thoroughly revised, but less coherent, version of this essay appeared as a preface to a variety of Grainger's scores published from 1930 onwards, starting with *Spoon River* (elastically scored for '3 single instruments up to massed orchestra') and *Jutish Medley* (elastically scored for '2 instruments up to massed orchestra'). That score preface is reproduced in Balough, ed., *A Musical Genius from Australia*, 125–31.

struments known to him—might have favored several 'despised' modern instruments, if he could have known them!) Let us not discourage any young
player from joining our experimental orchestras merely because the instrument of his choice does not happen to form a part of the conventional symphony orchestra.

Let us remember that at the time of the crystalization of the symphony
orchestra many of our most perfect modern instruments (such as the saxophone, the sarrusophone, the harmonium, the modern piano, the modern
pipe organ, the marimba, the ukulele) did not exist, or were not known in
Europe. That, in most cases, sufficiently explains their absence from symphony orchestras, but it certainly does not justify their absence from present
& future types of orchestra.

Let us rid ourselves of esthetic snobbery & prejudice in orchestra-
building! Let us take full advantage of the great richness of lovely new instruments available today—using them together with the lovely old instruments
sanctioned by 'classical' usage, where it proves effective to do so. Let us build
better-balanced, clearer-toned, more varied-colored orchestras than ever before. Above all, let us press into orchestral playing as many young music-lovers
as possible. Whether they are to become laymen or professionals, they need
some such experience of musical team-work if they are to become real musicians. In addition to getting to know some of the world's best music the budding musician needs the inspiration of hearing a grand cooperation of myriad
sounds surging around him, to which he joins his own individualistic voice.
This is the special experience of music, without which mere lonely practising
to acquire soloistic skills is esthetically barren & unsatisfying.

Let us use in our orchestras the vast mass of keyboard players (pianists, organists, etc.) that preponderate everywhere in our musical life. Pianists are more
in need of learning how to follow a beat, more in need of musical team-work (to
offset their all too soloistic study-activities) than almost any other class of musicians: use them 'massed', in smaller or larger groups, in our experimental &
study orchestras, letting them play on small, light, cheap, easily-moved upright
pianos (where grand pianos are not available) & on harmoniums & reed organs.
All these instruments are readily found & handled anywhere—only laziness
prompts a contrary belief! Harmonium & reed organ playing gives to piano students the legato-ear & legato-fingers they otherwise usually so sadly lack. More-
over, massed harmoniums & reed organs add a glowing, clinging resonance to
the orchestral tone, while massed pianos (the more the mellower, remember!)
provide brilliance, rhythmic snap & clearness of chord-sound.

The symphony orchestra uses many strings because string players
abounded at the time of its formation. Let us, in forming the orchestra of the

present & the future, try using large numbers of the instruments that most abound today: the mere fact that they abound (that they are widely liked & thus draw many beginners into musical habits) should be recommendation enough. If these instruments, under experimentation, prove orchestrally ineffective in massed usage, let us then discard such usage. But do not let us discard any instrument or usage of it without a fair trial.

My 'elastic scoring'[153] grows naturally out of two roots:

1. That my music tells its story mainly by means of *intervals* (rather than by means of tone-color) & is therefore well fitted to be played by almost any small or large combination of instruments, provided a proper *balance* of tone is kept.
2. That I wish to play my part in the active experimentation with orchestral & chamber-music blends that seems bound to happen as a result of the ever wider spreading democratization of all forms of music.

P.A.G., Sept. 10, 1929[154]

Source: 'Anent "Elastic Scoring"' (Grainger Museum, Melbourne).

77   [Letter to Roy Harris] (1937)

Roy Harris[155] (Jan 12,'37), writing about the plucked piano strings in Fickénscher's 'Evolutionary Q-tet',[156] writes: 'P.S. Do you believe that one of the tasks of composition is that of accepting the limitations implicit within a chosen medium?'

I answered (Jan 13,'37): Your question as to whether 'one of the tasks of composition is that of accepting the limitations inflicted [*sic*] within a chosen medium?' is a most fundamental & searching one. Each man must answer ac-

---

153. Grainger, in his final score prefaces, commented that '"elastic scoring" is naturally fitted to musical conditions in small and out-of-the-way communities and to the needs of amateur orchestras and school, high school, college and music school orchestras everywhere, in that it can accommodate almost any combination of players on almost any instruments'.
154. Written aboard the R.M.S. *Laconia*, returning from Europe to the United States.
155. (1898–1979), American composer. At this time, Harris was teaching at the Westminster Choir School (later College) in Princeton and giving summer courses at Juilliard.
156. The manuscripts of the *Evolutionary Quintet* by Arthur Fickénscher had been destroyed in the 1906 San Francisco earthquake. The Seventh Quintet, *From the Seventh Realm*, for piano and strings, used remembered materials from the lost *Evolutionary Quintet*. Grainger hailed the Seventh Quintet as 'pointing the way to our melodic future with prophetic powers' in his essay, 'Melody versus Rhythm' (1932/3). See Gillies and Clunies Ross, eds., *Grainger on Music*, 257.

cording to temperament, I suppose—don't you think so? My answer is strongly, 'No, I will not accept *any* limitations I can rightly or wrongly side-step'. I believe, with Busoni, that every composition is already an arrangement or transcription,[157] because no existing medium ever compares to the ideal medium dwelling in the composer's imagination. And then, I do not admit that plucking the piano strings (since Henry Cowell)[158] is outside the normal limits of the piano. I consider pizzicato as much a part of the modern piano as of the strings. I also feel that one of the things that makes the pre-Bach chamber music so superior (for those that know & like it) to all later chamber music is the fact that it was conceived *for music in general* & not merely for specific instruments. Incidentally (probably as a result of slavery to the limitations of the instrument) I feel that the modern instruments (with their lack of variety, of color & range) are too 'instrumental' & not 'musical' (in the sense of music being a wide, general, normal tonal experience close to the singing nature of voices) enough. Please forgive this lengthy answer, & please forgive my having bothered you about the 2nd piano for nothing.

Yours heartily, Percy Grainger.

Source: 'Roy Harris (Jan 12, '37)', in 'Nordic English. Thots on Tone-Art', dated 13 January 1937 (Grainger Museum, Melbourne).

⟶ 78   A World-Wide Tone-Wright ((Composer)) Guild (1945)

The leeches [doctors] have had to set up their guild to hinder quacks from mask-walking ((masquerading)) as trained leeches—so that people don't get killed off by know-nothing-y cures. (This is without going into the askment whether trained leeches or quacks do most harm. Any Tone-Wright [Composer] Guild would—it goes without saying—fail where the leech-guild fails. But if the Tone-wright Guild worked as well as the leech-guild works, I would be at-rest-set [content].) Ella & I have a good friend, Poultney Bigelow[159] (on the brink of 90, who allows himself the fun of acting witless about the old Kaiser & lots of other askments ((questions))); but

---

157. This view is most cogently argued by Busoni in his *Entwurf einer neuen Ästhetik* (1907).
158. Cowell's innovative approach to the use of piano strings is seen in works from the early 1920s onwards.
159. (1855–1954), American adventurer and author, friend of Ella Grainger since the 1910s.

who, at bottom, is kind & wise) who never can understand why Wagner, who wrote the 'Doppel-Adler' march,[160] is not to be found in Brockhaus (Brockhaus's Conversations-Lexikon), while Richard Wagner is. Bigelow most likely thinks the 'Double-Eagle' vastly better than anything Richard ever wrote. This is a far-stretched case. But there are heaps of mildly tone-liking folk who go to tone-fests ((concerts)), or listen to wireless, who rate Tchaikovsky best of all Symphony-wrights & who like Liszt's Liebestraum or 2nd Rhapsody, or Mendelssohn's 'Spring Song', or Dvořák's Humoreske,[161] way above Wagner & Bach, & who find themselves in a mind-fog when they read belittlements of Tchaikovsky, Mendelssohn, Liszt or Dvořák coming from looked-up-to pens. Then there is the host of half-lettered job-tone-men ((professional musicians))—band-bosses, piano-players, teachers, singers—who place Mozart above Skryabin, Wagner, Bach & Josquin des Prez & who are flabbergasted when a great over-soul [genius] like Delius says: 'When a man tells me he likes Mozart, I know [he is]'[162] a bad musician'. There ought to be some simple way of leading [them][163] out of the mind-fog they are in. If a man says he deems a farm-house a finer sample of build-art ((architecture)) than the best Gothic Cathedral, he is simply laughed at, that is all. Not that anyone would gain-say the right to *like* the farm-house better. All we set ourselves against is the right to forth-speak such liking in the form of a worth-mete-ment [evaluation]. Anent build-art, even the least-knowing man knows that size, style, richness-of-workmanship count for something—because he can see those howths [qualities] in a building. If the building has 5 towers, he can see & count them; but it may be doubted whether a tone-skill [man] can hear & count 5 tone-strands in a tone-bit. Anyone can count the stuffs used in a building (wood, thatch, stone, brick, metal), while it is doubtful whether even half-way tone-lovers can count the chord-types in a tone-piece. There is no need for every listener to be 'knowing' about tone-art; yet if millions of children are to be taught tone-art in the schools & still greater millions led to hear (in tone-shows & over the air) types of tone-art new to their ears, it would do no harm for the realm-sway ((government)) of each coun-try to offer its people some worth-mete-ment of tone-art stemming from the minds of the best tone-thinkers in each country—the tone-wrights.

160. Josef Franz Wagner (1856–1908), Austrian composer of the *Unter dem Doppeladler* (Under the Double Eagle) march, Op. 159.
161. Op. 101 No. 7, in G flat.
162. Three or four overwritten words illegible here.
163. About three overwritten words illegible here.

The otherhood between a tone-wright & a non-tone-wrighting tone-man is not a matter of being-type & heart-stir only. Every tone-wright who has dealt with singers, tone-tool-players [instrumentalists], band-bosses [conductors] knows the reason why these worthies don't write tonery—they don't *hear well enough* to do so. If band-bosses cannot hear wrong notes in chords (see No. [384-41]),[164] or hear when a voice is played an octave too high or too low (see No. [384-34]),[165] it is because their bodily ears have not been rightly trained, or because they are not rightly gifted (I will not talk of their 'inner' ears). From the standpoint of tone-art itself (as sundered from the trick of merely forth-sounding tonery, as [do] band-bosses, singers, players) tone-wrights are the only *skilled tone-men*; band-bosses, singers & players who are unable to tone-wright must be rated as *unskilled workers*, in this field. The gulf (in tone-skills—not merely in mind-picturement & selfhood) between a Cyril Scott (who can come away from the first forth-playment of a new Richard Strauss opera able to play by ear its themes, its new-typed chords, its key-switch-ments ((modulations))) & a Beecham (unable to rightset wrong notes in the parts of a new work, with its score before him (see No. 39);[166] unable to remember the roughest likenesses to the chords in a best-liked piece he had often time-beaten, as in the case of Delius's 'Appalachia' (see No. 41)) or a Stokowski (unable, even with the score before him, to hear when tone-tools thru-out a whole work are playing from a wrong part) seems bridge-less. These things being thus, in the tone-world, it behooves realm-sway-bodies ((governments)) to be-shield their country-men from the misleadingness & know-littleness of band-bosses as they shield them from the misleadingness & know-littleness of quacks in the leeching field. Just as leech-quacks do good work, & seem to help many people, in the leeching field, so, no doubt, do little-knowing & less-caring tone-quacks (band-bosses, singers, players) in the tone-field bring balm to many tone-lovers. I do not wish to see non-tone wrights harshly judged. But I do say: The skilled tone-men—the *only* skilled tone-men (the tone-wrights)—should be heard from. In each country, the realm-sway should call together a Realm-wide Guild of Tone-Wrights (every home-born tone-wright who has written 50,000 [*sic*] pages of tonery—which must in-count 25,000 of pages of works for string-&-wind-

164. 'Beecham's Wrong Chords in Delius's "Appalachia"', in 'Ere-I-Forget'.
165. 'Shavitch & Stokowski Both Flounder in "Molly On the Shore"', in 'Ere-I-Forget'. Concerning the relationship between cello and double-bass parts in *Molly on the Shore*, Grainger there commented: 'Band-bosses who cannot hear such things are not fit to lead a kindergarten group.'
166. 'Beecham's Cheek about "Colonial Song"'; see essay 69.

band, sing-host, room-music [chamber music], or of opera, or other highly-grand tone-type, being fit to be on a limb of the guild) whose task shall be to choose by vote, from their midst, a Realm-Tone-Spokesman for each year. During his year of spokesmanship this spokesman shall set forth his deemths ((opinions)) on tone-matters in a booklet (yearly) to be forth-printed by the Realm-sway and round-spread ((distributed)) free. The whole booklet should set forth the deemths of the spokesman-for-the-year only—his deemths should not [be] tampered with by the Guild-limbs ((members)). One of the aims of the yearly booklet should be to show how othery are the deemths of great tone-men. But however othery from each other, one thing will shine out: they will never same-deem with the folk-wise deemths. The folkmass (& the unskilled tone-men—the bandbosses, singers, players) must be taught to know that their views, their deems, their likings *never* are shared by the great tone-minds. Let the folkmass & the unskilled tonemen joy-quaff their own tastes & be as happy as they can in the tonery of their own choice; but never give them any grounds for doing themselves the honor of thinking that their thoughts dove-tail with those of the skilled tone-men. Each year the Tone-Spokesman for the year should make up a list of his ratings of the tone-worth of all (as nearly as may be) tone-wrights, from the earliest readable tonery to the very newest tonewrights. Where the tone-wrights are not known by name (as in the case of 13th year-hundred-y [13th-century] European tonery, tonery from outlying parts of the world such as Samoa, Africa, Madagascar, Greenland, & folksongs—which latter should be listed under their titles with name of gatherer, & the number he gave, in brackets) the music should be listed by title (as 'Sheepshearing Song', Somerset, Cecil Sharp; or 'Mampahory', Chant Malgache, French 'His Master's Voice') or by class or type (as 'Ceremonial Music, Bali'; or 13th-century partsongs, English, Worcester Cathedral Library—Dom Anselm Hughes).

The tone-worth of tone-wrights, & of their works one-by-one, or of folksongs, or of far-off ((exotic)) toneries might be meted along some such lines as: 1. Soul-life, 1 to 5 counts, 2. Tied-upness with life, 1 to 5 counts, 3. Many-typedness, 1 to 5 counts, 4. Beauty, 1 to 5 counts, 5. Change-shock-fulness, 1 to 5 counts, 6. Self-hood, 1 to 10 counts, 7. Out-findfulness, 1 to 10 counts, 8. Steadly color ((local colour)), 1 to 5 counts, 9. Well-sounding-ness, 1 to 5 counts, 10. Tween-realm-some skill-hoard-fulness ((international tradition)), 1 to 10 counts, 11. Puzzle-thoughtfulness ((complicatedness)), 1 to 10 counts. Let us see how my own tone-deemths [musical opinions] would add up under such a scheme:

Tone-wright, or Class	1	2	3	4	5	6	7	8	9	10	11	Total
Skryabin	5	3	2	3	1	10	10	-	3	3	7	47
Beethoven	2	5	3	3	3	10	8	2	2	4	3	45
Bach	5	3	5	4	5	5	8	-	5	10	10	61 [*sic*: 60]
Brahms	4	3	3	5	2	8	2	4	3	7	6	46 [*sic*: 47]
English folksong	5	5	4	5	3	10	5	5	5	5	5	57
German folksong	2	5	3	2	1	5	3	5	4	3	1	34
Javanese Tonery	5	5	2	5	1	6	8	5	5	5	6	53
Delius	5	2	2	1	5	2	10	3	5	5	5	45
Schönberg	3	-	2	4	1	10	10	-	4	8	10	52
Debussy	5	3	3	5	2	10	10	3	5	10	4	62 [*sic*: 60]
Norwegian folksong 'Fraanar Ormen'[167]	5	5	-	5	4	10	5	5	5	4	3	51
English folksong 'Sheepshearing Song', Somerset (Sharp)	5	5	-	5	-	10	5	5	5	4	2	51 [*sic*: 46]
Ole Bull's 'Saeterjentens Søndag'[168](song)	5	5	2	5	3	10	4	5	5	3	2	49
Mozart	1	3	2	2	3	5	3	3	3	5	2	32
Handel	4	4	3	4	3	8	4	3	4	6	4	48 [*sic*: 47]
Cyril Scott	5	4	4	5	4	8	8	4	4	8	5	59
Mde Lineva's coll. of Russian part-songs (folk-harmonies)[169]	5	5	3	4	3	7	10	5	4	6	8	60
Natalie Curtis's Negro ditto[170]	5	3	2	5	2	7	8	5	5	8	8	58
Gershwin	3	3	2	3	3	5	3	5	4	10	4	45
Wagner	5	5	5	5	5	10	7	3	5	10	10	70
Ravel	3	2	3	5	3	5	5	5	5	8	5	49

(*continued*)

Tone-wright, or Class	1	2	3	4	5	6	7	8	9	10	11	Total
Tchaikovsky	5	5	4	4	4	6	7	5	3	9	4	56
Japanese music	3	3	4	3	5	10	5	5	4	8	5	55
Rarotongan part-songs	5	5	3	5	2	10	10	5	5	8	10	68
Grieg	3	4	3	5	3	10	7	5	4	7	5	57 [*sic*: 56]
John Jenkins	5	2	3	5	3	5	4	2	5	10	10	54
Wm Lawes	5	4	4	5	4	10	10	4	4	10	8	68
M. Valérie White (songs)	5	5	3	4	3	5	2	5	5	4	2	43
Roger Quilter	4	3	3	5	2	7	4	5	5	5	4	47
Stephen Foster (songs)	4	5	3	5	2	8	5	5	5	3	-	45
African music (discs)	5	5	4	4	4	10	8	5	3	3	5	56
Arthur Fickénscher	5	3	2	5	2	6	10	-	4	10	10	57
P. Grainger	4	5	3	4	3	8	10	4	2	7	8	58
Duke Ellington	3	5	1	4	2	6	6	5	5	4	3	44
Puccini	3	5	3	4	3	7	2	4	5	4	-	40
Verdi (not late works)	2	4	4	2	4	4	3	4	3	2	-	37 [*sic*: 32]
Gounod	3	3	3	5	3	7	-	4	5	5	-	38
César Franck	5	3	4	5	4	10	6	5	4	10	6	69 [*sic*: 62]
Sibelius	4	5	3	3	3	5	-	5	2	5	3	38
G. Fauré	4	4	4	5	2	7	3	2	5	8	5	49

167. Norwegian hero-song, which Grainger described in 1952 as 'a folksong undragooned by rhythmic strictness' (unpublished 'Talk to American Guild of Organists, New York'; Grainger Museum, Melbourne).
168. 'The Dairymaid's Sunday' by Norwegian musician Ole Bull (1810–80).
169. Two-volume collection of songs of the Volga region by Eugenia Lineva (1854–1919).
170. Four-volume collection of *Negro Folksongs* by Natalie Curtis (1875–1921).

The above list is made out on the spur of the moment, without fore-thought, & it is clear-to-see it is full of flaws. If Bach is rated 61 [*sic*], then 70 is too high for Wagner. If Quilter is given 47, then 49 is too low for Fauré, & 45 scores too low for Gershwin if Quilter rates 47. On the other hand, 32 is *not* too low for Mozart—'the heartless tonery that caused the French Realm-crash ((Revolution))', as I like to call it. Ratings in English-speaking & other Blue-eyed Race-lands must not be overly swayed by fame-ratings in foreign lands. The great need in blue-eyed-race art-life is soul-size—not skill, not loveliness. The shallow thinking of war-fain lands *must not* be echoed in the art-judgements of our war-hating theeds [nations]. Last Saturday 25,000 people came to hear a whole evening of Gershwin's heart-throb-some, American-typed tonery. The next evening, only 13,000 turned up to hear Stokowski & me do an evening of Bach, Mendelssohn, Grieg, Debussy, Grainger & Antheil.[171] The writing is on the wall. And I hope the Spokesmen-of-the-Year of the Tone-Wrights' Guild will echo it in their ratings. The realm-sway should ask only one thing of tone-show-givers in uplinkment with the guild: that *the rating for the year* (by the guild's spokesman) be printed after each tone-wright's name on every tone-bill-of-fare printed for every tone-show of the year. So tone-show-goers would read: Beethoven (TG 45) Schönberg (TG 52) Saeterjentens Søndag (TG 49), César Frank (TG 69), song by Maude Valérie White (TG 43). The askment [question] will arise: should a masterpiece by a man who has written nothing (or next-to-nothing) else, like Ole Bull's 'Saeterjentens Søndag', be rated as high as a tone-wright who has written countless masterpieces (say Mozart or Handel). Why not? Should we not learn to rate a piece of tonery by its factful howths ((qualities)), & not be swayed by thoughts of what this tone-wright, or other tone-wrights, have done, or failed to do, in other works? Maybe songs, operas, oratorios, & other works built on texts should have a rating of their own, with no marks for 'well-sounding-ness' & the like? And maybe 'Soul-life' should be given a 1–10 rating (rather than 1–5) to give the Spokesman greater choice & stretch-litheness under this most meaningful heading. One why-ground why each theed ((nation)) should have its own yearly Spokesman & forthprint its own theed-y year-booklet, is to allow each country to unfold its own judgement of all the world's tonery & to work up its own steadly ((local)) right-from-wrong-sense in tone-art. It might be that a German or Spanish view of the

171. 15 July 1945, at the Hollywood Bowl in Los Angeles. Grainger performed the Grieg Piano Concerto in this concert, under Stokowski's direction. The concert also included orchestral versions of Grainger's *Londonderry Air* and *Molly on the Shore*. George Antheil (1900–1959) was an American composer and pianist.

worth of Javanese or Madagascan tonery would split away far from our own. Such deemth-splits [differences of opinion] are worth knowing about, when they come *from the hard-working tone-wrights in each land*, & from *no one else*! On top of making out the yearly list of tonewright-ratings, the Spokesman-of-the-Year should pen his summing-up of what has happened in his land during the year: 'Beethoven's 5th was given 783 times—too often. Bach's 6th Brandenburg only twice—too little. Rubin Goldmark's "Gettysburg Requiem"[172] not at all—shameful. Loeffler's "Hymn to My Brother the Sun"[173] only once—shamefully little.' One of the teachful points would be the othery ratings given to the big-boys from year to year: Beethoven, 1950, 43. Ditto, 1951, 73.

[on train] Kansas, July 18, '45

Source: 'Cure for "Sirre, Sirre"[174]-Blight in the Tone-World: a World-Wide Tone-Wright ((Composer)) Guild', in 'Ere-I-Forget', 384-38 (Grainger Museum, Melbourne).

172. (1916–19), for orchestra, by American composer Rubin Goldmark (1872–1936).
173. *Canticum fratris solis* (1925), for voice and chamber orchestra, by American composer Charles Martin Loeffler (1861–1935).
174. In the preceding section of 'Ere-I-Forget' (384-37), Grainger explains that 'Sirre, Sirre' (D'you see, d'you see?) was a popular song that Grainger's Norwegian friend Herman Wildenvej (Wildenvey) considered mirrored the condition of the day. Grainger saw the key issue (the 'Sirre-Sirre'-blight) as '2 unjusthoods clashing against each other: the unjusthood of badly treating the hard-worker (non-white-color), & the unjusthood of boosting the worthless man (of any class) to the level of the worthful (that is hard-working) man (of any class)'.

8

PERFORMER

79   [Letter to Mabel Gardner] (1901)

11 Taubenbrunnerweg, Frankfort o/Maine. April 4, 1901

My Dear Miss Gardner[1]

I cannot say how happy I was to receive a letter from you, & hear about you again. Mine is a fearfully busy life, otherwise I would long since have answered your welcome writing, but since December & this, plenty has happened for us. Early in December I gave a recital here,[2] which turned out an immense & unexpected success, & as it is no easy thing to achieve success in a big German musical centre like Frankfort, we are quite stuck up about my good luck. Of course, this brought other engagements, & I also have managed to get as many pupils as I can take. (Rather funny, me teaching, is it not?) I like teaching awfully & get on very well with pupils of all ages & types. But we have also managed to get ill lately, poor mother dreadfully so, having inflammation of the nerves of the spine, which has kept her in bed these six weeks, & she will not be able to get up for some time yet.[3] I also was knocked up in bed twice, but nothing serious. All this prevented our coming to London in February as we first intended,[4] but we will now come in May,

1. Mabel Gardner, later Mrs. Mabel Todhunter (1871–ca. 1945), had been Grainger's governess in Melbourne between 1888 and 1894. By 1927, when Grainger collected this letter, she was living in Hove, Sussex.
2. 6 December 1900, in the hall of the Hoch Conservatory. He performed a solo program of works by Bach-Liszt, Brahms, Schumann, Chopin, and Liszt.
3. The period 1899–1901 had been one of particular ill health for Rose Grainger. Her general health improved during the earlier London years.
4. The Graingers had visited Britain in 1900 and had intended to move there early in 1901.

as I have a really *splendid* engagement for early June in London, to play at Miss Devlin's[5] concert on the 11th. We are awfully happy about it. Father is very well & happy in Perth, W.A., & has just had some honors conferred on him, in connection with the Paris Exhibition, where he arranged the exhibs, & designed some furniture in West Australian woods, [ ].[6] By the way, did you receive the critiques of my Frankfort recital that mother sent? Mother sends her love to you all, we would both so like to see you when we come to England.

> With kindest to you & yours
>> Believe me
>>> Yours sincerely
>>>> Percy Grainger.

P.S. Still remember 'ME DIDNEY'[7]

Source: 'Two Old Letters of P. G.'s & One of Beloved Mother's Shown Me (Oct. 28, 1927) by Mrs Todhunter', Letter B, in 'Sketches for My Book "The Life of My Mother & Her Son" ', W35-75, entered 7 November 1927 (Grainger Museum, Melbourne).

⮞ 80   P. G.'s Powers during Australian Tour of 1926 (1926)

A stranger (Jean Sealey) writes, 26/10/26: 'I have often heard of the beauty of yr nature, now I know it is the truth; and you are great beyond realisation. . . . [8] I have a portrait of you taken in yr early youth, & then the fire & energy had not awakened that now animates you—and one wonders if you are real'.

It is easy to write nonsense about any artist, concert or tour, & I am not naysaying the maybeness of the above being nonsense. But it is more likely to be earned on the 1926 Australian tour[9] than at any other time of my life, any

---

5. See essay 34.
6. Grainger left this space blank. According to Eileen Dorum, 'A feature of this display [at the Paris Exhibition] was a staircase built with alternate steps of Australian jarrah and English oak, to demonstrate the superior wearing quality of the timber of the Western Australian eucalypt' (*Percy Grainger: The Man Behind the Music*, 35).
7. Grainger's nickname for Gardner. See her recollection of her Australian years with Grainger in Gillies and Pear, *Portrait of Percy Grainger*, 6–9.
8. Grainger's excision marks.
9. Grainger stayed in Australia for over five months, with his first appearance, a solo piano recital, in Melbourne on 5 June, and his last, a thirty-minute radio broadcast from Melbourne, on 15 November 1926.

other undertaking. For I was at the height of my powers. My gifts blossom best when they are unchallenged. I have always been a coward; so that my artistic inner-self cannot unfold itself in a one-against-t'other ((competitive)) life. Match me against my fellows & I show the white feather, play safe. But put me like a peacock on a roof, King of all I overlook, and I show forth my very best. I do not then (as some natures do) overreach myself, or grow over-bearing, carried away with my own greatness & thoughtless of others. Even in victorious hours I remain the unchanging coward, always with an eye to trouble, always sniffing danger. This cowardliness in victory seems to careless eyes like nobleness, give-willingness, warm-heartedness—tho it is not. Tho I admit that a certain kind of pride, sucked from early reading of the Icelandic sagas, would always (even if I were wholly unafraid) keep me seemly in victory.

When I first began to show myself a full-blown composer, around my 17th year, I felt myself a really great man. I felt I could spread to all sides, that I could tackle anything. It was a lovely feeling. It is a feeling that should [be] taken away from no begetsome ((creative)) artist, for it is best that his message goes out to the world from a high loving heart, untainted with fear & doubt. That is why every discerning state grant[s] life-long, state-paid, free livelihood to all its gifted ones the moment they prove their gifts in their early teens, or as soon as they do show them, if later. In my case, as soon as I had to earn my living, face the deed-ful outer world, I saw my giftedness melt like snow on warm ground. I need not dwell on my hardships as a concert player. I never had great natural gifts as a piano-player & I never had the nature to do things before massed folk. But even when it was a matter of coming forward as a composer, or training a choir, or leading[10] an orchestra, I was very uneven. At one moment (as when leading 'Molly' or 'Mock Morris' or 'Father & Daughter' at Balfour Gardiner's concerts), as if to the manner born, the next moment empty & wavering, lacking driving force. Think of that feeble choral rehearsal at Mrs [ ][11] in London, the truly terrible 'Warriors' rehearsals with NY Philharmonic in latest 1919,[12] my laughable unready handling of 'Marching Song of Democracy' in Bridgeport & New York in April 1923![13] Mostly after some real chance to show my mettle as a practical composer, conductor or

---

10. I.e., conducting.
11. Name illegible.
12. Grainger did not perform *The Warrior* with the New York Philharmonic at this time. The rehearsals may have been in preparation for performances of the work (the first since its première on 26/28 January 1917, in New York) with the Chicago Symphony Orchestra on 26/27 December 1919. Alternatively, Grainger may have confused the two orchestras.
13. Grainger conducted the Bridgeport Oratorio Society in performances of this work on 28 April 1924 in Bridgeport, CT, and on 30 April 1924 in New York.

leader in musical thought, I would end up saying to myself, 'You are a pretty ornery, middle-sized betwixt-and-betweener'. Year after year, many sour years, I have tried again & again to prove the greatness I saw so clearly in myself as a young man & have mostly stepped out of the ring a pretty small fry in my own eyes. But on this Australian tour my luck broke, for the good. The gods seemed with me wherever I went & even my mistakes seemed gifted ones— things that could be turned to the good with natural ease. Of course, I knew I was the *only really wonderful musician* in all Australia at the time. I knew it was the first time that a truly begetsome ((creative)) tonewright ((composer)) had kindled the flame of his own tone-art ((music)) before the very public eye. They had never witnessed the fire of the composer before—so different in its burning heat to the mere reflected glow of the mere performer, however well-in-tune. The blent-bands ((orchestras)), the choirs, the time-beaters ((conductors)) all were afraid of my works, anxious to shine in my eyes, all feeling amateurish & inexperienced along side me—the world artist. With such material I can work. By smiles & jokes & antics I could coax them into self-belief & by treating their unknowingness & feeblenesses as from no high horse I made them like me, wish to give me of their best. Then to the many rehearsals, going over the same works again & again, led me to know my scores fairly well—and usually I do not begin to know my scores as I should. And thus, as one high-mooded rehearsal followed the other, I began to take heart as never before, and my will began to rear its neglected head & to feel sure of its feet, until by the end of the orchestral & choral concerts I was a passionate force, hard to check. These concerts in all the 4 towns (Adelaide, Brisbane, Hobart, Melbourne), but most so in Melbourne, live in my memory as a riot of will—unbroken, unquestioned will.

I feel that I 'carried all before me', that I noted mistakes quickly & easily, that my conducting memory was ample & self-believing, that my grasp of the whole situation was manly & enough-some ((sufficient)), in short that I showed myself to be a great & gifted musician. This belief in my own powers left over from the Australian tour is a strong contrast to the hundreds of bitter memories of ungiftedness, un-enough-some-ness ((insufficiency)) I have harvested thru so many downhearting years—almost thru out my whole unhappy life, I might almost say.

Mind you, if the choral & orchestral concerts were a comparative walk-over after the gone-wellness ((success)) of the recitals, the recitals themselves were quite another test of courage. To come to the birth-land you have forsaken for another land, & to appear in one's birth-town in a rôle (that of a pianist) for which one feels one has no muchness of natural gifts, & to be ready to face not only the musical judgements of the may-be-ness ((possibility)) of one's own musical short-coming, but also rotten eggs & the uproar of hostile public opinion about other than musical things, to have to be careful every time one talks to an interviewer or holds a speech that one never calls Australia 'my country', but always only 'the country I was born in', to never let one's feelings run away with one along any lines, but to always move carefully as if with a sword thin-hung over one's head;—to show forth one's musical nature naturally & lovingly (for there can be no art without love, no reaching of the public's heart without some sure-enough swelling open of one's own heart) under these hardships & handicaps is a sore trial to such a timid mouse as myself, & how I came thru the 9 Melbourne recital programs I don't know, except by the old means; thinking only of the task at hand yet, in the background of one's mind, always ready to meet & welcome disgrace, prison— well knowing that one deserves far worse than those. That the Australian folk showed themselves forgiving & big-minded towards me, that they were willing & able to relish my art and even like my personality, that they were able to welcome me as an Australian artist & to point out Australian hownesses ((qualities)) in my musical make-up inspite of my being an American citizen & having blazoned forth that fact wherever I could, that even scandal-rags like 'Truth' did not bother to pick out the dirty spots in my life story—all these things are so much to the good, for the Australians. In me, alas, there is no heart-answer to all their goodness, kindliness, forgivingness, worthening-ness ((appreciation)) outside of the scared thanksgiving of the hunted hare that has (for the moment) side-skipped the hounds. I know I am unworthy of the good thoughts so many Australians seem to have about me, & I expect my truer, juster, worthenment ((appreciation)) to show up later, I know not how. But in spite of all my good luck in Australia I feel, I say, no heart-warming towards them beyond the above-said thankfulness. There is no Nordic folk amongst whom I feel less at home than amongst the Australians, no Nordic folk whose outlook I less share, no national hopes & aims that I could less easily make myself at one with than those of the Australians. I am that wretched creature that Byron holds up to scorn, the wretch who cannot say with a yea-saying ((affirmative)) heart-throb: 'This is my own, my native land'.[14]

But one thing must never be forgotten: that I was a true & passionate Australian, or at least a would-be Australian, in my young manhood, in the days when I was still a spirit-filled ((inspired)) tonewright, & that works like

14. The title of a poem by Walter Scott, the first three lines of which read: 'Breathes there the man, with soul so dead, / Who never to himself hath said, / "This is my own, my native land!" '

'Bush Music',[15] 'Marching Song of Democracy' & many others were awaredly ((consciously)) lit by a flame of being-filling Australianism. What, it would seem, cut me adrift from the Australian-ness for ever was the going to Scandinavia & the finding there of the things I had liked best in Australian pioneeringness, in Icelandic pride & truth-zeal, in German art-worship, in the finding in Denmark, for the first time in my life, true joy & the emptying of the cup of delight,[16] & in the farmer-art, family sagas, steadly ((local)) folk-speeches ((dialects)) & self-forth-showing of all the North that spirit and those wonts of inner-lore ((habits of customs)) that seem to me to be steering towards an uplift of mankind, a solving of human problems.

Aorangi, Nov. 30—Dec. 1, 1926

Source: 'P. G.'s Powers during Australian Tour of 1926', in 'Sketches for My Book "The Life of My Mother & Her Son"', W35-96 (Grainger Museum, Melbourne).

81   Native Art and Stage Fright (1938)

The strangely internationalizing, cosmopolitanizing influence of the arts seems to be rooted in the fact that art is the product of culture rather than of civilisation; so that one's particular civilisation, whatever it is, forms no bar to deep enjoyment and experience through the medium of the arts of peoples living under an alien civilisation.

In spite of (or because of?) South English forefathers, on both sides, my mother showed an unusual cosmopolitanism of taste, from girlhood on. When she and I were in New Zealand, on tour with Ada Crossley, in 1909, she went, by herself, into the museum in Christchurch and was fascinated by its display of S. African and other beadwork. Curiously enough, I happened to go to the same museum the same day and came home raving about the beauty of the beadwork[17]—not knowing my mother had been kindled by it too. She said: 'I was almost afraid to tell you about it. I was afraid you would

---

15. 'Sketch of Bush-Music Style', dated 29 December 1900, which Grainger returned to in 1901, 1922, and 1954, but never significantly developed. In a note of 14 July 1901 (Grainger Museum SL1 MG3/6), he commented that the work was 'to be a simple rise & fall . . . absolutely uneventful, plain-like'.

16. Grainger refers to the relationship with Karen Kellermann (née Holten) during his London years.

17. The Graingers visited Christchurch twice on this 1909 tour, during 9–11 January and ca. 28 February to 3 March. See another recollection of this Christchurch museum in essay 20.

think it silly of me'. So we entered a phase of intense mutual interest in South African and South Sea beadwork and kindred arts, buying at that time in Auckland (Eric Craig) and Sydney (Tost and Rohu[18]) most of the examples shown in this case.[19] Most of the African work had been brought back by soldiers from the Boer War, Tost and Rohu told me. While still on tour in Australia I did the bulk of the work (about 160 hours) on the beadwork necklace I gave my mother, finishing it in London. And on our return to London both my mother and I spent a lot of time puzzling out how the various types of native beadwork were made and making samples and copies of various styles. Among other things my mother made for Nina Grieg (widow of Edvard Grieg)[20] [was] a lovely beadwork table cover in South Sea style (using patterns from the 'Kanaka' bead-cuffs shown in the middle left of this case), using rather large red, black and white beads.

This love of beadwork and kindred 'primitive' arts (running alongside the overwhelming impression I had had of Maori hakas at Rotorua) and the boundless enthusiasm (never before or since aroused by any other music) I felt for the Rarotongan improvised partsongs[21]—preserved home-recorded phonograph records given to me by my seer-like friend A. J. Knocks[22] of Otaki, N.I., New Zealand—had a marked and lasting effect on my pianistic concert career. Up to this time (1909) I never once—either as a child, or as a man—done [sic] myself justice on the concert platform, owing mainly to paralysing stage fright. But now I said to myself: 'If I dislike the white man's civilisation as much as I think I do, why am I terrified when playing to white audiences? Logically speaking, I ought to be indifferent to them.' And actually from then on I lost, for life, a large measure of my art-destroying stage fright. Not, however, that I at any time overcame it sufficiently to play really accurately, expressively or naturally in public.

Percy Grainger, 9 December 1938

Source: 'Native Art and Stage Fright', Museum Legend (Grainger Museum, Melbourne).

18. Jane Tost (ca. 1817–1889) and her daughter Ada Rohu (ca. 1845–1928) were two prominent Sydney taxidermists.
19. Grainger wrote this early Legend as a commentary on one of the showcases holding native artifacts in his museum, then just being opened. His letters from the first half of 1909 are littered with drawings of beadwork, clothes, and ornaments. See Dreyfus, ed., *The Farthest North of Humanness*.
20. Nina Grieg remained a regular correspondent of the Graingers after her husband's death.
21. Grainger's *Random Round* (1912–15) attempted to capture the spirit of the improvised polyphony of Rarotongan part-songs.
22. Knocks gave Grainger these phonograph recordings in January 1909.

82   Call-to-Mindments about Delius Piano Concerto (1941)

Working up (Feb. 1941) the Delius Concerto for the Milwaukee forth-playment (March 9, 1941)[23] awakes call-to-mindments—all of them sad or nasty. A few days or weeks after I played this concerto under Thomas Beecham's bandbossry ((conductorship)) at the Torquay Festival (run by Basil Hindenburg—later Cameron—, then bandboss of the Torquay blent-band [orchestra]) of 1913 or 1914[24] Beecham & I were both at Mrs Chas. Hunter's (Hill Hall, Epsom Forest). During a lunch or dinner Beecham, talking to the table at large, was word-painting the festival & said, 'We did the Delius Piano Concerto, & our friend Percy' (looking at me) 'laid about him in great style'. (This he said in a tone-brotherly way; not aiming at be-littleing me at all.) But Mrs Hunter (suddenly showing an unfriendly slant towards me that I had never seen in the all the years I had played for her) took it up by answering in a loud (let-all-hear sort of) voice: 'Ah! Percy. I'm afraid you were thumping again'. I think Beecham spoke up for me, saying something like, 'Oh, not at all,' or the like; but I can't recall that close-upth ((detail)). Why was Mrs Hunter moved to 'turn & rend me'? I shall never know.

My deals with Mrs Hunter began years before that,[25] when Sargent (always great-heartedly wanting to put well-paid jobs in my way) asked me if I would be willing to play for Mrs Hunter for a lower than my wonted fee, saying that she gave many tone-arty parties but couldn't pay big fees—'her husband has plenty of money, but he doesn't like her to spend too much on music'. I answered that I would be delighted to do so, for any fee that he thot right. It may be that my wontsome [usual] fee for playing at parties then (1910–1909—or even earlier?) was £21-0-0, & that I same-deemed ((agreed)) to play for Mrs Hunter for £10 or £12 or £15. I cannot recall this now. I think she paid me by the size of the party. I feel sure that she paid me £40 for a party to which the Connaughts came & that fee was double my wontsome fee.[26] So I must have played for her for £20, I guess. When she offered me £40 for the Connaught party I said I didn't

23. Grainger performed the Concerto with the Wisconsin Symphony Orchestra, conducted by Sigfrid Prager.
24. An afternoon concert on 16 April 1914.
25. Probably in late February 1905.
26. This 'At Home', at 30 Old Burlington Road, took place on the evening of 27 June 1907. It was attended by, among others, the Duke and Duchess of Connaught and Strathearn. The Duke (1850–1942) was the third son of Queen Victoria and, at this time, Inspector-General of the Forces. Grainger was actually paid £50 for his performance.

want any larger fee than wontedly; but she said she wanted to pay me double for playing to royalty. All of which shows how give-willingly & big-heartedly Mrs Hunter acted towards me, & how there was never any struggle between us about fees. As a rule she would ask me to dine quite alone with her once in the off-season & ask me, then, to play to her, ask me about my tone-birthsome plans &, allroundly, behave as a friend. I did not feel 'at home' with her, for I never understood how anyone (man or woman) could want to be part of the 'sparkle-host' ((society)) & want to spend large sums on parties that could, instead, be spent on land-tilth [agriculture], the poor, art, or fact-search ((science))—the more so when one had (as Mrs Hunter had in Ethel Smythe[27]) a sister who was a great art-woman. (But no doubt Mrs Hunter spent big sums on E. Smythe's art too.) Yes, I felt Mrs Hunter was a kind of a friend—as far as any limb ((member)) of the sparkle-host could be.

Therefore, I was shocked & hurt to find her decry my 'thumping' before a table-ful of guests. (No doubt I did 'thump'.[28] Alfhild Sandby has written me that Herman was glad to give up playing with me in Denmark because he pain-felt my thumping so sorely. I have, it seems to me, never been a by-nature-ly *strong* player. For many years I felt 'weak' when playing in very large halls. So it stood to reason that I was trying to screw up my strength for many years. Nowadays I try to hold it back & try to sidestep thumping—having now, it seems to me, all the strength I need. But then I was 'building up' &, no doubt, often thumped mercilessly.) It would have been nicer if Mrs Hunter had told me, in a twi-talk, that my thumping was a bore. As it was, what she said that day angered me for life & I never, for a moment (in my dealings with her) forgot it or forgave her. It seemed to me an unfriendly blow at my play-for-pay life, & that I could ill brook.

I cannot get away from the feeling that this coolness to me all stemmed from her new-found closeness to Cyril Scott. It was a kind of 'gone-with-a-better-man-than-you' (as Kipling puts it) unfoldment. Some time before this (this Delius Concerto blow) Cyril had belly-ached about not earning enough & had asked me if I couldn't put some business his way. I said to him I didn't see why he couldn't get jobs from Mrs Hunter—maybe to play for her at a slightly lower fee than I did. He liked this plan & I offered him to Mrs Hunter as above outlined. They became thick as thieves & I think he played

27. Dame Ethel Smyth (1858–1944), German-trained English composer.
28. *The Western Daily Mercury* reported on 17 April 1914 ('The Torquay Festival'), regarding this Concerto performance, that 'The most delicate traceries with which the solo instrument clothes an orchestral theme, or the most fiery and passionate passages in which it has the leading part, were played alike by Mr. Grainger with perfect skill.'

for her a lot. No doubt it made a dint in her mind that she could have the playing of this over-soul (so much more graceful, inbornly skilful & self-hoodrich than mine—tho god knows that he, too, thumped unmercifully now & then!) for less money than mine & that that made her turn against me. Maybe it is inborn in us all to gloat when a good chance offers. It seems queer that she should have been moved to gloat (at having Cyril on tap) *just to me*, who had brot Cyril & Mrs Hunter together, & who was so happy at their getting on well together. It may be that Cyril told Mrs H. things about me that she found dislikable. (Is it not born in us all to belittle, up to a point, at least, our best friends? I see no harm in this, & I would unblinkingly belittle a dearest friend at one moment where I could warmly praise & upbuild the next moment. Life is, & should be, many-stranded.) Or it may be that Mrs H. grew to dislike (or somewhat dislike) me because of my broken betrothal to Margot Harrison.[29] Clear it is that Mrs H. (around this Delius Concerto at Torquay time) wanted to wound me. And wound me she did.

Later on, during the 1st world war, she took an unfriendly stand on my not joining the English army. Tho when I joined the USA army she cabled, 'Your friends are proud of you again', or some such sick words (1917). In other words, she acted like a foolish (& ½-unfriendly) woman. Around 1929 or 1930 or 1932 Cyril (loyally friendly to Mrs H. to her death—the English hold together in a way that I, as an Australian, am less likely to) begged Ella & me to call on Mrs H., in London. I said to him: 'I will never forgive Mrs H. but we will see her, if you urge it' (Cyril had stressed how much she still liked me. But I am not keen on friends who wish to get me killed in wars—friends who rejoice to hear I have donned army-togs). So we (Ella, Cyril, I) spent an evening with her. I played 'Marching Song of Democracy' on the piano. It was a bearable evening—a mirror-ghost of long-past evenings I had never liked at the time, & liked no better now; outcounted [except] that I now gloated over the thot that they were done with forever. Mrs H. (tho now ½-broke, so we were told) still lived in some style. But she died poor, Cyril says. Many women (against whom I had nothing, whom I rated as friendly) have seen fit to turn on me. Most of my sweethearts (Mimi, Karen, Margot, Lotta[30]) made up their minds, sooner or later (& always at a time when I was still wholeheartedly in love with them), that I was not worth sticking to. I guess there is something rootedly *unlikable* in my make-up from which stems this turning against me on women's part.

---

29. See essay 37.
30. Mimi Pfitzner (née Kwast), Karen Kellermann (née Holten), Margot Harrison, and Lotta Mills Hough, respectively.

So much for the 1st dislikable call-to-mindment linked with the Delius Concerto. The 2nd is a much sadder one. Around December 1921 (was it not?) I played the Delius twice with Walter Damrosch & the N.Y. Symphony orchestra—first in New York &, about 2 days later, in Brooklyn (Academy of Music).[31] I forget whether my mother was on hand at the New York forth-playment. She was in Brooklyn &, after the tonefeast, walked over with me, & some friends, to the subway, on our way back to New York (were we not at a hotel near N.Y. Central Terminal—the Belmont?[32]—for a few days) or White Plains. By the time she got to the subway she could walk no further & had to sit down on the inside subway steps to rest—our friends (Mrs Weichmann, Else Permin & others—was Lotta there?) waiting around till mother felt strong enough to walk on. The sight struck doom-awareness into my soul. The unwontedness of such a place to sit down on was, of course, part of my mother's always un-rut-wonted mind. But it also was proof of her great weakness, wornoutness, and hopewreckedness. If I recall aright (if the date really was Dec. 1921) this hap was sundry weeks before the endsome blow fell (Miss Permin's January letter, wanting to close her friendship with my mother).[33] But mother (thru Miss Du Cane's guest-stay at White Plains) was already doom-minded, foreboding-filled. This sight of mother sitting worn out on the Brooklyn subway steps (& my feelings of doom aroused by the sight) is the call-to-mindment that dogs any thot of, my naming of, the Delius Concerto.

I never played the Concerto to Fred (Delius), nor was he ever on hand when I played it in a tonefeast. (So I can never pose as knowing the tonewright's tone-wishes in this work, thank god!) There was talk of my playing it to him at Grez; but either I didn't have it in my fingers (I so seldom have anything in my fingers—my whole piano-playing life has been darkened by folk asking me to play pieces I never have learned, or cannot recall or play well at the moment) or there was no one there to play the orchestra on a 2nd piano. So I have no nasty call-to-mindments linking Fred & his concerto. Outcounting some bits (streaming, long-lined bits on the full blent-band [orchestra]) it is not the kind of Delius I love. It shows the European-mainlandlike Delius—the German Delius, unleavened by England & Grieg.

31. Grainger performed the Concerto in Brooklyn on 7 January 1922 and in New York on 8 January 1922. Since 1915 Grainger had performed many times under Walter Damrosch (1862–1950), an early advocate also of Grainger's compositions.

32. The Graingers were staying for the few days of these New York concerts at the Belmont on the corner of 42nd Street and Park Avenue.

33. Grainger's reports of the actions of Else Permin, Isabel Du Cane, Lotta Mills Hough, and his mother, leading up to his mother's suicide on 30 April 1922, are inconsistent in his various writings. He clearly suspected all three women of hastening his mother's decline in health and subsequent suicide. See, further, essay 20.

Am I wrong in thinking that Delius, before he met me, had not richly used the fund of Englishness & Grieg-swayedness that long lay buried in his mind? Can the Mass of Life, Seadrift, Life's Dance,[34] Appalachia be called English or Grieg-swayed? Yes, in spots—such as the 'Stars' chorus in Seadrift, the a cappella outburst in Appalachia. But as a whole, hardly. In these earlier works is he not what he often claimed to be: a Nietzsche-worshipping 'Good European'? But when he met me, heard me play farthest-northy Grieg works (such as op. 30, op. 66, op. 73[35]), heard me sing & play English folksongs, heard me champion Englishness & North-pinkiness ((Scandinavianism)) in tone-art, heard me play my English Dance, Green Bushes, Father & Daughter, Brigg Fair, Hillsongs I & II, and the like—did he not embark on a wholly new muchness of Englishness & North Pinkiness in his own art? Did my Danish worship & Jacobsen-worship not rebirth his own old Jacobsen-worship & lead to 'Fenymore & Gerda'? [36] Did my Norway worship not strengthen his own old Norway worship & lead to 'On Hearing the First Cuckoo in Spring' & 'The Song of the High Hills'? Did my 'Brigg Fair' not lead him to his first forth-heraldsomely English work 'Brigg Fair'? Did my Passacaglia-like forms (G. Bushes, Shepherd's Hey, Father & D., Scotch Strathspey & Reel, Bold William Taylor) not open up a form to him that proved more s[uita]b[le] to the treatment of folksongs or near-folksongs (such as his selfmade folklike themes in 'The Song of the High Hills' than his earlier-used variation form—thereby making English-like, North-pinklike tunes, phrases, themes more usable to him? Did the things I said, the things I played, not wean him away from Debussy-like, Wagner-like, late-19th-century-like tonebirthry & greaten his (already budding) Englishlike, Grieg-swayed, Northern-mooded tone-trend? Think of the utter Englishness of 'North Country Sketches', the Double Concerto, the first Cello & Piano Sonata, the Cello Concerto, think of the blended Englishness & North-pinkiness of 'The Song of the H.H.', 'On Hearing the 1st Cuckoo in Spring' as sidematched [compared] with the (mainly) European mainlandliness of the Piano Concerto, The Mass of Life, the Village Romeo & Juliet? In view of all this, am I not fact-up-borne in saying that Delius is my greatest sway-dom ((influence))? An oversoul will always take, steal, maw-work ((digest)) more than a lesser soul. Wagner took more than any man. Cyril Scott is a great hint-taker & so was Delius. So my hints, beliefs, thots, sample-deeds, fell on more life-taking earth in the case of Fred

---

34. Delius's symphonic poem, *La ronde se déroule* (1899), revised in 1901 as *Lebenstanz*.
35. Album for Male Voices (folksong arrangements), 19 Norwegian Folksongs (for solo piano), and *Stimmungen* [Moods] (for solo piano), respectively.
36. *Fennimore and Gerda* (1908–10), Delius's opera after *Niels Lyhne* by Jens Peter Jacobsen (1847–1885), Danish novelist and poet.

Delius than elsewhom. When I raised strong, one-sided, highly Graingerism thots to Fred, he would often echo them after me—re-saying my very words. This was not because he was copycatty, or weakminded. It was because, firstly, his mind was very wide & uptakesome; twaidly, because he & I thot as nearly alike as 2 artmen could. He, like myself, was an unravelable jumble of British, German & North-pinky sways. For him, as for me, America spelled art-birthing heartthrobs. He, like myself, was a god-naysayer, a sex-worshipper, a non-right-wrong-monger ((anti-moralist)). We both viewed the world touristicly—not as settlers, not as be-dwellers, not as broodraisers. We were at one in worshipping the sea, the hills, Icelandish sagas, Jacobsen, Nietzsche (he more than I), Walt Whitman, Wagner, Bach (in spite of his sometimes saying that Bach bored him), Grieg. We were alike in loathing (or more mildly disliking) Mozart, Beethoven, Hindemith, R. Strauss, & much else. We both had North English roots, strongfelt N. English moods. Both of us were selfish, sway-cruel—turning on even our kindest friends if an easy opening to do so showed. Both of us were 'bejahende Naturen' (yea-ful natures), almost uncheckable in our hunt for fun & joy. Both of us had the will to 'hector things then', both having little or nothing of the English will to 'only stand & wait'. Both were non-side-takers, giving our *whole* fealty to no one, to nothing, to no land.

And (I feel) we both helped each other more than the world will ever know. We alone (of all tonebirthers known to me) were foreshadowers of far-ahead British-German-Nordic togetherworkth. We alone drew our soulfood from the Colonial world (the old Colonial world of the sagas, the new Colonial world of the Nordic theeds [nations]). We alone were heathen ((god-naysayers)) yet wistful, pityrich & sorrowsharing. We were the art-twins of our timestretch [era].

Train, Portland → Los Angeles, Feb 18, 1941.

Source: 'Call-to-Mindments about Delius Piano Concerto', 'Deemths ((Opinions)) Book 1', section 8 (Grainger Museum, Melbourne).

➤ 83   The Lower the Fee, the Better I Play (1941)

There are tone-forthplayers & singers who do their best (so we are told) in the most be-famed opera houses, with the most bowed-down-to blent-bands ((orchestras)), when their fees are highest & when hearer-hosts are largest. All I can say is: such folk must be swollen-headed, or thick-skinned, or something. They must be brutes! What is the thought-path: 'Here is a frame worthy of my painting'? Are they so sure that what they bring is worthy of such spot-lighting? With me (cringing violet that I am—in some lines) t'is t'other way. I do my best where fees are lowest, listen-hosts are smallest. If there are only 110 listeners I say to myself: 'Most likely there is none here that will prick my bubble'. If I get $200 (or even $250) I say to myself: 'Likely I can play well enough for that'. But I think of a $700 fee (or a $1,000 fee! Have I ever had it?[37]) It is nerve-breaking. Can I be sure that I can cough up $700 worth of flawlessness, polish, host-holding skill? Hardly.

Kansas City Traingarth [station], Oct 28, 1941.

Source: 'The Lower the Fee, the Better I Play', 'Deemths ((Opinions)) Book 1', section 21 (Grainger Museum, Melbourne).

⤳ 84   Memories of Tchaikovsky Concertos (1943)

(June 12, 1943, Detroit, Roosevelt Hotel) Whenever I keyboard-swink ((practise)) at the 1st Tchaikovsky Piano Concerto[38] I recall my first strong mind-prints of the work—at the home of my piano teacher, Professor James Kwast, at Kronberg in the Taunus hills, a few miles outside Frankfurt. How did I become mind-stirred towards this work? Was it thru hearing Gabrilow-itsch (who then seemed to me a very sparkling player—much more so than in his American years) play it at one of the string-wind-band-y ((orchestral)) tonefeasts of the Frankfurt Opera House. Gabrilowitsch was just 20,[39] we were told, & I was greatly stirred at hearing him do this carry-away-some work. But whether that hearing was after or before the Kronberg call-to-mindments I cannot recall. Mother & I spent a summer in Kronberg (my paintings of the Kronberg castle-ruin & the later castle, and so on, are in the museum[40]) boarding at a breed group ((family)) called Green (how did he

---

37. During Grainger's first decade in the United States—the zenith of his performing career—his highest fee for a recital was in the $600–$700 range. He did once earn US$2,485 through a benefit solo recital for the American Red Cross in Boston (19 November 1917), but this money was given to the Red Cross the following month.
38. In B flat minor, Op. 23 (1874–75).
39. I.e., 1898–99.
40. Four of Grainger's Frankfurt-period paintings are reproduced in Gillies and Pear, eds., *The All-Round Man*.

come to have this English name?). James Kwast & his breed group were summering in Kronberg (was that why we went there?) & we saw much of them.
One day I was alone at Kwast's home (at least, he wasn't there) & was looking
thru the 1st movement of the 1st Concerto & was all enthralled with the
Russian bell-like (as it then seemed to me—I was always hearing bells in Russ-
ian tone-art) 2nd theme: ♩ | ♪ ♩ ♩ | ♪ ♪ ♩ ♪ | ♪ ♪ ♩ ♪ | ♩ ♪ ♩.

Kwast's house was on highish ground & the windows of his tone-art-
plying room overlooked the flat valley towards Frankfurt. Seen from his windows the many small, cabbage-shaped (dome-like) trees looked to me like an
untouched forest (Urwald) &, as such, stirred me greatly. As I looked out—all
full of the Tchaik. twaid [second] theme—a windstorm swept up & set the
tree-domes in a wild stir, as if they boiled. This touched me very deeply & I can
never think of the 2nd theme without thinking of Kwast's house & the sea of
swirling trees I saw from it. The maiden-forest (Urwald) & the Tchaik. tone-
art both spoke to me of the untamed all-stir ((nature)), & such things meant a
lot to me then, all strung up by Kipling's art, as I then was, with a worship of
all that was wild, deep-down, way-back, un-towny, un-townskillthy.

This day with the Tchaikovsky Nr. 1 (which is my only *root*-mind-print of
the work) was before Mimi (Kwast's elder daughter) & I became sweethearts (at
Kronberg, that summer). At the time of the windstorm in the treetops Mimi had
not yet at-come at Kronberg, so it seems to me—was she at a boarding school?
But it wasn't long after that windstorm that the Kwasts, mother, Mimi & I were
at [ ][41] one evening, & walked home thence thru the dark woods (full of glow-
worms) to Kronberg. I never flirted with girls. But mother said to me, 'Why
don't you take Mimi's arm & walk home with her?' (I always did what mother
told me. I guess there was not one love affair of mine, during mother's lifetime,
that was not started but by my mother giving me a 'go ahead' hint.) So I did, &
as we walked home thru the darkness & the glow-worms she told me of her un-
hope-fulfilled love for Hans Pfitzner.[42] Thus started our love-life. The first time I
kissed Mimi (& went home to Green's) I didn't sleep all night. I lay there crying
& grieving, feeling that I was faithless to my Australian childhood—I felt that
with this kiss, this opening up of sex-life, I was shutting the door on my Australian call-to-mindments. I felt I would never again be 'the same'.

When we went back to Frankfurt (when mother's teaching of English was
taken up anew in the Fall) the Kwasts (or at least, Mimi & her mother) stayed
on in Kronberg some weeks or months & once or twice a week I twi-wheeled
[bicycled] to Kronberg & back to see Mimi, trundling home in the dark, as I

41. Left blank by Grainger.
42. (1869–1949), German composer and conductor.

so well recall it. Those are all my fresh call-to-mindments (the swaying tree-tops, the glow-worms, my lovestir for Mimi, the sight of her sister's white limbs dashing about between the chestnut trees on the ruin side, near Green's, twi-wheeling home in the chilly Fall dark), with lots of bloom on them.

My first tonefeast in London was playing singles ((solos)) at Miss Devlin's tonefeast, summer 1902.[43] Shortly after that I played the 1st Tchaik. Concerto in St James's Hall.[44] A German time-beater [conductor][45] & some she-singer[46] wanted to make themselves known & gave a tonefeast with string-wind-band at St J. Hall. By paying a small sum (£25? £30? £50?) I was allowed to join in, playing the No. 1 Tchaikovsky. The time beater was, I think, a Saxon—a short, non-on-drawsome man, somewhat like Max Heymann at Bath, Edith Meadows's husband.[47] As I recall things he was not easy to play with—but then, I was un-wont myself. As always (the more so in those days) I played roughly, with lots of wrong notes & maybe a slip of call-to-mindment, here & there. It was a wretched business, like all my early tone-feasts. Yet I think it helped me to 'get on'. I think it helped me to get hire-jobs ((engagements)). Soon after, I had learned the 2nd Tchaikovsky Piano Concerto,[48] & this I played in Manchester, where Hans Richter[49] was kind enough to put me on there at the Hallé concerts.[50] In Manchester I stayed with Cyril Scott's friend [ ],[51] who soon after was put in prison for embezzlement. I didn't know, then, that the star-artist with a string-wind-band had to furnish the band-parts of a concerto. So I turned up at the rehearsal 'just as I was, without one plea'. The music-keeper ((librarian)) said, 'Where are the parts?' I had none. But Richter said, unhastily and kindlily: 'I believe we have it in the library'. And there it was. All was well until we came to the slow split ((movement)). In the middle of it I suddenly heard the string-wind-band play a scherzo I'd never heard before. This was an old forthprintment. The scherzo had been cut out of the forthprintment I had. Again Richter was very kind. 'Just listen till we come to the next part you know, & then we'll cut out the parts you don't know.' But it was a shock. It was a worse shock when, in the tonefeast, Richter took a theme (against which I had hard octaves to play) al-

43. Correctly, 11 June 1901. See essay 34.
44. 18 February 1902 at St. James's Hall, Piccadilly. Grainger had, the week before, played the Concerto twice, in afternoon and evening concerts on 6 February 1902 in Bath.
45. Emil Kreuz, later a deputy to Thomas Beecham.
46. Probably Eleanor Cleaver.
47. Max Heymann was then the musical director of the Bath City Orchestra. See essay 20.
48. In G major, Op. 44 (1879–80).
49. (1843–1916), Austro-Hungarian conductor, and the Hallé Orchestra's conductor since 1899.
50. 27 February 1905, at the Midland Hall.
51. Left blank by Grainger.

most double as fast as in the rehearsal. I was able to keep going, by playing very lightly & slovenly.[52] But, it nearly threw me off the rails. From such shocks a squeamish, scary make-up like mine never heals. Such things soured me on folkwise ((public)) playing for life. It was nobody's fault. But I was simply not made for such a rough life.

Source: 'Memories of Tchaikovsky Concertos', 'Deemths ((Opinions)) Book 2', section 51, dated 12 June 1943 (Grainger Museum, Melbourne).

85   Percy Grainger on Ideals (mid-1920s)

I am asked sometimes what the young pianist must do to begin a career; how he must start to establish himself as a pianist and musician.

Too often, I fear, he has his eyes fixed principally on the career and its emoluments rather than on the inner musical life he should constantly cultivate and enrich. The inner world must be paramount, must count for everything; the outer life will then take care of itself. That is to say, if he is true to himself, if he puts art first and self-aggrandisement and mere financial gain last, he is bound to succeed in the end. Opportunity will come to him in the right time and way when he is ready for it. With high aims and ideals ever in view he constantly prepares himself by diligent study. Careers are not made in a day, in a year or even two. They take time.

And time is a comparative terror. Mischa Elman[53] was a fine artist at sixteen—Paderewski[54] at thirty. Both were moved by the inner emotional urge to work out the life of the artist that they felt themselves called to follow.

The most vital asset for the young musician is emotion. He must be able to play 'with the heart', or his work is lifeless and dead. And he must be able to express this emotion in his playing, if he have it, or his performance will have no musical or (if you will) financial value. It soon becomes noised abroad and known whether a pianist's playing touches the heart and makes a sympathetic appeal. You cannot make an emotional appeal when playing unless you

52. Grainger received good reviews for the performance, *The Manchester Courier* ('The Gentlemen's Concerts', 28 February 1905) even noting 'the player's negotiation of the tremendous octave passages being especially clever.'
53. (1891–1967), Russian-born American violinist, who achieved débuts in Berlin, London, and New York by the time he was seventeen.
54. Ignacy Jan Paderewski (1860–1941), Polish pianist and composer, whose breakthrough came in Paris when he was in his late twenties.

love what you are doing, unless you love Art for itself, not for what it will bring you, not for what it will do for you.

But if you love Art with disinterested devotion, she will repay you with fourfold interest. Here is an illustration of this truth in my own experience. I early became familiar with the music of Grieg, and while much of it appealed to me strongly, I was particularly partial to the sets of Folk tunes, Ops 66 and 73.[55] These, belonging to his latest period, are little known and seldom played. But they interested me greatly, and I made them my own because I loved them.

Why Grieg Took to Him

Some years later I was in London and was invited to a function at Lady Speyer's on which occasion Grieg was present.[56] The conversation turned upon his own compositions. I spoke with enthusiasm of some of their characteristics, whereupon Grieg turned to me abruptly, asking if I played—if I were a pianist. Upon learning I was, he wished to know which of his compositions pleased me most. I mentioned these two groups, the Slåtter, Op. 66 [sic], and the set Op. 73 [sic]. He brightened at once, for it seemed just those were his favourites.

'Why,' he exclaimed 'No one knows these, no one plays them, and to think you know and like them best'.

When he returned to his home in Bergen, he was asked what had impressed him most on his trip. His answer was the fact that a young foreign pianist knew and could play his little known music.

All my further intercourse with Grieg hinged on this little incident, so trifling and yet so portentous. I was invited to visit him in Norway, and he seemed to delight in the feeling I put into his music. His friendship is a precious memory to me. I only speak of it here to show that it came to me because of my love for the least popular of his compositions.

I should like to bring out these little pieces in America, but don't know how they would stand being placed near larger and heavier works; they are so delicate and fragile in themselves.

How did I make the start which began my career? I can hardly say; it seemed to come by degrees, for one thing led to another. I think my dear mother helped most, for I was always so deep in work that I had little thought for anything else.

55. Grainger perhaps means the Op. 72 *Slåtter*, which he played more than the Op. 73 *Stimmungen*.
56. 15 May 1906. See essay 71.

We were living in Frankfurt in those early days. They were happy days, though we did not have a penny except as we earned it ourselves. And I can say that we lived from week to week, almost never having more ahead than would suffice to keep us a couple of weeks. My mother gave lessons and I added to our income when and what I could. I had at that time a very small repertoire and was working to enlarge it for I knew this must be done if I expected to do any pianistic work.

Source: 'Percy Grainger on Ideals', undated (mid-1920s; Grainger Museum, Melbourne), which formed part of 'Percy Grainger on Ideals', *Australian Music News*, 15/11 (June 1926), 45, 47.

⟫ 86   Grieg on Busoni's Lightning Octaves in Grieg Concerto (1949)

When Grieg was going over his piano concerto with me, the summer of 1907 in fore-readiment for the Leeds Festival of that year,[57] he asked me whether I could speed up the octaves at the very end of the first tone-bout ((movement)). I had to tell him that I couldn't (I could hardly play them trustworthily at the steady speed). He had heard Busoni close the tone-bout with gathering lightning speed & was wonderstruck at the tellingness of it & at Busoni's could-do-it-ness. So even in the stronghold of purest blue-eyed northern-ness one was dogged by skill-worship. The fact was that much of Grieg's worship (for one could hardly call it less) of me as a piano-player was rooted in my being somewhat of a Busoni, tho not a full Busoni.[58] It is because of all this that I say it was heaven sent lucky for me that darling Grieg did not live to hear me play his concerto in public. It was a heaven sent boon for me that out of all the world's be-famed tone-men *just one* had been genuinely stirred to write high praise-words about my filthy playing (thereby making my earning-path almost easy for life!) & that he never had to withdraw those praise-words, or drastically qualify them, as he undoubtedly would have had to had he heard me play before a hearer-host ((audience)). Not that he ever would have acted harshly or hard-heartedly to me, for it was not in his make-up to do so. But it would have been a grief to me to see that he saw he

---

57. 12 October 1907, with Grainger as soloist. Grieg himself was to conduct this performance in the Leeds Town Hall, but he died in the previous month and was replaced by Sir Charles Stanford.

58. See essay 106.

had picked the wrong horse. This grief I tholed ((endured)) at his hands as a tone-wright. (See 423-10.)[59]

Oct. 10, 1949

Source: 'Grieg on Busoni's Lightning Octaves in Grieg Concerto', in 'Grainger's Anecdotes', 423-9 (Grainger Museum, Melbourne).

87   Stanford Wanted to Take Me to the Norfolk, Conn. Festival, to Play His 'Down Among the Dead Men' Variations (1949?)

Between 1910 & 1913, it must have been, that Stanford wanted me to play his 'Down Among the Dead Men' Variations for piano & orchestra[60] (parts of which I doted on—but the bulk of it—no) at one of Stoeckel's[61] Norfolk, Conn. Music Festivals, where he was to conduct some of his music. But I (as a greedy Aussie money-earner & natural business man as regards my pianistic career) could not see myself making my bow[62] to America in such a patch-work quilt of good & bad as Stanford's variations are. So I said 'No'. And was I right, or was I wrong? A few years later, at the same Norfolk, Conn. Festivals, Stoeckel paid me $500 for the first performance of my suite 'In a Nutshell' (1916)[63] & the same a year later for my 'The Warriors'.[64] So it might be said that I showed very good judgement in refusing the Stanford offer. On the other hand, it was just with those 2 pieces (Nutshell & Warriors) that I sullied my fame in America. But it would have been sullied anyway—there was not a chance for a man like me to stay long in America's good graces. Stanford & America were as alike as 2 peas, as far as my inner art-life went. Both were nice enough as long as I played second fiddle, played other men's works & played into the hands of other men's vanities. Both gave me the cold shoulder the moment I made any sign of being a great man in my own right.

(1949?)

---

59. 'Grieg's Growing Fretfulness at My Tone-Works' (essay 71).
60. Concert Variations upon an English Theme, Op. 71 (1897–8).
61. Carl Stoeckel (1858–1925) and Ellen Battell Stoeckel (1851–1939), who started this chamber-music festival in 1899.
62. Début.
63. On 8 June 1916, conducted by Arthur Mees.
64. On 7 June 1917, conducted by Grainger.

Source: 'Stanford Wanted to Take Me to the Norfolk, Conn. Festival, to Play His "Down Among the Dead Men" Variations', in 'Grainger's Anecdotes', 423-20 (Grainger Museum, Melbourne).

➤ 88   Nina Grieg Thought Sostenuto Pedal Sounded 'Unclear' in 'Jeg går i tusen tanker' (1949)

One of the few things I can be proud of in my piano playing is my use of the sostenuto pedal ((organ-point-holding pedal)) in Grieg's 'Jeg går i tusen tanker'[65] (Op. 66, No. [18]). In the grand 3rd verse the clearness, yet carrying-on-ness, of the basses & other voices is masterly. Yet when I played it to Mrs Grieg in Copenhagen, 1922, all she said was [in Danish] 'The sound is unclear'. [In English] After all I have said of Nina Grieg it may be guessed that she had the finest kind of German officer steely grey-blue eyes. From [the] 'blue-eyed' race mankind let blue-eyed-race hero-deeds in art never look for fair treatment.

Oct. 10, 1949

Source: 'Nina Grieg Thought Sostenuto Pedal Sounded "Unclear" in "Jeg går i tusen tanker"', in 'Grainger's Anecdotes', 423-12 (Grainger Museum, Melbourne).

➤ 89   H. Allerdale Grainger (1953)

H. Allerdale Grainger,[66] Agent-General in London for South Australia around 1901–1906, thought he was an uncle of mine, but my father didn't know whether he was or wasn't. He was an impulsive North-English. Once he pulled the cable of a lift, to bring it down from above, & as the cage came down he put his hand in the case & caught the cable & stopped the cage—but made his hand all bloody! He liked to take me to the London Savage Club & set me to play, which I hated.[67] How I hate gatherings of professional men, actors, celebrities. They behave so cruelly. A young actor was asked to recite & was very boring in Shakespeare. In the middle they started clapping & silenced the poor young man, who looked so distraught. So (years later) when the Melbourne branch of the Savage Club invited me, I remembered this act of cruelty to the young actor & wouldn't go. I played Scott's 1st sonata (the one now

65. 'I wander deep in thought' (in Norwegian).
66. (1848–1923), former South Australian parliamentarian.
67. Starting with an early performance on 8 February 1902, Grainger occasionally played at the Savage Club in London.

called 'Handelian Rhapsody')[68] at the London Savage Club & H. A. Grainger said, 'it needs the knife'. Wasn't it also he who said, 'I wonder why young artists like yourself don't play really melodious music, such as "Home Sweet Home"'—a not stupid remark. (Is 'Country Gardens' my answer to that?)

K[ansas] C[ity], July 13, '53

Source: 'H. Allerdale Grainger, Savage Club, Scott Sonata "Needs the Knife", Cruelty to Young Actor, Melbourne S.C.', in 'Grainger's Anecdotes', 423-27 (Grainger Museum, Melbourne).

➤ 90   Cyril Scott's 1st Sonata at Bexhill (Suicidal Mood) (1953)

That same 1st sonata (now called, part of it, 'Handelian Rhapsody')[69] I played in a program on a pier in Bexhill, sometime around 1903–4.[70] As I sat & practised *I could not* remember the sonata, & as I heard the waves lapping under the pier & thought of my love of the sea & my hatred of the concert platform, & my love of my friend's composition & my unableness to play it well, I felt such a strong urge to drown myself in the sea & have done with it all—maybe the strongest suicidal urge I have ever felt. As I passed those tormented hours in Bexhill I did not dream that I would be blissfully & innocently happy nearby (Pevensey Bay)[71] about 24 years later.

(Kansas City, July 13, 1953)

Source: 'Cyril Scott's 1st Sonata at Bexhill (Suicidal Mood)', in 'Grainger's Anecdotes', 423-29 (Grainger Museum, Melbourne).

➤ 91   P. G. Rehearses 'Song of the High Hills' with Frankfurt Rühlscher Gesangverein (1953)

Before mother died (April 30, 1922) we had planned a tour for me in Norway, Denmark & Holland for the Fall. I carried out this tour, tho I was very lifeless. In Holland I saw old friends in an audience, but they never came round to see

---

68. (1901), revised in 1909. See essay 90.
69. Part of this early 1901 Sonata became *Handelian Rhapsody*, Scott's Op. 17, which was published in 1909, the same year that he published his official 'Sonata No. 1', Op. 66 (1908–9).
70. Perhaps on 13 December 1902.
71. See essays 41 and 42.

me, so disappointed were they. (It would have been like visiting a corpse.) But I did the first folksong gathering tour with Evald Tang Kristensen[72] in (August?) 1922, & there was nothing dead about that. The liveliness of the purpose (to phonograph the old tunes that still were left) & the liveliness of old E. T. Kristensen were my first contact (after my mother's death) with the *healing* forces of life. So when my Dutch tour was finished (mid-Dec., 1922) I went to take a holiday in my beloved Dordrecht, there to clean-write the tunes E. T. K. & I had gathered.[73] I was planning to stay there somewhat longer, before moving on to Frankfurt, when a wire or letter came from Delius asking if I could come at once to Frankfurt & rehearse the Rühlscher Gesangverein in his 'The Song of the High Hills', which was to be given in Delius's concert to take place in Frankfurt on his 60th birthday.[74] The conductor of the Rühlscher would not rehearse the work, because he was not to conduct it at the concert. The conductor at the concert was to be [ ],[75] but he could only come from Vienna at the last minute. I answered 'yes' & fared into Germany the very day the French occupied the Ruhr.[76] For sometime I had been wondering whether I should do more conducting. I had always conducted my own works, but not other composers' works, & I was wondering if I could do more for Nordic music if I did more conducting. I thought to myself: let this experience with the Rühlscher decide. If I do well & feel at home in the job I will go in for more conducting. But I will give up the idea if I feel ill at ease rehearsing the Rühlscher. (What happened was that I felt ill at ease & did badly in my rehearsing, of course. But I did not keep to my plan to let the Frankfurt experience decide. I just went in for more conducting, some of the first concerts being those with the Bridgeport Oratorio Society[77] & the Los Angeles Choral Society.[78] Was it a good move, this more conducting? I still don't know. If one's compositions do not 'slå an' (make a hit),[79] if they are not *liked*, I don't suppose there is much one can do. But whether it is better to accept defeat—as Cyril has—or to fight on, as I have, I don't know.)

72. Grainger had originally planned this collecting tour of Jutland with Evald Tang Kristensen for August 1914, but these plans had to be abandoned because of the escalating state of war.

73. Grainger's various transcriptions of Danish folk songs are listed in Kay Dreyfus, *Music by Percy Aldridge Grainger* (Melbourne: University of Melbourne), vol. 1 (1978), 293–95, vol. 2 (1995), 197.

74. Grainger appears to be misguided here. Delius had celebrated his sixtieth birthday on 29 January 1922.

75. Left blank by Grainger.

76. 11 January 1923.

77. On 28 April 1924 (in Bridgeport, CT) and 30 April (in New York), in both of which Delius's *The Song of the High Hills* (1911–12) was performed.

78. On 30 April 1926 (in Los Angeles), Grainger conducted a programme including Delius's *The Song of the High Hills* with the Los Angeles Oratorio Society.

79. In Danish.

The Rühlscher Gesangverein was as nasty to rehearse as a choral group could possibly be. They were poor readers, they talked all the time, & I am sure they hated the work. (After the Bridgeport Oratorio Soc. had sung 'The Song of the High Hills' & my 'Marching Song of Democracy' in Bridgeport & New York—1924—they lost one-third of their membership. So much disliked they the works—in spite of the fact that I had provided the New York Philharmonic Orchestra for both concerts, to the tune of about $12,000.) Someone who was at one of my rehearsals with the Rühlscher said to me: 'You don't understand the Germans. If you banged on the lid of the piano a few times, they would give you their attention.' I tried this in the next rehearsal & it had some effect. But one cannot act contrary to one's nature very long. There was a group of old ladies in the left back corner (2nd sopranos?) that had a bit by themselves very soon after the chorus starts singing. I had more trouble with those old ladies than with anything else. And when the Jewish-Danish conductor from Vienna had his first rehearsal with the choir & came to the spot where my old ladies became vocally exposed, he took one hate-filled look in their direction, made a big wiping-out-gesture & shouted 'Nicht mitsingen!'[80] Neither the conductor, nor Delius, made any bones about letting me know that they thought the chorus thoroly badly trained (by me), which of course it was.

Århus Kommunehospital, Aug. 15, 1953.

Source: 'P. G. Rehearses "Song of the High Hills" with Frankfurt Rühlscher Gesangverein', in 'Grainger's Anecdotes', 423-55 (Grainger Museum, Melbourne).

➤92   'The Bit You Played to Mark Hambourg' (Chopin Polonaise) (1953)

I played Chopin's A flat Polonaise[81] on the 1st Ada Crossley Australasian tour.[82] At the beginning, in Sydney, Melbourne, Adelaide, no doubt I played it complete. But in the 'smalls' I left out the section that turns into F minor off the octave Cs (about the 3rd page of the printed music),[83] partly to

---

80. 'Don't join in singing!' (in German).
81. Op. 53.
82. Lasting from 24 September 1903 (first Sydney concert) to 21 January 1904 (final Perth concert), including mid-November to early December in New Zealand.
83. Grainger appears to have left out bars 49–64.

shorten the piece (for the unspoilt ears of the smaller towns) & partly because I found this section hard to remember, when on the platform. But when we came back from the Gold-Fields (Kalgoorlie & Coolgardie)[84] we heard that Mark Hambourg[85] (who had just finished an Australian tour & was on his way to England) was to be present at our next concert in Perth. I debated with myself, should I let M. H. hear me play the Polonaise with the cut, or let him hear me play the 'cut' abominably. I decided to risk the latter. It went horribly of course. From then on Jacques Jacobs[86] always referred to the cut as 'the bit you played to Mark Hambourg'.

Århus, Aug. 17, 1953

Source: ' "The Bit You Played to Mark Hambourg" (Chopin Polonaise)', in 'Grainger's Anecdotes', 423-73 (Grainger Museum, Melbourne).

84. On 16–18 January 1904.
85. (1879–1960), Russian-born English pianist.
86. See essay 35.

9

COMMENTATOR

➤ 93   [The Expressive Potential of Music] (1901)

Music can express *one* type only at a time, for which reason *it can never become dramatic*. Thus in the drama, 3 distinctly different types may be brought onto the stage simultaneously, each standing out clearly & distinctly, whereas if we bring together 3 equally different types in music we do not get the impression of each of the 3 separately, but we get an entirely new type born of the 3, an intricate, in most cases, warring impression, in *no* way resembling any of the units of its construction, or its parallel in drama. In a landscape, a hill, a meadow, & a stream, will be each distinct, whereas relative contrasts in sound, united, would occasion a regular muffin-struggle.

But music can do what is denied the other arts, in that it can give the ensemble, the atmosphere, *without* any of the details (I mean, it can give the spirit of a landscape without the trees, can give the spirit of the trees without the branches, leaves, etc.), this being in fact the essence of musical possibilities, our highest right. Thus, I consider Impressionism an encroachment on the art of music, exchanging the office of painting (to express the underlying idea of a form thro its form) for that of music (to express the underlying idea of a form[1] without its form) in the same way I consider a certain musical school that has sprung up in Germany a false attempt to fulfil the functions of painting rather than that of its own art.[2] This school setting words to music frantically endeavours to follow the meaning of each single word (rather than devote the inwardness of its art & the whole emotional nature of the whole poem) so that if the word 'moss' appears in the text, 'moss' immediately grows

---

1. Grainger later added here the comment, 'has of course nothing to do with the "form" of music'.
2. Grainger is perhaps referring to Richard Strauss.

out of the depths of the piano, if 'sky' is mentioned, chords unmistakably 'blue' are the result, the accompanist thru-out performing 'The Lightning Trick'.

It is lowering to find so-called musicians so mistaking their duty towards their art. A writer in bringing before us anything ideal, noble, unreachable, must do so by touching on things that are material & graspable; even in speaking of God & Heaven, he must mention *names, facts, things*. With our art it is otherwise; our art is abstract, far from realities, is not limited to facts. (Imagination in literature & painting is merely the exchanging of the *known* forms & facts for those *unknown*.) Shall we discard our artistic birthright & attempt to follow other arts in lines where our very advantages force us to failure?

Thus, the love-music of *Tristan* loses continuity [so] that it may be dramatic. Here Wagner commits himself to an error of reasoning, for if we believe the *love-motiv* to represent *love*, the *Tristan-motiv* to represent *Tristan*, the *Isolde-motiv* to represent *Isolde*, then we must admit that, while the *Tristan-motiv* is playing, *Love* for the moment ceases, that *Tristan* gives place to *Isolde* while her motiv is played, & all 3 disappear while the *Death-motiv* reigns.

Surely this longing for the beyond to make possible the great desires (the *Death-motiv*) is meant to underly the whole scene, altho the dramatic entry given this motiv mentally convinces that this emotion has been absent to this present & has just arrived & is just being introduced by its motiv. Thus, the dramatic mode of expression Wagner had—to my mind—forced himself into, entirely spoils this as a *love* scene, though of course emotionally it is glorious. Love is not dramatic (only its results) & does not suddenly appear (for 30-second swags) to equally suddenly disappear. Rather is it a continuous thing to which interruption is death.

To my thinking, the *love-type* should have gone unbroken thro the whole scene, as also the individualities of Tristan & Isolde, also the veil of Death-desire, but above all the Love element should most certainly have been *ever-present*, & the breaking up of this act into many *mental ideas* I can view as nothing less than a complete failure. As above mentioned, this is the purely mental verdict. If, on the other hand, we go from the standpoint that the motivs *mean* nothing, & merely seek the emotional impression, we shall find it musically superb but must own to disagree with Wagner's doctrine of the purport of music. From this standpoint his application of philosophy to sound was a waste of time.

Sept. 13, 1901

Source: Untitled passage in 'Methods of Teaching and Other Things',[3] from section 58 (pp. [39]–[41]) (Grainger Museum, Melbourne).

➤ 94   After Reading Parry[4] (1902)

The point is that whereas the end of language is understanding of idea expressed, the end of music (is always, has been) is sympathy with emotion expressed, *understanding* being out of the question. Therefore, whereas in the case of language it is entirely necessary to determine on certain sounds (letters, etc.) for the purpose of attaching certain meanings to them, in music there is no like necessity for determining on certain divisions of pitch (notes), as no greater sympathy is felt towards underlying emotion. The argument of 'understanding' music is in any case untenable. All can feel music; none can *prove* that they understand a distinct meaning in it, etc.

Sept. 29, '02

Source: 'After Reading Parry (Preliminaries) (*Ev. of the A of M*)', in 'Methods of Teaching and Other Things', from section 58 (p. [38]) (Grainger Museum, Melbourne).

➤ 95   Donald Francis Tovey's Aunt (1953)

If I sense Balfour Gardiner's trouble when I hear that he knew Tovey at Oxford,[5] I sensed Tovey's trouble when I met his aunt [Miss Sophie Weisse][6] who, I am told, brought him up. ('The middle class is that part of society domineered by woman.') When I met Tovey's aunt she had just been hearing a Mengelberg performance of Bach's Matthew Passion in Holland & was loud in asserting how much better it was than any English performance of the work. I think she said something about English musical life being 'parochial'.

---

3. For other sections from this collection of Grainger's ideas from his early London years, see essays 46, 47, and 94, as well as Gillies and Clunies Ross, eds., *Grainger on Music*, 'Theme as Related to Form in Music' (1901), 5–12, and 'My Musical Outlook' (1902–4), 13–28.
4. *The Evolution of the Art of Music* (1896), by the English academic musician, C. Hubert H. Parry (1848–1918). This book was an enlargement of his *The Art of Music* (1893).
5. Balfour Gardiner and Tovey overlapped as undergraduates at Oxford during 1896–8.
6. Grainger left this space blank. Sophie Weisse undertook Tovey's general and musical education at the 'Dames School' for the children of Eton College masters and remained a strong influence over all aspects of his adult life.

(I always hate anyone who belittles music in England.) And then she turned around & said, 'Perhaps what we are doing in England is not so bad, after all', or words to that effect. Such people are at once unpleasantly humble & unpleasantly conceited. And however patriotic they may be about war, they certainly are not patriotic about music. Now the one thing I want to be most patriotic about is music; for it is the field in which I can do the most. Of course, one builds up for oneself a worry-some life by being patriotic about art, for most people look upon art as an international force, & do not understand excessive nationalism (such as mine) in art.

Århus Kommunehospital, Aug. 13, 1953

Source: 'Donald Francis Tovey's Aunt', in 'Grainger's Anecdotes', 423-50 (Grainger Museum, Melbourne).

96   Dr Russell's Statement: 'It's Too Early. You Must Wait Till You're Dead' (1941)

When I said to Dr Russell (that dear friend—but he was an Englishman; by which I mean: the world came first, his friends came twaid [second])—was it in 1926-ish?—that I hoped to build a Grainger Museum[7] very soon, he said: 'It's too early, Percikins. You can't build a museum devoted to yrself while you're still alive. It can't be done until after yr death.' But all I see, all that happens, drives me deeper into the belief that flag-keen ((patriotic)) men must do all they can to worth-show the worthwhile things of their own country, own race, without being afraid that others will dub them selfboasters. They should be much more afraid of being selfshamers, since self-belittlement is the deadly sickness of all our Pinkman [Scandinavian] peoples. Surely Bret Harte[8] & Mark Twain[9] have been famed long enough to make the silliest fool realize that it is poor business & foul flag-dullth to tear down a hotel they heartthrobcausingly put up in![10] One would think that everyone must see that to

7. The current Grainger Museum at The University of Melbourne, built in two stages (1935, 1938).
8. (1836–1902), American journalist and author.
9. (1835–1910), American author.
10. Grainger included with his text an unidentified Californian newspaper cutting entitled, 'Hotel Which Sheltered Early Day Authors Is Razed On Mother Lode'. It read: 'Mokelumne Hill (Calaveras Co.), Feb. 18 [1941]—(INS)—Historic Peek Inn, which gave shelter to such famous figures as Mark Twain and Bret Harte, was no more today. Mokelumne Hill workmen finished tearing down the old structure situated in the historic Mother Lode town fifteen miles north of San Andreas. On the site of the inn will rise a modern two story structure'.

keep standing an old mill like that shown in the bottom print-likish [newspaper copy],[11] or like the old barn in Grove Street in White Plains (torn down a few years ago—I took photolikths of it), is to build up gold-riches & mind-riches for the to-cometh ((future)).

It is not that Americans, Australians & Englishmen do not bow to fame—they bow low to fame as long as it is strictly nowy, for sample: to a living King, a wide-liked movie-star. But they are not aware of the worth of long-timey fame. They bow to the spread of fame thru space, but not to the spread of fame thru time! What a queer mind-squint! King Alfred (on top of being a much greater soul than Queen Elizabeth[12]) did as much for England as Queen Elizabeth. But he does not mean as much to the English as does she. The grand fact that his fame has lived longer than hers factfully makes him *less* thoughtworthy to English-speakers, queerly enough. But there is no strength, no to-come-th, no fairness, no fact-hunger in this, their mind-slant. It leads to nothing but self-out-wipedness. Will Americans or Australians or Britishers be-nay that Christ's (if they are his) thoughts holding sway for 2,000 years means nothing? That the mete-craft ((mathematics)) of the Greeks (if it was theirs) holding sway so long means nothing? If this is so, why shall the long-lasting heartsway of English-speaking bookmen or tonemen mean nothing? If the 'Peek Inn' (if it were kept standing as a pasthoard [heritage] piece) held the mindstirs of bookartlovers for many hundreds of years, would it be nothing? Even money-somely speaking: if it earnt more as the old 'Peek Inn,' than it will as a 'modern 2 story structure', spread over a hundred years, would that be nothing?

There is no rime or reason in the English-speaking viewpoint—if there were, I would bow to it. There is nothing behind it but knownothingness & the shortsightedness inborn in untrained minds. If Bruno David Ussher[13] (German Jew) says something about Goethe our weak-kneed English-speakers bow to his word, because they think he *knows*, & they are right, he does. If an English-speaking knower says something about Cadman[14] or Cowell or Scott they are a little less likely to bow to his word, because he is (in fact) less likely to know what he is talking about. So (if we English-speakers do not want to be forever trampled on in the world of art—if, in other words, we wish our gifts to have their rightful do-what ((effect)) on mankind, which

---

11. Beneath this essay, Grainger included two photographs from the *Salt Lake Tribune* (23 February 1941) showing a mill that had recently collapsed in Idaho.
12. The First.
13. American music critic, at this time with a regular column on film music in the *Los Angeles Daily News*.
14. Charles Wakefield Cadman (1881–1940), American composer, particularly interested in American Indian music.

is the only honest thing for any gifted man to wish), we must take set steps, much as follows:

1   factfully greaten our knowledge, our study, our workoutment,
2   never fail to forthtell to our folk what we know (if we really know it),
3   keep records, call-to-minders ((remembrances)), relics of all kinds, that tend to bring home to our wayward-willyish theeds [nations] the worth, the muchness & the howths ((qualities)) of knowledge. We must try to bring home to our folk the fact that greatness hinges on work & knowledge, not on luck or heaven-dropped 'gifts'.

Tho the Melbourne Pasthoard [Museum] is a cruel drain on my purse, tho the work (done & to-do) on it [is]¹⁵ more that I can ill spare cruel art itself, yet I don't think I ought to rue my self-altar-layment, laid on the altar of knowledge worship. I feel, more & more, that my pasthoard plans are unsidestepable.

Source: 'Dr Russell's Statement: "It's Too Early. You Must Wait Till You're Dead" ', in 'Deemths ((Opinions)) Book 1', section 11, undated (probably 23 February 1941; Grainger Museum, Melbourne).

➤ 97   Facts about Percy Grainger's Year in Europe (1923)

On arrival in Europe, in August 1922, I collected 80 Danish folksongs in Jutland together with Evald Tang Kristensen, Denmark's wonderful veteran folklorist, who is over 80 years of age. We travelled around the agricultural districts with a phonograph, getting the old peasants (some of them nearly 90 years of age) to sing their mediaeval melodies into the phonograph. Before leaving Europe this summer I again visited Mr Kristensen, this time to note down on paper the rest of the tunes we had collected the summer before.¹⁶ Amongst these melodies are several of striking beauty & archaic charm & I am making settings of several of the tunes for chamber music that I shall publish as soon as I can complete them.¹⁷ From Sept 8 to Dec 26 I gave piano

---

15. Some word(s) illegible here.
16. In total, Grainger undertook four visits to Jutland—in 1922, 1923, 1925, and 1927—to work with Evald Tang Kristensen. They collected over two hundred folk songs.
17. Hence, most notably, the *Danish Folk-Music Suite* (1928–41), consisting of arrangements of two melodies collected in 1922 ('The Power of Love' and 'Lord Peter's Stable-Boy'), a linked arrangement of melodies collected in 1922 and 1923 ('The Nightingale' and 'The Two Sisters'), and a medley of four tunes collected in 1922 and 1927 ('Jutish Medley').

recitals thruout Norway, Denmark & Holland, finding my old public (I had played in those countries every year from 1906 to 1914) as loyal & sympathetic as ever.

In December I was in London to hear a wonderful performance of Delius's 'Song of the High Hills' by the London Philharmonic under Albert Coates[18]—a truly unforgettable rendering of an exquisite & stupendous work. Thence, I returned to Holland & Germany to hold orchestral & chamber concerts & prepare my larger unpublished works for publication by Schott & Co. London, B. Schott's Söhne, Mayence,[19] Universal-Edition, Vienna. I found a thrilling degree of interest & sympathy in my compositions in Germany on the part of performers & publishers alike, & would have been greatly tempted to give orchestral & chamber concerts of my works in the chief cities of Germany, Holland & Austria had the manuscripts of my chief works not already been in the hands of the engravers. However, I am hoping to give such concerts in later seasons, my European impresario wishing me to return early in 1924 for this purpose; but this I am unable to do owing to the bookings Antonia Sawyer Inc. have made for me on this side.[20]

I heard many highly interesting concerts while in Holland & Germany, & much of the most extreme modernist music. In particular, I was interested in works by Arnold Schönberg, Franz Schreker, & Paul Hindemith. Schönberg I have always believed in since I first heard his 'Five Orchestral Pieces' in London in 1912.[21] Schreker's 'Kammersinfonie',[22] superbly given by Mengelberg in Amsterdam, is a work lovely in color in context. Of all the German composers Paul Hindemith impresses me the most.[23] This young genius has an almost Schubertian simplicity & facility of expression & natural sense of musical color. I feel that in Paul Hindemith Germany has returned to a *genuine musicality* (to a 'music for music's sake') that seemed to me much weaker in the years before the war. My feeling is that the musical life of Europe today is healthier, simpler, more vigorous, more sincere, & above all, *more musical* than it was from 1900 to 1914.

Europe is not only in an especially productive period, compositionally— it is also in a highly sympathetic receptive mood. This is shown by the warm response to Anglosaxon artists & their works. In Amsterdam I heard a most

18. The English conductor Albert Coates (1882–1953) had also conducted the première of this work in London on 26 February 1920.
19. Mainz.
20. I.e., in the Americas.
21. 3 September 1912, at a Promenade Concert in Queen's Hall.
22. For twenty-three instruments (1916).
23. See Grainger's later, perhaps more genuine, views on Hindemith's work in essay 82.

masterly interpretation of a Chopin Concerto by Ernest Schelling[24] & Mengelberg, also a most interesting work of Schelling's, & the reception accorded Schelling on both counts was hearty in the extreme. A Mengelberg performance of Rubin Goldmark's glorious orchestral 'Requiem' is one of the strongest impressions I received.

On my own tours I experienced a most refreshing response to the American & British works I played. When I played compositions by Dett, Guion, Carpenter, Griffes, Dillon, Balfour Gardiner[25] & others there was a certain spontaneity about the attitudes of the listeners which showed me that the so-called 'serious' work of music is as ready to capitulate to our classical English-speaking composers as the 'popular' public of all the world has to our jazz.

The Anglosaxon is the popular race in most parts of Europe at present & as this feeling is one of natural liking rather than of racial propaganda it is not surprizing that this liking manifests itself strongly in such an instinctive thing as the art of music. This attitude is strongly evident in the activities of the leading continental music publishers. The Universal Edition (Vienna) has secured all of Frederick Delius' recent works, large & small, while B. Schott's Söhne, Mayence, is publishing an opera, a ballet & several large orchestral works of Cyril Scott. Two large volumes of a German edition of Roger Quilter English songs [are] in the press,[26] & to my mind the time is ripe for European editions of the best American songs.

Head & shoulders above all the composers of Europe towers Frederick Delius, in my estimation. Great as his work always was, it has intensified in touching beauty & masterly powers during the last 10 years. Here is a truly great emotional soul, as well as a truly great musician, not concerned in the 'isms' or 'movements' of a brief day, but, while intensely modern & original on the one hand, on the other hand [he] combines the accumulated richness of past methods & eras into the wide scope of his creative scheme—in a similar way to what Bach did in his time. It is this type of the at-once progressive & conservative artist that touches the loftiest heights & depths of the soul in art. This Delius does in his 'The Song of the High Hills,' his Cello Concerto, his 'North Country Sketches' & others of his recent works. On the occasion

24. (1876–1939), American pianist and composer.

25. Including 'Juba Dance' by Canadian-born American Nathaniel Dett (1882–1943), 'Turkey in the Straw' by American David Guion (1895–1981), 'Tango Americain' by American John Alden Carpenter (1876–1951), 'Birds at Dawn' by American Fannie Dillon (1881–1947), and Balfour Gardiner's 'Prelude' and 'Humoresque'. Grainger's extant programmes for this European tour do not reveal a work by the American Charles Griffes (1884–1920).

26. Probably Quilter's five *Englische Lyrik*, published by Schott in 1924, and the *Drei Shakespeare-Lieder*, also published by Schott.

of his 60th birthday (Jan. 1923 [*sic*]),[27] 2 concerts of his works were given in several chief European centres, & the Delius Festival I then witnessed in Frankfurt was impressive not only for the majestic beauty of the works rendered but also for the great & spontaneous enthusiasm of the public. Delius is not merely the greatest English composer. He is one of the few towering international geniuses, acclaimed in all music-loving lands.

The part of my trip that had the deepest meaning for me, personally, was to visit again those spots & old friends, where & with whom, my beloved mother & I had been so happy in the past. The old places & friends that I saw in England, Scandinavia, Holland & Germany were as comforting to me as anything could be without the presence of my lifelong companion. In Denmark I had much joy in seeing Mrs Grieg. She was present at my recital in Copenhagen[28] & it was wonderful to see her looking so well (scarce altered since I first saw her with her great husband in 1906) despite her 77 years & a recent serious illness. She is, as ever, a real artist, thru & thru.

Source: 'Facts about Percy Grainger's Year in Europe for Interviews', dated 24 August 1923 (Grainger Museum, Melbourne).

➤ 98   ['The King Is Dead, Long Live the King': World, Racial and Tone-Art Loyalties] (1933)

The Germans & the French really still believe their fatherland is a fine place, altho they have been living there long enough to get sick of it & find out its lacks; but no, they cannot manage to get bored with their fatherland, as the English & the Northmen ((Scandinavians)) are able to get bored with their lovely lands, forsaking them for such less-likable places as Italy, the South of France (& America, in the case of the Northmen). The Germans are not able to get sick of their 'great masters' of tone-art—Weber, Beethoven, and so on. I guess they never really listen to these vulgar geniuses worthweighingly ((critically)). They just go on feeling 'loyal' whenever they hear the frightfully boring toneworks of their 'great masters' & that hinders the god-sent worm of boredom from gnawing their loyalty away. If they could shed their loyalty for a moment maybe they could hear the vulgarities & shallowness of Weber &

---

27. See essay 91.
28. 16 October 1922, at which Grainger performed Grieg's *Ballade*, Op. 24.

Beethoven for what they are & might then feel tempted to lend an ear to the many hundreds of things in tone-art that are finer & deeper, smoother & lovelier than the German 'great masters.' (When I studied the piano in Frankfurt with the Hollander James Kwast his little daughter Evchen (aged 10–12, & brot up quite German, of course), overheard her father holding forth thus about the gift from tone-pulse ((rhythm)) that he had met in his learners from sundry lands: [In German] 'The Germans don't have rhythm, the English don't have rhythm, the Americans and the French don't have rhythm. The Russians, the Scots and the Australians have rhythm, etc.' [In English] Evchen rushed in to her mother, nearby, in angry mood: [In German] 'It's dreadful how Papa is speaking about the Germans. The Germans don't *need* rhythm. The Germans need only to be loyal, true and gallant.') [In English] 'Perfidious Albion',[29] of course, is hindered by no such bootless handicap as loyalty.

The god of the English is boredom. This god whispers in the ear of the English: you are bored living in England, you are bored listening to Beethoven, you are bored with your father & mother, you are bored with your child, you are bored reading Shakespeare. So the English see their birthland, their Beethoven, their birth-givers [parents] & their children with the terrible sharp eyes of their God boredom, with the outcome that many of them great-trekk ((emigrate)) to Australia, Stravinsky [*sic*] & other new—& often less good—fields, thereby, however, widening the fan of the world's knowledge & been-thru-someness [experience]. And when they leave their breed groups ((families)), their birth-lands, their 'great masters', they leave them unloyally, with an open mind. But when Germans great-trekk to America or elsewhere, they take the [ ][30] of their old beliefs & loyalties with them. Almost every Jew, almost every German, is, & stays, a loyal bulwark of Jewishness or Germanness. He is blind & deaf to the new things he sees & hears. For him new thots, new beauties, new outfindments, new geniuses bloom in vain. He still believes in the rightness of the things & the great names he hears of first. He still believes in Homer, & Caesar & Napoleon & Goethe & Beethoven. He does not see that the world changes—not rootedly changes, but shows an othersome side, as the face of the day & the night are othersome sides of the same sun-world. In his heart, the German & the Jew stays [in German] 'loyal & true & gallant' [in English] to the end—however much he may joint-bargainsomely ((compromisingly)) have to hide the true color of his heart.

29. The idea of 'perfidious' England goes back to Jacques Bénigne Bossuet (1627–1704), although it was given additional currency by Napoleon Bonaparte at the end of the eighteenth century.
30. Two words illegible, and space for their 'translation' here left blank. Grainger appears to mean: the Germans took the stumbling block of their loyalties with them.

But the Britisher who great-trekks away from home & kin & the gods he was trained to worship, is a born & unblushing turncoat, upriser, weathercock. Think of Paul Jones,[31] Thomas Paine (the writer of *The Age of Reason*[32]—the man E. L. Masters has written a masterly poem on), Houston Stewart Chamberlain, Eugen D'Albert,[33] & a host of others. After the world war had got well under way, but before America had joined the banded-lands ((the allies))—in 1916, to be fact-neat ((exact))—I met a typetrue Englishman in California. He had become an American land-vow-taker ((naturalized American citizen)) & had written a play on the following askment [question]: 'What should an Englishman do who has taken land-vows to America ((become an American citizen)), if America should go to war with his birthland, England?' The writer's answer to this mind-nut-to-crack ((problem)) seemed to me almost rackpainfully ((agonizingly)) inbornly English: 'Such an Englishman, having taken American land-vows, should rush to war against his birth-land quicker than any American, to show the keenly-meantness of his land-vow-takement.' Here is the English open mind, the self-sown slave of the here & now. My mother always said to me that what frightened her in English-speaking folk was the speed & the zest with which they could rush to shout: 'The King is dead; long live the King'. It is a breath-taking gift; but is it not the frith-law [law of nature] that the frith-life lays upon us; & if we are deaf to this harsh behest do we not cut ourselves off from life & usefullness?

The German is loyal to Germany because he is unloyal to the world; the German is loyal to Beethoven because he is unloyal to tone-art. The German (& Jewish) eyes are 'near together' (as Kipling wrote in his [ ][34]) & do not see large issues. The German, the Frenchman, the Jew, the Italian (in short, the European mainlander) is willing to 'learn tone-art', is willing to go thru a stated mill, is willing to belong to a stated school of tone-art, because he takes a small view of tone-art, because he cannot even foggily guess at the hugeness & wild beauty of what music someday will grow to be. To him it is little more than a sort of 'Gebrauchsmusik'[35]—a lively noise that backgrounds ((accompanies)) marching, dancing & other dosomenesses ((activities)). But the typetrue English-speaking or Nordic view of tone-art, or any art, is gloryfully summed

31. John Paul Jones (1747–92), Scottish-born hero of the American War of Independence, on the American side.
32. (1737–1809), English-born supporter of both the American and French Revolutions, eventually indicted for treason in Britain. His *The Age of Reason* appeared in 1794, when he was living in France.
33. (1864–1932), Scottish-born German pianist.
34. Left blank by Grainger.
35. 'Utility music' (in German), term used in the 1920s and 1930s to refer to music 'with which we are directly involved' (Besseler), in contrast to 'autonomous' music.

up in Ruskin's[36] truth-soaked words, 'In art there is everything to learn, but nothing to teach'. That is why Nordic tone-art (Northmannish, British & American folksongs; American-Negro harmonies; the loving tone-weavings in D. A. Hughes's 'Worcester Mediaeval Harmony', or in John Jenkins's, Wm. Lawes's or Henry Purcell's angel-voiced string 'Fancies'; the wild beauty of much jazz; the angel-dreams of Grieg, Delius, Cyril Scott, Sandby & Vaughan Williams) is so close to the angels—'Angels, not Angles': because its ear is laid, not to the skill-tricks & well-seen-nesses of a stated school, of a stated system, but to the inner voice of mankind sounding lone-handishly ((individualistically)) thru each gifted man. The world war was the struggle between behest-power ((authority)) on the one hand, & lone-handishness ((individualism)) on the other. If the Germans had won there would have been a right, behest-hallowed ((authorised)) way of doing everything—a right way of making tone-art, a right way of saying 'good morning', a right way of sitting on a sofa, a right way of joy-quaffing life ((enjoying oneself)). As for the English, if there is a behest-hallowed way of doing things, they soon forget all about it.

Source: Untitled section, in 'The Aldridge-Grainger-Ström Saga', W37-55 to 37-57, dated 16 October 1933 (Grainger Museum, Melbourne).

➤ 99 [Parry's 'Judith'] (1935)

I have been looking at the words of Parry's 'Judith'.[37] Parry was indeed an old fool to have been taken by such a rotten text, dreary & wretched plot.[38] Such a choice shows how those 'old guard' boys were *really nasty* right thru. What is all this fawning on Jewish stories—a seeing of glamour in thots of this low race? It's all part & parcel of the nonsense that came into England with that Jewish Prince-husband ((consort)),[39] or at least it fitted in well with it. In fawning on the Jews & the Arabs (Byron, Moore,[40] a.s.o.) these half-artmen were (wittingly or not) making a stand against everything that was freedom-bringingly, self-enoughly, Northernly British. (Just like Ethel Smyth, said to have been in letter-touch with her German tone-forth printers ((publishers)) during the war, by way of Switzerland.) It is not merely that Parry & his ilk

36. (1819–1900), English writer and art critic.
37. Parry's oratorio (1888), for soprano, alto, tenor, bass, chorus, and orchestra.
38. The words are from the Apocrypha and by Parry himself.
39. Albert, Prince Consort (1819–61) to Queen Victoria.
40. Thomas Moore (1779–1852), Irish-born poet and friend of Byron.

were dull, little-gifted & stuckup. They were also wicked, traitor-some & un-wholesome in the sway they wielded. None of which hinders me from worth-prizing Parry's 'Blest Pair of Sirens'.[41] The text of 'Judith' has all that bootless & silly cruelness & harshness I hate in the Eng.-speaky world.

Source: Untitled section, in 'Nordic English. Thots on Tone-Art', dated 18 July 1935 (Grainger Museum, Melbourne).

100   [The Gifted and Half-Gifted] (1935)

I read in the latest forthprintment of Grove (Wordbook of Toneart)[42] that Albéniz, being a Catalan, could not enter in to many of the steadly ((local)) tone-styles of Spain, as de Falla can. Is not de Falla also a Catalan?[43] In any case Albéniz gives us Spain & de Falla gives us Spain & water. It is the old story, as with Grieg & Sinding.[44] When the all-gifted & the ½-gifted are lined up against each other, the half-artsome judges always better like the ½-gifted men. What these muffs like in Sinding & de Falla is that their toneworks follow the well-worn European tone-ruts & are not so one-bodysome ((personal)), selfladen, selfhoodfilled ((original)) & land-keen ((national)) as the output of the great ones—the Griegs & Albénizs.

We must not let ourselves be hoodwinked. When the ½-gifted judges belittle the oversouls ((geniuses)) they seem to guilt-state ((censure)) the lacks of these oversouls; but if we look into the cases, we will mostly find that it is the richness & sowth ((profusion)) of the all-great that they dislike—they feel uncomfy in the nearness of such flowing overmuchness & love for the simplehoods ((simplicities)) of the lesser artbegetters. It never fails: lukewarm about the truly great (Grieg, Tchaikovsky, Albéniz), but well pleased as soon as the apers ((imitators)) have whittled the oversoulhood ((genius)) down to middling sized, low-styled ((crowd-styled)) speech. The truth about the mock-highbrows is not only that they are so dull, empty & beadlelike—the worst is that they are unashamedly low-brow, eathouse-mooded. Only the toneworks that go with their meals please them.

Hobart, July 19, 1935

41. Parry's ode (1887), for chorus and orchestra.
42. The third edition of Grove's *A Dictionary of Music and Musicians*, ed. H. C. Colles (1927).
43. De Falla's mother was Catalan.
44. Christian Sinding (1856–1941), Norwegian composer, educated—as was Grieg—in Leipzig, but remaining more strongly in the German tonal sphere than did his compatriot.

Source: Untitled section, in 'Nordic English. Thots on Tone-Art' (Grainger Museum, Melbourne).

101   Balfour Gardiner's Judgement on Vaughan Williams [Holst and Bax] (1949/52)

It goes without saying that Balfour Gardiner was sharply worth-weigh-some ((critical)) about music. Also, he was very fickle in his tastes & likings. From about 1898 to about 1911 he almost worshipped Cyril Scott's music & writings. Around [ ][45] Balfour came to me & said: 'I've come to ask you to play your new compositions to Cyril, as you used to' (I had stopped doing this, for Cyril straight-way copied my newest tricks, & as he was publishing then & I was not, it seemed to me hardly fair to Australia). 'In the old days, when you played everything to Cyril as you wrote it, he was very inspired, & wrote wonderful works. And now he seems to have dried up.' (I had been away in Australia & New Zealand for nearly a year, 1908–1909.) That shows how keen he was about Cyril's muse at that time, & how willing to have Australia sacrificed for England. Yet by 1913, when he gave his first 'Balfour Gardiner Concert',[46] he had cooled on Cyril & his music to the length of not having anything of Cyril's on his first year's program.[47] That Cyril came into Balfour's twaid ((second)) year's program was due only to my saying that I would have nothing of mine done unless Cyril's music was done too. How keen he was on Bax & his music, at the time of the 'Balfour Gardiner Concerts', is shown by the following. Just after the first series was over Balfour said to me with some heat: 'I'm very dissatisfied with the way things have gone. Your & my pieces had far too much success & important works by Arnold (Bax)[48] & Gustav (von Holst)[49] & others never had a chance beside them. Next year I'm going to put your works & my works at the beginning & end of programs, where they

45. Illegible, probably 1910. See essay 25.
46. Correctly, 13 March 1912.
47. Grainger's memory here is faulty. Two works by Scott were performed in the first series, both in its fourth concert on 1 May 1912: *English Dance* No. 1 (ca. 1903) and *Helen of Kirkconnel* (rescored 1911), both conducted by Balfour Gardiner. There were no works by Scott in the 1913 second series of concerts.
48. The 1912 series' first concert had opened with *Enchanted Summer* (1910) by Arnold Bax, conducted by Balfour Gardiner. The 1913 series included two works by Bax—*Christmas Eve on the Mountains* (1911) and *In the Faery Hills* (1909)—both conducted by Gardiner.
49. The last concert of the 1912 series (1 May 1912) had featured Gustav Holst's *Beni-Mora* (1909–10), conducted by the composer (1874–1934). The 1913 series included three works by Holst—*Two Eastern Pictures* (1911), *The Mystic Trumpeter* (1904, rev. 1912), and *The Cloud Messenger* (1909–10)—all conducted by the composer.

can't make such a success'. I said, 'My dear Balfour, you can do what you like with your own works. But as I am the only Australian composer on your programs I am certainly not going to have my music discriminated against'.[50] 'OOHH' (with his arms shooting up in despair), 'how tiresome'.

Yet when I spoke to Balfour of Bax's music around 1948, he said, 'I dislike Arnold's music extremely' (or some such words), & he added, 'And he's terribly ambitious—all that business of being Master of the King's Music[51]— and he's always showing one photos of the Royal children, taken on lawn'. I understand that Balfour did a great deal, financially & otherwise, to launch Holst's 'The Planets'.[52] Yet the very last time I was with Balfour (1949)[53] & was telling him I had just heard 'The Planets' for the first time complete (or nearly complete) & how much I was struck by it, except that I thought that see-sawing back & forth on two chords was a bad habit, Balfour said, 'That's a most terrible habit of Gustav's'. I said I didn't know he had that habit & Balfour said, 'Oh, it ruins all his music'. The same thing seemed to happen over & over again: Balfour would seem to lose his art-heart to a given tone-wright [composer] for a few years, only to turn against that man & his work in the end. Maybe it was some self-awareness of this, his aesthetic fickleness, that made him unwilling to state his judgements upon his fellow-tone-wrights. He tried to wriggle out of doing so, if he could (especially with me, for he could see that I was mischievously trying to inveigle derogative [*sic*] statements out of him). But I caught him in Norway, 1939. Before that (1936?), lying on the beach at Pevensey Bay, I had tried to make him say what he thought of the music of Bax, Vaughan Williams, William Walton & others. But he just grew peevish, saying: 'This is getting too cerebral, Percy'. But in Norway, on that trip from Notodden to Bergen he took with the Sparre Olsens,[54] Ella & me, [in] 1939,[55] I caught Balfour off-guard. That was the morning we saw him striding along with great strides in the rain, his bald head shining wet, along the road from high up down to the hotel at Røldal. Later, the same morning, we had a long, rough bus drive, from Røldal to Hardanger, I think. We were

---

50. Gardiner placed works by other composers at the starts of each of his four 1913 concerts, but ended the first, on 11 February 1913, with Grainger conducting his own *Green Bushes*, and ended the last, on 18 March 1913, with his own *Shepherd Fennel's Dance* (1910). There were five other works by Grainger in the 1913 concert series, but no others by Gardiner.
51. Bax was knighted in 1937 and became Master of the King's Music in 1942.
52. Op. 32 (1914–16). Gardiner had paid for a private orchestral rehearsal and performance of the work by the Queen's Hall Orchestra, conducted by Adrian Boult, on 29 September 1918. The public première occurred over two years later.
53. Gardiner died on 28 June 1950.
54. Sparre and Edith Olsen.
55. In the midsummer of 1939.

thrown up & down like pancakes in a pan. And in the middle of this mind-addling jolt-bout I slipped a quick ask-ment at Balfour: 'What do you think of Vaughan Williams's music?' And like a shot out of a gun—before he had time to hide behind caution—came Balfour's answer: 'Vaughan Williams is a *miserable* composer'. These words were my reward for the whole trip. For the Sparre Olsens, Ella & I had just done the Bergen-[ ]⁵⁶ trip in the other direction a few weeks earlier, & we were doing it all over again for Balfour's sake—because when he heard of our first trip he had said, 'That is the kind of trip I would like to take'. And we had said, 'We will do it again, with you, if you like'.

Oct 19, 1949, & Sept 8, 1952

Source: 'Balfour Gardiner's Judgement on Vaughan Williams ("A Miserable Composer"), His Fickle-ness about Music, His Remark "Too Cerebral", His Censure on Holst's "The Planets", His Censure on Arnold Bax, "Your Works & Mine had Far Too Much Success" ', in 'Grainger's Anecdotes', 423-6 (Grainger Museum, Melbourne).

102   Grieg on His Romanticism, My Scientificness, re Folksong (1952)

When Grieg told me that the text that went with the old melody on which he built his Ballade (op. 14)⁵⁷ was a drinking song, totally unsuitable in mood to the lovely mood in his Ballade, I asked him why he didn't print this fact in a for-word to the Ballade—because I personally always like to see the incon-gruity of life shown up. Grieg said: 'That is the difference between you & me in our approach to folksong. I am always a Romantiker & you are a scientist'. That is true. But it is alas true that I feel piously (worshippingly) towards the personalities of the country folk who have preserved folkart for us thru the ages & consider no detail of their art-life & artistic point-of-view unworthy of preservation. Much the same start between the original folksong & what Grieg made of it is seen in 'Jeg går i tusen tanker' (see 423-12⁵⁸). The folk text that went with the folktune was a sentimental—not old—love-grumble: 'Wrapt in thought I wander & think of one I can't make mine'. But Grieg saw the chorale-like possibilities of the melody, so wrote 'Andante religioso' over the beginning. This (both in the case of the Ballade & in the case of 'Jeg går')

---

56. Illegible.
57. Correctly, Op. 24, Ballade in the Form of Variations upon a Norwegian Melody (1875–76), for solo piano.
58. Op. 66 No. 18, 'I Wander Deep in Thought'. See essay 88.

bears out what I always say: that Grieg brought more to folksong than he took from it. It is his middleclass, cosmopolitan sophistication brought to bear on folksong that made such a rich combination. It is significant what he told me of his years in Hardanger, or wherever it was: 'I wanted to like the peasants & to feel at one with them. But when the drinking bowl was handed around & I saw the stain of chewed tobacco on its rim I just felt sickened.' (Did Grieg tell this to me, or is it in some book?)

Sept. 10, 1952

Source: 'Grieg on His Romanticism, My Scientificness, re Folksongs', in 'Grainger's Anecdotes', 423-13 (Grainger Museum, Melbourne).

➤ 103   Mother Liked Sibelius. P. G.'s Estimate of Him & Other Nordic Music (1953)

One year when mother was with me in Norway (1912 or 1913?) & she stayed in Kristiania [Oslo] while I toured round, mother met Sibelius & heard him rehearse [the] National Teatrets Orkester[59] in his own works. Mother said he was a shy, sweet man—very gentle & quiet with the orchestra. Mother was unfailingly fond of geniuses. I never met Sibelius, & had no wish to, not liking much of what I know of his music. Yet the hymn-like tune in 'Finlandia'[60] seems to me the loveliest thing in 20th century music—the thing I would most naturally play when I sit down at the piano or reed-organ. It seems to me the truest expression of that feeling of weakness we blue-eyed people have in facing the hostile world of rough, harsh dark-eyed people. I also liked a dreamy little bit of Sibelius that Herman Sandby adapted for cello & piano, with double stops that Sandby could play so well.

But Sibelius as a whole rubs me up the wrong way—I am not fond of the Scandinavian-Finnish clumsiness & tweedishness in music. There must be something non-Nordic in me that makes me non-responsive to Sibelius or Carl Nielsen[61] & works of Vaughan Williams, & makes me prefer the Siciliana & Intermezzo in 'Cavalleria'. I think I must be deaf to non-sensual appeals. (I am not deaf to Cyril Scott's, Sandby's, Grieg's & Svendsen's[62] Nordicness, nor to the 'Lough Aruma' of Stanford, the 'Blessed Pair of Sirens' of

59. National Theatre Orchestra.
60. Op. 26 (1900), for piano and arranged for orchestra.
61. (1865–1931), Danish composer.
62. Johan Svendsen (1840–1911), Norwegian composer, violinist, and conductor.

Parry & much of Elgar. But I cannot bear the Scherzo of V. Williams's [ ]⁶³ Symphony.)

Århus Kommunehospital, Aug. 11, 1953

Source: 'Mother Liked Sibelius. P. G.'s Estimate of Him & Other Nordic Music', in 'Grainger's Anecdotes', 423-37 (Grainger Museum, Melbourne).

➤ 104   The Cheek of Band-Bosses
                ((Conductors)) (1945)

A year or so ago, when I dined with Sir Thomas & Lady Beecham in New York, Stravinsky & his wife were there, & a few others. The Stravinskys (he charmingly polite & nice-seeming) left first, whereupon Beecham felt called upon to say to his other guests: 'Stravinsky is the man who wrote a promising work—Oiseau de feu; a masterpiece—Petruschka; an attempt at a super-masterpiece—Sacre du Printemps; and after that, *nothing*!' I might say that the new version (Suite? For string-&-wind-band) of 'Le Rossignol' I heard Goossens make a sound-disc of in Cincinnati, half a year ago,⁶⁴ is a very pleasing form of nothingness. More mind-stirring was to hear that Stravinsky (tho born a Jew, as Beecham said) had become 'very devout' (Christ-believing).

[on train] New Mexico, July 19, 1945.

Source: 'The Cheek of Band-Bosses ((Conductors)): O. Fried, Mengelberg, Beecham (on Stravinsky)', in 'Ere-I-Forget', 384-35 (Grainger Museum, Melbourne).

➤ 105   Rudolf Ganz Praised Reger & Mahler
                to Busoni (1953)

Rudolf Ganz⁶⁵ is about as annoying a man as you could find, even amongst Jewish musicians—not the kind of man you would suspect to be able to tell a joke against himself. Yet he did actually tell me the following: one year he vis-

---

63. Left blank by Grainger. Cf. this lack of appreciation with Grainger's sycophantic letter to Vaughan Williams of 31 October 1948 in Gillies and Pear, eds., *The All-Round Man*, 221–24.
64. Recorded as *The Song of the Nightingale* by Eugene Goossens for HMV on 25 January 1945 with the Cincinnati Symphony Orchestra (DB6380/2).
65. (1877–1972), Swiss pianist and conductor. In the late 1890s, he studied with Busoni, who dedicated his First Sonatina (1910) to him.

ited Busoni in Europe & talked to Busoni about Max Reger's music. The next time Ganz visited Busoni he talked to Busoni about Mahler's music. Finally Busoni said: 'Now you've been to visit me twice, & each time you have talked to me about an untalented composer. Can't you find a talented composer to talk about?'

Århus, Aug. 11, 1953

Source: 'Rudolf Ganz Praised Reger & Mahler to Busoni', in 'Grainger's Anecdotes', 423-41 (Grainger Museum, Melbourne).

➤ 106   Busoni & P. G. (1953)

I knew nothing about Busoni when Mrs Matesdorf (a friend of Mrs Lowrey's) arranged for me to meet him at her house. I was to play for him. There is nothing I hate quite so much as playing to famous musicians (Gabriel Fauré,[66] Busoni, etc.). The only hope in such cases (for an ill-prepared & inaccurate player like myself) is to play something the celebrity has never heard. That is what I did in this case: I played Debussy's C sharp minor Toccata[67] (Busoni had heard no Debussy; this must have been the summer of 1904[68]) & my own settings of 'Irish Tune from Co. Derry' & my harmonisations of 'The Marquis of Huntley' Strathspey & Tulluchgoram Reel (both used, later, in 'Scotch Strathspey & Reel'). Strangely enough, Busoni seemed greatly taken with me, & was sweetness itself. (Such a man would like to behave like [an] angel. He could not help it that his antagonisms, his jealousies, his spite & scorn were so easily aroused.) He said he would teach me for nothing, if I would come to Berlin. I told him I was leaving for Australia in 3 weeks' time (1st Ada Crossley tour). 'Then come for 2 weeks', said Busoni. I stayed in Berlin with Mrs Kwast-Hiller (the daughter of Ferdinand Hiller, the divorced wife of my piano teacher in Frankfurt—James Kwast—the mother of my first sweetheart, who married Hans Pfitzner) at the boarding house she was running at [ ].[69] (For the haps linked up with Frau Kwast-Hiller, Evchen, Mrs. Lowrey on this Berlin visit, see 423-43.)[70] The first thing was I went to afternoon tea at the Busonis' & saw the strange assortment of 'the lame, the halt & the blind' he had thru. I suppose

66. Grainger played for Fauré at the home of John Singer Sargent in March 1908.
67. From Pour le piano (1894–1901).
68. Correctly, 1903.
69. Left blank by Grainger.
70. 'Frau Kwast-Hiller, Evchen, Mrs Lowrey in Berlin', essay 33.

Busoni's generosity (of which he had an overflow) made him collect cripples & unlucky ones. No doubt there was the other side too—the wish to be the undisputed master, the wish to have willing slaves. One could hardly hope that he would enjoy me long—me, a stiff-neck, able to draw my own ring of hysterical ones around me, however little I want it or like it.

That first afternoon at his place he asked me to play, & I suppose I did, the Debussy Toccata again. I cannot remember. I know I started the 'Irish Tune' & that he stopped me with, 'Don't let us have anything sentimental. Play those dance-tunes you played to me in London'. And I did the Strathspey & the Reel. Busoni had a new piano. After I had played I heard a girl say to Busoni: 'What a lovely tone. Is that the player or the piano?' He answered 'It's the piano'. So it was easy to see which way things were drifting.

Busoni gave me Beethoven's 32 C minor Variations[71] to work at. But it was just about a week before mother's birthday (July 3) & I was composing 'Mowgli's Song Against People'[72] as a surprise birthday gift to her. (To get the outside cover the right desert-brown hue we had to fill the bottom of a bath with coffee or tea & soak the outside cover-paper in it.) So as to make the gift an utter surprise to mother I had avoided being heard working at it, at home in London.[73] So I was thankful to be able to work at it full tilt in Berlin. So I put all my time into 'Mowgli's Song' & neglected the Beethoven Variations. At the next lesson with Busoni he said, 'Tell me, are you really *working* at these variations?' And I confessed I wasn't, because of the composition for my mother's birthday. He asked, 'When *is* your mother's birthday?' I told him, 'July the 3rd'. He said, 'Then come to me July 5th'. He was really very nice about it. But he sensed I didn't like the Beethoven Variations & asked me, 'Does such a work not interest you?' I admitted it didn't, altho I could see it was a work of genius. 'Then what *does* interest you pianistically?' Busoni's arrangements of Bach, I told him. And they did. And when I brought the Choral-Vorspiele to the lesson he said, 'Such things really suit you'. (I doubt whether any of his pupils played the Bach-Busoni arrangements as often as I, in concerts.[74] And none of his pupils or other admirers can have admired Busoni as a pianist more than I did, for I admired him without reservations of any kind & revelled in everything he did, pianistically. He was not a *normal* player, as Paderewski was, & even de Pachmann[75] was—un-

71. (1806).
72. Kipling Setting No. 15.
73. Grainger's first sketches for the setting dated from 25 April.
74. Grainger appears mainly to have played Tausig arrangements of Bach up to this point in his career.
75. Vladimir de Pachmann (1848–1933), Ukrainian pianist.

folding the composer's music straightly & faithfully. Busoni was a twisted genius, making the music sound unlike itself, but grander than itself, more superhuman. I cannot recall ever hearing or seeing Busoni play a wrong note. He did not seem to feel his way about the keyboard by touching adjacent notes, as most of us do. He smacked the keys right in the middle. As a composer he never interested me for one moment. I never heard a single musical phrase of his that had the least charm, or pith or meaning. Perhaps he sensed my unfriendliness to his own compositions & perhaps it was that that gradually changed his initial kindliness toward me into scorn & hostility.) On the whole, Busoni was nice to me up to the end of the Berlin period. He gave me a lovely photo of himself & wrote on it, 'To Percy, as dear as he surely will be great'. He also gave me a full score of a choral setting by Liszt of one of the psalms.[76] (He worshipped Liszt.) In Berlin his Swedish-Finnish wife[77] seemed to take a great fancy to me & her I considered a perfect example of the lovely-natured-ness to which Scandinavian woman-hood can rise. Her wide smiling face was like the sun shining & she certainly affected Busoni that way. When she was out of the house he would get sour & spiteful, but when the door opened & she appeared he rose with an exclamation of violent relief & greeted her with charming Italian manners. Busoni was a man worth being married to, for the presence of his wife transformed him utterly. She gave me my first J. P. Jacobsen books.[78] I had been busy learning Danish, but had read nothing much in Danish except the H. C. Andersen volumes Herman Sandby had given me, & the dictionary—also a gift from Sandby. Busoni was very sarcastic about my interest in the languages of small nations—Danish, Dutch, etc. 'What is all this interest in the art of small nations? Cannot you find enough to interest you in the literature of the great nations?' I answered (my ire being somewhat aroused), 'No, I can't. The large nations all seem to me to be warlike-minded. And I want to find out what are the influences that make some of the small nations happy in their peaceableness.' I think it was while I was in Berlin that Busoni asked me what books in English I could recommend. I mentioned 'Leaves of Grass' & Kipling's poems. A year or so later Busoni told me I was right about Walt Whitman, but not about Kipling.

When I got back from Australia things were never nice again between Busoni & me. I had to earn my living. Busoni would give a concert in Lon-

---

76. Liszt's setting of the eighteenth Psalm, 'Coeli enarrant gloriam Dei' (second version, 1870). This edition remains in Grainger's personal library (Grainger Museum, Melbourne).
77. Gerda Sjöstrand.
78. The first of these books was a volume of Jacobsen's poems.

don, but I would not be there because I was playing in the provinces. When I *was* able to go to one of his concerts he threw up his arms in mock surprise & said in a biting voice: 'London's society pianist has deigned to pay us a visit'. Busoni was scornful & teasing toward me, but not indifferent. He always wanted to hear what I had been composing & his comments on my compositions were thoughtful & type-aware. I remember he particularly liked the refrain to 'The Merchantmen'.[79] 'That is the most English thing you have written', he said. Around 1907, or soon after, I showed him 'Hill-Song II'. We played it thru in the 2-piano dish-up I had made & his reading was marvellous. [In German] 'That's a lovely piece. One would have to say: it's a lovely piece!' [in English] he said, in a rather sad, unwilling voice. But he criticised (& rightly) the way I had written the irregular rhythms—the way the rhythms were grouped inside the bar. 'If you have irregular rhythms they should be presented to the eye as straightforwardly as possible.' (This was a year or 2 before the irregular rhythms of the Cyril Scott Piano Sonata[80] (derived from me) were played in Germany & Austria by Alfred Höhn.[81] It is not unthinkable that Busoni was the culture-carrier, to Germany & Austria, of the irregular rhythms he heard in my 'Hill-Song II'. He might have talked about the irregular rhythms & his talk got round to Stravinsky. The point is: an Australian *did them first*, whatever happened afterwards & whoever was the culture-carrier.)

Once he took me to lunch in London & I ordered something sweet—a pancake maybe. I said, 'They say that teetotallers are fond of sweets because they get their alcohol out of the sugar'. Busoni said, 'You're fond of pseudo-scientific statements, aren't you?' Which was a fact.

To go back to the Berlin period (1904 [1903]) for a moment. Busoni was at his tiresomest when he took a few of us out to restaurants in the evening. He liked to go where there was some Italian man singing to his own guitar accompaniment, & then Busoni would very much play the Italian, as well as the great man condescending to the folk-level. I suppose it was only natural that Busoni (the Italian part of whose nature was still so well preserved) should want to relax in some Italianish way. But to my ears the singing & the commonplace chords on the guitar were boring in the extreme.

When I saw them in Berlin the 2 Busoni boys were as fair-to-see as children could be—fine-featured, bright-eyed, soft-limbed. And no wonder, with both parents so good-looking.

79. (1902–3), one of Grainger's unnumbered Kipling settings.
80. Op. 66 (1908–9).
81. To whom Scott had dedicated this Sonata.

The first time I knew that Busoni had become viciously hostile to me was when I played with Volkmar Andreae[82] (a composer as well as a conductor, & a delightful man) in Zürich, about 1911–1912.[83] I had rehearsed the Grieg Concerto with Andreae & his orchestra & we were lunching together. I thought Andreae looked at me queerly. At last he said, 'May I ask you something very personal?' What can Busoni have meant when he said to me: [in German] 'You'll make a laughing stock of yourself if you engage Grainger. He's only a charlatan. But you are certainly no charlatan.' [In English] I said, 'I suppose he meant just what he said'. And in the eyes of a pianistic giant like B. I must have seemed no better than a charlatan—an ill-prepared man earning money under false pretences. But I would be equally justified in considering B. a charlatan as a composer. There was no need for hard feelings on Busoni's part towards me—for our orbits never crossed each other. Each of us had what the other lacked. Busoni got brilliant results with next to no effort; I was slow & peg-away. Busoni impressed people immensely, but pleased few; I was able to please almost everybody (including B.), but impressed nobody. B. was a big-town artist; I a small-town artist.

There is the story of B. coming to Holland to fulfil 3 engagements, in Amsterdam, the Hague & Enschede.[84] Busoni was staying with some hifaluting [sic] family in Amsterdam. They asked him where he was playing & he told them. 'Why Enschede?' his hosts asked. 'Why, is there anything wrong with Enschede?' 'No, it's just a small manufacturing town.' So B. rings up his manager: 'I just wanted to say that I'm not going to play in Enschede'. 'Why not?' etc., etc. 'You are getting the same fee in Enschede as in Amsterdam & the Hague.' 'All the same, I won't play there', and he didn't. And that same year I was laying about 40 concerts (largely Enschede-like townlets) in Holland, I suppose. My patience & humble stamina must have been just as annoying to Busoni as his flashy pretentiousness was to me.

Then the war came & was very hard on Busoni, for his sympathies were with Germany, yet he couldn't stay in Germany because his nationality was Italian. So he came to America & hated everything.[85] He played the Liszt [ ][86] Concerto (which no one approached him in) with the N. York Philharmonic

---

82. (1879–1962), Cologne-educated Swiss musician, conductor of the Tonhalle Orchestra from 1906 to 1949.
83. 18–19 March 1912.
84. 140 kilometres east of Amsterdam, near the German border.
85. In fact, Busoni spent only the first nine months of 1915 in America before moving to Switzerland, where he saw out the war.
86. Concerto number left blank by Grainger.

Orchestra.[87] He played a Chickering[88] & it sounded simply stunning. But when I went round & told B. how marvellous the piano sounded he was furious. I'm not sure that he didn't think I was making fun of him. (These low-class, materialistic musicians who play pianos they despise just to make money & haven't the honesty to be in favor of the firm whose money they take! I understand business people better than artists.)

The Busonis lived near Riverside Drive, I think (or near Schwab's mansion,[89] near Richard Aldrich's[90]) & B. had surrounded himself with some half-talented composers & musicians, as usual. I was asked there one evening & Busoni asked me to play, but I begged him to excuse me, saying, 'I have been busy composing for weeks & haven't played the piano at all & I would hate to play badly to you who have been so kind to me'. He asked what I was composing & I told him, 'Marching Song of Democracy'. 'Democracy', he repeated, aghast. I suppose democracy was the last thing he wanted to make the world safe for. 'When did you begin it?' Busoni asked. 'About 1900', I said. 'Is it a very long work?' 'No, it will play about 8 minutes, I expect.' Then Busoni dropped into a most sympathetic & earnest voice: 'Then I sincerely hope you finish it this summer'. I (like the idiot I am, never suspecting sarcasm) said, 'Why?' 'Well, if you began it in 1900, & it's 1917 [sic] now, & it only plays 8 minutes, *then I sincerely hope you finish it this summer.*' By this time I was somewhat nettled, & said, 'Fancy, it doesn't seem to me to matter in the very least when I began it, or how long it takes to finish it, as long as it is good when it's done'.

Sometime after Busoni's death Mrs B. wrote me about a portrait of Busoni, asking if I could do something to get the New York Metropolitan Museum of Art to buy it. I knew no-one connected with the museum & am helpless in such matters. I asked her if she needed monetary help, but she said she didn't. Thinking of the J. P. Jacobsen books she gave me, & the advantages (the wonderful Bach arrangements) I had from contact with Busoni, I felt I was behaving meanly in not forcing my help upon her.

Århus, Aug. [11 &] 12, 1953

Source: 'Busoni & P. G.', in 'Grainger's Anecdotes', 423-42 (Grainger Museum, Melbourne).

87. Probably on 31 January 1915, when Busoni played Liszt's Concerto No. 1 in E flat major. In his correspondence, Busoni mentions that Grainger was present (letter, 31 January 1915, Busoni to Egon Petri, in Antony Beaumont, ed., *Ferruccio Busoni: Selected Letters* (London: Faber & Faber, 1987), 193).
88. Piano made by a firm based in Boston since the 1820s.
89. French chateau-style mansion built in 1901–5 for the industrialist Charles M. Schwab (1862–1939).
90. (1863–1937), music critic for *The New York Times* (1902–24).

➤ 107   My First Hearing of Fritz Kreisler, with Mrs Lowrey (1945)

I never did have any ease in picking winners in the tone-world. My race-feuds made me unjust in some cases. And I guilt-guess ((suspect)) myself for being begrudging towards anyone who did anything well, unless he was a close friend of mine. About 1903 Mrs Lowrey took me to hear Kreisler[91] in St James's Hall, saying to me, 'I think he is the coming man'. But I could hear nothing in his playing but out-of-tuneness & rasping bowing—a judgement I have never since gone back on. There was only one thing I liked about him: the way he came in, holding his fiddle by its head, & it low down by his knees, as if he meant to smash it. There was something cruel & wrecklustful about this that pleased me. I have always loathed the fiddle (a canary-like twitterer, not a man-high voice) & outsingledly all Jew-talk about fiddles worth gold-hoards (when I was sure that any one-pound-priced fiddle would sound just as well, or better). So I was happy to see this coarse-looking man come in acting (as it looked) unlovingly towards its wretched little tone-box. But that was all I did like.

I liked better a joke about Kreisler & his wife,[92] told as if it had taken place in Bournemouth. 2 silly tone-fond Englishmen were sitting in the Bournemouth glass-house (Pavilion) in readiness to hear Kreisler, & one said to the other: 'I hear he's a great artist, but that his tone isn't very big'. Mrs Kreisler, seated just behind him, tapped him on the shoulder, & said: 'Don't you fret yr liver. My Fritzie's tone's all right'. Such things sound funnier before one has lived in America. As a matter of fact, since knowing Mrs Kreisler, I don't think she is jolly enough, or witty enough, to have said a thing like that. But tone-loving & feelingful I think she is. Around 1920 I sat in the same box with her, at the Metropolitan Opera House, New York, listening to 'Parsifal'. And she seemed to thrill (as I did, you bet yer) to all the rack-painful discords in that soul-searing tonery, than which I joy-quaff nothing more.

[on train] Texas, Nov. 1, 1945

Source: 'My First Hearing of Fritz Kreisler, with Mrs Lowrey', in 'Ere-I-Forget', 384-49 (Grainger Museum, Melbourne).

---

91. Fritz Kreisler (1875–1962), Austrian-born American violinist and composer.
92. Harriet Lies, whom Kreisler married in 1900.

➤ 108   Melbourne Miss Rowe & Ernő Rappé's
Stolen Music (1953)

Before I first left Australia (1895) I knew 2 Miss Rowes, sisters to the one that taught singing in London.[93] One,[94] who sang Handel arias, I used to accompany, not far from Cliveden Mansions. About 40 years later she wrote me, saying her musical judgement must be very poor, for she thought the music she was sending me wonderfully beautiful, yet the composer's name was an unknown one. When it arrived it had some flowery name (Hyacinths, or something) & the composer's name on the cover was Ernő Rappé.[95] Inside, half of the music was Elgar's 'Salut d'amour' & the other half was that favorite 'moment musicale' of Schubert's. I wrote her that there was nothing wrong with her taste, only with the 'composer's' honesty. Another Jew (Joseph Hofmann[96]) similarly stole Julius Röntgen's old Dutch dances & put his name to them. When Röntgen's son Engelbert[97] upbraided him for this steal Hofmann said he thought the harmonies as well as the tune were antique. And, seeing one of them in Schering,[98] I'm not sure they're not. In any case, what queer behaviour in a rich conductor & one of the world's most successful pianists.

Aug. 16, 1953.

Source: 'Melbourne Miss Rowe & Ernő Rappé's Stolen Music', in 'Grainger's Anecdotes', 423-69 (Grainger Museum, Melbourne).

➤ 109   Balfour Gardiner: 'Obscure Successes' (1953)

Balfour was never cleverer than when he wrote (a year or so before his death) that composers should be content with obscure successes, as the local hat shop is. The hat shop is pleased if it sells a hat & a composer should not always aim at world fame, but be thankful if his work is done in some small

---

93. Nellie Rowe.
94. Probably Rose Rowe.
95. (1891–1945), Hungarian-born American conductor, also known as Ernő Rapee.
96. (1876–1957), Polish-born American pianist.
97. (1886–1957), Dutch cellist.
98. Arnold Schering (1877–1941), German music scholar. Grainger is probably referring to Schering's *Geschichte der Musik in Beispielen* (1931).

place. The arc-light of world fame need not glare upon everything a composer does.

Århus Kommunehospital, Aug. 19 '53.

Source: 'Balfour Gardiner: "Obscure Successes" ', in 'Grainger's Anecdotes', 423-82 (Grainger Museum, Melbourne).

✎ 110   Tonery (Japanese Singer, Javanese Tone-Tool, Pablo Casals) (1945)

This same Mexican breed-group (see 384-47[99]) was very tone-fond (or should I say 'tone-rutted'—for they simply followed a groove, a sham of tone-fondness being an easy way to 'rise' in the pomp-world ((society))), which caused me a lot of grief, for I never had anything I could play to such dark-eyed ogres. Yet I must say they were very all-to-bosom-clasping in their tone-range, for it was there I saw, & tried, my first Javanese gong-ring.[100] Each gong was double, the lower part of the gong giving out a note about a sixth lower than the note given out by the middle boss. Each gong had, below it, its own sound box. Its tone was very like the American metal marimbas & vibra-harps (which tied-in with my Kipling-fed mindstir in far-eastern tonery & the sway Mrs Ringer's Chinese tunes held over me—a sway fore-shadowed in my 'Eastern Intermezzo'[101] of some 3 to 6 years earlier), which may be said to be the birth of my marimba-worship, later fanned by what Daniël de Lange[102] in Amsterdam told me of Javanese tonery, by the tone-tools in the Leiden 'Etno-grafisch Museum', & still later by the Deagan tone-tools in Chicago.[103]

One day at this Mexican breed-group's house, the wife of the Japanese consul or theed-go-between ((ambassador)) sang Japanese songs, tone-back-grounding herself on the koto. It was the whiningest, howlingest sort of Japanese singing which today I might worship—I can't guess. But then (in spite of my be-Kiplinged heart-stir, my yearning to study tone-art in the far-east) it

99. I.e., Grainger's preceding recollection in 'Ere-I-Forget', which referred to a Mexican or South American family that the Graingers had visited in Kensington, London, around 1904.

100. Grainger drew a ring of nine gongs here and also represented the double nature of each gong (as Grainger goes on to describe).

101. For small orchestra (1898 or 1899); according to Grainger, inspired by his boyhood visits to Melbourne's Chinatown.

102. (1841–1918), Dutch music educator.

103. Grainger first visited the Deagan showroom in Chicago in Mar. 1915.

simply tore me with spasms of inner laughter. I shook soundlessly & had a hard time keeping myself from laughing out loud. Such is the change brought about by the years. Or *was* she (from a Japanese, or *any* standpoint) just a shockingly bad singer, & would I, even today, still find her singing unwithstandably laugh-rousing? I felt so ashamed of myself, wanting to be so keen on far-off tone-arts, yet turning out to be but a wont-some White Man, laugh-ready, unmannerly! And it was there we first met & heard Pablo Casals.[104] Mother (who always had easily-upwelling 'natural' good taste in art—a great change & shock ((contrast)) to me, whose taste-findings always had to come 'the hard way', mostly after a struggle with some foe-deemth in my past) was at once enthralled with his playing ('what a caressing, singing tone'), altho neither she nor I had ever heard of Casals. I scorned his playing, judging it weak & chilly beside the Northern keenness & fieryness of Sandby's playing; for Herman Sandby was there too, & played, if I mistake not. I am always riled if my friends are vied with in any way. I am a born henchman, a hopeless side-taker.

Maybe the father (of these girls) was Mexican theed-go-between ((ambassador)) in London, & that's why Casals (& Sandby) went there, why the wife of the Japanese theed-go-between sang there, & why they had the Javanese gamelan gong-ring (a left-overness of some theed-job in the Dutch East Indies?).

Train, Texas, Nov. 1, 1945

Source: 'Tonery (Japanese Singer, Javanese Tone-Tool, Pablo Casals) at This Mexican Breed-Group's House (Kensington)', in 'Ere-I-Forget', 384-48 (Grainger Museum, Melbourne).

➤ 111   Intelligence versus Education (1943)

We will never forget that best one: 'A high brow is a man who is educated beyond his intelligence' & now comes this one:

> You Said It! Intelligence appears to be the thing that enables a man to get along without education. Education appears to be the thing that enables a man to get along without the use of his intelligence.—*Albert Edward Wiggam*[105]

104. (1876–1973), Catalan musician, best known as a cellist. Grainger came to know Casals better in Holland in 1911.
105. Quoted in unattributed newspaper cutting from 1943, stuck into Grainger's handwritten article. Wiggam (1871–1957) was an American biologist.

Sometimes I feel very uneducated, & very unwilling to be educated. But when I read this sort of thing I feel a surge of wishing to range myself on the side of the unintelligent educated. Anything rather than Anglosaxon 'brightness'. What is my life & my art based on? On Bach, on Lempriere's 'Classical Dictionary', on Grove's 'Dictionary of Music', or Freeman's 'History of the Norman Conquest',[106] & on all sorts of 'Collections' (Sir Walter Scott's, E.T. Kristensen's, Linde[r]man's,[107] Landstad's,[108] Cecil Sharp's, etc.). No, no. Never class me among the talents, or among the Bobby Burnses, or among any folk whose heart is in the right place. I stand firmly for 'sophistry' & for the Japanese egg-with-in-egg rocked in the wife in the rocking-chair. I am for devices, not for instincts; for formulas, not for feelings. Appeals to my intelligence always make me furious. A man has a right to be as stupid as he likes. And I loathe all good-sort-cult (*gutekerl*-ism).

Sept. 29, 1943

Source: 'Intelligence versus Education', in 'Deemths ((Opinions)) Book 2', section 54 (Grainger Museum, Melbourne).

106. Edward A. Freeman's six-volume study was published between 1867 and 1879.
107. Grainger probably refers to Frank Bird Linderman's *Blackfeet Indians* (1935), a copy of which is found in Grainger's personal library, now held in the Grainger Museum.
108. Magnus Brostrup Landstad (1802–80) produced folk-music studies: *Norske folkeviser* (1853) and *Folkeviser fra Telemarken* (1925 ed.), both of which Grainger owned.

List of Sources

The following list presents, in alphabetic order, the source documents from which the essays of this volume have been drawn. For each source, the individual essays are listed in order of presentation within that particular source. As throughout the volume, essays with editorially introduced titles, rather than Grainger's own titles, are shown in square brackets. Essay numbers of the current volume are bolded. All sources are found in the Grainger Museum, Melbourne.

A comprehensive 'List of Grainger's Writings', by David Pear, is found as the Appendix to Malcolm Gillies and Bruce Clunies Ross, eds., *Grainger On Music* (Oxford: Oxford University Press, 1999), 377–85.

'The Aldridge-Grainger-Ström Saga': **1** [The Aldridge Saga Begins], W37-3 to 37-5, dated 28–29 Sept. 1933; **2** [Aldridge Family Strengths], W37-9, dated 30 Sept. 1933; **3** [Aldridge Family Weaknesses], W37-29, dated 13 Oct. 1933; **21** [Dr Henry O'Hara], W37-39 to 37-41, dated 8 Oct. 1933 (with additional paragraph of 7 Nov. 1933, W37-40); **45** [George Percy], W37-42 to 37-45, dated 11 and 12 Oct. 1933 (with later additions of 22 Oct. and 2 Dec. 1933); **98** ['The King Is Dead, Long Live the King': World, Racial and Tone-Art Loyalties], W37-55 to 37-57, dated 16 Oct. 1933; **4** [Frank and Clara Aldridge], W37-77, dated 30 Oct. 1933; **50** [The Centrality of Race], W37-91, dated 'Nov. 4?, 1933'; **51** [Pure-Nordic Beauty], W37-119 to 37-121, dated 15 Nov. 1933; **52** [A Flawlessly Nordic Way of Living], W37-141 to 37-143, dated 21 Nov. 1933; **53** [The Truly Nordic Life], W37-173 to 37-177, dated 3 Dec. 1933.

76 'Anent "Elastic Scoring"', dated 10 Sept. 1929.

20 'Bird's-Eye View of the Together-Life of Rose Grainger and Percy Grainger', 399-1 to 399-40 (complete), dated 5–9 Jan. 1947.

'Deemths ((Opinions)) Book 1': **56** Growing Nasty-Spoken as I Near My Sixties, section 4, dated 20 Dec. 1940; **82** Call-to-Mindments about Delius Piano Concerto, section 8, dated 18 Feb. 1941; **96** Dr Russell's Statement: 'It's Too Early.

You Must Wait Till You're Dead', section 11, undated (probably 23 Feb. 1941);
83 The Lower the Fee, the Better I Play, section 21, dated 28 Oct. 1941.

'Deemths ((Opinions)) Book 2': **84** Memories of Tchaikovsky Concertos, section 51,
dated 12 June 1943; **111** Intelligence versus Education, section 54, dated 29
Sept. 1943.

'Ere-I-Forget': **27** Walter Creighton & Cyril Scott, 384-1, undated (probably 24 Oct.
1944); **28** Walter Creighton on Roger Quilter's Hide-Fain-th ((Secretiveness)),
384-2, undated (probably 24 Oct. 1944); **26** My First Meeting with Cyril Scott,
384-3, dated 24 Oct. 1944; **29** Roger Quilter Failed Me at Harrogate, 384-4,
dated 6 Nov. 1944; **37** Sargent's and His Set's Set-of-Mind toward My Betrothal
to Margot, 384-14, dated 19 Nov. 1944; **32** Mrs L[owrey] and My Early London
Days, 384-19, dated 24 May 1945; **57** Put-Upon Percy, 384-33, dated 17 July
1945; **104** The Cheek of Band-Bosses ((Conductors)), 384-35, dated 18 July
1945; **78** A World-Wide Tone-Wright ((Composer)) Guild, 384-38, dated 18
July 1945; **69** Beecham's Cheek about 'Colonial Song', 384-39, dated 18 July
1945; **110** Tonery (Japanese Singer, Javanese Tone-Tool, Pablo Casals), 384-48,
dated 1 Nov. 1945; **107** My First Hearing of Fritz Kreisler, with Mrs Lowrey,
384-49, dated 1 Nov. 1945; **24** Karl Klimsch's Purse of Money, for Mother to
Get Well On, 384-66, dated 7 Nov. 1945.

97 'Facts about Percy Grainger's Year in Europe for Interviews', dated 24 Aug. 1923.

'Grainger's Anecdotes': **101** Balfour Gardiner's Judgement on Vaughan Williams
[Holst and Bax], 423-6, dated 19 Oct. 1949 and 8 Sept. 1952; **70** Balfour Gardiner's Criticisms of Sparre Olsen, Ravel, My 'Colonial Song', 423-7, dated 8
Sept. 1952; **86** Grieg on Busoni's Lightning Octaves in Grieg Concerto, 423-9,
dated 10 Oct. 1949; **71** Grieg's Growing Fretfulness at My Tone-Works, 423-10,
dated Oct. 1949, rev. 1952; **88** Nina Grieg Thought Sostenuto Pedal Sounded
'Unclear' in 'Jeg går i tusen tanker', 423-12, dated 10 Oct. 1949; **102** Grieg on
His Romanticism, My Scientificness, re Folksong, 423-13, dated 10 Sept. 1952;
68 Stanford Deemed My 'Irish Tune' Un-Irish & My 'Brigg Fair' Un-English.
His Disapproval of Vaughan Williams's Norfolk Rhapsodies, 423-17, dated
'1949?'; **67** My Dealings with Stanford anent His 'Four Irish Dances', 423-18,
dated '1949?'; **87** Stanford Wanted to Take Me to the Norfolk, Conn. Festival, to
Play His 'Down Among the Dead Men' Variations, 423-20, dated '1949?'; **89** H.
Allerdale Grainger, 423-27, dated 13 July 1953; **90** Cyril Scott's 1st Sonata at
Bexhill (Suicidal Mood), 423-29, dated 13 July 1953; **72** Sargent & Rathbone
Lost Interest in My Compositions When Publicly Performed, 423-33, dated 10
Aug. 1953; **34** Miss Devlin's Sweet Australian Ways, 423-34, dated 10 Aug.
1953; **7** My Father's Comment on Cyril Scott's Magnificat, 423-36, dated 10
Aug. 1953; **103** Mother Liked Sibelius. P. G.'s Estimate of Him & Other Nordic
Music, 423-37, dated 11 Aug. 1953; **73** Vaughan Williams's Praise of a Detail in
'Irish Tune From County Derry', 423-40, dated 11 Aug. 1953; **105** Rudolf Ganz
Praised Reger & Mahler to Busoni, 423-41, dated 11 Aug. 1953; **106** Busoni &
P. G., 423-42, dated 11–12 Aug. 1953; **33** Frau Kwast-Hiller, Evchen, Mrs

Lowrey in Berlin, 423-43, dated 12 Aug. 1953; **30** Balfour Gardiner Disliked What He Considered Political Falsification in Busoni & Harold Bauer, 423-44, dated 12 Aug. 1953; **22** Dr Hamilton Russell Called Me 'A Tiger for Work', 423-47, dated 13 Aug. 1953; **23** A Day of Motoring with Dr Russell, 423-48, dated 13 Aug. 1953; **95** Donald Francis Tovey's Aunt, 423-50, dated 13 Aug. 1953; **36** Eliza Wedgewood, Out to Buy Old Furniture from Folksingers, 423-52, dated 13 Aug. 1953; **91** P. G. Rehearses 'Song of the High Hills' with Frankfurt Rühlscher Gesangverein, 423-55, dated 15 Aug. 1953; **74** Delius Hostile to Harmonium Parts in My Chamber-Music Scores, 423-56, dated 15 Aug. 1953; **75** Mother Thought My Music Sounded like Hymn-Tunes, 423-57, dated 15 Aug. 1953; **108** Melbourne Miss Rowe & Ernő Rappé's Stolen Music, 423-69, dated 16 Aug. 1953; **92** 'The Bit You Played to Mark Hambourg' (Chopin Polonaise), 423-73, dated 17 Aug. 1953; **35** Jacques Jacobs on First Ada Crossley Tour, 423-74, dated 17 Aug. 1953; **31** Balfour Gardiner with Me in Norway, 1922, 423-80, dated 17 Aug. 1953; **109** Balfour Gardiner: 'Obscure Successes', 423-82, dated 19 Aug. 1953; **8** Mother's Experience with Scotch & Irish, 423-83, dated 19 Aug. 1953; **9** How Would We Ordinary Men Get On If the Clever Ones Did Not Destroy Themselves?, 423-84, dated 19 Aug. 1953; **10** My Father in My Childhood, 423-85, dated 12 May 1954; **58** The Things I Dislike, 423-87, dated 1 Aug. and 20 Aug. 1954; **62** What Is Behind My Music, 423-88, dated 16 or 17 Jan. 1954; **63** Why 'My Wretched Tone-Life'?, 423-89, dated 3–17 July 1953; **25** The English Are Fickle Friends, Tho Never Vicious in Their Fickleness, 423-102, dated 6 Nov. 1954.

5 'John H. Grainger', Museum Legend (with two variants), dated 15 Mar. 1956.

'The Love-Life of Helen and Paris': **38** On Board the 'Aorangi' ('My Fore-mood', 'In Auckland Harbor', 'I First See Helen', 'The Banjolele & the Bandleader', ' "No luck with Swedes" ', 'Talk in Writing-Room'), pp. 2–5, dated 4 Nov. 1927; **39** The Nordic Nature of My Love for Her ('The Nordic Nature of My Love for Her'; 'How H. S. Chamberlain's Book Swayed My Thots'), pp. 8–9, dated 4–5 Nov. 1927; **40** My Joy in Forming a Two-Some with Her ('My Joy in Forming a Two-Some with Her; My Pride in Her', 'My Feeling for My Race; Helen Seen as Race-Priestess, as Mother of Nordic Children', 'My Type is to Serve'), pp. 11–12, dated 5 Nov. 1927; **41** from Pevensey, pp. 29–33, dated 'mid-April 1928'; **42** [Sex-Life], from Pevensey, pp. 38–42, dated Nov. 1927 to 25 May 1928.

'Methods of Teaching and Other Things': **94** After Reading Parry, from section 58 (p. [38]), dated 29 Sept. 1902; **93** [The Expressive Potential of Music], from section 58 (pp. [39]–[41]), dated 13 Sept. 1901; **46** [For My Autobiography], from section 64 (p. [47]), dated 7 Aug. 1902; **47** [Art and Craft], from section 65 (pp. [47]–[48]), dated 8 Aug. 1902.

81 'Native Art and Stage Fright', Museum Legend, dated 9 Dec. 1938.

'Nordic English. Thots on Tone-Art': **64** Length (Size) in Tone-Art & Other Art, un-dated (probably mid-July 1935); **99** [Parry's 'Judith'], dated 18 July 1935; **100** [The Gifted and Half-Gifted], dated 19 July 1935; **77** [Letter to Roy Harris], dated 13 Jan. 1937; **65** The Strange Idea That I Compose for Piano & Then 'Arrange' for Strings, Orchestra, Etc., dated 29 Nov. 1937.

61 'Notes on Whip-Lust', dated 24 Dec. 1948.

85 'Percy Grainger on Ideals', undated (mid-1920s).

Photos of Rose Grainger and of 3 Short Accounts of Her Life by Herself, in Her Own Hand-Writing, reproduced for her kin and friends by her adoring son, Percy Grainger (private publication, 1923): **11** Dates of Important Events and Movements in the Life of Rose Grainger, 3–5, dated 30 Apr. 1923.

44 'Read This If Ella Grainger or Percy Grainger Are Found Dead Covered with Whip Marks', dated 21 Aug. 1932.

'Sketches for My Book "The Life of My Mother & Her Son"': **12** [How I Have Loved Her, How I Love Her Now], W35-4, dated 'early Sept. 1922'; **60** [The Goal of My Art], W35-22, dated 24 Dec. 1922; **13** Thought Mother Was 'God'. Something of This Still Remains, W35-62, dated 16 Nov. 1923; **66** 'The Inuit' at La Crosse, Wis[consin], W35-68, dated 19 Nov. 1923; **49** Money Spent on Ideals, Friends, Etc., 1920–end 1923, W35-73, undated (probably mid-1924); **14** Arguments with Beloved Mother, W35 appendix, dated 9 Feb. 1926; **15** Mother's Neuralgia in Australia, W35 appendix, dated 10 Feb. 1926; **16** Mother on My Love of Being Pitied, W35 appendix, dated 11 Feb. 1926; **18** Mother a Nietzschean?, W35 appendix, dated 17 Feb. 1926; **17** Beloved Mother's Swear-Words, W35 appendix, dated 16 Mar. 1926; **79** [Letter to Mabel Gardner], W35-75, entered 7 Nov. 1927; **6** [John H. Grainger in Adelaide], W35-77, undated (about 1933); **19** Thots of Mother while Scoring *To a Nordic Princess*, W35-88, dated 3 Mar. 1928; **48** The London Gramophone Co. (Now 'His Master's Voice') & the Joseph Taylor Folksong Records, W35-89, dated 22 Sept. 1932; **80** P. G.'s Powers during Australian Tour of 1926, W35-96, dated 30 Nov. to 1 Dec. 1926.

'Thots and Call-to-Mindments': **54** The Thots I Think as I Grow Old, p. [15], dated 25 Mar. 1937; **43** Ella's Rime-Piece 'In Search of Gold', pp. [16]–[17], dated 31 Mar. 1937; **55** [Fraud with Food, Fraud with Hair], p. [27], dated 18 July 1938.

59 'To Whoever Opens the Package Marked "Do Not Open until 10 Years after My Death"', dated 10 May 1956.

Select Grainger Bibliography

Balough, Teresa. *A Complete Catalogue of the Works of Percy Grainger.* Perth: University of Western Australia, 1975.

————, ed. *A Musical Genius from Australia: Selected Writings by and about Percy Grainger.* Perth: University of Western Australia, 1982.

Bird, John. *Percy Grainger.* 3rd ed. Oxford: Oxford University Press, 1999.

Blacking, John. *'A Commonsense View of All Music': Reflections on Percy Grainger's Contribution to Ethnomusicology and Music Education.* Cambridge: Cambridge University Press, 1987.

Callaway, Frank, ed. Percy Grainger Centennial Volume [Special Issue]. *Studies in Music* 16 (1982).

Clifford, Phil. *Grainger's Collection of Music by Other Composers.* Melbourne: University of Melbourne, 1983.

Clunies Ross, Bruce, ed. *Percy Grainger's Library.* Melbourne: University of Melbourne, 1990.

Dorum, Eileen. *Percy Grainger: The Man Behind the Music.* Melbourne: IC & EE Dorum, 1986.

Dreyfus, Kay, ed. *The Farthest North of Humanness: Letters of Percy Grainger, 1901–14.* Melbourne: Macmillan, 1985.

————. *Music by Percy Aldridge Grainger.* 2 vols. Melbourne: University of Melbourne, 1978, 1995.

————. *Percy Grainger's Kipling Settings: A Study of the Manuscript Sources.* Perth: University of Western Australia, 1980.

Foreman, Lewis, ed. *The Percy Grainger Companion.* London: Thames, 1981.

Gillies, Malcolm, and Mark Carroll, eds. Percy Grainger Issue [Special Issue]. *Australasian Music Research* 5 (2000).

Gillies, Malcolm, and David Pear, eds. *The All-Round Man: Selected Letters of Percy Grainger, 1914–1961.* Oxford: Clarendon Press, 1994.

————. *Portrait of Percy Grainger.* Rochester, NY: Rochester University Press, 2002.

Gillies, Malcolm, and Bruce Clunies Ross, eds. *Grainger on Music*. Oxford: Oxford University Press, 1999.

Langfield, Valerie. *Roger Quilter: His Life and Music*. Woodbridge, UK: The Boydell Press, 2002.

Lewis, Thomas P., ed. *A Source Guide to the Music of Percy Grainger*. White Plains, NY: Pro/Am Music Resources, 1991.

Lloyd, Stephen. *H. Balfour Gardiner*. Cambridge: Cambridge University Press, 1984.

Mellers, Wilfrid. *Percy Grainger*. Oxford: Oxford University Press, 1992.

O'Brien, Jane. *The Grainger English Folk Song Collection*. Perth: University of Western Australia, 1985.

Parrott, Ian. *Cyril Scott and His Piano Music*. London: Thames, [1991].

Simon, Robert. *Percy Grainger: The Pictorial Biography*. Troy, NY: Whitston Publishing, 1983.

Slattery, Thomas C. *Percy Grainger: The Inveterate Innovator*. Evanston, IL: Instrumentalist, 1974.

Index